1 MONTH OF
FREE
READING

at
www.ForgottenBooks.com

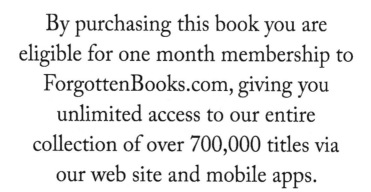

By purchasing this book you are eligible for one month membership to ForgottenBooks.com, giving you unlimited access to our entire collection of over 700,000 titles via our web site and mobile apps.

To claim your free month visit:
www.forgottenbooks.com/free268371

ISBN 978-0-331-03124-9
PIBN 10268371

For support please visit www.forgottenbooks.com

A PUBLIC HEALTH NURSE—1922.

(By courtesy of the Visiting Nurse Association of Detroit, Michigan.)

The Evolution of
Public Health Nursing

BY

Annie M. Brainard

Editor of "The Public Health Nurse"
Lecturer on Administration of Public Health Nursing in
Western Reserve University
President of the Visiting Nurse Association of
Cleveland, 1913
Author of "The Organization of Public Health Nursing"

Illustrated

Philadelphia and London

W. B. Saunders Company
1922

MADE IN U. S. A.

PRESS OF
W. B. SAUNDERS COMPANY
PHILADELPHIA

INTRODUCTION

There is an interesting chart in the Labor Museum at Hull House, before which the initiated visitor stands at thoughtful attention. Simply drawn, colored in yellow, blue and red, it illustrates the forty-five centuries during which the hand spindle was used by the busy housewife as she wove the clothing for her family. A briefer span indicates the period (1500-1850), when the spinning wheel was introduced; and then a very slender strip of red (A. D. 1850), shows the comparatively short space of time that steam has supplanted both distaff and wheel. Perhaps, in addition, this chart will eventually show that electricity has replaced all three older methods.

A somewhat similar chart might be made to demonstrate the development of public health nursing. The care of the sick as a Christian duty has been practiced for many years, but only since 1860 has any attempt been made to formulate a definite standard of scientific nursing care; while we have associated the two ideas of the prevention of illness and the care of the sick for less than a quarter of a century. "Health nursing" is a phrase coined by Florence Nightingale but not really understood until laboratory discoveries began to reveal the true causes of much of the preventable disease and needless waste of life. Consequently "public health nursing," although a comparatively new term devised to describe more fittingly an infinite variety of functions, is the extension of an old service variously known as neighborliness, sick visiting, and visiting nursing. As an organized movement, using trained workers, it is fairly new in many minds and countries today.

Therefore the writing of a twentieth century history of a movement thought to be less than fifty years old, is a difficult as well as a delicate task. The perspective that time, distance and cumulative evidence alone seem to give is entirely lacking when one attempts to discuss contemporaneous activities, but the world is changing with almost kaleidoscopic rapidity and history is being made so fast that it is well to record salient changes and outstanding facts. For while science is overthrowing established theories every few months, we still have to reckon with human nature, with preventable suffering, with sickness and death. Education is apparently to be had for the asking, but how many people think clearly, definitely, in terms of health? To vision the future wisely, one must attempt to evaluate the present properly, and the task of the true historian is to so relate the past with the present that our future work is more clearly outlined in the light of former mistakes or seemingly feeble beginnings.

The history of great movements, like great discoveries or inventions, is the same: the attempt or desire of a few to monopolize benefits or to bestow them. The public health movement of the past twenty years may not have been wholly altruistic, but we have all been its beneficiaries and the work of the public health nurse has been an important element in the success of this movement. Consequently a record of her work and of the people who have made it possible, will be a welcome addition to nursing literature and libraries. It is fitting that the author of this first history of public health nursing should be a former president of the Visiting Nurse Association of Cleveland and the editor, since its inception, of the first journal of public health nursing in America. To thousands of nurses and other readers that little blue-covered magazine never fails to make its monthly appeal. Briefly, perhaps it can be said to epitomize the secret of the strength of the public health nursing movement: the service given by interested laity to the public at large through the medium of trained workers. Although becoming more and more a service sought and paid by public funds, the keen interest of its first workers and directors, its guides and friends, has helped it to maintain standards and press on towards fields of greater usefulness, much as a well-conducted Parent-Teachers' Association energises and inspires an entire school personnel.

Miss Brainard's history touches far too briefly on the contributions of time, service and money that have made possible the firm establishment of much of the work described in her book. The Cleveland Group (as the former officers as well as present directors of the local association have been affectionately known for years), builded better than they knew when they planned a local seal that later became national; published a quarterly report that eventually became the official magazine of the National Organization for Public Health Nursing; and perhaps more far-reaching than all, gave hours of their time, thought, visions and ideals to struggling young workers, both nurses and physicians, who had been guided in the Cleveland traditions by former Cleveland students. The care of the sick in their homes, the alleviation of pain, the prevention of needless suffering, make an irresistible appeal to public-spirited citizens. That is undoubtedly why leading physicians and laymen as well as laywomen have given so freely of their skill and time. To name even a small number of internationally and locally prominent people who have aided in this development would be like writing names instead of placing stars on the service flag of a great university. But public health nursing owes a debt of which it is possibly not aware, to many prominent Americans whose names are not well known outside of the comparatively small groups in which their best work was done. In Cleveland, the late Dr. John H. Lowman; in Chicago, the late Dr. Henry Baird Favill and the late Dr. Theodore B. Sachs had a great deal to do with shaping the policies and guiding with scientific advice as well as kindly counsel, the work of young and struggling organizations. Nearly every community has names that it would honor in this way and perhaps some day a history will be written showing how much public health nursing work has been made possible, as well as stimulated and supported, by others than the nurses themselves.

For public health nursing is more than the care of the sick or the message of health: it is an attempt to coordinate the work of the nurse and her supporters with public needs. Scientific accuracy must be maintained, but at the same time scientific truth must be made comprehensible to simple people. Just as Darwin attempted to show that philanthropic effort springs from man's noblest impulses, but must not be allowed to remain satisfied with attempts at alleviation but must seek out and remedy preventable causes; so the history of public health nursing teaches us that pity first aroused compassion, compassion a desire to relieve, and this last an ever-increasing appreciation of the vast, unfolded field of possibilities in which a trained worker, backed by public interest, sentiment and funds, carries broadcast a message from schools, laboratories and workshops—becomes, in fact, a peripatetic teacher with true messages of hope and salvation. With an ancient, honorable lineage public health nursing is still in its pioneer stages. Its program is flexible, its standards capable of infinite elevation. To insure its success, which can be measured only by results in innumerable homes and communities, it must continue to have the support of the best element of every community.   It must seek to draw beneath its standard nurses with a spiritual vision of good to be accomplished, as well as nurses with the best possible technical training available.   An ample ancestry is sometimes too diffuse a blessing, but readers of Miss Brainard's history will realize more and more that traditions of honorable service are greater spurs to future work than vague rumors of an untold past can ever be.

EDNA L. FOLEY.

PREFACE

In writing this story of a great movement I have had constantly in mind that Public Health Nursing is no new thing, but rather the outgrowth and development of a very ancient practice.

What I have written, therefore, is not so much a history of fact, as an account of the origin of the work, its evolution, and the causes which underlie its development and have produced its variations.

I have tried to show how and why the early deaconess was the progenitor of the modern Public Health Nurse; how the growth of social self-consciousness reacted on the charities of the Middle Ages; how the industrial revolution brought about a re-adjustment of social conditions; and finally how the advance in preventive medicine and the development of the art of nursing, produced, and made inevitable, the Public Health Nurse.

The account of contemporaneous activities must, in the very nature of things, be vague and incomplete. History requires perspective and the work of today is too near to be properly evaluated. Neither has it been possible to give more than a passing glance at the work in foreign countries. Wherever possible, I have tried to seek the story of its growth at the source, and have consulted early records and reports, have talked and corresponded with many of the founders of the work, both in this country and in England, and have endeavored to corroborate all facts and dates. Both nurses and lay people have been most kind in giving me their aid.

In England, my thanks are especially due to Mrs. Dacre Craven, who, as Miss Florence Lees rendered such conspicuous service to the cause of District Nursing; to Miss Amy Hughes, former Superintendent General and Miss Peterkin present Superintendent General of the Queen Victoria Jubilee Institute for Nurses; to Miss Drysdale, of the District Nursing Association of Liverpool; Miss Andrews of the District Nursing Institution of Manchester; Miss Tisdale, Lady Superintendent of the Institution of Nursing Sisters; and to many others.

Were I to try to enumerate the nurses of America who have assisted me in collecting material for this book it would read like a roll call of all the prominent Public Health Nurses of the country; I must, however, give my special thanks to Miss Mary S. Gardner, Miss Edna L. Foley, Miss Lillian Wald, Miss Anne Strong, Miss Katherine Tucker, and Mrs. Reita Thelin Reed, all of whom have given me valuable assistance.

Among the lay people I am especially indebted to Mrs. William Jenks of Philadelphia, who, out of the store house of her memory, has given me many pleasant glimpses of the early work in that city; and to Miss M. Josephine Smith, Managing Editor of *The Public Health Nurse* for her assistance and coöperation at all times, and especially for the outline of the work of the English Ministry of Health which she in most part wrote herself.

Public Health Nursing with its tap root centuries deep in a soil rich with the sacrifice and service of religion and mercy, stands ready to bud and bloom anew, in response not only to those beneficent impulses of humanity which are a part of every age, but to those scientific discoveries and democratic principles of this present age which form a conspicuous part of the life of today.

Annie M. Brainard.

Cleveland, Ohio,
   August, 1922.

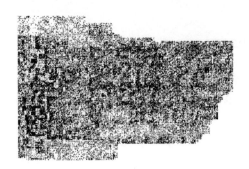

CONTENTS

The
Evolution of Public Health Nursing

CHAPTER I

VISITING NURSING IN THE DAYS OF THE ROMAN EMPIRE

Public health nursing is an outgrowth of visiting nursing, and as such we must look for its origin in the first century of the Christian era; for although human sympathy and love must have moved people to visit and care for the sick and suffering from the very beginning of time, still I think we can safely assert that the first *organized* visiting of the sick in their homes began in those early days when the primitive church established the order of deaconesses, and placed upon them the Christian duty of visiting and caring for those of their brethren who were sick or in need. "I was sick and ye visited Me," and, "Inasmuch as ye have done it unto one of the least of these My brethren ye have done it unto Me." It was natural that the earnest followers of Christ should have laid these words of their Master's to heart and, in founding the society which bore His name, should have placed this duty among the cardinal duties of the Church.

The work of these early Christian women may seem to have little bearing on the work of the public health nurse of the present; and yet, as we study its slow evolution through the ages we shall see that it has a very direct and important bearing and was the source of inspiration for all subsequent service of its kind.

It was the work of these early deaconesses of the church which inspired the deaconess movement in Europe during the early part of the nineteenth century, and which has remained its ideal to the present day. It was the work of the deaconesses at Kaiserswerth which, in turn, inspired Florence Nightingale, and that broad-minded layman, William Rathbone, to establish district nursing in Liverpool; and it was district nursing, transferred to America and given the broader term of visiting nursing, which, branching out to include all forms of social nursing and influenced by the world-wide movement for prevention and prophylaxis, developed into the public health nursing of today.

We go back to this early period, therefore, not only with an interest because of its historical importance, but with a feeling of reverence and gratitude for that love and charity which underlay it and was sufficient to inspire not only the women of that generation but the women of all succeeding generations, and to make possible a service to mankind that knows no creed, no bounds.

Love was the activating motive—pure love and undefiled—for those early Christian women, filled with the enthusiasm of the convert, eager to lay down their lives for the faith, labored with no ulterior motive. They carried on their works of mercy not with any thought of reward or atonement of their own sins, as became the case in later ages, but out of overflowing love for their neighbor, that the sick and needy might find relief, and that by ministering unto the least of these their brethren they might, in some small way, be ministering unto their Lord.

There were three orders of ministry in the early church—bishops, priests or elders, and deacons, the Greek word for deacon meaning simply *one who serves* and being applied indiscriminately to both men and women. The duties of the deacons and deaconesses were similar—namely, to assist in the ministry of the church, and especially to have charge of the poor and needy among their brethren. The service of the deacons (and presumably of the deaconesses as well) as carried on in the early part of the third century is quite minutely described by Clement, who says:

"He is to minister to the infirm, to strangers and widows, to be a father to orphans, to go about into the houses of the poor to see if there is anyone in need, sickness or any other adversity; he is to care for and give information to strangers; he is to wash the paralytic and infirm that they may 'have refreshment in their pains . . . he is also to visit inns to see if any poor or sick have entered or any dead are in them." (Christian Charity in the Ancient Church. Uhlhorn Book II, Chap. IV.

The deaconess was ordained to her office, like the deacon, by the laying on of hands; and the beautiful prayer, attributed to St. Bartholomew, which was used at her ordination shows that she entered upon her service with a feeling of sanctity and consecration.

"O everlasting God, Father of our Lord Jesus Christ, Creator of man and woman . . . Thyself look down upon Thy servant now admitted to the diaconate, and give her Thy spirit, and cleanse her from all pollution of the flesh and of the spirit, that she may worthily fulfil Thy work thus entrusted to her."

Such was the attitude of these first visiting nurses toward their work—they were set aside for a holy calling, consecrated to a divine ministry; they were following the command of their Master. No matter how hideous or how loathsome the task, they did it with joy and exaltation. They were filled with the enthusiasm of the convert, eager to show their love toward God and man and to prove by their humility and devotion that they were, in truth, sincere followers of Him Who spent His life in ministering to those in need.

Nursing, such as we know it, of course there was not. The care given to the sick by these Christian women probably consisted in bathing the fevered patient, dressing his wounds, giving him food and drink, and in other ways ministering to his comfort. It was purely palliative; it was to relieve suffering, not to cure or prevent disease; the day of the public health nurse was still many centuries away; and yet, although the motive which prompted their work was different, the same spirit of service to mankind animated these early pioneers, and what they lacked in science they made up for in tenderness.

The science of medicine at that period was as yet undeveloped and was closely bound up with occult sciences and superstition. Even the most intelligent people of the time believed that famine and plague, sickness and death, were caused by evil spirits which could be placated by offerings and supplications. In fact, this superstition continued far into the middle ages and was a source of anxiety to the Christians for many centuries. During the early years of the Christian era most of the great physicians in Rome were from the East and for that reason were unpopular.[1] Many people preferred to rely upon old prescriptions still preserved in Roman households, rather than to experiment with oriental novelties, or were quite content to follow the treatment carried on in the temples of Aesculapius, which taught the virtue of herb and mineral drug, of regular diet, of bathing, and above all the value of fresh air. These things were good as far as they went; but the proper diagnosis of disease was not yet possible, the idea of prevention was still far distant, and the treatment and nursing of the sick

[1] Ferrero Vol. V., p. 227.

was of the simplest kind and had little relation to cause or prevention.[1]

It would have been impossible, therefore, to have organized this early visiting nursing on the principles found practical and essential in the twentieth century. There was no profession of nursing, and therefore proper training of the nurse could not be required; physicians and the science of medicine were held somewhat in contempt, and it would have been impossible to insist that the patient be placed under medical care. Another modern principle, i. e., that material relief shall not be given by the nurse, was not only not followed, but the contrary was one of the basic motives of the work. The Christian had been taught from the very beginning to sell all that he had and give to the poor—to feed the hungry, to clothe the naked, as well as to visit the sick. In his mind the work could not be divided—"Charity" was "Love," and to have left the poor or suffering without material relief would have been unthinkable. Moreover, in those days they did not have the organized charities of the present day to turn to for clothing or food or other relief. The church was the one great charity organization, and the deaconess was the district social worker as well as the district nurse.

It had been truly said that the Roman age was no age of charity, though, on the other hand, it was an age of great liberality. But there was a vast difference between the liberality of the pagan and the charity of the Christian; the one sought personal applause or popular favor; the other sought not its own, but sought rather to help the down-trodden, to equalize conditions and to do good to all mankind. The poor man, as a man, was looked upon by the Roman with contempt, and to try to better his condition seemed money thrown away. "He does the beggar no service who gives him meat

1 Friedlander, Vol. I, p. 462.

and drink," says Plautus, "for what he gives is lost, and the life of the poor is but prolonged to his own misery."

The Roman of that day was practically without religious belief, which may, in part, account for his seeming indifference to suffering and his attitude toward the poor, for without hope of a hereafter or belief in the brotherhood of man what incentive is there to charity? The adage of the Epicurean could well hold sway: "Eat, drink and be merry, for tomorrow we die."

The masses, it is true, still held a kind of superstitious belief in the power of the gods and still attributed disaster of any kind to their wrath. But personal belief in the gods was waning; the practice of the old Roman religion languished and philosophy took its place. In this philosophy, especially as practised by a Marcus Aurelius or an Epictetus, we find perhaps the nearest approach to the teachings of Christ.

But while philosophy teaches in theory the universal brotherhood of man and the beauty of gentleness, justice, magnanimity and forbearance, it does not teach the selfless charity of the Christian, and preaches tolerance rather than love. Philosophy is a line of conduct based on lofty moral ideals, but there is nothing in it approaching that love and charity taught by Christ. The unfortunate, the poor, the sick, the suffering have no part in such a creed; therefore it is that in ancient Rome we find no philanthropy, no effort to investigate the condition of the poor or to alleviate in any way their suffering; no form of relief beyond the free and indiscriminate distribution of corn; and no charity worthy of the name.

The deaconess, therefore, in her ministration to the sick, was obliged to rely on the church for material relief, and on herself to investigate and procure whatever was necessary. The church was the great charity organization of the period. It had its special fund set apart for the purpose, the management of which lay in the hands of the bishop; the deacons and the deaconesses, in the rôle of district visitors and social workers, investigated the condition of the poor, reported cases of distress to the bishop, and made it possible to render to the sick or needy the kind of assistance required. Moreover, it was considered one of the duties of the bishop not only to relieve distress but also to visit the sick and to pray over them for their recovery, following the example of Christ and the Apostles.

And so we can imagine our pious deaconess, the handmaid of the Lord, faithfully fulfilling the work entrusted to her, caring for the sick, ministering to his needs and when human assistance seems to fail, calling upon her bishop to go with her to the house of pain and to give his godly aid by prayer and intercession.

In order to picture more clearly to ourselves the work of these first visiting nurses let us call to mind for a moment the Rome of that period, and the surroundings amid which they carried on their merciful calling. (Appendix I.)

The beauty and splendour of Imperial Rome has been the theme of many writers for ages past. The Eternal City! The city of marvels! With her marble palaces, her statues of bronze, her great amphitheatres, her glorious temples, her porticos, bridges and aqueducts, her green gardens and magnificent baths! It has all been painted many times.

But it is not in this Rome that we shall find our visiting nurse. Her work lay among the poor, and Rome had her slums as well as her palaces. In the Rome which she traversed the streets were narrow and crooked, the houses, flimsily built, towered menacingly above her, and the noisy crowd, pushing and crying their wares, jostled her on every side. This Rome was one continual bustle and confusion from morn to night, and then again from night to morn. "Here," says Martial, "the money changer clatters Nero's bad coin down on his dirty table, and there a workman is hammering Spanish gold on an anvil. . . . Peddlers peddling old clothes, linen and what not; carriers of pea-flour and smoking sausages; butchers with a reeking quarter of beef, and the feet, the guts, and the blood-red lung— each to his own screeching tune, proclaiming his wares."

It must have taken much of love, much of courage, to brave the dangers of these crowded, narrow streets in order to bring succor to the needy; but we may be sure that these ardent Christian women, eager to serve God, filled with that passionate enthusiasm which overcomes all obstacles, did not hesitate because of personal discomfort. Their duty was to search out the sick or dying and give them aid. It mattered little what difficulties they encountered. The spirit of self-sacrifice possessed them, their only thought was to do God's service.

While the rich of Rome lived on the hills in their splendid palaces, with marble pillars, frescoed walls, and splashing fountains; the poor, like the poor of every age, were crowded into dirty, squalid quarters in the lower and less healthful parts of the city. They lived in tenements closely resembling the tenements of our day, many of which were owned by landlords whose only thought was how to increase their own income and who, rather than spend money on repairs or improvements, would often let the houses fall to the ground, burying the miserable inhabitants in their debris. These huge buildings were called *insulæ*, or islands, because they were surrounded on all side by narrow streets, like islands by water. They rose four or five stories high, perhaps even more, for we read of the poor devil who climbs two hundred steps to his attic (Martial). If we take twenty steps as representing an average stairway from one floor to another it would give us some ten stories. That seems scarcely likely, however, and we are inclined to take the two hundred steps as a poet's license, though we may be sure that as many stories as possible were built, one on top of another, in order to increase the number of rooms for renting and thereby fill the landlord's pocket. The ground floor of these buildings was given over to shops, which overflowed into the streets, as so many shops in the narrows streets of old world cities do at the present day. They must have been lighted by doorways or archways, as there were no windows on the ground floor. The streets were very narrow, not more than eighteen or twenty feet wide, some only thirteen feet across. There butchers, bakers, money changers and wine merchants carried on their trade amid an intolerable din and confusion.

The upper floors were divided into many single rooms or lodgings, with small windows looking out on to the street or into the court around which the houses were built, and from which numerous stairways led to the rooms above.

The description of these *insulæ* calls forcibly to mind the *Bene Stabili* tenements being erected at the present time in modern Rome. These modern buildings are multiple dwellings, housing from eight to as many as a hundred and fifty families, and are built around one or more large courts. They are being put up with the express purpose of providing good modern homes for the working man, which can be rented at a price commensurate with his income.

The similarity between the old and the new probably ends with the ground plan, however, for while the modern tenement is well equipped with sanitary plumbing, gas and electricity and every modern convenience, the ancient buildings were probably devoid of everything that could have contributed to the well-being or comfort of the wretched inhabitant, and we can fancy that these single rooms were only used as a shelter into which they might crawl at night, or a place in which to cook their miserable meals when food was procurable.

Such was the Rome and such the homes in which the deaconess of the early church must have sought her sick and needy; and such the surroundings amid which she worked. We can picture her to ourselves, wrapped in the voluminous woolen cloak of the period, one corner fastened about her head, as she goes her quiet way from house to house through the noisy, dirty streets. We can see her enter a dark archway, cross the inner court and mount the rickety stairway that leads to the miserable rooms above. Here, in the midst of squalor and filth, she will find her patients, or, as she would have called them, her poor. She will not bring them scientific treatment, but she will bring them such ease and comfort as she can; she will not carry a bag with medical and nursing supplies, but she may carry a basket filled with bread and meat and perhaps a bottle of wine. There has been no record left of the cases she carried, but we may feel sure that the usual variety of diseases cared for by a modern visiting nurse were also cared for by her, even though she did not know them by name. She had her chronics—the infirm, the blind, the lame and the paralytic. There were wounds and putrefying sores of all kinds, for antisepsis was not known and a simple wound might easily become infected. There were fevers, and shaking chills, and tumors; and there must have been many burns, for fires were frequent and the great height of the houses and the narrowness of the streets must have made escape difficult and burns inevitable. And then there were the terrible plagues which broke out again and again and raged with such violence that whole cities were decimated.

The work done by these deaconesses and other Christian women of the early church in caring for the sick poor was the only kind of visiting nursing possible in those days, and when we compare it with visiting nursing as we know it today we feel that the inherent principles of both are the same and that their differ. ences are but the reflection of the age in which the work was done. Then, as now, its object was "to provide care for the sick poor in their own·homes and to give such other aid to the poor and needy as from time to time seemed desirable." (Constitution of the Cleveland V. N. A.) Then, as now, the work was organized, not individual, large cities being districted and each district under the special oversight of a deacon; and though the deaconess probably carried on her own piece of work in a more or less individualistic manner, never. theless, the whole philanthropy was under the care of the church, with the bishop at the head, and money or material relief, other than that provided by the worker herself, was only procured through application to the bishop. (Uhlhorn. Christian Charity in the Early Church.)

To teach hygiene and sanitation would have been impossible in an age when sanitation meant little beyond providing proper drainage, sewage and pure water for a community, and when hygiene seemed the prerogative of the rich only. As for the teaching of prevention, how could the prevention of disease have been taught to people who believed that sickness was caused by evil spirits and demons, or was sent to them as a just punishment for their sins? Moreover, the science of Preventive Medicine was then utterly unknown, and though a few intelligent and educated men may have realized that certain precautions might prevent certain diseases, the vast majority saw no relation between their daily mode of living and the sickness which might beset them; and the gentle deaconess probably had no wider vision than her humble patients.

Today we demand that only graduate and properly qualified nurses be employed in public health nursing;

in those days the only qualifications possible were an abounding love and faithfulness in the work undertaken. Today we insist that the nurse should not attempt to influence the religious belief of her patient; in those days the duty of the Christian was to turn all men to Christ, and the deaconess would have failed in the work entrusted to her had she neglected any opportunity to convert the heathen to the religion of Christ. Today we say material relief must not be given —that the patients must value the nurse's care for its own worth; in those days the distribution of alms and relief was one of the main duties of the deaconess, and her care of the sick would have meant little had it not been supplemented by gifts of food and clothing and other necessities.

We see, therefore, in this work of the primitive church, the germ of visiting nursing, and though it differed in detail and method the spirit was the same— the spirit of service to mankind.

CHAPTER II

VISITING THE SICK IN THE MIDDLE AGES

By the latter part of the fifth century the importance of the work done by the deaconess began to wane, and organized care of the sick in their own homes gradually disappeared. To be sure, we still hear of the deaconess in Rome as late as 800 A. D. (Tukes and Malleson— Monasticism. p. 42), and in Constantinople even as late as 1200, but the need for her assistance in the ministry of the church was no longer felt, and the women who bore the title were of a lower grade, with seemingly very different duties from those practised by the primitive deaconess.

Meanwhile, vast changes were taking place throughout Europe. The great Roman Empire had fallen, a prey to barbarian hordes; the wealth of the once proud people had been dispersed. The northern tribes which swept one after the other over Italy and southern Europe had not only sacked and burned many towns and villages and murdered their inhabitants, but, with reckless waste, had over-run and destroyed the cultivated fields as well, and where once vineyard, olive grove and ripening grain bespoke peace and plenty, desolation now reigned. After such an eruption of barbarians had raged over the country, the poor and homeless would crowd into the towns; swarms of mendicants appeared, and the sick began to display their infirmities in order to excite compassion.

Amid all this distress, poverty and political disorder the church, however, had grown with an amazing rapidity. Christianity had spread throughout the entire

Roman Empire, reaching out into Gaul and Germany and far-away Britain, and bringing to those then barbarous countries not only truth, but civilization as well. The Emperor himself had embraced the faith, and instead of persecution the Christian now enjoyed protection and special privileges. Money, too, began to flow in. Many wealthy people, having embraced the new religion, gave liberally to its support and, dying, bequeathed immense fortunes in money and lands. With all this wealth daily pouring into her coffers the church lost much of her primitive simplicity, and increased splendour and ritual began to appear in her services and worship. In every city magnificent churches, vying with the ancient pagan temples in grandeur and beauty, began to appear. Benevolent institutions for the swarms of poor and suffering arose on all sides— houses for strangers, aslyums for the poor and hospitals for the sick.

The ancient world had had no knowledge of hospitals, the nearest approach to them being the houses erected near the various temples of Aesculapius, where the sick might stay while they sought advice from the god, or followed the treatment prescribed. These houses, however, were more like inns than hospitals, and were not supposed to provide care or attendance for the sick.

The first hospitals—or hospices—also were not intended for the sick only, but were used as a refuge for all in need of an asylum—the stranger, the poor, the orphan as well as the sick. Gradually, as the number of applications increased, separate buildings for the various groups were erected, and the hospital proper arose. Many of the sick poor, therefore, who had formerly been visited and cared for in their own homes, now sought shelter and relief in these institutions, where they received not only medical treatment but food and lodging as well.

The first hospital in Rome was the Nosocomia or

House for the Sick, founded during the latter part of the fourth century by Fabiola, a wealthy Roman lady, who, having spent all her life in caring for the sick and poor in their own miserable homes, finally used her vast wealth to establish this first hospital for their benefit. She herself would often carry the sick into the house, would bathe and dress their wounds, and so gentle and tender was she that it was said the poor often wished to be sick if thereby they might only come under her care.

In 370 A. D., Basil, Bishop of Cesarea, had founded the celebrated hospital in that city, probably the first of its kind, and called after its founder "Basilias." This hospital soon became a model for other cities. It seems to have been built on the group plan. In the center was the church, around it, arranged in streets, were numerous single houses, some for the sick, some for the poor, others for servants, for work-shops, etc. The attendants in these hospitals were partly hired and partly volunteers. Some were called "Leaders." Their duty was to go out into the city and seek out the sick and suffering—as the deaconess had in former days—and, when found, to lead them to the hospital and there attend their needs. (Uhlhorn. p. 335) The volunteers were from every class, many of them being women of noble or even royal birth. These tender women, of gentle breeding, gave unstinted personal service; they would make the beds of the poor, give them food, dress their loathsome sores, and considered even the most simple duties, such as sweeping, cooking and trimming the lamps, as not beneath their dignity when done in the service of the poor.

These hospitals were soon found in all the principal cities of the Roman world. In Constantinople John Chrysostom caused two to be erected; Fabiola, as we have seen, built one in Rome; and Paula one in Bethlehem; and in Alexandria, John the Almoner had opened up, besides general asylums for strangers and the sick, *seven* special houses where poor lying-in women could find beds and necessary food and attendance during child-birth. Maternity cases seem always to have received special attention, both in their own homes and in institutions.

Almost co-incident with the rise of hospitals was the rise of the monastic life. As early as the third century many holy men and women, desiring to lead a religious life, had fled from the wickedness and temptation of the great cities to find refuge in the solitude of the wilderness. There, in the desert or on the mountains, they had lived as hermits, seeing no one, living on the simplest fare, and spending all their days in contemplation and prayer.

By the fourth century we hear of the first Communities of Anchorites, consisting of a collection of huts, not placed near together, as in cities, but scattered about at a distance from each other in the desert or on the mountain sides. (Tukes and Malleson. p. 10). In this drawing together of anchorites into communities we see the first embryo of the monastery, which finally found form under Pachomius, who, in 325 A. D., founded a religious house at Tabenna, an island in the Nile (Robertson's History of the Christian Church. Vol. II. p. 7), where a group of 1400 men lived the ascetic life under one roof and under one control. Pachomius became their abbas, or father, (abbot) and gave out a rule for the conduct of the community, thus becoming the founder of the true monastic life. His sister, Syncletica, at his suggestion, started a similar work for women and founded the first community house for nuns.

Monasteries were now erected in all parts of the world, and connected with them were usually hospices or hospitals for the care and entertainment of strangers and the sick. The nuns would look after the women, while the monks took care of the men. In this way the sick of the district were provided for and supplied with medical attention and nursing care—for the care of the sick, the stranger and the poor was a duty especially imposed upon the members of all monastic communities, and none who knocked at the gate for admittance or for help was ever turned away.

Many religious orders now arose; some were strictly cloistered, others uncloistered; some devoted themselves to religious exercises and contemplation, others to learning, others again to the care of the sick. Among these latter were many famous orders, some of whom gave nursing care to any who were ill, others again devoted themselves and their houses to the special care of certain diseases. Thus, the Order of St. Anthony treated the terrible inflammation of the intestines and the dysenteries known under the generic name of St. Anthony's Fire. (Note: St. Anthony's Fire is a name now more often applied to a form of erysipelas); the Johannists, who devoted themselves to the great epidemics of pestilences; the Lazarist who possessed remedies against leprosy, smallpox and pustular fevers; and the Templars, who tended particularly pilgrims, travelers and soldiers. (Science in the Middle Ages. Lecroix.) Thus, little by little, in all parts of the world we find institutional care supplanting the care of the sick in their own homes, and monks and nuns taking the place of the old-time deaconess, who, gradually but inevitably, disappeared, until by the sixth or seventh century she was practically unknown. (Note: The Order of Deaconesses was finally entirely ·abolished as a church order by the Synod of Orleans 553 A. D., which forbade any woman henceforth to be ordained as a deaconess.) [1]

[1] At the Lambeth Conference, 1920, resolutions were formally adopted approving the revival of the Order of Deaconesses. The following is one of the Resolutions relating to the duties of the Order:
"The office of a deaconess is primarily a ministry of succour,

2

For over a thousand years, therefore, namely from 600 to 1600 A. D., we find practically no organized care of the sick in their homes. There were sporadic attempts to establish associations whose main object should be to visit and tend the sick poor, but many of them were short lived, most of them were local, and those that prospered and survived for any length of time usually developed other activities, relegating the care of the sick to a secondary place, and considering it not so much from the standpoint of benefiting the sufferer or nursing and helping the patient, as from the more selfish standpoint of a means of salvation, and as an atonement for sins committed.

During these long, dark ages the progress of civilization throughout Europe was slow. The earlier centuries were filled with violence and brutality. Most of the country was wild and uncultivated—vast tracts of primeval forest, desolate moors and dark marshes abounded. It was dangerous for even men to go forth from castle or fortified towns unarmed or alone. The women were kept closely sheltered within the guarded castle or still more closely cloistered behind the convent wall. Constant wars were carried on between the nobles—war became, in fact, the normal state,—and, as warfare at that time consisted chiefly in destruction the butchery of peasants, the devastation of the lands and the destruction and pillage of villages and towns was continuous. Passions were intense and customs more brutal than today. Society consisted of but two classes, the clergy and the nobles—the peasant, the artisan, the tradesman were ignored—they were but the workers who produced the means of existence for the upper classes. The "social question" did not exist.

bodily and spiritual, especially to women, and should follow the lines of the primitive rather than of the modern diaconate of men. It should be understood that the deaconess dedicates herself to a lifelong service, but that no vow or implied promise of celibacy should be required as necessary for admission to the Order."

The people of the middle ages were not concerned with improving the condition of the poor. Health was a matter of luck, sickness a visitation from God. The church continued to bear practically the whole burden of public charity, helped out by charitably inclined individuals; but the general condition of the peasant remained the same from one generation to another and no hope or thought of betterment appeared.

It must be remembered, however, that even the rich and noble of those days lived hard, bare lives, devoid of any of the comforts which modern civilization deems essential. Their homes were cold, gloomy and bare, their food, while abundant and hearty, was coarse and heavy, lacking even the refinements and delicacies of the more cultured Romans; and luxury, such as the older civilization enjoyed, was practically unknown.

Therefore, while the ordinary hardships of life were in many respects greater for all alike than they are now, on the other hand the disparity between the luxury of the one class and the poverty of the other was probably not so great as in modern times.

Not only was mankind harsh and cruel in those days, but nature herself seems to have been unkind. During the eleventh, twelfth and thirteenth centuries the number of floods, earthquakes and cyclones that visited Europe was appalling. Season after season, harvest and vineyards were destroyed, houses demolished, roofs carried away, towers beaten down, and men, women and children killed by the falling buildings. These frightful visitations of nature naturally brought terror to the hearts of the people, who in their ignorance knew neither how to account for them nor how to meet the disaster. The floods, perhaps, did the more lasting damage, destroying crops and leaving disease in their wake. These floods, which seem to have come with great frequency—we hear of them in 1185, 1195, 1196, 1205, 1206, 1213 and 1219—destroyed the growing

crops and limited the production of food. Consequently we hear of oft recurring famines. It was estimated that men actually died of hunger one year in
every four, for famine in those days meant, not merely
privation and misery, but death.

Pestilence followed in the train of flood and famine.
"Epidemics ran an unobstructed course among the
anæmic and squalid people in the undrained and un-
paved cities, where houses were nothing more than leaky
hovels and streets veritable sewers." (Social France
at the time of Philip Augustus by Achille Luchaire. p.
5) These dirty streets and dark, damp houses were of
course a breeding place for all kinds of contagious
diseases, and, as the middle ages knew no preventive
or combative measures, they usually ran a frightful
course.

The Black Plague of 1348 was probably the most
destructive of all those terrible epidemics. It seems
to have come originally from Asia into Italy, passing
thence into Western Europe and England. Its ravages
were frightful. Whole districts were depopulated, the
scourge falling with equal violence upon the towns,
with their filthy, undrained streets, and the peasants,
working in the open country amid fresh air and sunshine. Some historians estimate that one-third of the
population perished from this plague. Others say that
one-half died. The poor naturally succumbed more
readily to the disease, for not only were they undernourished, but their houses, both in town and country,
were superlatively unsanitary, being dark and damp,
with little air and no sunshine. At that time there were
practically no public sanitary measures, and the public
health was unconsidered. The results of this terrible
epidemic, however, seem to have awakened the authorities to certain dangers, and in some places the houses
and streets, or even the quarters of the town in which

the disease had raged, were closed and certain precautions were observed.

At the time of which we write, the practice of medicine was largely in the hands of the monastic orders, (Science and Literature in the Middle Ages—Paul Le-Croix. p. 142) who mixed up the use of herbs and relics, science and religion, with astounding inconsequence. Prayer, holy water, pilgrimages, and the touching of relics were relied upon with even greater faith than medicine.

When the son of Philip Augustus fell ill of dysentery in 1191, the monks of St. Denis, followed by an immense crowd, came to the palace where the sick child lay, carrying in their arms the sacred relics—the crown of thorns, a nail from the cross, and an arm of St. Simon. With these the monks traced a cross on the abdomen of the little sufferer, and immediately all danger of death disappeared (Luchaire). Surely it was the faith that made whole! Perhaps this is more readily understood when we remember that to the men of the middle ages "natural scourges," such as the plague, famine, flood, drought—were only visitations of the power of God or the saints, to which they must submit, or try to avert by some pious act.

The church also had supervision of midwifery—the women who followed this calling being properly licensed by ecclesiastical authorities; but the requirements seem to have been more ecclesiastical than surgical—for one of their principal duties was to see that no child died unbaptised, and if no priest was at hand and the babe in danger of death, they themselves were to administer this sacrament.

Bearing in mind a picture of the middle ages, we can readily see that there was no possibility of visiting nursing in any but a very restricted sense. What little was done was carried on by a few uncloistered religious orders, or by Christian women who practised it as a form of charity, and whose activities were confined to the poor on their own estates or in their immediate neighbourhood. Many a noble lady of the manor felt the care of the poor among her lord's dependents as a duty incumbent upon her, and especially when illness occurred do we find her descending from her castle hall to seek out the sick and helpless in the village or nearby country districts and, when found, caring for them with her own hands, washing their bodies, cleansing their sores, providing them with food and other necessaries, and doctoring them with what skill she might possess.

Of these women, however, we have only occasional glimpses. Most of them practised their good deeds unheeded and died unsung. A few names, however, stand out conspicuously and their work is indicative of the kind of work done; Genevieve, a simple shepherd girl of Nanterre near Paris, whose charity in time of fever or famine was unequalled; Radegonde, Queen of France, who "loved to serve the sick poor with her own hands"; Margaret of Scotland, who distributed all she had for the use of the poor, who washed the feet of beggars, and herself nursed the sick. It was her daughter Matilda—good Queen Maud—who in 1148 founded the Hospital of St. Katharine in London, whose charter included nursing the sick poor in their homes, and which, many centuries later, was adopted as the Corporate Ancestor of the Jubilee Institute for District Nursing.

One of the most celebrated women of this transition period was Elizabeth of Hungary (1200), who, dying at the still youthful age of twenty-four, yet left behind her a reputation for gentle, sweet charity, which has gone down the ages and made of her a saint.

Besides these individuals, who carried on a sort of personal visiting nurse work, we hear of much visiting of the sick poor in their homes by members of the various so-called *secular* or *active* religious orders, which, though more or less confined in its application and forming usually a small part of the work of the orders concerned, cannot be entirely overlooked in surveying the field of visiting the sick in their own homes during the middle ages.

A great number of these active orders sprang up—especially during the twelfth and thirteenth centuries—as a spontaneous reaction against the repression of the older church orders. Some of them were mere congregations of men or women pledged, perhaps, to do good, and especially to care for the sick or serve the poor, but who were not required to take perpetual vows or to renounce the world. Others took perpetual vows but were uncloistered and found their work outside the convent walls, going wherever the need called. Some of them enjoyed from the first the sanction and protection of the church; others were organized without the church, as lay societies, and by their resistance to ecclesiastical control often aroused strong opposition and even persecution.

Among the earliest of these nursing orders sanctioned by the church was that of St. John of Jerusalem, or the Knights Hospitallers, founded in 1050 to care for the many poor pilgrims who fell ill from the fatigues and hardships suffered during their long journey to the Holy Land. In this order there were women as well as men, the vow of the Hospitaller Nuns being, "To be all their life, for the love of Christ, the servants of the sick poor." (Helyot-Ludlow. p. 143).

One of the oldest and most persistent of the secular sisterhoods was that of the Béguines. The name may have been taken from the old Teutonic word to *beg* or pray, so that the Béguines (and later a similar order of men, the Beghards) may have been simply "praying women" or "praying men." (Ludlow. p. 117) The origin of this order is lost in obscurity. Thomasin tells us that the Béguines were known as early as the seventh century (Tukes and Malleson p. 156). Mosheim says that the name Béguine was used in Germany and Belgium in the tenth century to designate those widows or unmarried women who, without renouncing the world or taking vows of perpetual poverty and chastity, yet lived a religious life of prayer and labor either in their own homes or in a common dwelling (Ludlow. p. 117).

The story of its origin, however, which is given the widest credence is that it was founded by a priest of Liège, Lambert le Bégue (the Stutterer), in 1184, and from him adopted the name of Béguine. This man, an earnest Christian and ardent reformer, aware of certain evils which had crept into the monasteries, and realizing that it was possible to live a religious life and to devote oneself to good work without entering into the strict rule of the established church orders, suggested the founding of a community of women, who should live together, but with greater freedom than in the other orders, and who should devote themselves to good work without giving up their property or taking perpetual vows.

The idea evidently filled a wide felt need and met with hearty response. Lambert le Bégue owned a large tract of land without the city. This he presented to the newlyformed organization and erected on it a church which, on March 26th, 1184, he dedicated to St. Christopher. About the church were then built small, simple houses in which the women lived, usually two or three together.

The new sisterhood flourished exceedingly, spreading throughout Belgium, Northern Germany and into Switzerland and Northern France, until by 1250, a little over fifty years after its establishment, we hear that in Cologne alone there were a thousand Béguines.

As soon as a Béguinage became firmly established there was added a hospital where the sick and infirm of the town could receive care; but not only did the sisters nurse the sick in their hospital, they went out to nurse the sick in their own homes as well, to watch by the dying and to wash and lay out the dead.

Their dress scarcely differed from that ordinarily worn by other women of the period, but was coarse and without ornament.   They took no vows, preferring "to remain inviolably chaste, rather than to promise to be so; to obey without binding themselves to obedience, and to use their property in reasonable outlay for the poor, rather than to give it up entirely."

In France and Germany the Béguinage usually consisted of a single building divided into separate cells, but with common refectory and dormitory (Ludlow). In Belgium, on the contrary, it consisted of small, simple houses, built in streets about the church, like the original Béguinage, and with separate buildings for hospitals, workshops, etc., the whole being inclosed by a wall.

The whole movement of the Béguines was a reformatory effort towards greater freedom for women, and it is to be noted that it attained its greatest strength in Northern Germany and, especially, in Belgium, where the free life of the people was always asserted.

Because of their greater freedom and their independence of church rule the Béguines endured much clerical opposition and even persecution.   Council after Council, bull after bull, denounced and excommunicated them as heretical.   Despite all opposition, however, the people upheld them—they were too useful and too much in harmony with the spirit of their country to perish before the canons of a Council or papal bull, and it was impossible to stay the movement.   By the beginning of the fourteenth century the whole number of Béguines was estimated at 200,000.

After the Reformation many of them embraced the doctrines of Luther, others became Tertiaries of St. Francis or St. Dominic. At present, members of the Order are to be found mostly in Belgium, where they still live their old independent and self-supporting life, devoting themselves to good works, among which is always counted nursing the sick in their homes.

The Grey Sisters, or Sisters of Mercy, founded in 1222, was a Tertiary Order that resembled the Béguines in many respects. They were uncloistered, they devoted themselves to good works, and especially to nursing the sick in their own homes; and they had the same healthy Béguine spirit of independence. When, in 1696, the Bishop of Nancy tried to compel their cloistration they appealed for help to the civil power, as had the Béguines three centuries before, and like them were upheld in their contention and continued to pursue their free, uncloistered life, serving the community in which they lived.

The Sisters of the Common Life, a little group of women who gathered about Gerhard Groot during the middle of the fourteenth century, stirred to good works by the eloquent appeals of this impassioned preacher, was another lay association that closely resembled the Béguines. It has been said of them that "they were eminently Visiting Nurses." (Nutting. Vol. I, p. 274.) The Brethren of the Misericordia, founded in Florence in 1244, and still existing there today, was a remarkable order of home visitors. They wore black gowns and masks, in order that they might not be recognized, and went about among the poor, nursing and succoring the sick, and bearing the dead to the grave for burial.

The Alexian Brotherhoods and Sisterhoods were especially required to "visit the sick and if need be keep and nurse them in their sickness when haply required to do so." (Bull of Boniface IX, 1395.)

The Damsels of Charity, a short-lived Protestant society of women, founded by Prince Henry de la Mark
in 1560, was organized to "succor in their own homes
the aged and sick poor." And, finally, the Sisters of
St. Charles of Nancy—a lay order founded in Toul in
1652, in memory of a young man who had given his
life caring for the sick during a terrible pestilence—
were specially required to nurse the sick poor in their
homes and to serve in time of epidemics.

But it takes a good deal of imagination to call any of
these various efforts towards caring for the sick in their
own homes *Visiting Nursing.* The members of the
different religious orders, and the merciful ladies of
the manor did indeed visit the sick poor and did minister to their wants and nurse them as best they knew
how, but nursing, as such, was unknown in those days;
there was no organization of the work as a special philanthropy; there was no effort to remedy evil conditions;
no thought of improving sanitation or teaching hygiene;
no suggestion of prevention; no progress or cooperation
in the work done. Each was a spontaneous, desultory,
sporadic effort, each was an individualistic attempt
to do good; each was put forward as a Christian duty
and followed in the hope of eternal salvation. Visiting the sick became a popular form of penance; it
offered every opportunity for the practice of the Christian virtues—humility, gentleness, compassion—it was
accounted an atonement for sin, and glorified the individual who practised it, if it did not greatly benefit
the sick among whom it was practised. On the whole,
visiting nursing had retrograded rather than progressed.
It was no longer done systematically, as in the days of
the early deaconesses; towns were not districted, as in
primitive times; and there was practically no investigation of cases for relief.

Visiting the sick in the middle ages was not a science—it was a work of mercy, a Christian duty that

ranked high amid the many deeds of personal charity practised in those days for the sake of one's soul—and one sometimes questioned whether much of it was not done for spiritual reward, rather than for the good of the suffering patient.

However, it would be wrong to belittle the good done by these well-meaning visitors of the sick poor. We must remember the rough times, the sheltered lives of the women and the misery of the poor, which was accepted as inevitable. We must remember also that the great movement for social reform had not begun and that the unconscious acceptance of conditions as they were prevented any organized effort to improve them; and, finally, we must remember that the science of medicine was still struggling for recognition, and that anxiety for one's soul far outweighed anxiety for one's body. Instead of criticizing the shortcomings of the work as viewed from a modern standpoint, we should rather marvel at the great piety which prompted this hard service; at the self-sacrifice which faced unflinchingly the most frightful plagues and the most disgusting conditions; at the tenderness which at least brought consolation and ease, if it did not bring permanent relief. Without the aid of the nursing sisters and other Christian women of mediæval times the suffering of the sick poor would have been even greater than it was, and the cause of visiting nursing would have died utterly.

CHAPTER III

THE BEGINNINGS OF SOCIAL REFORM

With the dawn of the seventeenth century a new epoch in social history is opened up. We are now to see the first, feeble beginnings of that great movement' for social reform which in time was to revolutionize society; and, side by side with the awakened consciousness to the suffering of the oppressed and the responsibility of those in power to reform conditions, comes the organization of what might well be called the "first Visiting Nurse Association"—namely, the Order of the Visitation of Mary, which was simply a voluntary association for friendly visiting and nursing among the poor, the members of which were "to visit the sick daily, bathe, dress and care for them, and take home their linen to be washed."

The seventeenth century saw not only a great advance in social understanding, but in science and literature and general culture and refinement as well. The dark ages were well passed; the brutal attitude toward the less favored portion of mankind which had prevailed for so many centuries was giving way to a better understanding of the causes of poverty, and therefore to a better understanding of the poor themselves. Although humanity had still to struggle through long years of suffering, dawn had come, and a glimpse had been caught of that brotherhood of man which teaches that all men are born free and equal and are entitled to an equal chance.

The discovery of America and the opening up of new fields of adventure and thought had widened man's outlook and contributed to increase his general stock of knowledge. Such men as Bacon, Shakespeare, Corneille, Racine, Molière brought philosophy, literature and the drama to their highest level. The natural sciences, also, made rapid progress. During the century a brilliant group of doctors and chemists succeeded in divorcing medicine proper from its long connection with alchemy and occult science, and new knowledge and the application of knowledge, scattered the shadows which for so long had hampered its advancement. New remedies were discovered. In Paris the growing of plants for medicinal purposes was studied in the Jardin des Plantes, and a wider use was also made of mineral as well as vegetable compounds. "Remedies became really remedial," though the doctor himself was still trembling on the borderland of servitude, and was classed among the middle-class people, along with the butcher, the grocer, the apothecary, etc. However, he held his own intellectually and still struggled on to raise his profession to the first rank, where it naturally belonged.

In spite of this general advance in medical knowledge, however, the simple rules of hygiene remained strangely unrecognized. "To take a bath was to confess oneself ill" (Social Life in France. Hugon. p. 102), and although there were many famous medicinal baths in Italy, France and elsewhere, where hydropathic treatment was given for all kinds of maladies, the use of the bath as a purely hygienic measure was not practiced. The value of fresh air, too, was little understood. When a person fell ill the doors and windows were immediately closed, for there was a universal fear of cold and draughts, and people willingly bore the discomfort of a stagnant and impure atmosphere rather than venture to let in the colder air from outside.

Mme. de Maintenon tells of a servant of hers who, being sent to inquire after a sick friend, was quite unable to enter the sick room on account of the horrible air; "the patient, poor man," says she, "did not wish them to open so much as a shutter, thinking it would harm him, which was perhaps true." (Hugon. Social Life in France. p. 143.)

In spite of this blindness to what, to us of today, are the commonplaces of health and hygiene, there was a tremendous increase in the sum total of knowledge— and along with this widened intellectual horizon came a higher standard of living and comfort. Food was better, more varied and more wholesome; housing was better, even the homes of the poor being more comfortable and less unsanitary, and there was greater security of life and property.

In England, Elizabeth's beneficient reign had brought her people to an advanced state of well-being, and though pauperism in that country had unfortunately become a permanent evil, still the general wealth of the country and of the people had greatly increased. The merchants and landed gentry were rich, farmers were prosperous, and even the artisans and laborers, with higher wages and without a corresponding increase in the cost of food, were much better off than heretofore. The condition of the really poor was already being investigated, and it was now considered the duty of each and every citizen to contribute his share toward the alleviation of the worthy poor. By 1601 the first English Poor Law prescribing a compulsory poor rate tax in every parish was passed and the relief of the poor became no longer an individual problem, dependent upon voluntary acts of Christian charity for solution, but a national duty exacting a compulsory contribution towards its alleviation.

In France, however, conditions were not so prosperous. During the sixteenth and early seventeenth centuries religious intolerance and the fatal ambitions of the great families, in addition to financial and other disorders, had reduced France to a state of atrophy almost impossible for us to realize. In the country the peasant lived on his land as best he could. The wars, which followed one after the other without interim, the heavy taxes and the lack of consideration by the State, made his lot a sorry one. In the cities the poor fared no better. The artisan lived obscurely in back streets, or slept in the attic of his master, often going to bed hungry, always candleless. His working day was a long one, sometimes seventeen continuous hours.

Warfare, famine and plague—that devastating trio— still stalked through Europe. The price of food rose, until in 1652 a loaf of bread in Paris cost 1 een or about $1.20. In some parts of the country the poor ate acorns, roots and grass. Later, corn became somewhat cheaper, but it took many years before conditions were again normal.

In 1649, during the worst of the famine, the Abbess of Port Royale writes as follows:

"This poor country is a horrible sight; it is stripped of everything. The soldiers take possession of the farms and have the corn threshed, but will not give a single grain to the owners, who beg for it as an alms. It is impossible to plow, there are no more horses—all have been carried off. The peasants are reduced to sleeping in the woods and are thankful to have them as a refuge from murderers. And if they only had enough bread to half satisfy their hunger, they would indeed count themselves happy." (Hugon. p. 172) Three years later she again writes: "All the armies are equally undisciplined and vie with one another in lawlessness. The authorities in Paris are trying to send back the peasants to gather in the corn;[1] but as soon as it is reaped the marauders come to slay and steal and disperse all in a general rout."

Of course the class which suffered most under this

[1] The refugees had flocked to Paris and in 1652 there were 100,000 beggars in the capital.

general misery was the poor, both the peasant in the country and the artisan in the city. The famine bread which they ate was made of barley and oats mixed with straw. The Jesuit *Rélations* of 1651 say that in one parish the poor subsisted on "straw mixed with earth" and that their staple dish was "mice which the inhabitants hunt, so desperate are they from hunger."

Nothing worse than this occurred during the middle ages, and we are not surprised to find that the plague continued its ravages through the land. The history of its triumphal march is one long tale of horror. It broke out in 1606 and again in 1623; from 1630 to 1635 it raged without interim, and in 1650 became more virulent than ever before. Hospital service was entirely inadequate and many people died on the street or without care in their own homes. In order to meet this distress, poverty and sickness there was great need of some form of organized charity. That, however, did not then exist. But, just as through the ages evolution has produced the eye, when sight was needed; or the ear, when hearing was required; so now this great need at last produced an organization to cope with it which from a small beginning, grew and spread until it reached out to the uttermost parts of the world. I need not say I refer to St. Vincent de Paul's Sisters of Charity.

St. Francis de Sales, however, was the first to enlist the sympathies and help of the great ladies of the period and to induce them to give their time, as well as their money, to an organized service for the sick poor. This organization was called the Order of the Visitation of the Virgin Mary. In founding this Order he was fortunate in having for his co-worker a woman as experienced in visiting nursing and as wholly consecrated to the work as Mme. de Chantal, who became the first head of the Order and the leader and director of all its good works.

3

In reading the life of Mme. de Chantal one feels as though she had been especially trained for the work which lay ahead. She was born in the ancient town of Dijon, of a good and prominent family, and given the name of Jeanne in honor of John the Almoner, on whose festival she first saw light. Her father, though a faithful adherent to King Henri IV, was a staunch Catholic. He early taught his little daughter the Catholic tenets, and carefully instructed her in the controversal points between Catholic and Protestant beliefs. As she grew older Jeanne wished to enter a cloister, but her father objected. "Christian virgins," he said, "should remain in the world and edify it with their virtues."

She was married at the age of nineteen to the Baron de Chantal, a distinguished officer in the service of Henri IV, and her married life seems to have been filled with domestic love and happiness.

She lived a busy, active life managing her household and the estates well, learning to know the poor people about her, and practicing the charity which her heart and religion prompted.

She rose at dawn and after attending to her devotions and ordering her household, devoted the remainder of her day to the management of the estate and the care of the poor who lived on her husband's domain. Her charity was boundless. She often said "I can with more confidence ask of the Lord to grant me my necessities, when for love of him I have bestowed alms on the poor."

Mme. de Chantal was not unusual, however, in her mode of life or the charity which she practiced, unless, perhaps, in the quality of her work. Women were expected to really manage their households in those days and girls were taught in the schools those duties which would be theirs in after life. The education of girls was at that time occupying the minds of many. Fenelon, in a letter on the education of girls says: "In order that a house should be well managed the mistress of it should be familiar with the nature of every servant's duty, so that she may command reasonably and with justice—" and Mme. de Maintenon, who founded the school of St. Cyr for poor girls of noble birth, said in an address to them on their duties and responsibility: "Families living in the country should do all that in them lies to set a good example to their tenants. The mistress should rise at six in the summer and seven in the winter, and say her prayers, and take a turn to see that all are at their appointed work. She should then complete her toilet and go to Mass. The day should be devoted to household tasks and necessary visiting. A walk may be taken in the evening—. A good woman will visit the poor after vespers on Sunday, and send them the food left from her table."

Mme. de Chantal, however, did not confine her visiting of the poor to Sundays, and the account of her work among them shows that she had a much higher sense of her duty toward them than merely to bestow upon them the food left over from her own table.

After some eight years of happy married life, the Baron was accidentally shot while out hunting, and Mme. de Chantal was left a widow. Her grief was intense, and she resolved that from henceforth she would devote herself entirely to the poor, the Church, and to her children. Soon afterwards she moved with her children to the home of her husband's father near Autun. Here she practiced her charity unrestricted, not only distributing alms, but visiting the sick and poor of the parish undeterred by summer's heat or winter's cold— "She loved to visit and serve the poor, and confessed that the most tedious day was that on which she found no fitting opportunity to exercise charity—Seldom did a day pass in which some hours had not been devoted to the sick poor in their own homes. She dressed their wounds, cleaned.them, made their beds, gave them clothes, which were kept in readiness, took home their linen, boiled it to free it from vermin and other impurities, mended it, and then returned it to them. All the neighboring sick were known to her, for she had requested that so soon as a poor person fell ill she might be informed of it. She visited and assisted them, and was often present at their agony; when they were dead she washed and laid them out" (Kavanagh. p. 146).

In the year 1606 Mme. de Chantal went to her Chateau at Boubilly where she found her people affected with a fatal dysentery and she devoted herself to them with the passion she carried into everything she did. "She rose with the dawn, visited the nearest houses, returned to Mass and breakfast, and then went forth again afternoon and evening. The dysentery lasted seven weeks; during that time it is computed that Mme. de Chantal laid out from two to five corpses daily; at last she fell ill literally from fatigue" (Kavanagh. p. 149).

In this way did she pass her novitiate, so to speak, for the great work ahead of her. She cut off her hair, and dressed in a plain serge dress, with white linen sleeves and collar, the nearest approach to the religious garb which she had once wished to put on. Wherever there was sickness, sorrow or poverty needing help there she was to be found and the people called her "the Saint of Monthelon"—the name of her father-in-law's house.

In 1603 while on a visit to Dijon Mme. de Chantal had met Francis de Sales—the Bishop of Geneva—who was giving a course of Lenten services in that city. A deep and understanding friendship sprang up between them.

Francis de Sales had long had in mind to found an Order "mild in rule but evangelic in Spirit" to which ladies of delicate health or those unable to bear the austeries of the established Orders, might be admitted and spend their time in tending the sick and poor. In Mme. de Chantal he saw the person he had been looking for to head the new community. He did not speak at once, however. He waited and tried her out; he studied her character and her ability; and not until 1610 did he finally take up the plan definitely with her. His idea was to found a congregation of women, without external vows, in which the Sisters would be free to go out to visit the sick poor, and minister to their needs in their own homes, a life which he felt was more profitable and more productive of good than the more restrained and inactive life of the cloister. He suggested to his friend Mme. de Chantal, that she should lead this community, which he planned to found in his native town of Annecy in Savoy. She joyfully acceded to the proposal. By this time her eldest daughter was married, one of her younger daughters was dead, and the other she proposed taking with her to Annecy, while her son, a lad of fifteen, no longer needed her care or direction, for in those days the sons of the nobility were often launched into the world at a still earlier age. She determined therefore to part from her family in order to give herself up to a religious life. "Mme. de Chantal was a mother full of tenderness, her children loved her passionately, none better than the young son she was about to leave— He twined his arms around her neck and intreated her not to go; seeing at length that his prayers would not avail he laid himself down on the threshold of the door and said: 'I cannot detain you, but, if go you must, pass then over the body of your child.' She stepped over him, then returned weeping. A clergyman, tutor to her son, thought he saw her wavering and reproved her. Her only answer was 'I am a mother.'" This son was killed while fighting the Huguenots. He left a widow

and an infant daughter, who afterwards became the
brilliant Mme. de Sévigny.

Madame de Chantal arrived in Annecy on Palm Sunday, 1610, and on the following Trinity Sunday was
founded the new Order of the Visitation of the Virgin
Mary—whose members were to visit the sick and afflicted as Mary visited Elizabeth. Mme. de Chantal
and the little group of Sisters at once started about their
work. They went forth daily like the visiting nurse
of today, to visit and relieve the sick poor in their
homes. It is told of them that "one day the Bishop
being confined to his room owing to a hurt received in
one of his legs, saw two Sisters going past and called
them in. 'You are going to tend the sick,' he said, 'and
here is a sick man with a wounded leg; will you
take pity on him?' The Sisters were proud to minister
to their venerated founder, but their agitation, half
pleasure, half shyness, caused them to set about their
work with tremulous hands, and they consequently put
the good Bishop to not a little unnecessary pain. He
would not betray them, but after the operation was
over, and he had thanked them for their services, he
added 'when you dress the wounds of the poor, my
daughters, you must try and steady your hands and
not tremble so much nor be in such a hurry, for it is
rather tender work.' " (Life of St. Francis de Sales,
by Farrer).

Unfortunately the little community carried out its
original plans for only five years. In 1615 Francis de
Sales was, after much hesitation, finally persuaded to
abandon his first idea and to permit the order to adopt
the principle of cloistration imposed on all religious
orders of women by the Council of Trent. It cost him
much to desert his sick poor, and he used often to say
"Can anything be more unreasonable than to call me
the Founder of the Visitation: I have done exactly
what I did not wish to do, and have undone all I did

wish for." (Life of St. Francis de Sales, Farrer. p. 202.)

But although Francis de Sales was the first to enlist the sympathy of the public in an organized effort to nurse the sick in their own homes, it remained for Vincent de Paul to introduce the modern principles of relief, and to place visiting nursing on a plane which it had never before reached. His conception of charity was a new one; he believed that not only the rich and influential, but the humble as well should contribute toward the relief of distress: he showed that it was not money or material relief alone that counted, but brotherly sympathy and personal service as well: he taught that promiscuous giving was harmful, and that one must investigate the condition of the poor, must find out their needs, must ascertain the causes of the poverty and wherever possible remedy them, and must get the unemployed work and put them in such a position that they might be able to help themselves. This was a great step in advance over the pauperizing charity that had prevailed for so many centuries. He realized also the right of the poor to their family life, and the benefit to be derived from a recognition of the family unit, and urged that whenever possible the home be kept together, even if it were necessary to pay the rent for a time, or to lend furniture. These were certainly very modern ideas.

Vincent de Paul was first and foremost a philanthropist. The distress and suffering of the poor touched his heart; like St. Francis d'Assisi of old he held all men, even the humblest and weakest, his brothers, and longed to help and comfort them. He realized, however, that the personal service of one man would go but a short way to meet the need and, therefore, instead of going out himself, as one field worker, he set himself to organize large groups of men and women, who, spreading out in organized units, might multiply indefinitely and form a band of workers numerous enough to encircle the globe. His whole movement for social reform was well systematized, and from the first he was looked upon, not only as the founder of his various charity organizations, but as their director as well. The enthusiasm and earnestness of Vincent de Paul kindled a like enthusiasm in those who heard him preach, and as the century advanced the interest and energy in charity work displayed by the public throughout France was astonishing. Various charitable organizations and societies were started by private individuals working independently, and a number of books and pamphlets were issued for their guidance. In 1651 an excellent book, entitled "L'Aumône Chrétienne et Ecclésiastique" was published; another followed in 1652 called "Exhortation sur les secours des pauvres," and a third appeared soon after with the simple title "Le Chrétien Chari table."

Visitors of the poor were told to find out the reason for the poverty and if genuine, to help the people to help themselves; money, they were told, should be given only under exceptional circumstances, and brotherly love should be the motive power.

Vincent de Paul's first effort for succoring the poor was the establishment of his Society of Missioners in 1617. These Missioners were priests trained for their special work among the poor, and whose vows were taken annually. The work done by these Mission Priests was varied. At first they worked in the country districts only, but by 1627, when France was torn by war and its entraining miseries, their efforts were confined to no localities, no boundaries, and wherever there was distress, in town or country, there these self-sacrificing men were to be found.

The following description taken from the *Rélations* of 1651, gives a vivid picture of the famine and the work done by the Missioners.

"Of the 450 sick persons (in St. Quentin) whom the inhabitants were unable to relieve, 200 were turned out, and these we saw die one by one as they lay on the roadside. A large number still remain, and to each of them it is only possible to dole out the least scrap of bread. We only give bread to those who would otherwise die. The staple dish here consists of mice, which the inhabitants hunt, so desperate are they from hunger. They devour roots which the animals cannot eat; one cannot, in fact, put into words the things one sees—not a day passes but at least 200 people die of famine in the two provinces. We certify to having ourselves seen herds, not of cattle, but of men and women, wandering about the fields between Rheims and Rhétel, turning up the earth like pigs to find a few roots; and as they can only find rotten ones, and not half enough of them, they become so weak that they have not strength enough left to seek food. The parish priest at Boult, whose letter we enclose, tells us he has buried three of his parishioners who died of hunger. The rest subsisted on chopped straw mixed with earth of which they composed a food which cannot be called bread. Other persons of the same place lived on the bodies of animals which had died of disease, and which the Curé, otherwise unable to help his people, allowed them to roast at the Presbytery fire."

Of course disease and plague followed these conditions and nowhere were the Missioners more untiring in their efforts to relieve distress than in the villages where the pestilence raged most fiercely. They tramped the muddy country roads, with their mules heavily laden with bedding, seed and gold and when they came to a house where the tenants lay ill or dying they entered, nursed and comforted them, and buried the dead. Many of these Missioner priests died in consequence of their exposure to the contagion.

Vincent de Paul's greatest work, however, was the

establishment of the Sisters of Charity, an Order which still exists, and still inspires the world by the gentleness, the sweetness and the modest earnestness of its members. It was while he was at Chatillon in the year 1617, the same year in which he started the work of the Missioners, that Vincent de Paul first conceived the idea of the *Dames de Charité*. One day a lady approached him and asked that he recommend to the charity of his congregation a poor family lying ill on their farm in the nearby country, and greatly in need of care and attention. His appeal found ready response—in fact, so many undertook to relieve and help the sick family, that Vincent de Paul, with his usual clear-sighted vision, soon realized that unless the ardor of these charity workers was properly directed and systematized, it might easily do more harm than good. He suggested to a few of the ladies that they form themselves into a voluntary association for the practice of charity, and without taking external vows, declare themselves willing to devote a portion of their time and money to the task of visiting and relieving the poor in their midst. The idea took ready hold, and the ladies were called *"les Dames de Charité."* Their work consisted mainly in visiting nursing among the sick poor.

St. Vincent himself taught them the fundamental principles—"Lay off your jewels and fine clothing to visit the poor," said he, "and treat them openly, respectfully, and as persons of quality. To send money is good, but we have not really begun to serve the poor until we visit them."

The ladies would go from cottage to cottage visiting their patients in turn. Everywhere they were received with gratitude. They would make the sick man's bed; give him food and prepare his medicine; exhort and console the dying or the sorrow stricken, and give whatever other help or comfort was possible. Material relief was only given, after a thorough investigation had shown it to be justifiable. The new organization soon spread throughout France, and groups of the *Dames de Charite* were to be found at Soisson, Meaux, Senlis, Chartres, Châlons and other towns, as well as in the larger cities, including Paris itself.

By this time medical, as well as nursing care, was becoming available for the poor. Doctors gave their services freely, and in times of epidemic often gave their lives as well, for even the best of them had hazy ideas as to protection from infection. The medical charities at Paris were directed by one Theophrastus Renardot, who had established an association for the purpose in 1612. In 1640 the King, realizing the splendid nature of this physician's work, gave him letters patent and a free hand to do what he liked for the poor. Four years later he and five others, likeminded with himself, gathered together a number of doctors who agreed to set apart two days a week to visit the sick poor and to prescribe remedies which were furnished by the faculty. (Hugon. p. 183.) We see therefore the elements of an almost complete visiting nurse service—the doctors, to diagnose the case; the ladies, to give the bedside care; and the charity association, to investigate conditions and give material relief.

Slowly but surely the thoughts and ideas of men were converging toward the point where organized district nursing would become inevitable, but the time for its final establishment was still a long way off.

For ten years the work of the *Dames de Charité* went on as originally planned. New groups were organized in various places; but having no central control nor general supervision, the work gradually became unstandardized. Vincent perceived that the ladies were not all animated by the original spirit, and were not all carrying on the charity as the Association desired. He saw the need of a person to whom he could confide the task of visiting the various places where the Sister-

hood had been established, and who could supervise the
work and teach the *Dames* the new method of charity,
which he felt to be so important. Such a person he
found in Mlle. Le Gras. He suggested to her that she
should assume the direction of the work in the field.
She eagerly accepted the proposition, and in 1627 became what we might well call the first Supervisor of
Visiting Nurses. Mlle. Le Gras was a lady of noble
birth. She had married a gentleman whose ancestry
was not of ancient date; she therefore had, according
to the usage of that day, no claim to the title of Madame
and was always called Mademoiselle. At the time that
Vincent de Paul suggested to her the supervision of
the *Dames de Charité* she had been a widow for two
years. Her original intention had been to enter a convent, but her health was somewhat delicate and after
talking to Vincent, and seeing the work that was being
done by his Ladies, she decided to abandon her first
idea and, to accept the position suggested and devote
herself to good works in the world instead of behind the
cloister wall.

This was in 1627. Mlle. le Gras immediately took
up the task of visiting the various places where the
Ladies were working. Before starting out on a visitation tour she always took written instructions from
Vincent de Paul, as to what she should do, and how
best to do it. She was generally accompanied by two
or three other ladies, all together "travelling roughly
and faring poorly in order to better sympathise with
the poor." On arriving in a village she would collect
the women who composed the charitable sisterhood, and
would give them instructions which they so often required. She would accompany them on their rounds
and help and advise them in their ministrations, assisting them in making the beds of the sick, preparing their
medicine and food, and pointing out how best to relieve
their distress. This plan was continued for some five

VISITING THE SICK IN THE 17TH CENTURY.

(Reproduced from Cecile Hugon's "Social Life in France in the 17th Century," by permission of the publishers, Messrs. Methuen & Co., Ltd.)

or six years, but even this supervision of the work, while it helped greatly, did not seem to meet all the difficulties.

Seventeen years had now elapsed since the establishment of the first Sisterhood at Chatillon. The work, though meeting a great need, was yet hampered by many inconveniences which it seemed impossible to entirely overcome. "The husbands of the Ladies objected to having their wives exposed to the danger of breathing impure air, and of bringing home the contagion of disease." The zeal of the Ladies flagged; they hesitated to render the personal service which the work required; they hired servants to fill their places. In consequence the sick were neglected, and the Sisterhood began to decline.

Vincent de Paul reflected. He knew that if matters were left as they now were all his previous efforts would be lost. Never had there been greater need for organized relief and care of the sick. There was a famine in the land that year, 1633, and the plague had been raging without cessation for three years. Hospital service was entirely inadequate to meet the need, and it was necessary to supply means for caring for the sick poor in their own homes. He could not let his organization fail. He must think out some way whereby its flagging zeal could be resuscitated and the work of the Ladies supplemented. But why restrict the work to ladies alone? Were not the humbler classes equally responsible and equally capable of rendering the care required? He bethought him of the many sturdy peasant girls, simple and good; not able perhaps to enter a convent, but anxious to devote themselves to God's service. Could they not be pressed into the work? The plan was tried and proved more of a success than he had dared hope. The girls were called the Servants of the Poor. At first they worked under the Ladies of the various parish Sisterhoods, and assisted them in all the care of the patients, probably doing the more menial and rougher tasks.

Each group, however, was still working independently and lacked the unity which comes from a central government, a common spirit. To remedy this defect, Vincent de Paul selected three or four of the most promising country girls, and placed them under the special guidance and instructions of Mlle. Le Gras. The experiment proved a success and spread with extraordinary rapidity. The number of humble workers increased constantly and were soon found in all parts of France. The people called them *les Filles de Charité*.

St. Vincent de Paul had not thought of founding a religious order, but when he found that he had in some way unwittingly done so, he sought to establish it on a sure foundation. He knew that his Sisters must be uncloistered for their service required the greatest freedom of action. He decided also that their vows should be taken for one year only "so that they might always possess the merit of liberty." These vows were renewed each year, if the Sister so desired. St. Vincent wished that the Sisters should be in the world but not of it. He taught them that the presence of God was to be found wherever the service of God was performed, and that they could create about themselves the atmosphere of the·Convent.

"Nuns must need have a cloister, but the Sisters of Charity must go everywhere," said he, "your monasteries are the homes of the sick; your cell a hired room; your cloister the streets of the city or the wards of the hospital. Let obedience be your solitude, and the fear of God your grating; and a strict and holy modesty your only veil."

Thus arose the Sisters of Charity whose loving, gentle service to the sick and suffering has made of them the very embodiment of that charity which "seeketh not its own" and whose example has been an inspiration to all who know them.

And so we begin to see events—world-wide conditions —pointing toward the fulfilment of an idea which first had birth in the early days of Christianity. Not that those first impulses in the early church were identical with the impulses and reasoning of the later day; not that the originators had in their minds the wide, sweeping and varied movement which has finally spread through the whole of civilization—but the idea of human brotherhood, of love of one's neighbor, of responsibility for the bodily and material needs of one's fellow creature, originating in Christian love, held within itself the seed of that mighty tree, which today, in this twentieth century, is spreading its shade over all the world.

During the 17th, 18th and early part of the 19th centuries, three mighty movements were slowly arising which were mainly responsible for the evolution of what is known as district nursing. These movements were at first unrelated, and were carried along quite independent lines of activity. But as the small mountain streams, starting from widely separated springs, and at first slowly meandering down the mountain side, faltering in their descent, finally converge into one mighty river, so the various activities which led to district nursing started in widely different fields, including religion and science, finally came together in that great movement for human welfare, which has changed and bettered living conditions for hundreds of thousands of human beings and is still sweeping on in its beneficent course.

During the eighteenth, and especially the nineteenth centuries these forces took on a new and impelling strength, and contributed to—or might almost be said to have made inevitable—the founding of public health nursing. These three movements were:

(a) The New Humanity, which arose from an awakened consciousness to the evils under which a large portion of mankind was living and to a realization that those in power were responsible for improving the condition of the poor.

(b) The growth of Medical Science, which had developed from a purely curative application of its principles, into a *preventive* as well as curative science, embracing sanitation, hygiene, inoculation and all the more recent application of modern medicine; and

(c) Nursing, which from a desultory and inexpert care of the sick, whether in their homes or the hospital, developed into a profession, with technical rules and laws governing its practice.

These three movements are of so great importance in the history and evolution of public health nursing that we shall devote a chapter to each of them.

CHAPTER IV

THE NEW HUMANITY

The nineteenth century was ushered in by what a modern writer calls "three great revolutions"—the Intellectual Revolution, which opened up new avenues of thought and showed the deeper relation between cause and effect, opportunity and growth, poverty and disease; the French Revolution, which, together with the American Revolution, spread the doctrine of independence and the rights of man, and taught that all men are born free and equal and are entitled to life, liberty and the pursuit of happiness; and, finally, the Industrial Revolution—perhaps the greatest revolution of any age —which overthrew all previous methods of industrial production and, by substituting machinery for human hands, utterly changed the lives of countless men, women and children, and brought about conditions of poverty, over-crowding and disease which after a century of battle we are still fighting, and which today form one of the largest fields of activity for the public health nurse.

It is with this last revolution that we are chiefly concerned, for it was the conditions of poverty and suffering brought about by it which awakened that active spirit of the "New Humanity" which, in turn, started a multitude of philanthropies and public health activities for the betterment and protection of the masses, of which District Nursing has proved to be one of the most far-reaching and persistent.

Up to the end of the eighteenth century the production of industry was carried on more or less as it had been for thousands of years. What was known as the *domestic system of manufacture* prevailed. That is, the work was carried on mainly in the homes of the workmen, and the whole family entered into the labor of production. Most of the people still lived in the country or small villages where, in their neat thatched cottages set in the midst of little gardens or green fields, the workman pursued his trade in comfort and in peace.

Even the artisan who lived in the town was surrounded by many of the conditions which made the life of the rural worker so comparatively pleasant. The country-side was near at hand, for the cities were small, and there was no smoke nor grime, no huge factories with whirring machinery, no crowding. The town workmen were not then huddled together in sunless courts and alleys, but lived in small stone or brick houses where, like their fellow workers in the country, they and their families carried on the business of carding, spinning, weaving and sometimes dyeing—a varied and therefore a pleasant and healthful life, amid surroundings that offered something of pleasure and much of comfort.

Toward the end of the eighteenth century, however, a sudden and overwhelming change occurred. A series of marvellous inventions appeared one after the other, which completely revolutionized the whole system of production, substituting machinery for hands, factories for homes, and bringing in their wake a host of evils from which we have not yet recovered.

It is easy now to argue that it was a beneficient revolution, for in this day we see the result of the increased production and the greater comfort and luxury made possible to millions of men and women by the comparatively cheap articles turned out by machinery. But in those early days it was otherwise. All that could then be perceived was that the home worker had been deprived of his labor; that his independence was gone; that he was virtually the slave of the factory manager; and that instead of the simple family life and work, which enabled even the humblest workman to bring up his children in health and happiness, he was now condemned to work in crowded, noisy factories under the eye of an often tyrannical overseer; and to live in dirty, close tenements, where family life was impossible, and even decency hard to attain.

The various inventions were of course in the end of great benefit to mankind, but the changes which they brought among the working classes in those early days were little short of tragic. It was as though a huge juggernaut, in the form of an iron monster, had appeared to crush out in the most ruthless manner the hopes and lives of the humble, diligent and self-respecting workers of the land.[1]

These great inventions followed each other in quick succession. The first, the "Spinning Jenny," a wooden frame with eight spindles, which enabled the worker to spin eight threads at a time instead of only one, was invented by James Hargreaves in 1765. Four years later Arkwright invented a spinning machine to be worked by water instead of by hand. Crompton followed in 1779 with his "mule," a hybrid of the two former inventions, which greatly increased the speed of production. Finally, in 1785, Watt's invention of the steam engine was applied to the machinery used in factories, and the modern method of manufacturing

[1] "Once our English artisans were famous throughout Europe. They were spread among the country villages. Each workman was complete of his kind, in his way an artist; his work was an education to him as a man. Now he is absorbed in the centres of industry and is part of a machine. In the division of labour a human being spends his life in making pins' heads or legs of chairs, or single watch wheels, or feeding engines which work instead of him. Such activities do not feed his mind or raise his character, and such mind as he has left he feeds at the beer shop and music hall."
(The Earl of Beaconsfield. J. A. Froude. Chap. X.)

was fairly established.   Huge buildings were now erected to house the machinery, and here, in these hastily
constructed mills and factories, amid the noise and jar
and rattle of this primitive machinery, with no arrangements for health or even decency, the workers of all ages
and both sexes were crowded from early morning until
late at night, and then again from night to morning.

The spinners and weavers and other workmen from
the rural districts flocked into the cities where these
factories were established, deserting their villages and
domestic industry—for there was no competing with the
"iron men" as the machines were called.   The country-
side was deserted, the hum of the spinning-wheel was no
longer heard in the little cottage, and the few weavers
left behind eked out a penurious living.[1]   The workman, instead of working quietly in his home, was now
forced to work all day long in the crowded, badly ventilated mill, with the throb and whirr of the machinery
sounding constantly in his ears and the fear of the overseer in his heart.   Instead of living peacefully in the
little cottage, with its bright flowers and garden plot, his
home was now the ugly, dingy tenement, built close to
the factory, with its tall chimneys and belching smoke,
in order that the workman should waste no time in going to and fro from his work.   Moreover, these "iron
men" could often be handled as easily by women, or
even children, as by a man.   Therefore, as the wage
for such labor was small, women and children were
pressed into the work, leaving the home—or rather,
the miserable room which took the place of home—deserted and comfortless.   Dr. Aikin, writing in 1795,
pictured the evil effects arising from the employment
of so many women and girls in factories and mills.
He maintained that domestic life was endangered, the
women folk becoming ignorant of all household duties.
"The females," he said, "are wholly uninstructed in

[1] See Silas Marner by George Eliot.

knitting, sewing and other domestic affairs requisite to make them frugal wives and mothers. This is a great misfortune to them and to the public, as is sadly proved by a comparison of the laborers in husbandry and those in manufactury in general. In the former we meet with neatness, cleanliness and comfort, in the latter with filth, rags and poverty."

As the need of more and more labor in the factories increased, and as child labor was cheap and sufficient, a terrible system of what was virtually child slavery appeared. Pauper children from the parish workhouses were regularly collected by the overseers of the poor and ostensibly apprenticed to the factories. The treatment of these children was brutal in the extreme. Their hours of labor were very long—little children of five, six and seven years of age often working fifteen or sixteen hours a day. "In stench, in heated rooms, amid the constant whirling of a thousand wheels, little fingers and little feet were kept in ceaseless action, forced into unnatural activity by blows from the heavy hands and feet of the merciless overlooker." (History of the Factory Movement, by Alfred.)

Their only wage was food of the coarsest and lodging in some near-by cellar or garret. They slept in filthy beds *"which were never cool,"* for as one set of children was sent to its daily—or nightly—work, another set of children was placed in these dirty, unaired beds. Not only were pauper children employed, but poverty and wretchedness had so blunted the natural feelings of fathers and mothers, that little ones of five, six and seven years of age were often forced by their parents to work in the mills and to contribute their mite to the family purse. Child labor was encouraged, and the sufferings of those innocent victims of the industrial revolution was extreme. Mrs. Browning, in her poem "The Cry of the Children," voiced the growing indignation against these horrible practices.

In the factories, where not only the children but men and women as well worked for twelve, sixteen and eighteen hours constantly, conditions were appalling. There was little ventilation, no sunlight and the most horrible crowding. Malignant fevers, bred by these unsanitary conditions broke out; while overwork, insufficient clothing, scanty food, vitiated air produced puny and stunted bodies and lowered resistence to infection. The suffering was acute, and the result was seen not only in the frequent spread of epidemic fevers and the early death of many children, but also in the pale, anæmic faces of all the workers, and the crippled and deformed bodies of many. In fact, even at the present day we see the result of these terrible years of suffering in the poor physique and low standard of health of the average English factory workers.

These terrible conditions of poverty and suffering could not go on for long unnoticed. Moreover, men began to realize that it was not enough to notice and give temporary relief, not enough to sympathize and comfort, but that they must act—must search out the hidden underlying causes of all the misery, and go to work in a systematic and constructive way to remedy the evil. The people themselves also, though downtrodden and suffering, were no longer unthinking nor utterly helpless—the various political revolutions had opened their eyes to their own power; there was a new spirit of liberty abroad; the working man, in his ignorant and groping way, was beginning to realize that he was the victim of conditions that could be changed, and he clamored for a change. Riots occurred, and the first union of working men began to take form. A distinct and wide-spread feeling of indignation against prevailing factory conditions began gradually to assert itself. Philanthropists and political and social reformers worked together to obtain the passage of protective laws, which might in a measure relieve the situation.

As early as 1816 an effort had been made toward factory reform, and a committee appointed to investigate the condition of children employed in factories. Evidence of terrible overwork and unsanitary conditions was brought forward, but little or nothing at that time was accomplished. In 1819 a second commission was asked for, and finally an Act passed, which provided that children under *three* years of age should not be employed in factories, that twelve hours a day be the limit of work for those under sixteen years; that time for meals be allowed, and, as a sanitary measure, that walls and ceilings be whitewashed at least twice a year. This law, however, had little effect and was constantly evaded.

So things went on from bad to worse. Social reformers, however, were in earnest—they were not willing to lie back and rest while thousands of children were compelled to labor from 12 to 16 hours a day, and while men and women were living and working under conditions of stress and hardship which made a healthy, normal life impossible. They realized that they were in truth their brothers' keeper—and they would not desist in their efforts. New advocates for the cause appeared, first and foremost among whom we may mention Richard Oastler, a Yorkshire man of the middle class; and Lord Ashley, who later became the Earl of Shaftsbury, and whose name is associated with many humanitarian and philanthropic movements throughout a long life.

Richard Oastler threw himself heart and soul into the cause of the factory workers—he labored among them day and night and endeavored to awaken in their minds a sense of their own responsibility. "You must manage this cause yourself," he would cry. "Collect information, publish facts, let your politics be—*ten hours* a day and a time book!" (Gibbin. p. 397). He was assisted in his campaign by Mr. Saddler, a member

of Parliament who in 1831 introduced into the House
a Ten Hour Bill.   Again, however, little was accomplished, and it was left for Lord Shaftsbury to finally
put it through, although even his efforts did not at
first avail.   Lord Shaftsbury, however, reintroduced
the Ten Hour Bill and many witnesses of the abuses
it sought to remedy were brought forward.   The evidence obtained was overwhelming.   One witness assured the Commission, with unconscious self-condem-
nation, that *children under five were never employed.*
Further evidence brought out, however, that children
over five were often employed from five o'clock in the
morning until ten at night; that during that time they
were constantly on their feet; and that they were so
cruelly treated and beaten that they dared not for their
lives be late to their work.   Several cases of deaths
through such treatment were cited by witnesses.

These stories of the evil conditions existing were too
horrible and too thoroughly proven to go longer un-
remedied.   The people were finally aroused.   Lord
Shaftsbury's bill was brought to vote and passed, and
a few improvements in factory conditions established.
This bill of 1833 prohibited night labor to persons under 18 years of age; children from 9 to 13 years were
not to work for more than 48 hours a week; and young
persons, 13 to 18 years, only 68 hours.   Children
under nine were not to be employed at all.   Not
until 1847, however, was the cry for a ten hour work-
day heeded, and even then the law passed applied only
to women and young persons.—Men were still employed at will for 12 hours or more, the legal working
day being from 5:30 A. M., to 8:30 P. M.

Though this legislation was far from ideal, it was a
great step in advance.   There was some protection offered for women and children; there was a legal working day established, and, perhaps best of all, the public conscience had been awakened, evil conditions could

no longer be hidden, there was an unofficial inspection constantly going on, and from henceforth all factory employers realized that they must meet at least the minimum requirements of the law, and that it did not pay to ignore popular sentiment.

But factory reform was by no means the only manifestation of the "New Humanity" which had made its appearance. Many other abuses and evil conditions were brought to light and reforms instituted. Indeed the social legislation carried through during the first half of the 19th century was in itself a revolution.

One of the first evils investigated was that of the prison. John Howard in the 18th century and Elizabeth Fry in the early 19th, were indefatigable workers in the cause of prison reform. The treatment of prisoners was found to be inhuman, the prisons themselves filthy, and breeding places for disease of all kinds—in fact one disease—in reality typhus—was so prevalent that it went by the name of "gaol fever." Another abuse that aroused sympathy in the hearts of a few far-sighted men was the treatment of the insane. An investigation revealed the most horrible conditions. Poor lunatics were treated like dangerous animals, were chained and beaten, and left in dark rooms and cells alone like felons. Lord Shaftsbury, a young man of only 22 years of age at that time, 1828, took up their cause as his first social work, and through a long life labored for the better care of these poor unfortunates. Although their treatment still continued to be based on repression and incarceration, their condition was somewhat ameliorated, and many abuses were done away with.

Other evils attacked were bad housing, and poor sanitation (of which more in another chapter); lack of education; the miseries of little chimney sweeps; and the frightful conditions attendant on the employment of women and children in the mines.

All this social work for bettering the conditions of the poor was the outgrowth of a new point of view—a new kind of philanthropy which saw, not only the evil under which men, women and children lived and labored, but saw also that these conditions could and must be improved. It was doubtless the result, at least in part, of that great evangelical movement begun by the Wesley brothers in the preceeding century, which was based on a passionate love of humanity, a love which, like the love of the early Christians, their prototype, sought out the poor and oppressed, the afflicted and the sinner, and endeavored "to remedy the guilt, the ignorance, the physical suffering, the social degradation of the profligate and the poor." (J. R. Green, "History of the English People.")

Philanthropy during this period was so wide-spread that many thought it was becoming a mania. There were ragged schools, and Sunday schools and night schools; there were district visiting societies, and mothers' meetings, and temperance unions, and a Society for Improving the Condition of the Working Man; and there were Bible-women and parochial mission women—the forerunners of the parish deaconness and the parish nurse. The various commissioners appointed by the Government to study into the condition of the poor in relation to the different evils investigated, and the full and widely read reports of their findings, brought the subject before the people in a way that had never before been possible. People began to see how the other half lived. There was a widespread impulse to help and uplift the degraded masses—the poor and their suffering were constantly in the thoughts of men, and there was a well-nigh universal desire on the part of thinking men to better their conditions. Therefore, when in 1859 a philanthropic gentleman in Liverpool saw the benefit conferred on a sick member of his own household by the tender ministration of a trained nurse, it was in keeping with the spirit of the times that he should have visualized the benefit which a similar care might give to the sick poor in their homes, and that he should have inaugurated a system of district nursing for their benefit.

Slowly but surely the appointed time for this service was drawing near. The idea of a new type of work does not spring full-fledged from the brain of one man. It is the slow growth of ages. Many needs, and many thoughts, and many efforts go towards its final formation. And so with district nursing. Had it not been that the cause of the poor was close to the heart of the great philanthropists of the nineteenth century, the service of the trained nurse might even yet be the prerogative of the rich only.

CHAPTER V

SANITARY SCIENCE AND PREVENTIVE MEDICINE

During these years in which the spirit of the "new humanity" had been at work inspiring the great social reformers, and arousing the public conscience to its responsibility for the evil conditions under which so many of the people lived, other forces in the evolution of public health nursing had also been at work, namely; (1) the new idea concerning sanitation and its relation to health, and (2) the application of medical science to the prevention as well as cure of disease.

The therapeutic value of fresh air, cleanliness and wholesome living was becoming better and better understood. The various investigations into the condition of the working classes, which had been ordered by the government from time to time, had drawn the attention of the public to the prevalence of disease in the poorer quarters of the town, and had shown up, in a startling manner, its relation to unsanitary conditions.

It was becoming generally recognized that before any permanent reduction in fever, or any lasting improvement in the health of the people, could be effected, there must be a civic house-cleaning, so to speak, a general over-hauling of existing conditions, and the introduction into the life of the people of those healthful surroundings which alone would make possible the health to which they are entitled.

Gradually the realization was reached that there was need for sanitary, as well as for social, legislation; that the latter, in fact, included the former. The cry for "social reform" was well-nigh universal, the demand for "social justice" was becoming insistent. But social justice means an "equal chance for equal health," which, in turn, means healthful living conditions for the poor, as well as for the rich.

We see, therefore, beginning with Lord Shaftsbury's Factory Bill of 1833, a long series of Acts having to do with the welfare of the working people, with sanitation, with housing, with the prevention of disease, with the protection of the weak, and the care of the sick. These Acts became a working part of the law of the land, and were the foundation for all future public health and social legislation. "No individual planned this significant sequence," says Sir George Newman, "no single factor explains its emergence. It represents a new social spirit, a new application of science to the life and labor of man."

Medical attention for the poor was no new thing. We have seen how in Paris during the 17th century the doctors had taken turns in caring for the sick poor, and had given of their service most unsparingly. In London, too, the members of the Colleges of Physicians gave their advice gratis, where desired, to all their sick neighboring poor "within the City of London or seven miles around" (Kirkman Grey. p. 132, History of English Philanthropy).

Also, there were the hospitals, which since the days of the early Basilias had been open freely to the sick poor. Besides the hospitals there were the dispensaries. In 1777 the Royal Dispensary, the first in London, for the express benefit of the poor, was opened, and so popular was it that within thirteen years no less than ten others had been opened in the same city.

But the medical treatment available to the poor from these various sources was only available *after* the person had already become ill. The physician was called into the home only *after* disease had already entered.

No attempt was made to prevent the disease, no attempt made to teach the poor the principles of hygiene and sanitation in their relation to disease. The various societies for visiting the poor, many of which were started during the last decade of the 18th century, had, it is true, included among their other activities the teaching of cleanliness and thrift to the poor, and may therefore, be considered as the first organization to teach hygiene and sanitation, or in other words, public health; but it was not until many years later that the possibility of the actual prevention of disease was really taught to the poor in their homes, and even then it was not the physician but the *nurse* who carried the message.

In the meanwhile, the science of medicine itself was making rapid progress. A better knowledge of the human body; a better understanding of the signs and symptoms of disease; and especially the discovery by means of the microscope, of the disease-producing bacilli, had made possible a more scientific study of many diseases, especially in connection with cause and prevention. But although the germ theory was fairly well established, and inoculation and the use of antiseptic measures were beginning to be understood and practiced, still at this period *prevention* in most cases meant *sanitation*.

The earliest of the "Fathers of Prevention," as Sir John Simons called those physicians who first taught that "prevention is better than cure," was Richard Mead, who was born in England in 1673 and lived to the good old age of eighty-one. He was physician to St. Thomas' Hospital, London, and the undisputed leader of his profession in his day. He believed heartily in prevention, and taught the scientific principle that cleanliness is the best preventive against contagion.

In 1720, England was threatened with an epidemic

of cholera, and at the instigation of the Government, Dr. Mead published a little book entitled, "A Short Discourse Concerning Pestilential Contagion," which contained much excellent advice, and outlined a course of action which shows the soundness of his judgment and the modernness of his views.   In it he discusses various precautionary measures, which, in his opinion, would mitigate the danger of contagion and prevent the recurrence of the "pestilential diseases."   Cleanliness and common-sense were his basic principles.   In the past it had been the practice, in times of plague, to quarantine infected houses, marking them with a cross, and to shut up in them the sick with the well, keeping them imprisoned for at least a month after all trace of the disease had disappeared.[1]   This was probably the best they could do with the limited knowledge of those days.   But Dr. Mead realized that "it savored of punishment rather than of compassionate care," and tended to make people conceal their illness rather than suffer the penalty for having contracted it.

He suggested, therefore, that instead of "Penalizing infected families" a reward should be given to the person who first discovered and reported any case of infection; and that, instead of imprisoning the unhappy ones, the sick should be removed to some place outside the town where they could safely and properly be cared for; and the well be disinfected and allowed to go at large.   Dr. Mead had little faith in the efficacy of fumigation as a disinfectant, though he admitted that "smoke of sulphur" might have some effect as "it abounds in an acrid spirit which is found by experience to be very penetrating."   On the other hand, he laid great stress on cleanliness, and insisted that "whereas nastiness is a great source of infection,· so cleanliness is the greatest preservative."   All these

---

[1] Daniel Defoe's book on The Plague in London is interesting reading in connection with this practice of closing infected houses.

recommendations sound very modern; especially a further recommendation that "all unnecessary assemblies should be avoided," a precaution which was insistently urged during the great influenza epidemic of 1918–1919.

Other contributors to the growing science of sanitation and the new "Science of Health" were; Sir John Pringle (1707-1782) whose study of hygiene in the British army showed the great part played by filth and foul air in the propagation and spread of such diseases as dysentery, gangrene, typhus, etc; Dr. James Lind (1716–1794) whose study of the cause and prevention of typhus fever showed that typhus was but another name for hospital fever, jail fever, ship fever, etc.; and that all were caused by the same filthy and unsanitary conditions; and finally, to mention only one more of the pioneers who laid the foundation of Preventive Medicine, Dr. Lettsom (1744–1815) who in his little book "Hints towards Promoting Benevolence" devotes one section to "Hygiene" and after describing various modes of disinfection, dwells on the value of fresh air as a preventative of disease; bewails the fatal aspects of the window tax; and points out the necessity of washing the body all over once a week.

Gradually the attention of the public was being drawn to the fact that dirt meant disease; that unless the cause of sickness was removed, medical care was of no avail; and that, in order to protect the public health the authorities must have power to initiate and to enforce sanitary measures.

As I have already observed the many investigations into the conditions of the poor, carried on by the various Commissions appointed by the Government, to study the factory conditions, the working of the Poor Law, the state of the prisons, etc.; had brought vividly before the public the terrible conditions under which the greater part of the laboring classes lived. Moreover, several special investigations into the causes of certain local epidemics had made apparent the close relation which existed between these wretched conditions and the recurring epidemics of cholera and of fever which continued to claim such a heavy toll of lives. The realization that these epidemics were, in most cases, preventable, made their recurrence a crime for which the nation itself should be held accountable; and in 1831, during the epidemic of cholera in London, the Poor Law Commission addressed a letter to the Home Secretary "Indicting preventable disease as a fertile source of destitution and death" (Morris' History of Public Health. p. 26).

In the winter of 1837, there was an unusually severe epidemic of fever in Spitalfields, which excited such alarm that the Poor Law Commissioners sent three prominent physicians, Dr. Arnott, Dr. Southwood Smith and Dr. Kay, into the district to investigate as to the possible causes of the epidemic. After a thorough study of conditions these physicians reported that the filthy and crowded state of the tenements where the poor lived, and the poisonous atmosphere caused by lack of drainage and the accumulation of putrifying matter, were the outstanding causes of the disease; and they added that conditions were so bad that not only did the inhabitants of these localities suffer from the fever and die, but that many of the physicians and relieving officers who had been forced to work in these quarters, had also contracted the disease and died.

About this same time another investigation was made in Liverpool, where it was found that sixty-three cases of fever had occurred in one year in a small court containing only twelve houses. The place was visited and it was discovered that the court was inundated with fluid filth which had oozed through the walls from the

5

adjacent cesspools (Report into Sanitary Conditions of the Laboring Population of Great Britain, by Chadwick).

In the summer of 1839 some bad cases of fever occurred in a section which had always hitherto been considered healthy. Attention was therefore attracted to the spot and upon investigation an old, half-choked drain was discovered, which had caused a shallow stagnant pool of fetid matter. Measures were immediately taken to carry off this nuisance by means of proper sewerage, and from the hour of its removal no fresh cases of fever occurred.

The findings in these several investigations were so startling and the evidence so conclusive, that there was no longer any doubt as to the causes of the epidemics, nor any doubt as to where the responsibility lay. It was a matter for the public authorities to take in hand. But the public authorities lacked power to act. It was clearly a situation where legislative action was necessary, but in order to secure that legislation it was necessary to educate the people so that they would understand the need, and demand the remedy. Again Lord Shaftsbury was instrumental in arousing a public protest. He not only himself investigated conditions, but he published an article in the Quarterly Review detailing, in no uncertain terms, the things he had found. "We have penetrated alleys," wrote he, "terminating in a cul-de-sac, long and narrow like a tobacco pipe, where air and sunlight were never known. On one side rose walls several feet in height, blackened with damp and slime, on the other stood dwellings, still more revolting; while the breadth of the wet and bestrewed passages would by no means allow the full expansion of our arms.—Pass to another district, there you will see flowing before each hovel, and within a few feet of it, a broad, black, uncovered drain, exhaling at every point the most unwholesome vapors.

If there be not a drain, there is a stagnant pool; touch either with your stick and the nephetic mass will yield up its poisonous gas like the coruscations of soda water."

He exposed, also, the shameful crowding in the homes of the poor, caused not only by poverty and lack of quarters, but by the extortionate rents charged for the wretched dwellings. He found hundreds of human beings living in a dozen small houses; men, women and children sleeping in alleyways or under bridges. In the fourteen houses of Wild Court (Drury Lane), nearly one thousand persons found shelter. He saw why people became a prey to disease, and why fevers were rife and contagion spread even to the homes of the rich. He pointed out how futile it was to try to raise or help the masses unless at the same time they were provided with decent homes; and how more than futile were the efforts of physicians or medical officers unless the unsanitary conditions of the poor quarters of the city were rectified.

The result of all this agitation was at last felt, and, after much effort on the part of a few public spirited men, an Act of Parliament was finally passed in 1848 which established a General Board of Health, with power to form local Boards of Health throughout the kingdom, and to enforce certain measures for the protection of the public health.

Although public health activities at this time, and for many years to follow, were concerned chiefly with environment, that is, with the removal of filth, refuse and nuisances, the providing of pure water, the proper disposal of sewage, etc., nevertheless, this Act of 1848 was of epoch-making importance, and marked a new era in sanitary requirements.

The new Board, consisting of Lord Ashly (the future Lord Shaftsbury), Mr. Edwin Chadwick (whom Sir Malcom Morris calls "the true begetter of the

Public Health Act of 1848), and Dr. Southwood Smith (who for so many years had been interested in sanitary matters), was active from the very start. A general overhauling of sanitary conditions was instituted, and a group of splendid sanitarians and health officers appeared. Dr. John Simon, the first medical officer of London, was undoubtedly one of the most able among them. The care of the public health was to him a sacred charge. He realized also that it is "Public Opinion that fills the sails of the Ship of State," and that, in order to secure legislative power to carry on the work of sanitation and to protect the public health, the people of the country must be educated in sanitary matters.

This he undertook to do in a series of brilliant Annual Reports which contained a mass of interesting and instructive information, and which were widely read by the whole country. In these reports he pointed out how filth diseases were being inflicted on hundreds of innocent and helpless people because of carelessness on the part of the public; that the poor were atrociously lodged, and that until more healthful and sanitary homes were supplied, it was useless to try to cope with disease. He showed that the employment of women in factories had a marked effect on the increasing rate of infant mortality. He insisted upon the need of sanitary measures to prevent industrial disease; measures to insure proper ventilation in workshops; to prevent overcrowding; to prevent or at least to mitigate, the evil effects of dust, and poisonous gases in the dangerous trades; and, finally, he pointed out that sanitary effort is primarily an effort to prevent disease, and that unless the people did their part, not only in making but in following the laws pertaining to sanitation and hygiene, it was impossible to attain a high standard of public health.

And so in this growing science of sanitation, and

in this still newer science of preventive medicine, do we see yet another factor in the slow evolution of public health nursing. Prevention was beginning to be the watchword for health. It would no longer be possible to work among the poor without endeavoring to remove the causes of their distress.

Now that it was recognized that sickness was the result of bad living and dirty homes, it followed naturally that the visitor to the poor would try to teach them some of the simplest principles of hygiene and sanitation; and by demonstration, as well as precept, endeavor to instill in them a desire for a better standard of living. Although for many years yet the work of the doctor and the nurse was to be mainly curative, and they were still looked upon as the people to be called in *after* instead of *before* illness had made its appearance, still the word "health" was to a certain extent beginning to replace the word "disease," and the day was approaching when Florence Nightingale could speak to an understanding audience of the training of "health nurses" as well as "sick nurses."

CHAPTER VI

KAISERSWERTH AND THE ENGLISH SISTERS

During all these centuries the early deaconess of the church had not been forgotten. The remembrance of her work and self-consecration was still an inspiration to many. During the Middle Ages the Roman Catholic sisterhoods had, as we have seen, carried on a certain portion of her ministry to the poor, and had been responsible for such nursing as there then was. After the Reformation the lack of these sisterhoods was felt in the Protestant churches, and many of them, turning back to the primitive church for an example, instituted deaconesses of their own, assigning them duties which usually included serving the poor and nursing the sick.

As early as 1530 the church in Minden had decreed that "an order of district nurses and visitors for the poor be established" (Nutting Vol I. p. 526). In 1568 the office of deaconess was recommended in the reformed church at Wesel,—though it was not actually established until twelve years later; and in Amsterdam we find that at the time of the Pilgrim Fathers, there was in the church, besides pastors, teachers, and deacons, "one ancient widow for a deaconess who did them serve many years. . . . She did frequently visit the sick and weak, especially women—and if these were poor she would gather relief for them of those that were able." (Chronicles of the Pilgrim Fathers of the Colony of Plymouth, by Alex. Young. p. 455.)

These movements however, were more or less local-
ized, and the various Roman Catholic sisterhoods,
among which the Sisters of Charity and the Béguines
were still the most active, continued to represent the
only large groups of women organized to nurse the sick
poor in their homes.

The Protestant countries, especially England, felt
keenly the lack of these nursing Sisters. Travelers
visiting Catholic countries and coming in contact with
the Sisters of Charity or the ancient order of the
Béguines, would, on returning home, expatiate upon the splendid work which they did, and regret
that their own homeland had no similar nursing orders.

Southey in 1815 visited the Béguines at Ghent and
wrote home that it was "an institution reasonable and
useful, as well as humane and religious"; and in 1825
Dr. Gooch, a well known English physician, visiting
these same Béguines, was so struck with their general
efficiency in visiting and nursing the sick poor, that
he recommended, in an open letter, that a similar community, or an order like the Sisters of Charity, be
established in England, and the members taught the
rudiments of nursing, so that the poor, when ill, need
not be without care. "Let all real Christians join
and form an order of women like the Sisters of Charity in Catholic countries," he said, "let them be selected
for good, plain common sense, kindness of disposition,
indefatigable industry and deep piety; let them receive
—not a technical and scientific—but a practical medical education. For this purpose let them be placed,
both as nurses and pupils in the hospitals of Edinburgh
and London, or in the country hospitals. Let them be
made as familiar with the best remedies (which are
always few) as they are with barley-water, gruel and
beef tea—let such women, thus educated, be distributed

among the country parishes of the kingdom and be maintained by parish allowances,—let this be done, and I fearlessly predict that (country priests) will no longer complain that their sick flock suffer from medical neglect."

No results followed this appeal, however, and it was left for a young but earnest Lutheran pastor, in the little town of Kaiserswerth on the Rhine, to establish the first Protestant sisterhood which should include among its many activities the ones outlined by Dr. Gooch, and should prove the source of inspiration for a work much broader and farther reaching than any of which the good doctor had dreamed.

When in 1822 Theodor Fliedner, a young man of twenty-two, was appointed pastor to the little church at Kaiserswerth, a small village on the Rhine, he little realized how great a work was to result from his pastorate there. He probably saw ahead of him no greater service to mankind than the care of his little flock, and no broader influence than that of a simple, pious, country minister. But the humble are sometimes more influential than the ambitious; and great good sometimes results from seeming disaster. The parish was a poor one, most of his parishioners being either peasants or workers in the big silk factory, the only industry of the little town. When therefore, only four months after his installation, this silk factory failed, leaving a large part of the population without means of support, and making it impossible for them to pay even the small salary promised him (about $135 a year), it seemed as if his work in Kaiserswerth must end, and the little community be doomed to struggle on without a spiritual guide.

Theodor Fliedner, however, was a true shepherd of his flock, he would not desert his sheep. After some thought and much prayer for guidance, he resolved to start out, staff in hand, on a tour of the country, having in mind to visit the richer parishes of his own and other lands and to ask their aid in financing the work in his own poorer community.   It was an appeal for home missionary work, and proved highly successful.   His travels took him through Germany, Holland, Belgium and into England.   In Holland he was much impressed by the order of deaconesses which he found established among the Mennonites, a small but earnest evangelical society; and in England he was even more strongly impressed by the work being done by Elizabeth Fry among the prisoners at Newgate. "In both these countries," said he, "I became acquainted with a multitude of charitable institutions, for the benefit of both soul and body; I saw schools, almshouses, orphanages, hospitals, prisons and societies for the reformation of prisoners—At the same time I observed that it was a living Christ which had called almost every one of these institutions and societies into life."

His mission abroad was successful and he returned home with sufficient funds to carry on the work of the little parish.   Money, however, was not the only thing he had gained.   He had brought back with him a wealth of new ideas regarding social work, and from henceforth he was constantly revolving in his mind how he might best serve his fellow-man, by works, as well as by prayers.

In 1828 he married Frederika Münster, a good and pious woman who, until her death in 1842, was a faithful wife, a devoted mother, and an able help-mate in all her husband's undertakings.   When we learn that during these fourteen years of her married life she not only aided him in all his parish work, but bore him ten children as well—we can scarcely be surprised at her early death.

Under her husband's direction Frederika Fliedner started a Woman's Society for visiting and nursing the sick poor in their homes. There was much poverty in the little parish, and no provision for dealing with illness when it appeared, so this little society met a great need.

Other social work was also undertaken; a refuge for discharged women prisoners provided; an infant school opened up; and various other activities inaugurated; but it was not until 1836, fourteen years after his tour abroad, and eight years after his marriage, that he started the hospital and training school for deaconesses, the institution which brought him the most lasting fame, and proved the most far-reaching in its results.

The idea of a hospital and the training of good Christian women as nurses had lain dormant in his mind for many years. The work done by the Women's Society was far from sufficient to meet the needs of the parish. The members were all hard working German "Hausfraus" with their own large families to care for, and the little visiting and nursing they were able to do was far from adequate.

"The state of the sick poor," said Fliedner, many years later, "had long weighed on our hearts. Did not that terrible saying of our Lord's apply to us? 'I was sick and ye visited me not'?" Another idea also was germinating in his mind. Did not the Apostolic Church create an order of deaconesses? If so, why should not the modern church revive the institution? The primitive deaconesses cared for the sick and visited the poor; why should not a modern deaconess be trained to do a similar work? No sooner had the idea taken definite form, than he and his good wife set to work to carry it out. "We now looked quietly about for a house for the hospital—Suddenly the largest and finest house in Kaiserswerth came into the market—It was true the price was $2300 and we had no money. I bought it, however, with good courage on the 20th day of April 1836, and at Martinmas the money was paid."

There was some opposition to so novel an undertaking as the founding of an order of deaconesses. The Protestants doubted—"did he wish to set up nuns and convents in their church?" The Roman Catholics thought they saw in his hospital a proselyting scheme. The best answer to the latter fear was, that though there were Protestant doctors in the place Pastor Fliedner selected for his hospital the one Roman Catholic physician in Kaiserswerth, because he was the most skilful. The Fliedners now set to work to furnish their hospital with what furniture they could procure—a few beds and chairs, the necessary cooking utensils, and six linen sheets—and on October 13th, 1836, it was opened with one patient, one nurse, and a cook. In the course of a month four more very sick patients were received, and before the year was over sixty had been cared for in the hospital and twenty-eight in their own homes in the village. Applicants for admission as deaconesses also applied, and by the end of the first year seven were in training.

These girls were all either from the peasant class, or were the daughters of small tradesmen. Like St. Vincent's Sisters of Charity, they came from sturdy country stock and brought with them robust bodies, clean minds, and a simple piety which saw the hand of God in all their leadings. The rules for admission were few. Applicants must be twenty-five years of age or over, of good character, and good health. After three years of training they were consecrated to their work by the laying on of hands and a blessing.

Their dress was a plain blue cotton gown, a white apron, large turned down collars, and a white muslin cap with a frill around the face, tied beneath the chin with a large white bow. Out-of-doors, they wore a long black cloak, and a black bonnet over their cap.

The course of instruction was simple but practical. The probationers were taught the essentials of housework; the making of beds, sweeping of rooms, cleaning, dusting, serving and cooking. They also were taught bookkeeping, letter writing, and reading aloud. This last accomplishment might be an interesting and useful addition to the training of a modern private duty nurse.

After this preliminary instruction the pupil was obliged to decide whether she would be a teacher or a nurse; if the former, she entered the infant school and went through a certain preparation to fit her for teaching; if the latter, she went into the wards of the hospital for her training as a nurse. Compared with the training considered necessary for a nurse today, that given at Kaiserswerth was, as Florence Nightingale declared, "nil." The sanitary arrangements, too, were most inadequate; "hygiene horrible," said the truthful Florence, but hastened to add, however, "Never have I met with a higher tone, a purer devotion—there was no neglect."

Besides the regular work in the hospital wards there was a certain amount of instruction in visiting nursing, carried on in the village under the superintendence of Frau Fliedner, who would accompany the pupils from house to house, showing them how best to care for the sick poor in their own homes. This instruction was found valuable even in the early days of the Institution. Not long after its establishment an epidemic of virulent fever broke out in some of the nearby German towns. Knowledge of this epidemic reached Kaiserswerth and four deaconesses were at once sent to one of the villages where the suffering was most acute. They found some twenty-five fever patients in the most alarming condition. A mother and four children, in one hovel; four other patients in another; and so on, all lying on foul straw, or on bedclothes that had not been washed for a week, almost without food, utterly without help. Many had died already. The healthy had fled; the parish doctor lived four German leagues away and could not come every day. The first care of the Sisters was to introduce cleanliness and ventilation into the narrow cabins of the peasants. They washed and cooked for the sick; they watched every night by turn at their bedsides; and tended them with such success that only four died after their arrival, and the rest were convalescent, after four weeks' stay. (Deaconesses in Europe, Bankroft. p. 88.)

The daily life at Kaiserswerth Institute was simple in the extreme. Every hour was filled with its regular prescribed duties and an atmosphere of love and zeal prevailed. Frau Fliedner superintended the practical work of the students and the Pastor had charge of the spiritual side. No vows were taken, but seldom if ever did a probationer desert when once her hand had been set to the plow.

In 1842 Fliedner's wife died and was greatly mourned both by her husband and by the deaconesses, who had found in her a mother, as well as a teacher. Two years afterward Fliedner applied to Amalia Sieverking for someone to take charge of his hospital.

She recommended Caroline Bertheau, a former friend and pupil, who was then serving in the hospital at Hamburg. This young woman so pleased the Pastor that he asked her not only to be his superintendent but to be his wife. They were married at once—and again Fliedner was fortunate in finding a devoted helpmate in his wife.

At about this time, or somewhat earlier, a new phase of the work was undertaken, namely, parochial nursing. When a church would apply to Fliedner for a deaconess to nurse the sick in its parish, the pastor would send one out with homely words of advice and admonition. "It is your duty," he would say, "to

give your first service to the poor. If you happen to
be forced to choose between them and the rich, go to
those who cannot recompense you, for they are the
ones who need you most."

These parish deaconesses, "Geimeinde Diakonissen"
they were called, visited the poor and the sick in their
homes, going from house to house and following, as
far as possible, the example laid down by the early
Christian deaconesses. They were very popular, and
because of their experience in the care of the sick, as
well as in the household management, were able to
render the greatest assistance in time of need. They
were expected to give a regular report of all their
labors to the clergymen, to the diaconate, and to the
Ladies' Charitable Society, when such existed.

Besides the regular graduated deaconesses, there
gradually developed a large number of lay graduates,
the "Johannister Schwestern," so called because the
Society of St. John of Jerusalem paid for their training. These were women of every age and social position, married or single, who had at some time in their
life taken a six months' course at the Kaiserswerth Hospital. They are not in any way to be confounded with
the deaconesses proper, but in the parish work throughout the country they formed a reserve army of lay-work-
ers, whose slight hospital training made them efficient
"aides" in time of need, and who helped to spread
the doctrine that hospital training was a necessary prelude to successful nursing of any kind.

Meanwhile, the fame of the institution at Kaiserswerth was spreading far beyond the confines of the little
village where it had originated. In other towns and
other countries, movements for the training of women
to nurse the sick, especially the sick poor, were started;
and various orders of Protestant deaconesses or sisters
founded, though at no place was there such a varied

program of work, nor so large and comprehensive a plant, as at Kaiserswerth.

In 1841, "The Institute of Deaconesses or Protestant Sisters of Charity" was founded in Paris, the object of which was to instruct and direct women who should "devote themselves to the relief of bodily or spiritual misery, particularly to the care of the sick, the young, and the poor" (Ludlow, Deaconesses and Protestant Sisterhoods, Edin. Review, Vol. 37, p. 442).

Besides the regular deaconesses this Institute taught other women who, not wishing to enter the order, were yet anxious to receive instruction in the different fields of charitable activity which might be open to them, especially that most appealing of all charities, the nursing of the sick poor; thus a class of lay-nurses for the sick, of a lower order than the deaconesses sprang up in Paris, somewhat similar to the Johannister Schwestern of Kaiserswerth.

A similar institution was opened in Strassburg, in 1842; with an affiliated house at Mulhausen which placed special accent on the training of the deaconess for parish work. These parish-deaconesses would start out early in the morning, each to her own particular section of the city, and there carry on their work of district nurse and district visitor among the poor, returning at night-fall to the central house.

In Switzerland, also, several institutions for the training of deaconesses were opened at about this same time, all of which had as their especial object the "training of women for the care of the sick"; the one at Eschallen setting forth as its main object "the care of the sick in their own homes" (Ibid, Edinburgh Review, 1842).

In England Mrs. Fry, whose prison reform work had, perhaps, been the original inspiration to Fliedner for all his social reform, was, in turn, herself inspired by the work at Kaiserswerth; and in 1840, founded the "Society of Protestant Sisters of Charity," for the purpose of supplying nurses to the sick of all classes in their own homes.

The Dowager Queen Adelaide was asked to become a Patroness, which she readily consented to do, asking at the same time that her name might be added to the list of Sisters, so that she might be called upon to act as nurse in an emergency.

Their first Home was in a small house in Raven's Row, White Chapel; but after one or two moves, they finally settled, in 1850, at 4 Devonshire Square, where the Society still exists under the name of "The Institution of Nursing Sisters." Its work became quickly known and grew rapidly, applications for nurses coming in from all classes of individuals, including the clergy, who asked for nurses to work in their parishes.

In 1841, an application was received from a doctor, who appears to have been very much in advance of his time. He applied for a nurse to work from a Dispensary, his idea being that her work would be mainly of a preventive nature. She was to instruct the poor people how to perform the ordinary duties of the sick room, such as how to stop the bleeding from a leech bite, and how to make poultices and fomentations. She was to inquire if all the children of the family had been vaccinated, and was to report all cases of blindness, idiocy, or any other abnormality and she was to teach cheap cooking, and perform other duties now being arranged for by the English Ministry of Health.

All this is the more remarkable when we remember that at that time there was not even a Central Board of Health, and that the great illuminating Report on the sanitary condition of the Laboring Population of Great Britain, which so aroused people to the need of preventive measures, did not appear until the following year. It goes to show, however, that while these great public movements towards an improved system of public health activities were slowly evolving, there was a constantly growing private initiative along the same lines, which helped to increase popular knowledge, and did much to make possible the passage of the sanitary laws which followed.

These nursing Sisters were at first untrained; within a few years, however, a system of training was worked out whereby the nurse-candidates were sent to various hospitals for a regular course of instructions. At first this was for a period of six months; increased later to one year; and so on, until today, all Sisters of the staff have received a full three years training in recognized hospitals.

This Sisterhood, though thoroughly religious in spirit, was secular in character. There were no vows, and the "placement" of a sister on the staff was accompanied with no formality beyond the saying of a prayer composed by the foundress, Mrs. Fry.

Other English Sisterhoods followed, among which we may specially mention, the "Park Village Community" started under Dr. Pusey's guidance in 1845; and St. John's House Sisterhood, founded in 1848, and which was the first *purely nursing* order in the Anglican Church.

The Park Village Community, however, was the first distinctly religious English Sisterhood. Dr. Pusey, with several other priests and laymen of the English Church, had long had it in mind to form a society of "Soeurs de Charité" in the Anglo-Catholic Church. They knew that there would be opposition to such a course, under the impression that it savored of Romanism, and therefore, at first, it was suggested that it might be started merely by the employment of women in hospitals and lunatic asylums "in which last Christian nursing is so sadly missed," said Dr. Pusey. Dr. Hook agreed with the idea, and wrote; "I am always

6

an advocate for establishing works before principles.
Let the good be done before we tell people why and
how it is done."

This was in 1840. Four years later, however, the
desire for the establishment of an English religious
sisterhood had become so strong, that a meeting of
prominent churchmen, among whom were Lord John
Manners and Mr. Gladstone, was held in London, at
which it was resolved that steps be taken, at once for
the "Establishment and permanent maintenance" of
such a sisterhood; and first among the works of mercy
which the sisters were to engage in, was mentioned,
"visiting the poor or the sick in their homes."

A paper circulated and signed by this group of fourteen prominent men, in order to solicit funds for the
maintenance of the sisterhood, gives a succinct statement of the need and the plan.

The works of mercy contemplated were such as:

1: Visiting the poor or the sick at their own houses.

2: Visiting hospitals, workhouses or prisons.

3: Feeding, clothing and instructing destitute children.

4: Giving shelter to distressed women of good character.

5: Assisting in the burial of the dead.

It will be seen from this outline that the original
idea which animated the founders of the Institution
was to minister to the sick and suffering.

On March 24, 1845, the little community, to be
known as "Sisters of Mercy," was inaugurated at
17 Park Village, London. The house was small, containing on the ground floor a parlor, a recreation room,
and an oratory, the upper floor being divided into
six "cells"; the kitchen was used as a "refectory."

The sisters wore a distinctive dress, dropped the
title of "Miss" and were simply known as "Sister Anne"
or "Sister Jane" or "Sister Mary." They rose at 5

A. M. and retired at 10 P. M. Three hours in the morning, and two in the afternoon, were spent in visiting the poor; the rest of the day being devoted to religious exercises, some housework and a little recreation and meals.

Such was the origin of the Park Village Community or "Sisters of Mercy" whose rule was founded somewhat on the lines of St. Francis de Sales' Order of the Visitation, and whose prime work consisted in visiting the sick poor in their homes. No training was given, however.

The St. John's House Sisterhood was founded in 1848, with the express design of improving and raising the character of nurses for the sick in hospitals, among the poor and in private families. These Sisters were given a very thorough training, according to the light of that day, in King's College Hospital, and were especially instructed in all such matters as would best fit them to be nurses and visitors of the sick poor. Their first home was at 36 Fitzroy Square in the district of St. John, the Evangelist, from which the Society took the name by which it has ever since been known.

St. Margaret's Sisterhood was still another Anglican Order, whose members devoted themselves to the care of the poor. Many years later, when District Nursing was well established and the well-trained Queen's Nurses were found in all parts of Great Britain, one of the older Sisters of St. Margaret wrote: "How we ever managed to help our poor sick people before those invaluable nurses came I cannot think. We did the little we could ourselves just in our own parish, but it was but a tiny drop in the ocean of sickness and misery. How it rejoices the hearts of everyone to see the bright, cheery, kindly face of the nurse going about on her errands of helpfulness, and accomplishing on a very large scale, with trained skilfulness, what we used to attempt, on a very small scale, with anxious unskil-fulness." (Memoirs of a Sister of St. Savior's Priory. p. 304.)

We see, therefore, that not only was there a general awakening to the miseries of the poor, and the simul-taneous appearance of all kinds of organizations for the alleviation of these miseries, such as Sunday schools, ragged schools, mother's meetings, visiting societies, and nursing Sisterhoods; but there was also a growing feeling that people must be trained for their work; and, especially when it included the care of the sick, that the workers should receive a definite training in hos-pitals.

"We have works of love and mercy for the best of our women to do," said Mrs. Jameson. "But we must have them such as we want them,—not impelled by transient feelings, but by deep abiding motives; not amateur ladies of charity, but brave women, whose vo-cation is fixed, and whose faculties of every kind have been trained and disciplined to their work." (Commun-ity of Labor, by Mrs. Jameson.)

Nursing was beginning to be looked upon as a voca-tion, as a "calling" to a high duty, which demanded, not only the love, self-sacrifice and self-consecration, thought sufficient in the middle ages, but a novitiate of training as well, a training of mind, and of hands, but particularly of hands.

Nevertheless, although the general principle that training is necessary in order to make a competent nurse was accepted, the knowledge of what that training should be, and how best attained, was vague; and it was left to Florence Nightingale to show the way, and to demonstrate that nursing, and especially that most important branch of nursing, the care of the sick poor in their homes, was no amateur work, but required knowledge, patience, self-denial, tact, kindness, and an abounding love for one's fellow-creatures.

CHAPTER VII

FLORENCE NIGHTINGALE

Florence Nightingale was born on May 12, 1820, in the beautiful city of Florence. Her parents were English people of position and wealth, and from her birth Florence was surrounded by every luxury which money and love could procure. Her childhood was passed in the country, the summers at Lea Hurst, Derbyshire, an estate inherited by her father shortly before his marriage; and the rest of the year at Embley Park, Hampshire, a beautiful English home surrounded by "old oaks and beeches, thickets of flowering laurel and rhododendron, and profusion of flowers and scents." As an indication of her early interest in the subject which was later to engross her life, stories are told of how, at the age of six, she copied into a little book which she herself had made, a medical prescription with instructions as to the dose; and how, a few years later, she bandaged a poor dog's broken leg and nursed him back to health. But, as Sir Edward Cook has said, in his incomparable Life of Florence Nightingale, "Other children have tended wounded animals and had their pill boxes and samples."

It is, nevertheless, true that at a very early age she realized the aimlessness of her life and longed to consecrate it to some work which would occupy all her faculties and contribute to the welfare of man and the service of God. Many other young girls, however, have also been filled with this same longing; have had a period of religious exaltation, and have worked hard among the poor or sick in order to satisfy the name-less discontent which they interpreted as a religious "call." The difference between them and Florence Nightingale is that the majority of young people are later caught by the glamour of the world and turn aside from the "call." Florence Nightingale never turned aside.

As we have indicated, the state of life to which she had been called seemed to point to a gay girlhood, a happy marriage with someone of her own social rank, and the more quiet pleasures of an English country home. The young lady ought, according to all prece-dent, to have been content with pretty clothes, balls, concerts, travel and a little visiting among the poor in the village as a salve to her conscience. She ought, according to her catechism, to have done her duty in that state of life to which it had pleased God to call her, and to have thanked God that her "state of life" was such a pleasant one. Strange to say, Florence Nightingale did not consider it a pleasant one. To her it seemed an oppressive life, a narrow life, a life in which she could not expand to her full measure, could not use the faculties with which she had been by na-ture endowed. It was a life of selfish inactivity, and she longed for action, though at first she did not see clearly the line of action, she should pursue. But though she rebelled fiercely against the life of luxury and inactivity to which she was condemned, and cried out in bitterness against the restraints of home, she sub-mitted herself to what seemed the inevitable, and en-deavored, so far as in her lay, to be a good and obedient daughter.

I have said that though impelled to action she did not see clearly what work she wished to pursue. How-ever, in later life she herself said "the first thought I can remember and the last, was nursing work" (Cook. p. 106), and certain it is that her mind was early impressed by the suffering of the sick and the miseries of the poor. A friend, who visited at Lea Hurst, recalls that Florence Nightingale would often be missing in the evening and on search being made, she would be found in the village, sitting by the bedside of some sick person. (Cook. p. 41).

Had she lived in the days of the early Christians, she would undoubtedly have been a Deaconess in the church; had she lived a few centuries later, her aspiration and interests would probably have drawn her into some one of the active religious Sisterhoods; but living as she did, in the early part of the 19th century, a century quick with the growing unrest of women, though still hampered by the Victorian idea of domestic duty, she was forced to work out her own salvation and was able to open up a new field of work for the interest and energies of womankind. That her lead should have been along the line of sanitary and nursing reform was in keeping with the times in which she lived. She was a girl of thirteen,—a most impressionable age,—when the great Factory Bill was passed. If her mind was as keen and alert in early girlhood as it proved itself in later life, she must have followed, with a quickening sense of personal responsibility, the dreadful findings of those days.

She was seventeen when the terrible epidemic of fever broke out in Spitalfields and she must have read with a beating heart, the report of the Commissioners on the preventable causes of the disease, and the unnecessary suffering of the stricken ones. Of that same year she wrote, "God called me to His service on February 7, 1837." (Cook. p. 15) Did these happenings in the great world outside her door have their influence in shaping her life and work? Who can doubt it? Moreover, the need of better nursing care for the sick and the lack in England of Sisters of Charity, had long been felt.   It was the suffering of the sick poor that suggested to Mrs. Fry the founding of her Institute for Nursing Sisters, and the inefficiency of the nurses of that day which suggested the founding of St. John's Sisterhood for the better training of nurses.

Is it not logical to suppose that so sensitive a mind as that of Florence Nightingale should have been impressed by the unnecessary suffering of the sick and should have felt the call to reform conditions a personal one?   However, although from the age of seventeen her principal interests seem to have centered around "sick folk," hospitals and nursing sisterhoods, it was not until some years later that she realized that in nursing only, could she fulfill the true purpose of her being.   One of the first definite allusions to the desire which now filled her soul was in 1844 when she asked Dr. Howe, "If I should determine to study nursing and to devote my life to that profession, do you think it would be a very dreadful thing?"   "Not a dreadful thing at all," he replied, "I think it would be a very good thing."

She was then twenty-four years old.   Though she longed to nurse the sick she did not wish to do so as an amateur, giving only her leisure hours to the work. She wanted to devote her whole life to it, and as she said to Dr. Howe, to *study nursing*.   Hitherto, it had not been considered necessary to study nursing.   Anyone was looked upon as competent to nurse the sick, without training, without aptitude, without even the virtues of sobriety or trustworthiness.   The women into whose hands the care of the sick was, at that period, delegated were, as a class, ignorant, gossiping, full of old wives' superstitions,—when they were not actually vicious,—and the only skill they possessed was that gained from practical experience. Almost invariably they drank. Indeed drunkenness was looked upon as a natural consequence of their occupation. Even the medical men of the day considered it inevitable. "The duties they have to perform are most unpleasant," said one doctor, "and it is little wonder that many of them drink."

Florence Nightingale, however, felt otherwise. She realized that the care of the sick, more than almost any other work, should be in the hands of women of good character, responsible women, who could be relied upon to do what the doctor ordered and to do it with intelligence. Not only did the comfort of the sick require tenderness, watchfulness and skill, on the part of the nurse, but the very life of the patient might depend upon the careful carrying out of the doctor's instructions. Life is sacred; to protect it, to minister to it, to save it seemed to her a mission worthy to be ranked among the highest a woman could follow.

Thus, for many years, revolving in her own mind the ways and means by which she could best accomplish her purpose, did Florence Nightingale pursue her cherished dream. At last the way seemed clear. She would go to Salisbury Hospital for a few months as a nurse, to learn the practice of nursing, and then return to Lea Hurst and care for the sick in the little village of West Wellow, "Making such wondrous intimacies, under the shelter of a rhubarb powder and a dressed leg!" (Cook vol. 1, p. 44.) She even had the dim idea that later she might take a small house in the village and establish a Protestant Sisterhood.

Her family, however, had little sympathy with her ambitions. Her mother was terrified at the idea. "What! Enter a hospital where she would be exposed to all kinds of dangers both physical and moral!" It was preposterous. The idea of nursing in the village, romantic and sentimental; the whole thing unfitting a lady. "It was as if I had wanted to be a kitchen-maid," said Miss Nightingale. And so in bitter disappointment the plan was abandoned.

In 1847, she wintered in Rome, where she made the acquaintance of Mr. and Mrs. Sydney Herbert, the friends who were to have perhaps the greatest influence in her after life; and again in 1849, she traveled abroad visiting Greece, Egypt and Germany. New friends, new scenes, new interests did not, however, turn her from the call to God's service which she now heard so clearly. A deep-seated conviction cannot be uprooted by foreign travel, nor an over-powering interest be supplanted by social gaieties, the latter form but the surface of life, the underlying life of the mind goes on untouched. Her mind still dwelt on the idea of nursing and she used every occasion to further her knowledge on the subject.

She visited hospitals in Italy, France and Germany; she compared their methods of nursing and administration; she studied reports and papers on sanitation, health, hospitals and sisterhoods. She was very much interested in certain Reports of the Kaiserswerth Institute and longed to visit it. During her travels in the year 1849 her desire was fulfilled. She had the unparalleled pleasure of a fortnight's visit at Kaiserswerth. Two years later she returned for a stay of three months.

We can well understand with what enthusiasm she must have entered upon her training in this establishment and how happy she must have been at last to have realized her heart's desire. "The world here fills my life with interest and strengthens me in body and mind," she writes. And again, "I find the deepest interest in everything here. This is life. Now I know what it is to live and to love life. I wish for no other earth, no other world but this."

The reality had equalled the dream. There was

no longer any doubt in her mind as to what she should do. A year or two later she visited Paris and made a study of the hospitals there, herself entering the Maison de la Providence and going with the Sisters on their rounds of duty.

She was now thirty-three. She had never faltered in her purpose. She was at this date probably the most thoroughly trained nurse in England. Not only was she trained in nursing technique but she had studied and compared the systems of nursing as carried on in the various hospitals of France, England and Germany, and had, herself, had practical experience with the nursing Sisters of France and the nursing Deaconesses of Germany. Besides her experience as a nurse, she had untiring energy, great executive ability and a passionate desire to concentrate her life to the work which from her girlhood had never ceased to beckon to her. Above all, she was a woman of broad education and fine culture. She had reached an age when even her parents realized that she was entitled to lead her own life, and to follow the dictates of her own conscience.

There was, therefore, little opposition when, in 1853, she accepted the position of Superintendent of an "Establishment for Gentlewomen during Illness." At last she was free! Free to follow the work for which her soul had so long pined. This espisode was however, but the prelude to a far greater work; was but the final preparation for a task, the magnitude of which was at first, not realized.

In the autumn of 1854, letters from the "special correspondent of the *Times*" began to appear in that paper describing the unspeakable suffering of the soldiers in the Crimea; stories of privation, sickness and death; stories of the lack of the most common necessities; stories of the needless suffering of the sick and wounded; and, finally, stories of the utter lack of nurs-

ing care in the Army Hospitals. "The soldiers have
to attend upon each other," said one report; and again,
"the manner in which the sick and wounded are treated is worthy only of the savages of Dahomey—not only
are surgeons not to be had, but there are no dressers or
nurses to carry out the surgeon's directions." "Why
have we no Sisters of Charity?" asked the writer.
"There are numbers of able-bodied and tender-hearted
English women who would joyfully and with alacrity
go out to devote themselves to nursing the sick and
wounded, if they could be associated for the purpose,
and placed under proper protection."

The appeal went to the heart of Florence Nightingale.
Here was the opportunity for which she had been waiting; here was a work in which she could serve God by
serving man. On October 14, the day on which the
appeal was made, she wrote to Sydney Herbert, Secretary of War, offering her services. On Ooctober 15,
the Secretary wrote to her asking if she would be willing
to head such an expedition of nurses. "There is but
one person in England that I know of, who would be
capable of organizing and superintending such a
scheme," said he. These letters crossed each other
in the mail. The preliminary arrangements were soon
made and one week after the first suggestion was made
Florence Nightingale and thirty-eight nurses, recruited
from the Roman Catholic Sisters, the Anglican
Sisters, the St. John's House, and from various English
hospitals, started on their long journey to the near
East.

It is not our part to tell the story of those wonderful
days which followed. The history of Florence
Nightingale's work in the hospitals of Scutari and the
Crimea has already been fully and vividly told.
She found disorder, a lack of the commonest necessaries
for comfort, and the most frightful suffering among the
sick and wounded; she installed systems of order, sup-

plied needed articles from her private funds, and, assisted by her thirty-eight nurses, brought tender nursing care to the sick and suffering. She opened up extra diet kitchens to supply proper food for the sick; reorganized the sanitary arrangements; introduced rules and regulations among orderlies and attendants; rebuilt old wards to relieve over-crowding; worked among the patients all day, and wrote letters and reports half the night. It was a life of constant activity, great responsibility and tremendous difficulties. There was no time now for self-searchings or passionate repinings. Every minute was filled with the service for which she had so long pined. The call had come, the work was at hand, and she proved herself equal to the opportunity.

After nearly two years of labor, both mental and physical, such as only one deeply impressed with the necessity of the work could have endured, Florence Nightingale returned to England. She returned to find herself famous. Her name was on everyone's lips. She was the popular heroine. Almost the popular saint. But applause and public recognition were not what Florence Nightingale desired. She still wished for work, and though broken and often unable to rise from her bed, she plunged into new activities, and proved herself a reformer, an organizer and a leader of brilliant capabilities. The story of her work in connection with the re-organization of the Army Medical Department and Army Hospitals; the Sanitary Commission for India; with reformers, sanitarians, statisticians; as general adviser in all matters pertaining to hospitals, sickness, health and nursing in general, is full of keen interest. But it is to her work as the founder of modern nursing that we must confine ourselves. For years she had realized that nursing was a calling for which the most careful training and preparation was necessary; for years she had longed to raise it from the despised condition to which it had sunk, and to place it among the skilled professions which would attract to its ranks the type of woman who alone should be in charge of life and death.

Although her wonderful achievements in the Crimea, as well as at home, had all been the outcome of her knowledge and ability as a nurse; and although she had shown to a sympathetic public that a gentlewoman of education and training could follow with distinction the calling to nurse the sick; she had as yet done nothing to prove her contention that nurses should be carefully trained for their work and that the training should embrace something more than a mere routine to be learned by experience alone.

Good nursing—good so far as it went—had long been connected with religion and had been carried on by Sisters, both Catholic and Protestant; it was now to be linked with science, and to become one of the most valued contributions to the health and well-being of mankind.   Great strides in scientific discoveries had been made; the new science of sanitation was clearly allied to health and disease; it was a natural outcome of the times that nursing should have developed along scientific lines.   That it should have had a leader such as Florence Nightingale was a good fortune that cannot be over-estimated, and was the cause of its phenomenal revolution and advance.   The old idea of a good nurse was that she should be a kind, motherly sort of person who had some experience in taking care of the sick; could make gruels, and beef-tea; knew how to make a poultice or a mustard-plaster; was strong enough to lift the patient if necessary, and who was willing to sit up all night and "watch."   It was expected that she would be something of a gossip, and that her bodily comforts should be very well looked after.   It was not expected that she should be held responsible in any way, for the actual well-being of the patient. Even the medical men expected nothing more than a "hand" to carry out their behests.

"A nurse is a confidential servant, but still only a servant," says one. "She should be middle-aged when she begins nursing; and if somewhat tamed by marriage and the troubles of a family, so much the better." (Nursing Sisterhoods and Hospital Schools for Nurses, Dr. La Garde.) "As regards the nurse or 'ward-maids'" says another, "these are in much the same position as housemaids, and require little teaching beyond that of poultice-making which is easily acquired, and the enforcement of cleanliness, and attention to the patient's wants." (Facts Relating to Hospital Nurses, J. F. South, Nutting. p. 181 vol. II.)

How different was Miss Nightingale's idea of a nurse! In the first place, she believed that a good nurse must be a good woman. That was fundamental, but goodness alone was not sufficient. She must be technically trained as well; must know what to do and how to do it. "It has been said scores of times," wrote Miss Nightingale, "that every woman makes a good nurse. I believe, on the contrary, that the very elements of nursing are all but unknown." (Notes on Nursing, Florence Nightingale.) Besides goodness and training, Miss Nightingale believed that a nurse must have a special "call" to her work, must love to nurse the sick, that otherwise she could not endure with fortitude the terrible suffering and sickening sights with which she would be constantly surrounded.

Her ideas on training were very clear and very definite, and were based on knowledge, gained by experience, as to what a nurse could and could not do. "Training is to teach not only what is to be done, but how to do it," said she. "The nurse's eye and ear must be trained. . . . The most important practical lesson that can be given to nurses is to teach them what to observe, how to observe—merely looking at the sick is not observing—it takes a high degree of training to look so that looking shall tell the nurse right, so that she may tell the medical officer aright, what has happened in his absence. . . . Life and death may lie with the good observer. . . . Training is to teach a nurse to observe exactly—to know exactly—to tell exactly."

This training, this "handicraft of nursing" as she called the technical training of a nurse, Miss Nightingale felt could only be learned in the wards of a hospital, at the bedside of the patient. There was another side of the training, however, the theoretic side, so to speak, which she felt could be taught by precept and example. She herself wrote a little book, "Notes on Nursing," a classic in nursing literature, which taught in clear concise language many of the things the nurse should know and do. In this book she laid great stress on sanitation, cleanliness, fresh air. "The very first canon of nursing," she wrote' "is this; to keep the air the patient breathes as pure as the external air, without chilling him." In this day such a statement seems axiomatic; in that day it seemed revolutionary. A sick-room was expected to be a close room. There was a real fear of fresh air for a sick person, especially night air. But, as Miss Nightingale said, in her quick, conclusive way, "What air can we breathe at night but night air?" "Never be afraid to open the windows," she preached—a preachment that was not fully heeded for many years.

A second canon of good nursing, as outlined in her "Notes" was cleanliness. "Very few people, be they of what class they may, have any idea of the exquisite cleanliness required in the sick-room," said she, and then went on to show that there are other ways of having uncleanliness in a house besides visible dirt. Old papered walls, dusty carpets, and uncleaned furniture came under her disapproval; water and sewers and cellars, may contain the germs of disease; slop jars and toilet vessels, may poison the air; the nurse must keep an eye on all that. "The greatest part of nursing consists in preserving cleanliness," said she. And when she comes to the dangers of infection, and the precautions to be observed she says; "True nursing ignores infection, except to prevent it. Cleanliness and fresh air from open windows, with unremitting attention to the patient, are the only defence a true nurse either asks or needs."

But the great point in good nursing, the point to which she kept reverting as prominently essential was trained, keen, quick, observation, which could only be attained by a clear, trained and educated mind.

The opportunity to put into practice her theories as to nursing education was given to Miss Nightingale as a direct result of her work in the Crimea. In 1855, while the popular enthusiasm over her work among the soldiers was at its height, a fund for the establishment of a school for nurses was started, the fund to be presented to Miss Nightingale as a grateful recognition of her great services to the country. It was at a public meeting where the first plans for raising this fund were made that the soldier's letter was read which gave rise to Longfellow's famous poem and the title of "The Lady with a Lamp."

"What a comfort it was to see her pass even," wrote the soldier. "She would speak to one and nod and smile to as many more; but she could not do it to all, you know. We lay there by the hundreds; but we could kiss her shadow as it fell, and lay our heads on the pillow again, content."

Subscriptions to the fund poured in, contributions coming from every class, nine thousand pounds being subscribed by the soldiers themselves.

"The result of voluntary individual offerings plainly indicates the universal feeling of gratitude which exists

among the troops engaged in the Crimea," wrote the
commander of the forces.

Upon her return to England after the war, Miss
Nightingale's time and energy were, as we have seen, so
absorbed by her work with the Government in reor-
ganizing the Hospitals and Medical Department of the
Army, that she was unable to give her attention to the
founding of such a school as the fund contemplated.

After much delay, however, owing to these public
duties, as well as to ill-health, arrangements were made
to open, in connection with St. Thomas' Hospital, the
first training school for nurses, the plan being that the
hospital should provide the facilities for the training
and the fund pay the costs.

Her reasons for selecting St. Thomas' were many.
It was one of the oldest and richest hospitals in the
country, having been established in 1213; it had, for
over a century had nursing Sisters in charge of the
wards, which assured a better type of nursing than
that often found in other hospitals; the resident Medical Officer was in sympathy with the plan, an attitude
by no means universal; and above all, the matron, Mrs.
Wardroper, who would have personal supervision of
the Nightingale probationers and guide them both in
their technical and moral training, was a woman after
Miss Nightingale's own heart. She was a gentlewoman
of decided character, a strict disciplinarian and an
astute judge of character. In writing of her some
years later, Miss Nightingale said, "Her power of
organization and administration, her courage and discrimination in character, were alike, remarkable. She
was straightforward, true, upright." Such a character would have appealed to Miss Nightingale and she
must have felt a sense of comfort that her cherished
plan was to be placed in charge of one so strong and
wise.

Arrangements were at once made for the proper

housing of the new pupils. Miss Nightingale had always maintained that a nurse, in order to do good work, whether in hospital or field, must have a good home in which to live. This principle was carried out in her training school. The upper floor of a new wing recently added to St. Thomas' was fitted up as a Home for Nurses, each probationer being given a separate bedroom, with two rooms for the Sister in Charge, and a common sitting room for all.

Advertisements for candidates were inserted in several papers, and on June 15, 1860, the school opened with fifteen pupil nurses, who were to have one year of training in the wards of the hospital after which they were expected to remain with the hospital for one or two years as full fledged nurses. It was not expected that they should go out as private nurses, but rather that they should act as a band of trained women who in turn, should train others.

The nurses wore a brown dress with white caps and aprons. The schedule of instruction was carefully worked out. They were to be taught the technique of nursing by practical experience at the bedside of the patients under the supervision of the Sisters in charge of the wards. This training included the taking of temperatures, the making of beds, the bathing and feeding of patients, the dressing of wounds and sores, the moving of the helpless and the many other needs of a bed patient.

"She has to make and apply bandages, line splints, and the like," wrote Miss Nightingale when describing the training given to a Nightingale nurse. "She must know how to make beds with as little disturbance as possible to the inmate. She is instructed how to wait at operation, and as to the kind of aid the surgeon requires at her hands. She is taught cooking for the sick; the principles on which sick wards ought to be cleansed, aired and warmed; the management of convalescents;

and how to observe sick and maimed patients so as to give an intelligent and truthful account to the physieian or surgeon in regard to the progress of cases in the intervals between visits." And finally, their moral conduct and their deportment in the sick room was carefully supervised, the latter including punctuality, quietness, trustworthiness, personal neatness and cleanliness and order of the sick room itself.

Besides the technical training in the wards, the nurses were given lectures by several of the visiting physicians on such subjects as the principles of medicine and surgery, chemistry and the like.

A systematic course of reading was laid down, hours of study arranged, and a most elaborate and exhaustive system of marks instituted. At the end of the year those who passed their examination were placed on the hospital register as certified nurses.

Thus was started the first training school for nurses, and thus was inaugurated the modern system of nursing. While others had for years been endeavoring to raise nursing by establishing sisterhoods, by appealing to religious motives, by trying to secure good and honest women to care for the sick. Florence Nightingale had used as her slogan "training, training, and yet more training." Moreover, as Sir Edward Cook has pointed out: "She was able to do, on a larger scale, and on a scale and in a form which attracted general attention, what others had attempted on a smaller scale and in obscurity." By her work in Scutari she had attracted the plaudits of the world, the eyes of all were upon her.

The school which she founded was carried on by the money given her by the people; it was in reality, the peoples' school. Every Englishman had a personal pride in the "Nightingale Nurses." Everyone knew about them; everyone wanted them. Other hospitals wished to imitate St. Thomas' and begged for a Nightingale Nurse to start a school of their own.

The knell of the "Sairy Gamp" [1] type of nurse had sounded. From henceforth nursing was on a different plane. More and more it assumed the character of a profession; more and more it allied itself with science; more and more it called to its ranks women of education and culture. Florence Nightingale had shown the way and had opened up a new career to women for all time.

[1] See Martin Chuzzlewit by Dickens.

CHAPTER VIII

THE FOUNDING OF DISTRICT NURSING

So wise a man as King Solomon has said: "There is nothing new under the sun." If we examine carefully, we will find that what we call a new idea, a new invention, a new principle, is usually merely an old idea in a new dress, an old invention with a new development, an old principle with a modern application. The progress of the world is merely the evolution of the original matter into more complex forms; civilization is the application to life of the more fully recognized laws of nature; and the *new* is but the *old* changed, transmuted, transfigured by a wider understanding of the great principles which underlie the whole fabric of creation.

And so it is with district nursing: they say that the first district nursing was started in Liverpool in 1859, but district nursing is as old as the Christian Church. The work started by William Rathbone was but the work of the early deaconesses, modernized and brought into keeping with the spirit and knowledge of the times. It was charity, plus science, carried on by the renewed art of nursing. Charity had learned much since the days of Phoebe. St. Vincent de Paul had taught that true charity does not distribute alms indiscriminately, but tries rather to help the poor to help themselves; the "new humanity" had taught that universal brotherhood is but a name, unless it seeks to remove the causes of one's brother's degradation; and

the new science had taught that disease and suffering
are not a visitation from an angered God, but are the
direct results of our own carelessness in not following
the right principles of hygiene, sanitation and healthful living; and finally, the care of the sick had been
raised from the despised occupation of unskilled, untrustworthy women, and placed in the hands of women
of refinement and character, who looked upon it as a
vocation, and were trained, not only to the gentle ways
and tender touch of the early nuns and deaconesses,
but to the scientific care and treatment of the patient
as well.

The time was ripe for the development of just such
a form of charity as appeared under the name of District Nursing and had it not developed in Liverpool under the inspiration of Mr. Rathbone, it would have developed with equal certainty in some other city, under
the guidance of some other friend of humanity; for
when the time has arrived for the emergence of some
new development, some new application, of an old idea,
nothing can long hold it in abeyance.

It is a far cry from the work of the deaconesses in the
first century to the organized work of the district
nurse in the nineteenth; and yet both were prompted
by the same spirit, carried on by the same energy, the
latter modified only by the newer knowledge, the wider
brotherhood, and the more liberal spirit of the times.

William Rathbone, to whom we must accord the
credit of inaugurating district nursing, was a citizen
of Liverpool, England. A man of broad experience
and philanthropic interest, his mind had long been
filled with the problems of the poor. At the early age
of thirty, he became a visitor for the District Provident Society of Liverpool, and each week he visited the
members of his district, one of the poorest and lowest
in the city, tramping through the alleys and squalid

courts and calling from door to door to collect the penny and six-penny savings of the poor. This intimate association with the poor in their own homes gave him, from the first, a personal knowledge of their sufferings and their needs. "Visiting, as he did, the same set of families from week to week, and in many cases from year to year, he learned something of the homes, the habits, and the difficulties of the very poor. He saw them under normal conditions, and, as the Provident Society there undertook also the work of a Relief Society, he was brought into still closer contact with them in times of sickness and distress." (Memoirs of Mr. Rathbone by Eleanore Rathbone. p. 140)

Many years later, when speaking of his early work he said that of no other work with which he had ever been connected was he so sure that it had done good and not harm. The fear, lest charity should do harm instead of good, seems to have haunted him during his entire life, and was probably one of the many reasons why his work was always so constructive and modern. "If it is difficult to prevent one's wealth doing oneself harm," he said, "it is almost as difficult to do good with it—so easy to do harm to others."

Though generous to a fault, he seldom gave pecuniary help, unless obviously necessary, without a careful inquiry into the case, and then kept a detailed and permanent record of the inquiry. When he entered his father's business as quite a young man, he found that the numerous applicants who came to their business office for help, were a constant source of annoyance. His conscience would not let him turn them down, neither would it permit him to dismiss them with a small sum of money which might do more harm than good. He, therefore, instituted a plan of referring all needy applicants, to the local Relief Society with instructions to investigate the case and, when worthy, to give substantial and constructive assistance.

He believed thoroughly in personal service, and believed also that only through personal contact with the poor could relief be successfully and helpfully distributed. He was much interested in a system of relief work which was worked out in Elberfeld, Germany, whereby, two hundred and fifty lay-visitors, in a town of fifty thousand inhabitants, had apparently checked the rising tide of pauperism, and by sympathy, counsel and discriminating relief had succeeded in practically abolishing poverty. This system seemed to prove to him that the one principle under which relief giving could be successful was this personal contact between the giver and the recipient, the visitor and the poor, and that its continuity could only be assured by the proper division of labor through the appointment of a sufficient number of visitors, so that busy men could do the work without serious interference with their own personal business, and would go on doing it—"not only a few for a short time, but a great number and persistently."

He eventually succeeded in persuading the Liverpool Relief Society to adopt the Elberfeld system in a somewhat modified manner. The town was divided into districts, and the districts into sections and a committee of "Friendly Visitors" placed in each district. The preliminary inquiries were made by paid agents, the case being then turned over to the care of the friendly visitor for the section in which it occurred, who dealt with it in a kindly, personal manner under the direction of the committee. This sectional arrangement, namely, the placing of one visitor in one specific section of the city, had the same advantage that we find today in the placing of one general public health nurse in a small district—it enabled them to thoroughly know and be known by the inhabitants of the few streets in which they worked, and gave them a local and intimate knowledge of people and conditions which was of great assistance in determining the needs and the merits of the case.

Mr. Rathbone was not only thoroughly constructive in all the charitable work which he understood, but he endeavored to conduct it on business principles. He deplored the use of fancy balls, bazaars and other desultory methods of raising money, and the amount of time and energy which the managers of charity so often consumed in collecting the funds necessary for its support. "People give less in obedience to principle than under a sudden impulse of feeling"; said he, "less to fulfill an obligation, than to relieve themselves of an uneasy, though vague, sensation of compunction."

He wrote a book on the subject which he intended to call "Method versus Muddle and Waste in Charitable Work," but which upon the insistance of his friends was ultimately published under the more pompous title of "Social Organization of Effort in Works of Benevolence and Public Charity, by a Man of Business."

In 1859, his wife died, after a long and painful illness. During those weeks of suffering she had been greatly eased and comforted by the care of a trained nurse. After her death it occurred to Mr. Rathbone's mind that if skilled nursing could bring such relief to a patient for whom everything was provided that wealth and affection could suggest, what untold comfort and help such service would bring in those less fortunate homes where ignorance and poverty must combine to increase the inevitable suffering of those whom disease had laid low.

Mr. Rathbone was a man of action as well as of vision. He decided to try out at once, and at his own expense, the experiment, and to see whether or not much of the suffering and misery of the sick poor could not be alleviated by proper nursing, and home conditions improved by instruction in hygiene and sanitation.

Mrs. Mary Robinson, the nurse who had been attending his wife, was asked whether she would undertake to nurse poor patients in their homes in a restricted district of Liverpool. She consented, and was accordingly engaged for an experimental period of three months, and provided with the necessary appliances for ordinary bedside care. Arrangements were also made for furnishing the nourishment and medicines which might be needed in order to procure the best results from her nursing. Mr. Rathbone realized that it would be impossible to nurse the poor in their own homes without at the same time considering and endeavoring to better, their physical and moral surroundings. The nurse was, therefore, instructed to give not only nursing care to the patient but to teach the families how to care for their own sick, how to keep their homes clean and tidy, and how to live clean, healthy lives. From the very beginning, therefore, district nursing was bound up with social work, and the district nurse became, perforce, a social worker as well as a nurse. This educational work and constructive policy was the new element in the old charity of visiting the sick, and was, as we shall see, the only thing which made ultimate success possible.

The conditions which the nurse found among the people whom she nursed, were worse even than she had anticipated. The misery and squalor were appalling, the suffering intense, and the apparent hopelessness of giving relief, weighed heavily on her heart. Although accustomed to sickness, suffering and death she felt she could no longer endure the strain of this new work, and at the end of one month, returned to her employer and begged to be relieved from the remainder of her engagement.

But Mr. Rathbone, with greater courage and greater faith, urged her to persevere. He showed her how much relief from suffering her care brought to the sick; how her teaching and example must, in time, bear fruit; and that the satisfaction of knowing she had been instrumental in putting even a few families on their feet, and of blazing the path in a new field of work, would compensate her for all her present discouragements.

He finally prevailed upon her to continue, and at the end of the three months' time she found his prediction entirely fulfilled. Not only had she been able to give great passing relief and comfort to the sick, but she had, in that short space of time, been enabled to do much permanent good, and to raise the standard of living and health in many families.

Instead of giving up the work, she now wished to continue, and to devote herself entirely to nursing the sick poor in their homes. Thus, Mary Robinson became the first district nurse.

The results of the experiment were more satisfactory than even Mr. Rathbone himself had dared hope. Let us quote his own words: "The effect, indeed, was far beyond anything that could have been expected," said he. "Patients who, in the special circumstances of the case, had been given up as hopeless, and others who, without the assistance of skilled nursing, would have been hopeless even in well-provided homes, were restored to health by the aid afforded. The good thus accomplished spread far beyond the person of the sufferer; the nurse, in restoring to health the breadwinner, or the mother, often restored to independence and tolerable comfort the whole family, which had depended for food or for care upon the sick person. Not only was the further spread of physical weakness and disease arrested, but, more than this, the help given, tended to prevent the moral ruin, the reckless.

ness, the drunkeness, and crime which so often follow upon hopeless misery. Within the space of a few months, she had attended two cases in which the wife's sickness had thrown a whole household into disorder, and the husband, unable to face the wretchedness which he knew not how to remedy, had taken to drink. After the nurse had shown what might be done to restore order and to lessen suffering, the husbands, who were well-meaning, industrious men, took heart again, left off drinking and were saved, together with their families, from the utter state of degradation, wretchedness and collapse into which they were sinking when the nurse came to their rescue."

The results of the experiment were, in fact, so satisfactory that Mr. Rathbone was now determined, not only to continue the work of Nurse Robinson in the district already laid out, but to engage other nurses and extend it to other parts of the city. He at once, encountered two great difficulties; first, the attitude of the public in regard to the undertaking, and second, the impossibility of obtaining enough trained nurses to carry on the work if established.

It is almost impossible for us in this day to realize the feelings with which the public looked upon this new form of philanthropy. Most of the people were aware of the conditions under which the laboring classes lived; many of them had been drawn into social work and, themselves, had glimpses of the misery and suffering of the poor. The good which one or two women might accomplish in the midst of all this distress, seemed to them so small—the effort futile. As for nursing the poor in their own wretched quarters, what could be accomplished when every condition for health was lacking?

The following quotation from the work of a physician on the care of the sick shows the general feeling at that time. "It is evident that the essential conditions

of rational and successful sick nursing such as good
air, light, warmth, bedding, good food, etc., are altogether wanting in the homes of the poor.   Of what use
are the gratuitous supply and regular giving of medicines, if every necessary is wanting for ordinary,
healthy living?   It is not that the nurse shrinks from
the privations and injurious influences existing in the
cottages and hovels, but it is the impossibility of being
useful under such circumstances that render home
nursing unattainable for the poor.   One can comfort
them in their cottages, and give them food and medicine, but to nurse and heal them there with any hope
of success cannot be done."

Such was the attitude of the majority of thinking
people.   Only a few had a wider vision.   Mr. Rathbone, however, was not discouraged.   "It is a work,"
said he, "which is not immediately understood.   We
all know that the poor may enjoy the care of the
hospitals or medical attendance, more or less free of
cost, by means of benefit societies, the Poor Law, or
free dispensaries.   Many feel that a patient's chances
of recovery would be seriously diminished in his own
miserable and unwholesome dwelling, and that for the
sick poor the hospitals and workhouse infirmaries afford
the proper and only suitable means of relief."   "How
can the poor be nursed in their own homes with any
hope of cure? you ask.   Their narrow, stuffy rooms, the
sick often lying with those in health, the bustle and
disturbance of daily occupation, the comings and go-
ings, the crying of the children, the noise, the heat, all
contribute to make recovery difficult, if not impossible.
How can you hope to accomplish any good from the
occasional visits of a trained nurse?"

To each of these objections Mr. Rathbone offered a
convincing answer: "First, there frequently occur
cases of serious illness, which are either unsuited, or
are not admissible into general hospitals; cases, for

example, of chronic disease combined with extreme poverty. Such are some classes of incurable diseases, as cancer, consumption, (in its later stages) and paralysis, bronchitics, rheumatism, ulcers, etc., etc., and many diseases connected with confinements.

"Secondly, the invalid often objects—or his family objects—to his removal from a place which, however wretched, is still a home. The comfort to the sick and to all the family which the nurse is able to give, the relief of knowing that the invalid need not be removed to the hospital, the restoration of order, the awakening of new hopes and the introduction of a· more cheerful element—such are the happy results of the nurse's work, which help to abate the bitterness, the feeling of having been abandoned by God and man, so deplorable and yet so natural in those who, often without any fault of their own, find themselves plunged in inexpressible wretchedness.

"Thirdly, there are not, and there never can be hospitals large enough and numerous enough to take in all cases of grave illness among the poor.

"Fourthly, the work, done by district nursing is, in proportion to its results, far less costly than that done by the hospitals."

These arguments, finally prevailed and sufficient funds were secured to guarantee the opening up of more districts. Unfortunately, the second difficulty was less easily overcome. Money and interest were assured, but where were the trained nurses to carry on the work? Mr. Rathbone applied to the Nightingale School St. Thomas' Hospital; and to St. John's House. He conferred with friends, he applied to the various hospitals; all in vain. Trained nurses were very scarce in those days and the few existing were already busy in hospitals or private nursing. None could be spared to nurse the poor in their homes.

In his dilemma he consulted Florence Nightingale,

hoping that she might use her influence to procure the needed number. She was obliged to tell him, however, that it would be impossible to procure any from the present source of supply, and advised him to set up his own training school for nurses in the Liverpool Royal Infirmary, with the understanding that a certain number of the nurses, when trained, should be reserved for work among the poor.

The authorities of the Royal Infirmary had already realized the need of better nursing in their institution, and as a step toward the improvement of the nursing standard, the matron had been empowered to pay a salary of sixteen pounds (about eighty dollars) a year, to any nurse who deserved it. This salary was certainly not large, and yet no more than four nurses could be found worthy to receive it. Any ordinary nurse of that time, if paid more than the usual salary of ten pounds (fifty dollars) would most probably have spent the surplus in rioting and drunkenness and been dismissed after the first quarter day.

A training school for nurses was, therefore, needed in Liverpool not only for district work, but quite as much for the Infirmary, as well as for private work. In spite of the very apparent need, Mr. Rathbone had great difficulty in persuading the Committee that the establishment of such a school would be wise. One of the great difficulties seemed to be that there were no suitable accommodations for either nurses or probationers. This obstacle Mr. Rathbone quickly disposed of by offering to put up a building as a Home for Nurses, and to present it to the Infirmary. His offer was accepted, and on July 1, 1862, the nursing of the Royal Infirmary was handed over to the new Committee of the "Liverpool Training School and Home for Nurses," and a year later, the new building on Ashton Street, was opened.

The three main objects of the training school, as set forth in the prospectus were:

1: To provide thoroughly educated professional nurses for the Royal Infirmary.

2: To provide district nurses who should attend the poor in their own homes.

3: To provide sick nurses for private families.

The work was placed under the superintendence of Miss Merryweather, who had been given a short training at St. Thomas' Hospital, and the practical experience and instruction was carried on in the wards of the Royal Infirmary. The success of this effort was so satisfactory that Mr. Rathbone was encouraged to try the experiment in yet another quarter.

Sir Edward Cook, in his "Life of Florence Nightingale," speaks of district nursing as the natural sequel to the reform of workhouse nursing. As a matter of fact, workhouse nursing was rather a sequel of district nursing. At this period, the care of the sick in the workhouses throughout England was in the hands of the female pauper inmates, untrustworthy, untrained and often vicious women.

The Liverpool Workhouse Infirmary, on Brownlow Hill, was no worse than others of its kind, but conditions there were, nevertheless, very terrible. The nursing was all done by able-bodied pauper women selected from the inmates of other parts of the workhouse. Now one knows that an "able-bodied woman" rarely enters a workhouse unless there is something radically wrong with her. Either she is vicious, or physically incapacitated, or mentally deficient. That these pauper nurses were found to be of a low and vicious type, brutal, and usually given to drink, is not, therefore, to be wondered at. Even the best of them were thoroughly ignorant; the patients remained unwashed, and the bed-clothes unchanged for weeks at a

8

time; gentleness with the sufferers was unknown; oaths and foul language was the common tongue; and when not unavoidably engaged in the task of caring for their patients, these old women would gather around the fire and gossip by the hour, while they sipped their tea, or, more likely, something stronger.[1]

Mr. Rathbone suggested that paid trained nurses be placed in the Infirmary. The Vestry objected, fearing that the expense would be too great. Mr. Rathbone and his party argued that the cheapest way to treat the sick was to cure them; so that those who might otherwise become chronics and a permanent expense to the authorities, might be enabled to go out and resume their work. It was finally decided to give Mr. Rathbone's suggestion a trial. The plan was to secure about a dozen trained nurses from the Nightingale School, about the same number of probationers, who, with a certain number of able-bodied women from the Workhouse to act as assistants, should carry on the nursing in the male wards; more nurses for the female wards to be added later if the experiment proved a success. The next question was how to secure a satisfactory Superintendent of Nurses. This was a difficult matter, for good women, suitably trained for the position, were very scarce, and yet the success of the whole undertaking would depend, almost absolutely, upon the person in charge.

With the assistance of Miss Nightingale , they finally succeeded in securing the services of Miss Agnes Jones, and the selection proved a satisfactory one in every respect. Agnes Jones was the daughter of an Irish Colonel, and the niece of Sir John Lawrence. Of good family, young, beautiful, highly educated and witty, she was essentially the new type of nurse, whose espousal of the nursing profession filled her contempor-

[1] See Oliver Twist by Dickens.

aries with much amazement and fear—That women
of refinement and culture could, out of love for humanity, become nurses, and devote themselves to this arduous, dangerous and exacting occupation seemed little
short of incredible and was called "romantic," "sentimental" and "unfeminine."

Miss Jones, however, was not only rich, attractive and
highly cultured, she was intensely religious, as well, and
like her leader, Miss Nightingale, she felt a "call."

She had taken a course of training at Kaiserswerth,
in 1860, after which she joined Mrs. Ranyard in her
Bible-women's Mission work in London. While with
Mrs. Ranyard the project of training a corps of nurses
to live and work among the poor was often discussed,
and when, in 1868, the year of Agnes Jones' death,
Mrs. Ranyard first established the Nursing Branch of
the Mission, she regarded it as, in a certain sense,
dedicated to the memory of her former companion.

In 1862, Miss Jones entered St. Thomas' Hospital
and took a year's course in the Nightingale School of
Nursing. She was, therefore peculiarly well fitted to
assume the position now offered. She had received
as much training as was possible for a nurse to procure
in those days; she had had a year's experience in social
work among the poor of London, which in a measure
gave her an understanding of the class of human beings
she was now to care for; and her beautiful Christian
spirit made it possible for her to face trials and discouragements, which, to another, would have seemed
well-nigh insurmountable, but to her seemed merely a
part of the "Father's business," to which she had been
called.

The work was started on the 16th of May, 1865, with
twelve nurses from St. Thomas' Hospital, eighteen
probationers and fifty-four old pauper women.

In less than two years after the arrival of Miss Jones

and her staff, the Guardians announced their intention of never reverting to the old system, and of charging the rates with the expense of the new.

But the work proved too much for the strength of the delicate girl who had so valiantly undertaken it. She contracted typhus fever, and, worn out with her exertions during the past three years, died, "at her post" on February 19th, 1868.

"In less than three years she had reduced one of the most disorderly hospital populations in the world to something like Christian discipline, such as the police themselves wondered at." (Una and the Lion, by Florence Nightingale; Good Words, June 1868.)

The experiment was considered eminently successful; in ten years' time the system of employing pauper nurses in any workhouse or infirmary was a thing of the past; and in 1897 their employment was forbidden by law.

CHAPTER IX

THE FOUNDING OF DISTRICT NURSING IN LIVERPOOL (continued)

Nurses were now obtainable for work among the poor in Liverpool. The Royal Infirmary furnished the first ones and paid their salaries. Later nurses trained at the Workhouse Infirmary, were also employed. The city was divided into districts, each district being provided with a nurse, who worked under the direction of a Lady Superintendent, or sometimes, under a committee of Lady Superintendents.

This plan of districting the city was probably based on the plan followed by the Liverpool Provident Society, and, also the one which Mr. Rathbone had considered so advantageous in the work of the Elberfeld Relief Society. Placing the work under the superintendence of untrained ladies, indicates the general feeling of the times, that nursing was still in the hands of women who needed the oversight and assistance of lay people in order to keep it from danger of corruption. Moreover, the experience of the "ladies" in social work was considered greater than that of the nurse, the latter's training having been along the purely professional lines of bedside care. The social side of her work was, for many years, to be learned only in the hard school of experience.

Although the Lady Superintendents were supposed to supervise the nurse's work, they were not required to have any training in, or knowledge of, nursing itself.

They were usually selected from among the wealthy and philanthropic ladies of the city, and were expected to provide (either themselves or through subscriptions) the board and lodging of the nurse, and the medical comforts required by her patients. They were also expected to visit the cases under treatment, so as to see that the nurse was working faithfully, and that each case was receiving proper care. They also kept a record of all cases carried, and an account of all expenses incurred. Furthermore, they were expected to be always ready with sympathy, assistance and advice when needed,—which was often. "The work presented numerous opportunities of assisting the nurse in what may be fitly described as the social and reforming aspect of the work. It brought the ladies face to face with, and enabled them to understand, the terrible realities of poverty and disease, the remedies for which, without their assistance would have been quite beyond the powers of the nurse." (William Rathbone, A Memoir.)

Within four years the whole city was divided into eighteen districts. Each district was made more or less conterminous with parishes so as to facilitate the co-operation of the clergy in the work of ministering to the sick, although it was kept on a purely undenominational basis.

In beginning the work in a new district, a meeting was usually called of the clergy, the ministers of the various religious bodies, medical men, and other people living in the vicinity whose interest or co-operation might be helpful, in order to explain to them the nature and object of the work, and to ask for their assistance and support. They were invited to recommend cases to the Lady Superintendent or to the nurse, being at the same time requested to use this power with discretion, as the object of the work was to help the needy, not to pauperize the independent.

The Lady Superintendent herself, was provided with a map of the district, a nurse's register book, and forms of recommendation and applications. The nurse was also supplied with a register, and it was the duty of the Lady Superintendent to examine the nurse's register from time to time, to consult with her on new cases, and to hear her report of old ones. She was also expected to arrange for the supply and distribution of all medical comforts and appliances, and to keep a list of all articles loaned and expenses incurred.

It will be seen, therefore, that the office of "Lady Superintendent" was no sinecure. She was expected to be responsible for the work in her district, and in honor to her, we must acknowledge that she was eminently so. She found the money to run the work, she kept the accounts, the records, and other data. She discussed "case work" with her nurse, and besides she kept that close personal touch with the work, and with the patients themselves, which enabled her to continue her service year after year without, in any way, losing her interest, or allowing her service to become perfunctory or coldly official. As proof that this type of organization worked well in Liverpool and held the interest and continuous support of the same people year after year, without interruption, and without the need of other stimuli to arouse a flagging zeal, we may cite the fact that in 1898, nearly forty years after the founding of district nursing in Liverpool, it was found that six of the Lady Superintendents in that city had held the office for over thirty years, while in many other cases the position had been handed down from mother to daughter and was looked upon as an honorable, though perhaps arduous, civic duty. (The six ladies were Mrs. William Rathbone, Mrs. C. Langton, Mrs. H. B. Gilmour, Mrs. Paget, Mrs. G. Holt, Mrs. R. D. Holt,— William Rathbone, A Memoir. p. 163.)

While the Lady Superintendent thus carried a large share of the responsibility, the nurse also had her regular, defined duties which were carefully worked out. The following extract from Mr. Rathbone's little book on District Nursing, gives a general outline of what these duties were.

"The district nurse was expected to devote at least five or six hours a day visiting the sick. She was to investigate as soon as possible all cases recommended to her by the proper persons and in proper form; to take the recommendations to the Lady Superintendent to be filed by her, and then to report upon the cases and take the Superintendent's decision upon them at the earliest opportunity. She was to report any case in which she judged that additional nourishment would hasten the recovery of the patient; any case which would be better dealt with in a hospital or workhouse and any case in which the neglect or disobedience of patients or their friends made her efforts fruitless. She was to render all the assistance which the medical man might require in any operation, and to do whatever was necessary for the patient, and which but for her would be left undone. In the homes of the sick poor this includes, of course, many things not generally supposed to come under the title of nursing at all, but which, in their case, are most important accessories to it; such offices, for example, as cleaning the sickroom of lumber and unnecessary furniture, sweeping floors and lighting fires. It was the nurse's duty, moreover, to teach the patient and his family the necessity of cleanliness, of ventilation, of regularity in giving food and medicine, above all the implicit obedience to the doctor's directions, and herself set an example of that neatness, order, sobriety and obedience which she was to impress on others. She was exhorted to regard as sacred any knowledge of family matters which might come to her in the course of her duties, to avoid and discourage scandal, and especially to interfere in no way with the patient's or other people's religious opinions. As a rule, the doctor and the nurse could seldom visit the patient at the same time unless by special arrangement, and to avoid the inconvenience resulting therefrom a slate and pencil were hung up in the patient's room, on which the doctor could write his instructions and make an appointment with the nurse, and on which she could enter any fact or ask any questions which she might think necessary."

The burden of providing the medical necessaries fell from the first, upon the different districts—practically upon the Lady Superintendents and their friends and supporters, an arrangement which might seem to demand too large a contribution of their free services from these generous and charitable voluntary agents, but which was considered necessary to secure careful administration.

Every system of district nursing runs a risk of becoming merely a new system of distributing relief among the poor. It is far easier, more agreeable, and more popular, to give relief than to nurse. But the primary object of the founders of the institution was distinctly to provide nursing for the sick. They specially wished to guard against the possibility of a sort of competition arising between the nurses and the relieving officers or the agents of charitable societies. They intended to supply medical comforts only in so far as might be absolutely necessary to make the labours of the district nurse effective. At first they did not succeed in altogether maintaining the observance of this important principle. The outlay for nourishment and stimulants rose rapidly in several districts. "It was more than questionable whether any real and equivalent good was obtained by so large an expenditure. At least it was work for relieving agencies and not for nurses to undertake, and, whilst it seemed likely to pauperize the patients, it certainly imposed too heavy a tax upon the Lady Superintendent and her friends, out of whose pockets the cost was being defrayed. The best check upon this waste was found to be a spontaneous one, and resulted from the growing efficiency of the nurses themselves. The more efficient each one of them became, the more plentiful was the supply of cases which really called for her professional help, namely, for genuine nursing as distinct from giving relief."

At first it was very difficult to get the nurses, especially the less efficient, to observe the rules laid down for relief giving. In one district it was estimated that about one thousand dollars was paid out in one year for relief and medical comforts. This is readily understood, for even in these present days, where associations for almost every kind of need under the sun have been organized,[1] and where it is a comparatively simple matter to turn over to the proper authorities the giving of relief or the procuring of certain comforts and assistance, we find the socially-untrained nurse loth to delegate these pleasant duties to another. For it is pleasant to be able to give comfort and material relief to those who are suffering or in want. It is pleasant to see the smile of gratitude or the look of relief on the faces of those one is trying to help. Besides, a nurse comes to know "her people" so intimately she is their friend as well as helper; it naturally seems to her that she is better acquainted with their tragedies and their needs than any outside relief society or social worker, and therefore, that she should know better what to give and how to give it. Especially was it hard in those early days of social work; for at that time the relief societies were expected merely to dis-

[1] Rural districts are still often without the proper authorities for relief giving, and the Public Health Nurse must therefore either be trained to give the relief herself or better still try to organize a committee that will do it for her.

pense relief on application, such relief usually taking on the tangible form of money, fuel, food or warm clothing, which, from the nurse's point of view, could so much better and more quickly, be distributed by herself. It was recognized by only a very few far-sighted people that there was a social problem involved in the giving of any form of material help, and that, in order not to break down the independence of the self-respecting man, or contribute to the destruction of the home, material assistance, whether in the form of money or the things which money buys, should only be given after careful investigation had shown that it would help rather than injure the family welfare.

Mr. Rathbone was particularly insistent on this matter of non-relief-giving. Even sick relief he felt should not be given indiscriminately, and the nurses and Lady Superintendents were urged, over and over again, not to pauperize their patients by giving even medical comforts unless actually necessary.

Florence Nightingale also preached against this same danger. She saw that "if district nurses begin by giving relief they will end by doing nothing but giving relief." "It is utter waste to have a highly trained and skilled nurse to do this," said she. Moreover, she saw clearly the demoralizing and pauperizing effect of indiscriminate relief-giving and the danger of providing those necessities which the head of the family, be he ever so humble, should naturally provide. "How often a drinking man will go all to drink if you support as well as nurse his sick wife, is perhaps little thought of," said she, "and also what efforts such a man will make not to drink, when his wife is sick, if you help him to help himself, and her to maintain his independence; and if you make his home, by cleanliness and care, less intolerable." And again she says, "To set these sick people going again, with a sound and clean house, as well as with a sound body and mind, is about as great a benefit as can be given them—worth acres of gifts and relief. This is depauperizing them."

That these same arguments are used today in defining the special functions of the public health nurse, shows the fundamental correctness of the principles on which district nursing was builded. "Sometimes, as in the case of the sickness of the bread-winners, adequate and continuous material relief may be a most important element in restoring the family to normal living. Sometimes, as in the case of non-supporting husband, the giving of material relief, relieving them of the consequences of his evil doing, may result in a further break-down. Sometimes, it is as necessary for social as well as for medical workers to see an individual suffer because out of that suffering will come eventual recovery." (Extract from "The Interdependence of the Nurse and the Social Worker," by Margaret F. Byington, "The Public Health Nurse." vol. 9, p. 21.)

Not only was relief-giving discountenanced from the first, but another principle, which has ever since been found to be fundamental, was insisted upon, namely, that the nurse should not interfere with the religious convictions of her patients. That the value of this principle was recognized even in that day is the more remarkable when we remember that hitherto, most of the visiting nursing among the poor had been carried on by nuns, sisters of charity and deaconesses and in England, by Anglican Sisters and Bible-women, and was, therefore, closely associated with religious instruction. Even the work of the laypeople among the poor had been mostly parochial, and had been closely connected with religious teaching, either by the members of the established church or those of the non-conformist chapels. That such an innovation as the severance of religious instruction from the visiting of the sick poor

was, at first, looked upon askance by a few, is evidenced
by the attitude of Miss Agnes Jones, when she was first
asked to become Superintendent of the Royal Infirmary, to prepare nurses for district nursing.   In answer
to the invitation she asked: "Is its foundation and
corner-stone to be Christ, and Him crucified, the only
Savior?—I shall not embark in any work whose great
aim is not obedience to the command: 'Preach the gospel to every creature.'"

But it was soon seen that non-interference in religious convictions did not mean that district nursing
was in any way divorced from religion or that it was
not founded on the very teaching of Christ that one
should love one's neighbor as oneself.   Mr. Rathbone
was a broad but truly religious man.   When only seventeen years of age, he was so impressed by a sermon
he heard on the text, "The poor have the gospel preached
to them," that he was strongly tempted to take up the
life of a city missionary.   And many years later he was
still able to say, "I feel now, as I felt then, that had
I possessed the necessary powers successfully to carry
Christ's gospel of peace and hope and purity to the
toiling and suffering, it would have been a success far
nobler, worthier and more to be desired than any other
whatever." (William Rathbone, a memoir. p. 70.)
William Rathbone practiced a religion that expressed
itself in deeds rather than in words. "He interpreted
his own discipleship of Christ very literally, as something that should not only govern the inward spiritual
life, but should condition and direct his activities of
every kind.   The ultimate, implicit aim of all public
work, conducted in the right spirit, was in his view, to
make the condition of national, civic or individual life
a little less out of harmony with the ideal of a kingdom
of God on earth."   (Ibid) Such a religion was broad
enough to take in all shades of spiritual conviction,
and the district nurse was expected to live such a re-

ligion and to preach it by her daily acts, but whether
as Jew or Gentile, Catholic or Protestant, mattered
little. Florence Nightingale, also, never ceased to
speak of nursing as a direct service to God.

One other fundamental principle was insisted upon,
and that was that the nurse should be thoroughly well
trained. The work was started by a "trained nurse"
and when Mr. Rathbone wished to extend it he was so
persuaded that only women with a proper nursing education should undertake it that he established a training school for the purpose, and as we have seen,
insisted upon as thorough a course of training as was
procurable in those days. And again we see that Mr.
Rathbone's attitude was based upon, and coincided with,
the opinion of Florence Nightingale, who, speaking of
requirements for district nurses, said: "Training and
efficiency—training which must continue all her life;
efficiency always increasing every day."

In the matter of health education it may be felt by
some that the work of the present day public health
nurse is very different from that of the earlier district
nurse; that the latter puts all the accent on the bedside
care of the sick, while with the former the educational
factor is the most important phase of the work. And
yet if one studies the subject carefully, one will find
that the difference is not a change, but a natural growth,
coincident with the growth of preventive medicine.
From the very beginning, Mr. Rathbone had insisted
that the nurse teach her patients the value of cleanliness, order and fresh air, and instruct them in matters
of sanitation and hygiene, as well as how to care for
their families in health and in sickness. And Florence
Nightingale, as we know, always laid great stress on
sanitation. "A district nurse," says she, "must nurse
the room as well as the patient, and teach the family
to nurse the room."

When we call to mind the crowded, unsanitary condition of the majority of working-men's homes in those days; when we recollect that at the time district nursing was started, the first Public Health Act had been in force only eleven years; we can better understand the value of this phase of the nurse's work to public health in general.. And as proof that she did, indeed, teach hygiene and sanitation, and was entitled, even in that early day, to be called a public health nurse, we may cite the words of Dr. Hope, the medical officer of Liverpool, in 1909, who said, "My experience and observation enable me to say that the influence for good of the district nursing staff is by no means confined to the patient; their presence in the houses of the poorer classes is a guarantee of an improvement in the general household arrangements'; cleanliness and order take the place of the dirt and neglect which have previously existed. These experiences are so frequent and so constant that for years past I have regarded the district nursing staff of the city as a valuable accessory to public health works.

To show what the great founders of modern nursing considered to be the functions of the district nurse we cannot do better than to again quote from Miss Nightingale.

"First," says she, "a district nurse must nurse. She must be of a yet higher class, and of a yet fuller training than a hospital nurse, because she has not the doctor always at hand; because she has no hospital appliances at hand; and because she has to take notes of the case for the doctor, who has no one but her to report to him. She is his staff of clinical clerks, dressers and nurses.

"Secondly, she must nurse the room as well as the patient; put the room in nursing order; that is, make the room such as a patient can recover in; bring care and cleanliness into it, and teach the inmates to keep up that care and cleanliness. And it requires a high

stamp of woman to do this; to combine the servant with
the teacher and with the educated woman, who can so
command the patient's confidence as to let her do this.

"Thirdly, a district nurse must bring to the notice of
the Officer of Health or proper authorities, sanitary defects, which he alone can remedy. Thus, dustbins are
emptied, water-butts cleaned, water supply and drainage examined and remedied, which look as if this had
not been done for one hundred years." (Taken from a
pamphlet, "On Trained Nursing for the Sick Poor,"
by Florence Nightingale.)

It is because district nursing was builded on such a
solid foundation, was carried on with such forethought
and discrimination, that its growth has been so phenomenal. The work being done today is in its essentials the same as that started over sixty years ago in
Liverpool and the rules then laid down have been
found practical and fundamental.

District nursing was now well established in Liverpool, but as the work grew those in charge began to feel
that it lacked co-ordination. Each district was a separate unit, an individual piece of work. There was
no esprit de corps, among the nurses; there was no way
in which one nurse could benefit from the experience of
another. The standard of work in each district depended entirely upon the training and ability of the
particular nurse in charge, or the initiative of the
Lady Superintendent of the district. The idea of
placing the nurses in centrally located homes, under the
supervision of technically trained nurse-superintend-
ents was suggested as a possible way of remedying the
defect.

Florence Nightingale was particularly enthusiastic
over the idea. She felt that by offering only lodgings
to the nurse, as had been done in the past, they were
prevented from procuring the best type of woman; that
on the other hand, if a real home were provided, a home

which would give what real family homes are supposed to give, namely, a bed-room for each, a dining-room and sitting-room in common, all meals prepared and eaten in the house, a head of the home, who should be thoroughly trained in nursing so that she might intelligently direct and advise the nurses in their work, as well as act as a chaperone and house-mother; such a home in fact, as any mother of whatever class would be willing her daughter should enter, then and then only, would a very much finer and higher type of women be attracted,—the type of woman in fact which the work demanded.

She had seen the beneficial effect of such a home-like atmosphere on the deaconesses and their work at Kaiserswerth; she knew that the improved condition of hospital life, the making of the hospital into such a home as good educated young women could live in with comfort, had, more than any other factor, raised the tone and character of hospital nursing; and she felt that district nurses, whose lives were harder and more exposed, needed the comfort and help of a good home more, even, than their sisters in the hospitals.

One other thing she pointed out,—and this is a matter which public health nurses at the present day would do well to consider,—and that was, that a district nurse ought not to live in a way which requires her to do housework, or to be responsible for the care of her own home, after business hours. "If a nurse has to find herself," said Miss Nightingale, "to cook for herself when she comes home dogtired from her patients, do everything for herself, she cannot do real nursing; for nursing requires the most undivided attention of anything I know, and all the health and strength, both of body and mind. If then, she has to provide for herself, she can only be half a nurse." (Trained Nursing for the Sick Poor," by Florence Nightingale.)

9

When an idea was warmly espoused by Florence Nightingale it was usually carried through. Whether or not in this particular instance she herself was instrumental in securing the change is not material—certainly her approval of the scheme would have had great influence with those in charge of the work. In any case, the change was made, and the nurses, instead of living separately in lodging-houses as hithertofore, were collected together and placed in a house in Eldon Place, which thus became the first District Nurses' Home.

A trained nurse was put in charge as matron of the Home. The change proved a success, and gradually other "Homes" in various parts of the city were opened, for it was found that not only must the number of inmates be limited, in order to preserve the character of a real home, but also that the house must be centrally located, so that the nurses would not have too far to go to reach their various districts. Eventually there were four homes, located in the four quarters of the city and known as the Central Home, the South Home, the North Home, and the East Home. Each was placed under the care of a nurse-matron whose duty it was to care for the housekeeping and general management of the home and to keep all the books and accounts. She was also expected to visit each new case and to judge whether or not it was a proper one for district nursing care. If in doubt, she consulted with the Lady Superintendent. She was also expected to instruct the nurses as to the particular care of their cases, to receive reports, and to keep a record of the same. And she was to call on the physicians, clergymen, Sisters or any others working among the poor, in order to explain to them the service the nurse was prepared to render and to co-operate with them in their work wherever possible.

The respective duties of the matrons and the Lady Superintendents were not definitely laid down, but it

was generally understood that while the matron should
have charge of the strictly professional side of the work,
the Lady Superintendent would still continue to exercise a general supervision over the whole, and should
pay especial attention to the so-called social side.

The Homes proved a great success.   The common life
lived by the nurses increased the zeal and created the esprit de corps which was formerly lacking.   In their intercourse with one another, they would eagerly discuss
points of interest in their work and would dwell
with satisfaction upon cases which they had been able
to carry through successfully, even when the illness was
grave.   From the matron the nurses gained advice, encouragement and intelligent and sympathetic criticism;
and in the Home itself they found the congenial com-
panionship, the rest and recreation which they so much
needed to counterbalance the hardship and depression
of their work.

And so at last, we find the work of visiting and caring for the sick poor safely placed on a sure and solid
foundation.   It is no longer dependent upon the passing caprice, or desultory effort, of a few amateur women,
but it is in the hands of brave, strong, competent trained
nurses.   Bedside care and health teaching go hand in
hand; the service is offered to all, without restriction
to creed, or church; the work is not only a charity,
based on the old, old precept "love thy neighbor as
thyself," but is also a public service based on scientific
principles for the protection of the health of the people.
It not only gives passing relief, but it endeavors to
give permanent cure, and it is not too much to say in
the words of the Right Honorable Charles Booth:
"Wherever the nurse enters, the standard of life is
raised."

CHAPTER X

THE SPREAD OF DISTRICT NURSING

The success of the novel experiment being carried on in Liverpool could not fail to attract the attention of other cities and soon similar experiments were being started in various parts of England, especially in the large industrial towns, such as Manchester, Lancaster and Birmingham, where the suffering among the laboring classes was most acute. Manchester, one of the largest and most crowded of these industrial centers, was the first to follow the lead. In 1859, the same year in which Mr. Rathbone first sent out Nurse Robinson to minister to the sick poor in Liverpool, Mr. Charles Herford, a Manchester business man, engaged a nurse to work in the Ardwick district, one of the poorest and most conjested of the city. This should have been a favorable locality for beginning such an undertaking and Mr. Herford thought the services of a nurse would be of great use, but the plan was misunderstood and after a short time was discontinued.

Three years later, a Biblewoman undertook to do some nursing among the poor in the Cathedral district, but it was a parochial effort, its object being mainly religious and the work done probably consisted only in giving such bedside comfort and care as a kind heart and gentle hand could confer. It was not until 1864, two years after district nursing was firmly established in Liverpool, that Manchester started the "Nurse Training Institution," as it was then called, to provide nurses for private homes, as well as for the poor in Manchester and Salford—a large industrial suburb of Manchester.

The Institution was organized on lines somewhat similar to those followed in Liverpool, although the founders were advised—"not to slavishly copy the District Nurses' Home in Liverpool," but to found one on their own ideals. This they did, though they were indebted to Liverpool for much valuable advice. Early in 1865, four selected women were sent to London, and after passing through a practical course of training at St. Thomas' Hospital and King's College Hospital, they returned to Manchester in December of that year and immediately set to work. A house was ready for them in Grosvenor Street and a lady who had spent some time in the Liverpool Home was appointed matron. The number of nurses soon increased, many of them having been trained in the Brownlow Infirmary under Agnes Jones, and the work spread rapidly.

The nursing of the sick poor in their own homes was a special department. The salaries and board of these nurses were defrayed by the Institution, but their lodgings were provided by ladies who undertook the supervision of their districts. These ladies and their friends also supplied funds for medical appliances and extra nourishment as in Liverpool.

There were many difficulties at the outset and for a time the doctors had to be implored to send cases. Gradually, however, the good work done was recognized, and in 1879, a Home for District Nurses was opened in Ardwick. It was felt that nurses living together and supervised by a matron, who was herself trained, would work more economically and efficiently and cover a larger area than when isolated and doing their own housework and cooking. A second Home was opened in

Salford in 1887, and others in Hulme in 1890, in Harpurpey in 1893; in Bradford in 1895.   Ardwick, Salford and Harpurpey have all since had houses built or
given for the purpose. During the year 1906-07 the
matron of the Bradford District Home was Nurse
Cavell who, during the great war, was executed by the
Germans in Belgium.

But district nursing was not confined to large industrial centers; many of the smaller towns and rural
communities undertook similar work, either under
the direction of philanthropic men and women, or as
parochial work in certain parishes.

In 1865, the town of Derby through the individual efforts of Dr. William Ogle a prominent physician of the place, started an interesting and somewhat unique piece of district nursing work. There
were, at that time, no trained nurses in Derby, and Dr.
Ogle, realizing the tremendous good that would result
from their presence, determined to found an association which should have as its object the training of
nurses for work in the public hospitals, for private
cases and for the care of the sick poor in their homes.

Before starting the association he visited all the institutions in England where nurses' were at that time
being trained, with the idea of obtaining first hand information on the subject.   He also conferred with Miss
Nightingale—as anyone undertaking any form of nursing work did in those days—and was thus prepared
to start his own piece of work on the best and firmest
foundation.

The first nurses here also were trained at the Brownlow Infirmary, Liverpool, and the district branch of its
work followed more or less the principles found good
in that city—the districts being much smaller, however, and less congested than in the larger town, and
therefore more easily handled. The one innovation
which Derby introduced, and which was later recom-

mended for all district nursing associations was the placing of a *trained nurse* as "Lady Superintendent" who not only gave out the medical comforts, etc., required as in Liverpool, but also supervised the nursing by making a weekly visit in the homes of the patients and inspecting the quality and grade of care given.

Besides these and many other associations and institutions there were many individual workers carrying on a form of district nursing in various parts of the country. During the cholera epidemic of 1866, many women, especially the Sisters from the Anglican Sisterhoods, impelled by a desire to relieve the suffering among the poor, had gone forth to nurse the stricken ones in their own homes; and after the epidemic was over had remained, realizing that the need of their presence did not cease with the cessation of that particular disease, but that sickness in some form was ever present in the homes of the laboring classes, and the care of the sick poor a never-ending need.

In this way a form of district nursing was started in many towns and districts where, hitherto, it had been unknown, but in most cases was carried on by untrained women who did not follow, indeed did not know, the principles laid down by Mr. Rathbone and his followers.

In London, especially, many such women were working, and it was the desire on the part of a few leaders in the philanthropic world, to co-ordinate and standardize this desultory, untrained nursing, which led to the founding, in 1868, of the East London Nursing Society, the first in London organized solely for the benefit of the poor.

This society was started through the united efforts of the Hon. Mrs. Stuart Wortley, Mr. R. Ingram and others interested in the welfare of the poor, and had as its object the placing of trained nurses in the various districts of East London where the deep poverty and consequent suffering made their service especially desirable. Arrangements were made for providing nursing comforts and special diets for the sick. The nurses were placed in different parishes in the east end, and were expected to live each in her own district. Money, however, was lacking, and the work of the Society did not develop as rapidly as had been expected: at the end of six years there being only seven district nurses working under its supervision.[1]

In the same year in which the East London Nursing Society started its work, another and similar effort was attempted by another and different organization in other parts of London. The Bible and Domestic Mission, founded by Mrs. Ranyard in 1857, had for years been sending out its Biblewomen to read and pray among the poor in the various parts of the city in an effort to raise the moral condition of the people and to bring to them the comfort and solace of religion. In their ministry they constantly came in contact with sickness and physical suffering and for some years. Mrs. Ranyard and Agnes Jones, who was her co-worker for a year or more before taking up her work in Liverpool, had discussed the feasibility of training a corps of nurses to live and work among the poor, ministering to their bodily needs, as the Biblewomen did to their spiritual. In 1868, therefore, the idea took form and the Nursing Branch of the Biblewomen's Mission was established.

The first nurses were taken from the ranks of the Biblewomen and were untrained in nursing technique, though their previous close contact with the poor under all kinds of circumstances and under varying conditions was looked upon as a useful apprenticeship to their new undertaking, and as giving them an intimate understanding of the needs of the poor, if it did not give them training in the care of the sick.

With the exception of two or three nurses sent out by the East London Nursing Society, then just begin-

[1] Appendix II.

ning, and a few more sent out to various districts
and parishes by St. John's House, by the Nursing
Sisters of Devonshire Square, and by two or three
other Sisterhoods, London was practically without real
nursing care of any kind for its sick poor in their
homes.

Even untrained care, therefore, seemed better than
none, and though the work of the Biblewomen was at
this time limited, and did not aim to do much more
than relieve suffering, it did fill a gap until more fully
trained women could be procured.

In writing of this early work of her Biblewomen
nurses, Mrs. Ranyard described it at the time as follows:

"Our Biblewomen to the number of 200 are now
over all the Postal Districts of London, and our Nurses
are following in their wake as fast and as far as our
means allow; there are no women more really wanted
at this time in London, and in all large towns, than
Biblewomen nurses, if we may judge by letters we are
constantly receiving. In every poor street there are
some diseased and deformed people needing the help
they cannot give themselves or secure from others.
They comprise a multitude in our great city, who cannot be received into the wards of either workhouse or
hospital; there is not space for them. In the early
stages of their illness they have probably been taken
to some hospital or infirmary, but in a few months
have been discharged incurable. Cases of paralysis, of
rheumatism, of asthma, of consumption, of cancer, and
of scrofula in its many forms, are constantly treated
thus. In our visitation from house to house, we are
constantly distressed with the scalds, burns, broken
limbs, and emaciated forms of the little ones. The
mere administration of food, as relief, is a very small
part of their (the nurses') duty. They have constantly
to fight with disease born of dirt and neglect. The
poor in their one room seldom need a person watching

with them all day, and they cannot afford to feed her; but they do want the mercy of the skilled hand, that can cleanse and dress their wounds, refresh the bed on which they lie so wearily, and supply the clean linen."

The training which the Biblewomen nurses received is described as follows: "We seek first a godly woman, unencumbered, if possible, with family care of her own, and yet having a motherly and missionary heart. We employ her first in Bible work for three months amongst the lowest poor. Next, of course, comes hospital training. She must reckon no service that is needful, distasteful and learn to perform all that is required in Miss Nightingale's list of duties; and although a far longer probation is considered requisite for a nurse in a hospital, still the fit woman who goes with a mind to learn all she can, will pick up much useful knowledge in three months; quite as much as we have found required for our purpose, and will then often be able to teach the poor in various ways how to nurse themselves, which is by no means an unimportant part of her duty.

To her training in the surgical and medical wards we add that of passing three or four weeks in a lying-in hospital; and even after that, we cannot feel full confidence in a nurse till we have proved her by her practice in our Bible districts, for the women themselves often say that they learn in the first six weeks after they begin their out-door work more than they ever learned in the hospital; and still the hospital is the indispensable preparation."—(Nurses for the Needy, by Mrs. Ranyard.)

This idea that a woman could "pick up" sufficient nursing knowledge by merely working in a hospital for a few months was universal at that time; and the further feeling that a little knowledge was sufficient to fit one for nursing the poor was also prevalent.

The good common sense of the leaders in the Bible-women's Mission however taught them what they could and what they could not allow their nurses to do, which saved them from the danger of undertaking cases in which their lack of training might have proved disastrous. Again we quote from Mrs. Ranyard:

"One of the first things we learned affecting such a nurse passing from house to house, was the division of the work that she could do from that which she could not. She could not, unless set apart to it, nurse infectious diseases, because she would, of course, spread it from one family to another. Measles, small-pox, scarlatina and contagious fever were, therefore, beyond her bounds, though she might in many cases carry help to the door, and give most useful previous instruction to the poor mothers how, in such cases, to nurse their own children. A very wide circle of non-contagious disease remained in her care. Bad legs, incident to the much standing of the labouring classes, cancer, tumours, dropsy, abscesses, ulcers, skin disease and putrefying sores; a great part of them uncared for, except as the sufferers were out-patients of hospitals, or served by ignorant relatives.

Such cases alone presented an unending field for the practice of all the nursing that could be learned in the surgical wards of hospitals; while paralysis, epilepsy, rheumatic fever, with affections of the heart, spine, lungs, stomach, and liver, developed in young and old by bad smells and unfavourable conditions and atmosphere of lodgings, are always swelling the list; besides which, there again remain the important department of the 'prevention which is better than cure' in the cases of poor mothers recovering from their confinements; teaching them how to care for themselves and their babes at a period when suffering so perpetually arises from the want of that care."

Many of these patients were chronics, some few

were acute and some were surgical cases requiring after care. "They often undergo operations of more or less importance, which, if not of sufficient magnitude to warrant their being received into the hospital, often need the attendance of a nurse who has been trained to such dressing and cleansing of the wound as will insure the successful result of the doctor's treatment. And, alas! in the homes of many, the helpful hand is not found. Our nurses have often discovered a piece of dirty ticking or even sacking, aggravating an open sore, and how gladly have they displaced it with the soft lint or clean rag and healing lotion which our kind friends supply to the Mother-house for their use."

But though willing to start at once with a "ready to hand agency," as she herself called the first untrained Biblewomen nurses, Mrs. Ranyard fully realized that for good constructive work in district nursing, hospital training was essential, and as soon as possible arrangements were made for a three months' course of instruction for her nurses in such hospitals as Guy's, Westminster and the London Hospital.

The work grew rapidly. By June 1869 there were eighteen nurses at work under a central superintendent and certain local ladies, and the number of visits made had increased from 5000 the first year, to 27,690 the second year.

The nurses were at that time drawn entirely from the humblest rank but were all earnest and devoted Christian women, religion taking the place of education, and devotion the place of training. Although in this present day the Biblewomen Mission has among its nurses many women of refinement and education, the feeling is still general that the Mission does not wish to, in any way, limit the class. "It is character that is needed primarily," said the Hon. Superintendent in her report to the Jubilee Congress in 1909. "No merely professional aptitude is considered sufficient.

There is need for a strong personality, common sense, breadth of view, and *devotion.*"

But while the accent was from the first placed on the religious character of the nurse, and the principle that Christ crucified should be, as Agnes Jones expressed it, "the corner-stone of all her work," nevertheless, hospital training was by no means undervalued.

As we have seen, the Mission began at once giving its nurses a three months' course, and, as standards rose, the *Ranyard Nurses,* as they were called, rose with it, until at present, though the Mission has never affiliated with the Queen's Institute, it nevertheless, bases its standards on those of the Institute, and its nurses, like their sisters the Queen's Nurses, are required to have a three years' hospital training besides a six months' course in district nursing under supervision, and a certain amount of social training, taking up such subjects as "Principles of Relief," "The Poor Laws," Public Health Acts, "Charitable Agencies," etc.

But in the days of which we speak, though training was at last recognized as desirable, very few of the women who were doing nursing among the poor received any whatsoever. A few were given a one year's course in the hospital; others were sent to a hospital for a few months, "to pick up what they could, and then put into lodgings to find out any sick in their neighborhood needing their care"; and the rest, like the women of the Middle Ages, went forth filled with the spirit of devotion but lacking in the most elementary knowledge of scientific nursing.

Nursing the sick poor was still looked upon in great measure as a religious rather than a professional occupation. Good women, who would not have felt themselves qualified to go into private homes and nurse for wages, still felt that the impulse to do good was sufcient guarantee of their ability to nurse the sick poor. The majority of the nurses, moreover, had been drawn

from the lower middle class; only a few were gentlewomen, and these were mostly in administrative positions in charge of nursing institutions or schools of
training; the rank and file, the "field nurse" was almost universally of humble origin, often of the same
class as the poor patient whom she nursed. These
nurses had not the education necessary to understand
the principles of hygiene and sanitation which they
were expected to teach, nor had they the intelligence
and initiative necessary to meet the various emergencies constantly arising in district nursing, when in the
homes of the poor the commonest articles of convenience are often lacking and when a nurse must impro-
vise utensils to meet the need. "There is nothing to
clean with among those poor people, Ma'am; no proper
brushes or dusters or anything," said one of these nurses
when criticized for not keeping the patients' room clean
and tidy.

Many of the nurses boasted, moreover, that they
could cure the patient without calling in a doctor, and
some tried it, with dire results. Miss Lees, in her report on district nursing, of which we shall soon speak,
quoted the following case as typical: "I was taken by
a nurse to see a man whose hand had been poisoned,
but who, as he absolutely refused to go into a hospital
or to see a doctor, the nurse herself had 'treated,' and
was not a little proud of it! She seemed utterly un-
aware that the diseased hand, although preserved to
the man, could never be of any use to him, and that
his whole health had been affected by it. I persuaded
her to use her influence to induce her patient to place
himself under a good surgeon, telling her that she ought
to have done so from the first, and to have refused
'nursing' him in any way whatever unless he would
do so. There was little doubt from his appearance that
his whole health was so seriously damaged that it might
end in his having to exchange his life for his hand."

These facts were beginning to be known and a certain undercurrent of feeling manifested that district nursing, as then carried on, was not entirely satisfactory. True, it relieved much suffering—but it aimed to do much more. Were these so-called nurses really teaching the poor the things they were supposed to teach? Were they even giving them the nursing care that their condition required? It is a dangeous thing to trifle with a human life; were these untrained women, by assuming to have medical knowledge, perhaps doing more harm than good? Even if they were doing good, were there enough of them to make any impression on the great mass of poverty and ignorance found among the people whom they served?

There was a difference of opinion. Those who saw only their own small corner of the globe felt that the work was well-done, and that the need was being properly and sufficiently met; others, with a wider vision, and a more profound appreciation of the need, felt that the few workers in the field were as a drop in the bucket compared with the vast field of sickness and suffering about them; and that while a kindly visit and friendly smile might brighten a sick room, that only trained hands and intelligent minds could successfully cope with the situation. Moreover, each piece of work was local, unrelated, unstandardized. It needed to be made national; to be more widely distributed; and to be standardized both in its nursing requisites and social aspects. Unless steps were speedily taken to provide for these needs and to see to it that the rules of health, order, cleanliness and ventilation were properly taught and insisted upon district nursing would soon fall back into the merely palliation work of the past, and the ideals of its founder be lost forever.

CHAPTER XI

THE METROPOLITAN AND NATIONAL NURSING ASSOCIATION

About this time, *i. e.*, early in the year 1874, the Order of St. John of Jerusalem called a committee to consider the question of providing more fully trained nurses for the sick poor. Miss Florence Lees, a trained nurse, actively interested in district nursing, was present as an Honorary Associate of the Order; and the meeting was held at the house of Lady Stanyford, also a member of the Order. The committee heartily endorsed the suggestion, and on the 25th of June, 1874, a public meeting was held, under the auspices of the Order of St. John of Jerusalem, with a view to establishing a National Association for securing better nursing. Sir Rutherford Alcock, K. C. was in the chair and such well-known philanthropists as the Earl of Shaftsbury, the Duke of Westminster, Mr. Rathbone, Mr. Wigram, etc., were seen on the platform. Our old friend the Earl of Shaftsbury, moved the first resolution, *i. e.,* "That, with a view to securing better nursing for the sick poor, as a sanitary and preventive measure, an association be formed, in accordance with the suggestions of a committee of the Order of St. John of Jerusalem, for training and providing a body of nurses for that object in London and the provinces; and that a Home be established where nurses in training in the London Hospitals, or employed as district nurses, may lodge, and where a register of trained nurses requiring employment may be kept."

FLORENCE L. CRAVEN NÉE LEES.

First Superintendent-General of the Metropolitan and National
Nursing Association for Providing Trained Nurses for the Sick
Poor. England, 1875.

The resolution was passed and the new association formed under the name of "The National Association for Providing Trained Nurses for the Sick Poor."

The Association was to have a central committee in London, with sub-committees in each county, and subscriptions were to be solicited from the public. It was felt that by having one central organization with branch committees in various parts of the country cooperating with it, that a standard of work could more easily be maintained, and assistance more easily rendered when new work was to be undertaken.

It was also clearly pointed out that the new organization did not wish to supersede in any way already existing institutions, but to co-operate with them, and to endeavor to meet, so soon as public support would permit, the acknowledged national need of properly trained nurses for the sick poor. The first step was to ascertain clearly the needs of the city of London; what nurses were available for the work; what training was necessary; and how the work was being conducted in London and other parts of the Kingdom.

A Sub-Committee of Inquiry was, therefore, named with Mr. Rathbone as its chairman, and Lady Stanyford and Miss Florence Lees, as Honorary Secretaries. At Miss Nightingale's suggestion Miss Lees was placed in charge of the investigation and asked to visit and inspect the chief nursing institutions where there were district nurses—such as the Liverpool Association, the Biblewomen's Mission, the East London Society, etc.

Miss Lees is described by Kinglake as—"the gifted and radiant pupil of Florence Nightingale." She had been one of the earliest pupils of the Nightingale School; had studied at Kaiserswerth, Dresden and Berlin, and was a woman of superior education and refinement. Miss Nightingale herself spoke of her as "A

10

genius of nursing." Mr. Rathbone was intensely interested in the work of the committee, and himself
defrayed the expenses. After nearly a year of exhaustive labor, the committee presented the result of
its investigation in a long and interesting report.

When the Committee first set to work little was
known as to the actual state of district nursing either
in London or elsewhere; so little, in fact, that many
people questioned whether London stood in need of any
more district nurses than she already had. No one
knew just how many were at work; nor what training,
if any, they had had; nor what kind of service they
were rendering. It took months of constant, untiring,
searching, industry and inquiry, to collect the facts;
but after they were collected, the Committee was able
to say, with pardonable pride: "We now know exactly what nursing is done and by whom, and what
training the nurses have had. We know what districts
are poorest and most suffering. We know the name
and address, the nature and professed character
of the work of every nursing or nurse-training
institution in the capital. We have seen, through the
eyes of a trained nurse of the very highest grade, the
actual working of the best organized district nursing
systems in London and in other towns; their effects;
their shortcomings; the difficulties they have to encounter, the means they take to meet these difficulties."

The first thing the Committee had done had been to
send out some seven hundred or eight hundred circular
letters to the clergy and medical officers of London, [1]
asking them whether there was a nurse in their district
and, if so, what her training had been and whether
the work she did was satisfactory. These letters elicited
an almost unanimous testimony as to the value of the

[1] Appendix III.

district nurses' services, wherever she was employed, *provided* she had been trained, and was thoroughly in earnest in her vocation. A few of the medical officers expressed doubts as to whether real nursing of the poor in their own homes, considering what those homes are,—how wanting in cleanliness, ventilation, quiet and every condition generally regarded as requisite for the proper treatment of sickness,—was possible. For that reason, many maintained that only in a hospital could they be properly cared for, and that there was little real nursing that could be given, or was needed, in the districts.

The Committee agreed that the hospital is the right place for serious, acute cases, and for severe accidents; and that the workhouse infirmary could take care of chronic cases that are friendless, penniless and helpless. But even then there are many that cannot be cared for in a hospital, nor in an infirmary and, as proof that there were always plenty of really sick people to be found in their homes who really needed nursing care, pointed out that neither in Liverpool, nor in London where real nursing had been attempted, had there ever been a lack of real nursing work for the nurse to do. "Even where it is alleged that they do not nurse but give relief the very reports show that there was plenty of nursing to do had they but known it. Of the Liverpool district nursing cases in 1873, numbering 3572,—326 were sent to hospitals, 246 otherwise taken off the books, and of the 3000 left, 547 died. A death rate of 18.2 per cent after the list had been weeded of its heaviest cases by the hospital, implies very serious illness and very grave need of real nursing."

The Committee, however, did not stop at sending out circular letters. Miss Lees made personal investigation in nearly every district, town or village in which district nursing of any kind was being carried on; accompanying the nurses in their rounds; writing out detailed reports of each visit; and, like her leader, Florence Nightingale, basing her deductions upon the actual facts and statistics procured. These reports of the work done by the various organizations in that day are very illuminating. In her report on London Miss Lees says: "—As to the district nursing work actually done in London and the suburbs at present, we may briefly state that there are about 100 such district nurses engaged, here and there, among a population of three-and-a-half millions,—of this number (100), one-third can hardly be said to be trained at all. One-half the entire number consists of the Biblewomen Nurses, who receive three months' instruction of a more or less perfunctory nature in a general, and one, in a lying-in, hospital. The small remnant, about one-sixth of the whole, enjoy a training of from three to twelve months."

The actual number of district nurses working in London was found to be 115. These nurses were working under 15 different societies. The following table gives a detailed account of the figures:

Institutions in London employing Dis. Nurses	No. in work	Length of training	Remarks
East London Nursing Soc.	7	1 year	
St. John's House Sisterhood	2	1 year	
Biblewomen's Mission Inst. of Nursing Sisters Devonshire Square	57	4 months	The no. 57 includes 3 in training, and 4 pioneers i. e. supervisors.
	20	not trained	
Nat. Ass'n for Providing Nurses for the Sick Poor	1	1 year	
British Nursing Ass'n.	1	1 year	
Eight various Sisterhoods Catholic and Protestant	27	none, to a few months.	

The report then proceeds to analyze the quality and

amount of service rendered by each organization or Society:

"The well-known Society of St. John's Sisterhood, of Norfolk Street, Strand, established in 1848, which undertakes the nursing of King's College and Charing Cross Hospitals, and has done so much for raising the standard of nursing generally, numbers 25 Sisters, 112 nurses, and probation nurses—only two of the staff are stated to be regularly employed in district work in London."

"The most extensive organization of District Nursing amongst the poor in their own homes in London is that of the Bible and Domestic Female Missions, 13 Hunter Street, of which Mrs. Ranyard is the head. A body of Biblewomen has been at work in the Metropolis for upwards of seventeen years, and the Biblewomen Nurses form a branch of the original institution, arising from the need which the Biblewomen found to exist in their visitation from house to house.—The Biblewomen Nurses are insufficiently trained; they are taught to regard their nursing duties as subordinate to spiritual objects, and their efforts are chiefly directed, of course, to those who have had either a religious education or religious impressions later in life, and whose homes consequently present a different aspect to those of too many labouring people; for among the poor cleanliness is indeed next to godliness, and the two are not often separated.   Therefore, the work of the Biblewomen falls, as a rule, in favored spots and under special conditions; they nurse no contagious diseases, and consequently their work confines itself in a great measure to monthly nursing, chronic and surgical cases, a limited and by no means most difficult class of nursing."

The work of the East London Nursing Society seems on the whole to have been the best organized; of this the report says: "The plan of the East London Nursing Society is to find some lady of means, willing to undertake two duties,—first, to provide the funds neces-sary to lodge a district nurse and provide medical com-forts, etc., for the sick; secondly, to act as superintend-ent and counsellor of the nurse when settled in the district to which she may be appointed. The Society then takes up the position of providing a suitable trained nurse—her wages and a great part of her dress—who, with others, is under the constant supervision of a trained matron, who visits the patients from time to time with the nurse, advises with her as to the various cases, and gives directions."

It may be worth remarking, as illustrating the in-terest, almost enthusiasm, of some of these nurses, that the matron stated that one of the most difficult duties she had to perform was to get the nurse to leave the patients she had had the care of, and take the needful annual holiday for the benefit of her own health.

This Society, begun, as we have seen, in 1868, was doing good and careful work though the Nurses' Home had been given up, and each nurse was then living in lodgings provided for her in the district where she was employed. Their great difficulty seems to have been to obtain funds to maintain and extend the work.

Of the various Sisters doing district nursing, Miss Lees says, "Whatever may be thought of their ec-clesiastical aspect, we are bound to say the duty they do, and the self-sacrifice it involves, are features that claim notice and often compel admiration.—Generally it may be said of the Sisterhoods that many districts have no other nurses amongst the sick poor, and can get none."

Referring to the difficulty which some of the societies seemed to meet in trying to attract nurses to district work, especially if they supplied private nurses as well which was very generally the case, the report says:

"Some societies which began with a special regard

to district nursing have gradually declined into private work. They offer, as a rule, a higher renumeration and the nurses being employed continually in houses where comfort, and in many instances luxury, prevails, it can be no matter of surprise that comparatively few institutions can successfully combine the two sorts of employment. And it is still rarer to find a nurse, who, with occasional chances of attending to patients of a wealthy class, can change her occupation so far as to do the harder duties of nursing the sick poor amidst the squalor and misery of multitudes of London homes, where every sense is offended."

But the committee wished to know not only how many nurses were actually working in the various districts of London, how they were trained, and by whom supported; they wished also to know just what kind of work the nurses were doing, whether they were giving real bedside care and teaching the rules of health, or whether they were simply swelling the list of friendly visitors and becoming mere distributors of material relief. To ascertain this information it was necessary to go about with the various nurses in their rounds of duty, and to personally inspect the work they were doing. No better person could have been chosen for this difficult task than Miss Lees. She was a highly trained and experienced nurse, and she possessed the intuition, tact and power of keen observation which enabled her to see below the surface, and to obtain information which a less tactful or acute person would have been unable to procure.

The first thing, in point of importance, perhaps, that she discovered was that the majority of the nurses were not sufficiently well trained to be entrusted with the care—especially the unsupervised care—of sick people. In many cases there was no doctor in charge and the nurse, in her ignorance, would give so-called "treatments" which were actually harmful in their

results.   Many of them had no idea of disinfection or
even proper cleanliness in the case of the sick and ran
great risk of spreading the very diseases they were
supposed to nurse and prevent.—"In all cases of scarlatina or other fevers that I visited with different
nurses," said she, "I was much struck with the fact that
the nurses did not seem to have the faintest conception
of the necessity of disinfecting a room while the patient
was ill.   They seemed to think that that was the duty
of the sanitary officer and could only be carried into
effect when the patient was cured, or dead.   I visited
several convalescents from scarlatina, with nurses, who
then proceeded to other cases without having used the
very commonest of precautions against carrying infection, such as washing their hands afterwards, not
sitting down in the room in which the patient is, etc.,
—I will give an instance which struck me particularly.
We had just visited a case of spotted typhus in a house
where the whole family, with one exception, were recovering from the same fever, and yet the nurse went
straight from this house to one where a mother was
nursing her baby!—In one instance she went from
a case of erysipelas to another surgical case of crushed
foot, and was proceeding to take the bandages off it
when I stopped her by the half-jesting exclamation,
'Oh, you wicked woman; remember what you've just
been doing, and that you have not washed your hands
since!' "

Such utter disregard of the commonest precautions
fills one with terror, and one wonders whether those
ignorant women did not, indeed, do more real harm
than good.   Another great and universal fault that
Miss Lees laid bare was that, as always, district nursing tended to degenerate into mere charitable relief—
giving to the sick poor instead of doing for them; and
that in London, where little supervision was given
and where much poverty and consequent need certainly

existed, this tendency was greatly exaggerated. She tells of one visit she made with the nurse who, after bathing the patient and making the bed, then left, after giving her "tea, sugar and two shilling, six-pence in money." Again, "we visited a paralyzed woman. Nurse lifted her out of bed, and then made it and gave her a new blanket." She said most of the nurses had their *baskets* filled with things to give away—jam, tea, sugar, arrowroot, etc.

She also found that the nurses fell far short of their duty in regard to sanitary instruction and preventive measures; that they carried too many cases at one time; and that they did too many other things that were not nursing, to be able to nurse properly. The one recommendation on which she laid the greatest stress, as a remedy for all these evils, and in her mind, as the essential condition for any efficient District Nursing, was the employment of a professional Lady Supervisor, who would be in charge of the nurses in an area containing a certain number of districts; would receive the reports of the nurses; and, periodically, inspect their work and go the rounds with each of them. Miss Lees pointed out that this supervisor should be a lady of education and breeding, as well as a nurse of the highest order, having received as complete an education in the duties of her profession as men in the training for their professions, and should be able, therefore, to direct and instruct the ordinary nurses in the technique and science of their calling, as well as to secure their deference and obedience, because of her superior position.

As to the various systems of organization and administration, the Liverpool system of District Nursing was described as the most complete of its kind in existence; though even there, little sanitary reform or sanitary instruction had been possible; the reason given being that, where the nurses were drawn from the same class as the patients themselves, as was the case in Liverpool, it was next to impossible to exact the patient's obedience.

The work done in Derby was pointed out as being the most successful in *pure nursing*.

"Of the various district nursing systems investigated, that of Derby has been in pure nursing, the most successful in its results. The nurses—not half-a-dozen— are under a *trained* Lady Superintendent, who alone gives the medical comforts, etc., required, and who inspects weekly the work done by the nurses under her charge, and *daily* arranges what that work shall consist of for each nurse. Fevers and contagious diseases are nursed by a Fever Nurse who is not allowed to visit any other patients. She brings a daily report of her cases to the Lady Superintendent—the said report being delivered verbally over the low garden wall of the Nurses' Home. The Lady Superintendent calls at the house of each patient to ask the relatives 'what nurse has done for them?' But she does not enter the room. The doctor reports to the Lady Superintendent if the sick person and room are dirty and neglected by the nurse."

Further on, however, Miss Lees explained one reason why in Derby they were able to give this better nursing care. "The poor were better housed, and not so degraded as in Liverpool. The nurses lived with their own families in their own homes. Among the very poor they did not seem to do much actual nursing, but among the better class of the poor, *e. g.,* small shopkeepers, etc., they did actually 'nurse,' and, so far as I could judge, the patients were left nearly untouched by their relatives until the arrival of the nurse.—All the cases where nurses actually did anything for their patients were people who could well have afforded (it seemed to me) to have paid some small sum weekly for her services.—As far as I could learn no district nurse visited more than twelve cases a week. All fevers were reserved for the care of one nurse, who was not permitted to enter the 'Home,' but made her report and received her directions in the open air over the wall of the garden, and the Lady Superintendent heard from the parish doctor as to how far she filled, or failed in her duty. No 'medical comforts' or nourishments of any kind could be given by the nurse.—One thing struck me very much, *i. e.,* that there did not seem to be one-tenth of the disease, misery and destitution in any nurse's district that there was in any one district in Liverpool or London."

The principal conclusions at which the Committee arrived were briefly outlined as follows :

1 : That there exist only two organizations in London which have succeeded in employing trained nurses, in nursing the poor in their own homes to any considerable extent—the *Bible and Domestic Female Mission.* which, as a corollary to its general religious work, employs fifty-two Biblewomen nurses (chiefly in care of chronic cases and monthly nursing) ; and the *East Londone Nursing Society,* which has seven district nurses at work in general nursing. There are about 100 nurses employed in such work in London, but of these, one-third are untrained, and can be of little service except in the administration of nourishment, medical comforts and general relief to the sick poor.

2 : That the hospitals as nurse-training schools, do not, under their existing arrangements, afford such means of training nurses for the sick poor at home as ought to satisfy the requirements of this Association.

3 : That the present system of district nursing is open to grave objections. It has done infinite good, and relieved incalculable suffering; but it has a tendency to degenerate into mere distribution of relief, and that not always well regulated.

4 : The chief faults in the operation of that system are :

(a) Too much relief and too little nursing.

    (b) Too little control and direction and consequent lapses into slovenliness and neglect, sometimes dangerous to the very lives of her patients on the part of the nurse.

    (c) Too little supervision or discrimination as to the class of cases to be allotted to the nurse, and consequent neglect of some and danger to others.

    (d) Too little communication between the nurse and the doctor. Very often, indeed, the doctor does not attend the nurse's patients, and she becomes their doctor rather than their nurse, and when the doctor does attend the nurse is as often absent as present.

    (e) Too little instruction given to the patient's friends and family in regard to the care of the sufferer, to ventilation, cleanliness, disinfecting, etc.

5. A scheme was then outlined, the principal provisions of which were:

A training school in close connection with a hospital on the principle of the Nightingale School at St. Thomas' and under the regulation suggested by the trustees of that school.

A District Home in the vicinity of the hospital, inhabited by four or six nurses under charge of a Superintendent (responsible to the head of the training schools), which would take in hand the district nursing of the region immediately surrounding it, and in which the trained nurses might serve an apprenticeship to district nursing; in fact, a Model Group of Nursing Districts.

The supply of nurses to other districts, in connection with religious or charitable organizations or individuals willing to be responsible for the expenses other than the nurse's salary, and to accept the general regulations laid down from time to time by the Association. Provision, either for the combination of four or more such districts into a group under a professional Superintendent, or for their regular inspection by an experienced lady-nurse reporting both to the local employers and to this Association.

A year's training should be given in the hospital and from three months upwards in the original District Home.

6. To obtain payment for the nurses' service from patients would, in very many cases, be most desirable, and would, it is believed, promote the employment of the nurse by a large class above the very poor, who are quite as deserving and equally unable to procure such aid.

7. Should the means fail at the outset of establishing such a Hospital Training School as above mentioned, the alternative would be to make arrangements with such of the existing hospital or hospitals as contain the best organization for the purpose, and having obtained a sufficient number of trained nurses to establish a model District Nurses' Home under the charge of a trained superintendent. In this case, the first step would be to appoint a Superintendent duly qualified as a trained nurse and experienced in the management of a nursing staff. It is possible that a sufficient number of already trained nurses might be obtained to enable her at once to commence the district home and school on a small scale; but even if that were not possible, she would be well employed in selecting qualified women for training in the hospitals, and during their period of training, herself gain experience in district work. [This was the plan eventually adopted.]

In concluding their report the Committee again stated that they wished in no way to supersede existing organizations but desired to establish a standard for district nurses and nursing, which might be applied by the Association not to London only, but eventually to all England—perhaps ultimately to the United Kingdom—and be truly national in character.

This truly wonderful report was made public on June 11th, 1875, and was so widely read and excited so much interest and enthusiasm in the cause of District Nursing that a second edition was published in order to meet the ever increasing demand for it.

The general principles of the report were at once accepted by the Council and, at Miss Nightingale's suggestion, Miss Lees herself was asked to act as Superintendent-General.

In accordance with the recommendation of Miss Lees it was decided to recruit the nurses entirely from the class known as gentlewomen. This recognition that district nursing required the very highest type of women, was not a new thing. As far back as 1832, when Amalia Sieverking founded the society of "the Friends of the Poor," in Germany, she discovered that women of the higher classes had more influence and could carry on the work of nursing the sick poor more successfully than women from the humbler walks of life.

"I thought at first," she said, "that they [middle-class women], would understand better the needs of the poor, but I am now certain that a wider culture contributes much to the solidity of judgment." (History of Nursing,—Nutting. Vol. 1, p. 545).

Although the recommendation was ultimately accepted it was at first strongly opposed by all the members of the Council, except the Duke of Westminster. Even Miss Nightingale was skeptical of the wisdom of such a step. "I don't believe you will find it will answer," said she, "but try it—try it for a year."

There were good grounds given for the recommendation, however, chiefly that in nursing the poor in their own homes the nurses were placed in positions of greater responsibility in carrying out the doctor's orders than in hospitals; that women of education would be more capable of exercising such a responsibility; and that nurses recruited from the class of gentlewomen would be able to exercise a greater influence over their patients than women of a lower rank, and would be better fitted to instruct them in the rules of sanitation and hygiene.

That the decision was a wise one was ultimately proved beyond dispute. Many years later, Miss Lees in writing of gentlewomen as district nurses said: "I have always found gentlewomen of good birth and breeding more ready than women less delicately reared to perform the most trying and repulsive services for the sick poor which could in any way add to their comfort or well-being." And again, "If, as a nurse, I am capable of judging nursing work, I can fairly say that the *nursing* services rendered by these ladies have been the highest attainable."

The new association changed its name to "The *Metropolitan* and National Nursing Association for Providing Trained Nurses for the Sick Poor," and began at once to plan for its financial support. It was estimated that in order to launch so large an enterprise a capital fund of 20,000 pounds ($100,000) must be immediately raised and an income of 5000 pounds ($25,000) a year assured. The public was appealed to and certain bankers in London and the country designated to receive subscriptions. The East London Nursing Association which had been founded with the same object as The Metropolitan, viz; the providing of trained nurses for the sick poor in their own homes, at once placed its entire staff at the disposal of the new association, turning over, as well, its subscription lists, which amounted to about $1500 a year, together with a special subscription from its treasurer of an additional $1000 for at least two years.

Besides the seven district nurses of the East London Association, distributed in different parts of East London, Miss Nightingale, who was much interested in the new Association, undertook to procure six trained nurses to start work at once in the Central District, under Miss Lees; and the Trustees of the Nightingale Fund, with a view to promoting the training of nurses in district work, agreed to maintain at the expense of the Fund, not less than four trained nurses to work in the southern part of the city under a District Superintendent. With these definite resources, both in funds and personnel, and the prospect of much more, the Association felt safe in starting its work.

A small furnished house at 8 Queen's Square was taken and occupied for a few months while the permanent Central Home at 23 Bloomsbury Square was being repaired and put in order. Two "Nightingale Probationers" were provided "to make a start" and the Parish and Infirmary doctors sent in cases.

The Central Home in Bloombury Square was opened in December 1875, the poor in the surrounding district, and also in those districts formerly nursed by the East London Society, being cared for under the personal direction of the Superintendent-General.

The uniform adopted and worn by the Metropolitan Nurses was simple and practical though it seems strangely old-fashioned and ugly to our modern ideas. The dresses were brown Holland trimmed with bands of dark blue linen, with large apron and over-sleeves of the same material to be worn when on duty. The dress itself was not changed until evening. Out of doors they wore a large dark-blue cloak—of blue alpaca in summer—and a black straw bonnet, trimmed with black silk, piped with pale-blue silk, lined with white muslin, and with a stiffly crimped muslin border and wide white muslin strings. Their bonnets were worn when on duty and only removed with the apron and over-sleeves. Each nurse had, moreover, a sort of Chatelaine of leather with pin-cushions, scissors, and dressing forceps attached; and carried a small morocco hand-bag containing disinfectants, hand towel and soap, surgical dressings, etc.

The training of the nurses was, from the first, looked upon as one of the fundamental duties of the Association, and was most carefully supervised by Miss Lees, than whom no better person could have been chosen. The candidates were first carefully selected by the superintendent herself, and remained for one month in the Central Home, observing and going about with the nurses, in order to learn the general nature of district nursing. They were then placed in the hospital where they remained for one year, after which they again returned to the Central Home for a six months' special course in district training under the superintendent, who accompanied each nurse to every new case, and taught her how to extemporize useful appliances; how to place the room in order; and also—a procedure they could not learn in a hospital—the care of the mother and infant after birth; and how to nurse and disinfect in contagious disease. They also received lectures of a more advanced type than they had been able to receive in hospital, where the instruction was necessarily adapted to the understanding of women of a lower grade and education.

These lectures were on anatomy, physiology, (the latter introducing some lectures on the diseases of women) and hygiene, also the peptonizing of foods. Nurses had to read up for these lectures, and at the end of each course, undergo an examination by the lecturer. After finishing this training they were then placed on the roll of trained district nurses of the Association.

11

The experiment was a success—it was found that
gentlewomen of good birth and breeding were more
ready than their more humble sisters to perform the
menial tasks so often required in nursing the sick
poor; also, as Miss Lees had foreseen, that they exerted
a better influence and commanded more respect and
obedience from their patients than women drawn from
a lower walk in life; and finally, that the nursing
technique was better and more intelligently administered, and that their better education and mental equipment enabled them to teach in a clear and forceful manner the principles of hygiene and sanitation, and to
meet any emergency which might arise in a quicker and
more intelligent manner.

Much of the success of the Association must be
credited to Miss Lees, who from the first brought to
it her enthusiasm, good judgment and trained experience, and who inspired her pupils with her own high
ideals as to what a district nurse should be.

Eighteen years later, when speaking before the International Congress of Nurses, held in Chicago, at the
World's Fair, Miss Lees—then Mrs. Dacre Craven—
outlined her idea of a district nurse and we cannot do
better than to quote her in full:

"District nurses should feel themselves beyond and
before all things, the servants of the sick poor. They
instruct—but *practically* and by *example*. District
nursing means, the care of the sick poor in their own
homes, where there are no proper appliances, and where
the nurse can rarely see the doctor,—in some cases, not
at all. She must know how to put the room of each
patient into such good sanitary conditions that the
patient may have a fair chance of recovery, and how
to extemporize hospital appliances where these are required. She must be so well trained in nursing duties
as not only to know how to observe and report correctly
on every case under her charge, but to allow no change

to pass unnoticed; and to be able to apply, provisionally, suitable treatment, until the medical man shall have arrived. She must know how to purify the foul air of the room without making a draught; to dust without making a dust; to ice drinks without ice; to filter water without a filter; to bake without an oven . . . She must be content to be servant and teacher by turns. . . . A district nurse must have a real love for the poor and a real desire to lessen the misery she may see among them; and such tact as well as skill that she will do what is best for her patients even against their will. No district nurse should ever give alms or relief of any kind, beyond the highest of all—that of nursing service . . . A nurse's business is to nurse—but she has also to teach the poor those sanitary laws which are household words with the well-to-do.—" (Proceedings of the International Congress of Nurses, 1893.)

In other words, Miss Lees showed that a district nurse must be a woman of great intelligence and initiative. She must be not only well-trained in nursing technique, but she must possess an intellectual understanding of her work so that she may safely assume responsibility for the care of her patient when necessary. She must have love, tact, sympathy and a quick mind; and, finally, she must have the ability to teach and to command the respect and obedience of her patients.

All this means that a district nurse must be a woman of superior intelligence, education and character. District nursing, therefore, is one of the highest types of nursing. It has called to its ranks, as Miss Nutting has said, "the very flower of the profession"; it has opened up a calling which combines service to God with service to one's fellow-men; and brings with it a satisfaction and an interest which compensates for all the hardships it may entail. "It is a life in which love and human sympathy have so large a share that patients cease to be mere 'cases' and may be termed rather the friends and children of these 'servants of the sick poor.'" (Article entitled "Servants of the Sick Poor," by Mrs. Dacre Craven, presented at the International Congress of Nurses in Chicago, 1893.)

The Metropolitan Association had then succeeded in doing what its founders had hoped for. It had set up a *standard* of training and efficiency for district nurses; it had made possible the attainment of the standard by establishing a Home, where nurses could be trained in the technic for district work; and, lastly, by precept and example, it had shown the world what good district nursing should mean, and had dragged it back from the slough of mere relief giving by untrained workers into which it was so fast degenerating.

In a letter written to Miss Lees by Florence Nightingale in 1876, one year after the establishment of the new National Association, Miss Nightingale expressed her satisfaction in the results attained and set her seal of approval on the work done. In this letter she says: "As to your success—what is not your success! To raise the home of your patients so that they never fall back again to dirt and disorder, such is your nurse's influence; to pull through life and death cases which it would be an honor to pull through with all the appurtenances of hospital or the richest in the land, and this without any sick-room appurtenances at all; to keep whole families out of pauperism by preventing the family from being broken up and nursing the bread-winner back to health; to drag the noble act of nursing out of the sink of relief-doles; to show the rich and poor what nursing is and what it is not; to carry out practically the principles of preventing disease, its causes and the causes of infections which spread disease; last, but not least, to show a common life able to sustain the workers in this saving but hardest of work, under a working head, who will personally keep the training and nursing at its highest point. Is not this a great success?"

And so at last we see the care of the sick poor in their homes placed in the hands of trained workers—women selected for their high character, and trained in the scientific principles as well as the manual duties, of their calling. And although, as yet, the bedside care of the patient overshadowed the instruction given, nevertheless a strong accent was being placed on the preventive, as well as the therapeutic value of their services, and Miss Nightingale and other leaders in the profession, were beginning to talk among themselves of "Health Nursing" and "Health Missioners."

CHAPTER XII

QUEEN'S NURSES

In 1887 the British Empire celebrated the fiftieth anniversary of Queen Victoria's accession to the throne. It was a wonderful and impressive demonstration of the "far flung battle line" of British dominion. From India and Australia, from South Africa and Canada and New Zealand and the Islands of the Sea came kings and princes, viceroys and governors—black, white, yellow and half-breed—to do homage and reverence to the great Queen, who for so many years had ruled over them as a mother over her children.

Among the many demonstrations of the respect and affection in which the Queen was held, was a popular subscription fund of 76,000 pounds, raised by the women of England; and it was significant of the growing interest in nursing that this Women's Jubilee Fund, like the Nightingale Fund of some thirty years earlier, should also have been devoted to the advancement of nursing and training.

In 1879 Miss Lees had resigned her position as Superintendent-General of the Metropolitan Association, in order to marry the Reverend Dacre Craven, Mr. Craven was soon after elected Hon. Secretary to the Association, and it was entirely owing to his initiative that the Queen's Jubilee Committee recommended that at least a portion of the Women's Jubilee Fund be devoted to the training of district nurses, as the Nightingale Fund had been to the training of nurses in general.

In order to give the members of the Jubilee Committee a clear and definite idea of the work for whose benefit he suggested the Fund be used, Mr. Craven sent to each, a copy of the Report of the Metropolitan Association; a copy of Mrs. Craven's article on district nursing entitled, "Servants of the Sick Poor," as well as a copy of Florence Nightingale's letter to Miss Lees, when Superintendent of the Metropolitan Nursing Association, in which she spoke most enthusiastically of the work done by the district nurses and the consequent benefit to the sick poor.

Mrs. Craven, also, lent her aid in promoting the idea, and wrote a special letter to the Queen urging, not only that the Women's Jubilee Fund be devoted to the advancement of district nursing, but also that the funds of St. Katharine's Hospital be again used for the care of the sick poor in their own homes, as originally intended, and that the new undertaking be incorporated with the old. This letter was presented to the Queen by one of her ladies-in-waiting and received careful consideration.

Queen Victoria had followed with much interest the inception and development of district nursing among the poor, and ardently desired that the humble subjects of her realm should enjoy, equally with their richer neighbors, the supreme comfort and advantage of trained and skilful nursing in time of sickness.

Such nursing she knew could only be assured by a National Organization, equipped to give a training in district work which would standardize the service; and large enough to supply a sufficient number of these trained nurses, and to properly supervise their work in all parts of the kingdom. With this in mind, therefore, and following the recommendation of the Committee, her Majesty decided to use 70,000 pounds of the Woman's Jubilee Fund for the establishment of an

Institute for the Training and Supervising of District Nurses, with which any properly qualified nursing association already established might affiliate, thus gathering into one standardized system all the unrelated work of the country, and making the cause a royal and truly national one.

The Fund was placed in the hands of three trustees, the Duke of Westminster, Sir James Paget, and Sir Rutherford Alcock—men already interested in district nursing, and well acquainted with its needs—and a provisional committee appointed to work out the details of the scheme.

In September 1889, after many months of preliminary labor, the "Queen Victoria Jubilee Institute for Nurses" was finally established by royal charter, and a President and Council appointed to carry on and promote the work.

Following the suggestion of Mrs. Dacre Craven the Institute was connected with the ancient charity of St. Katharine's Hospital, an ecclesiastical institution formerly occupying the site of St. Katherine's wharf, but later, when the present wharf was built, removed to Regent's Park. This hospital was founded in 1148 by Queen Matilda, wife of Stephen. In 1273 it was chartered by Queen Eleanor, widow of Henry III, and again in 1351 by Queen Phillipa, wife of Edward III at which time the visitation of the sick and poor in the neighborhood was especially imposed upon the members of the Corporation most of whom were women of noble birth dedicated to the service of God.

It was at first intended to call the nurses trained by the Institute "Jubilee Nurses," but, again at the suggestion of Mrs. Craven, the name, "Queen's Nurses" was substituted, and by this name they have ever since been known.

It was deemed wise to utilize, so far as possible, all the valuable experience already gained by the various existing District Nursing Associations throughout the country, by inviting them to affiliate with the Institute, and to co-operate in working out the plans and ideals of its founders. The Council, therefore, drew up a "form of affiliation" which was submitted to the committees or trustees of District Nursing Associations, wherever it was felt that such affiliation would be desirable. The fundamental conditions for affiliation were: (Appendix IV)

1: A uniform standard of qualification and training for nurses.

2: That in large towns nurses should reside in Homes under a qualified Superintendent, and should nurse only under the direction of a medical practitioner.

3: While not excluding poor patients able to pay something, the service to be confined to the poor.

4: That the work should be absolutely non-sectarian, and that the nurses should give no money or relief of any kind except under special circumstances and with the approval of the Superintendent.

All the principal associations of the country at once sought affiliation with the Queen's Institute. The advantage accruing to them by affiliation were many. They were able to obtain help and advice, and often temporary financial aid, from a group of experts in district nursing. They were also supplied with fully trained Queen's Nurses as rapidly as the Institute could turn them out. Finally they had the great advantage of regular inspection by a Supervisor of the Institute, by means of which a uniform standard of efficiency and training was assured.

The great advantage of inspection from without is manifest. It is difficult for an individual to perceive his own short-comings, and the same is true of a group of individuals, namely, an Association. So used are they to the *status quo* that they do not perceive its defeets. The accustomed eye becomes pur-blind—it needs the clear vision of a stranger from without, to survey, as it were, the entire field; comparing one town with another; measuring all by a recognized standard; able to see where one fails and where another may be improved; and with authority to recommend changes. This regular inspection of every affiliated association, from the large city association, with its forty or fifty nurses and its trained superintendent, to the solitary nurse working alone in the remotest part of the country, has been, therefore, one of the fundamental principles of the Queen's Institute from the very beginning. And this inspection is not resented, rather is it welcomed. "The inspector comes as a friend, alike to the nurse and the Committee," says Miss Hughes, former superintendent-general of the Institute, "visiting the cases, seeing the books and helping, by her experience and advice, to smooth over any little difficulty that may arise." But though the inspector might suggest changes, she had no power to enforce their acceptance. Neither did affiliation with the Institute in any way effect local management, each local committee or association supporting as far as possible its own work, and making its own rules and regulations, *provided only* that the conditions of affiliation were maintained. Even when an association failed to meet requirements, the Institute had no power to enforce a change, its only weapon being the power to drop any member from its roll of affiliated societies should it fail to come up to standard. This power, however, was seldom if ever put to the test, most of the nursing associations realizing that the Institute was wise in its judgments and anxious only for the best results. Whenever, from time to time, as the years went on, an affiliated association was forced to sever its connection with the Institute, it was usually found to be for financial reasons—because funds could not be found to support a Queen's Nurse, or because it was impossible, under existing conditions, to live up to the rules and regulations laid down in the form of affiliation.

As the training of nurses in the theory and practice of district nursing was to be an important part of the work of the Institute, one of the first duties of the Provisional Committee was to establish and develop model training centers in connection with District Nursing Homes, in various parts of England, Scotland and Ireland. The Metropolitan and National Nursing Association was already carrying on a similar work, well organized and with an admirable system of district training. It had at that time nine Homes in London and several in the country. Arrangements were, therefore, made with this association to utilize its Central Home in Bloomsbury Square as the Central school for the Institute, where practical experience in district nursing could be given to the pupils, and plans were laid for a supplementary course of lectures to be given by distinguished professors of medical science, on subjects especially bearing on the duties and work of district nurses. In a short time similar Central Homes were opened in Edinburgh, Dublin and Cardiff. The Scottish Branch of the Queen's Institute had, from the first, its own Council and Executive Committee, and conducted the work of training and inspecting the Queen's Nurses in Scotland, the Central Home being located at 29 Castle Terrace, Edinburgh, with later, branch Homes in Glasgow, Aberdeen, Dundee, Paisley and elsewhere, where training was also given. The work in Ireland and Wales, on the other hand, together with that in England, was placed under the direction of the Central Council in London; although Wales soon had a Central Home for training, at Cardiff; with several Branch Homes; and Ireland established two Central Training Homes, one in connection with St. Patrick's Protestant Cathedral, 101

St. Stephen's Green, Dublin; and the other at St. Lawrence's Catholic Home, 34 Rutland Square, in the same city.

This training for Queen's Nurses was in no way intended to be a supplementary course in hospital work, only nurses thoroughly trained in hospitals being accepted as probationers. Rather was it a course to teach the nurse how to apply, in her work among the poor, the knowledge she had gained during her hospital days; instruction in how to give the most perfect bedside care without even the simplest of sick-room requisites; instruction in how to teach the ignorant poor the common rules of hygiene and sanitation, so that they would understand and practice them; and instruction in social aspects of the work, so that the nurse, in turn, might better understand her patients and help them to help themselves.

Not only did the city associations seek affiliation with the Institute, but soon country villages and hamlets were also begging for "Queen's Nurses." Rural nursing had always been a serious problem, midwifery and maternity, care being the most pressing need. As early as 1643 we hear of the wife of a country clergyman, the Rev. Abraham Colfe, who included among her other charitable duties, the care of women at the time of child-birth. "She was," wrote her husband, "for about forty years, a willing nurse, midwife, surgeon, and in part, physician to all—both sick and poor—without expecting reward." Again in 1782, the Rev. Mr. Dolling, having seen the danger and unnecessary suffering to which the women of a certain small parish under his jurisdiction were exposed because there were no midwives nor even nurses to be had, raised a subscription in order to send a woman to a lying-in hospital in London where she might be trained in the necessary care of maternity patients. After three months passed at this hospital the woman returned to

the little village where she attended the wives of the
laborers for a small charge; and it is said of her that
during all her service she never had an accident.   This
experiment was so successful that it was adopted by
numerous other villages and hamlets and the "village
nurse and midwife" soon became a well-known institution in certain parts of the country.   In some villages
a "maternity-bag" was also provided, the bag containing baby garments made by the children in the schools
for the poor.   (Report on Bettering Conditions of the
Poor,—K. Gray. p. 236.)   These first village nurses,
however, were local; and vast stretches of countryside
and hundreds of scattered, lonely villages, remained
without any nursing care whatever, except that offered
by inexperienced, though kindly-meaning neighbors.

In 1883, Miss Broadwood, a lay woman of independent character and broad sympathies, had become greatly
concerned over the number of broken-down women
whom she met in the villages near her own home, and
had set herself to work out a remedy.   Let us quote
her own words regarding the beginning of her work:
"One day I went to call on a neighbor with whom I
was very well acquainted.   I found her lying in a beautifully clean bed with her new-born baby, and I said:
'Who have you got looking after you?'   She replied,
'My husband.'   Her husband was a wood-cutter and
he attended her when he came home from work.   I
asked her who attended to her when her husband was
at work.   She replied that Caleb did.   'I learned him
to make gruel before I was laid up,' she said.   Caleb
was a boy of twelve years of age.—Another case was
that of a woman who I thought was going to die in my
arms.   She had called in a neighbor at the cost of 10
shillings and at the end of a week she had got up and
come down to do her washing.   You may imagine the
condition she was in.   Before I could get her into a
carriage and drive her to the Cottage Hospital she had

collapsed in my arms.   Her health was ruined for life."
(Report of the Jubilee Congress of District Nursing.
p. 167.)   These cases and many others like them so
impressed Miss Broadwood with the tragedy of the sit-
nation that she determined to do all in her power to
bring nursing care to the helpless woman in the villages
and isolated rural districts of the country.   She realized that trained nurses were best, but argued that if
trained nurses could not be had, partly trained women
would be better than nothing.   She at once set herself to work to procure this training for women of the
village class who, when trained, could return and minister to their sisters in the humble cottages of the
country districts, not as visiting nurses, but as resident
ones, willing and able not only to nurse the patients,
but to help with the housework and take the mother's
place while she was ill.   Of course she met with much
opposition.   Miss Broadwood, however, could not be
dissuaded.   She felt that these cottage nurses would
be of inestimable value.   She knew that, in the poor
country districts which she had in mind, sufficient
money could not be raised to support a fully trained
district nurse, but that a humble cottage nurse of the
village class, with a special training in maternity care,
and perhaps in some cases in midwifery, would be of
invaluable assistance and could be supported on a provident basis; and finally, she believed that half a loaf
was better than none.   She tried to obtain training for
her women in the various hospitals of London, but was
unsuccessful.   She tried again at the workhouse infirmaries, but there also she met with rebuff.   But Miss
Broadwood was not discouraged.   She bided her time.
At last it arrived.   Let us again quote her own words:
"It was put into the heart of Sister Catherine Twining
to write to me, after she had seen a letter of mine in the
Times newspaper, saying that she would attempt the ex-

periment that I had begged other trainers of nurses to attempt. Sister Catherine, who was then working with one other nurse in the slums of Plaistow, a place that had grown up over the unhealthy swamps of Essex, was contending against the evils of a dreadful amount of fever and sickness together with attending the mothers. She undertook to accept two of my pupils."

With the help of a doctor, Miss Broadwood drew up an outline of the course of instruction she wished her cottage nurses to have. It consisted of, "such elementary instruction as is given at ambulance classes in dressing wounds, bandaging, applying fomentations, poultices, leeches, etc., also in the use of the clinical thermometer, enema apparatus and catheter, urine testing, noting pulse, moving the bed-ridden and feeble, preventing and dressing bed-sores, making the beds of patients, preparing invalid cookery, hygiene, and observation and noting down of symptoms." The instruction was not to include assistance at serious operations, such as could not be properly treated in a laborer's cottage but was to include sepecial training for maternity cases. The training lasted from 4 to 18 months according to the requirements of the women.

This work of training cottage nurses begun by Miss Twining at Plaistow, has continued to the present day, and the "Maternity Charity and District Nurses' Home" started by her at that place is still the principal training school for the modern "village nurse."

These modern village nurses were, like the cottage nurse, a compromise. The desire on the part of those interested in rural districts, that country people should have Queen's Nurses, led to the formation of County Nursing Associations which should, whenever possible, employ nurses with, not only a full hospital training, but with district and midwifery training as well—in other words specially trained Queen's Nurses,—and become affiliated with the Institute.   The main objects of these associations were:

(a) To promote local interest in providing trained nurses and midwives for the sick in their own homes throughout the country.

(b) To raise funds locally for the support and training of such nurses within the county.

(c) To establish nursing centers as far as may be throughout the county.

(d) To seek out and train suitable women in accordance with the regulations of the Queen's Institute.

Unfortunately many districts could not raise the funds to support a Queen's Nurse.   For such districts, therefore, the county associations were to undertake to train women, free of cost, as midwives, giving them additional instruction in elementary sick nursing and to supply these so-called "village nurses" to the rural districts in need.   In order to affiliate with the Institute, however, the county associations employing village nurses were required to appoint a Queen's Nurse as Superintendent, who would be responsible for the adequate and constant supervision of the practical work of these nurses, and would, herself, be under the direction and inspection of the rural superintendent of the Institute, thus forming with other Rural Queen's Nurses the Rural Branch of the Organization.[1]

This employment of partially trained women as nurses in rural communities has met with much opposition and much criticism; and yet, in its practical application, the scheme seems to have been a success. The women are carefully chosen, the training given is standardized and consists of a certain minimum of re-

[1] There is now no Rural Branch of the Queen's Institute.   It has been merged into the whole.

quirements[1] and when training in midwifery is given,
as well as elementary training in simple general nursing, their usefulness in the scattered, isolated rural districts of the country cannot be gainsaid. Moreover,
when they are affiliated with the County Nursing
Association, which in turn is affiliated with the Queen's
Institute, and are under the constant and careful supervision of a superintendent, who is herself a Queen's
Nurse, they cannot go very far astray. Miss Amy
Hughes, former Superintendent-General, and one of the
foremost graduate nurses of the country, says: "There
are certain centers where the village nurse is the right
woman in the right place," and perhaps we must leave
it at that.[2]

The Queen's Institute has at the present time (1922)
2432 of these women employed by County Associations
and working for them under inspection. All of these
women are certified midwives, and all are under the
supervision of a Queen's Nurse.

The total number of nurses connected with the Institute (Jan. 1, 1922), including Queen's Nurses, those
in training, Village Nurses and Midwives, was 5478.

The establishment of the Queen Victoria's Institute
for Nurses undoubtedly gave a great impetus to district nursing throughout the Kingdom, and at the
present day, there are a few localities where their services are not available.

We find them in the lovely villages of southern Eng-

[1] In the last annual report of the Jubilee Institute it says
that the minimum training for a village nurse should be twelve
months and that it is desirable for the pupil to stay for an
additional two months for instruction in health work.

[2] The Queen's Institute has laid down a rule that no district
with a population of 3000 or over may employ a village nurse,
the reason for this being that the amount of illness amongst a
population of that size is more than can be efficiently cared for
by a nurse who is partially trained only.

12

land, on the wild coast of west Ireland, in the high-
lands of Scotland, as well as in the slums of London,
or the crowded districts of great industrial cities.   All
over Great Britain, in town and country villages one
comes upon the sign, "District Nurse" or "Nurses'
Home."

In the large cities the nurse lives in a Home, under
a superintendent, as advised by Florence Nightingale,
and by her successor, Florence Lees; but in the quiet
village, nestled away in the heart of rural England,
she may have her own little cottage, and her own fire-
side.   There, with her little maid to clean the house
and cook her meals, she finds the rest and homelike
comfort her work makes desirable.   There when her
work is done, we may find her seated before the open
grate fire enjoying her cup of tea and toasted muffins;
and there she entertains her friends and leads her
normal life.   Misery and suffering are still met with in
her daily round of duty, but whether in the city Home
or in the country cottage, the English district nurse
now finds a pleasant and congenial homelife, and Mr.
Rathbone's prophecy is more than realized.

Of the enormous possibilities opening up before the
Queen's Nurse of the future, we scarcely dare to speak.
The widespread interest in matters pertaining to public health is giving to her work more and more an educative and preventive character.   Maternity and child-
welfare work, school nursing, and the care of the tuberculous, mental hygiene and the combat against social
disease, are all being increasingly undertaken in connection with general nursing among the sick poor.

Upon the district nurse, therefore, entering as she
does into the homes of the people, depends in a very
large part, the education of the people in matters of
health and sanitation.

She, better than most, can see the first symptoms of
disease, and, by careful instruction and care, forestall

its development; she, whose kindly ministrations give her such wonderful intimacies with the poor and ignorant, can best teach them, not only to nurse their sick, but how to prevent them from getting sick; and by showing them how to live, can implant in their hearts a desire for better things.

Upon the ability of the Queen's Nurse to seize these opportunities; to ally herself with the new thought, and the new schemes for the betterment of the nation's health; and to prove herself not only a good bedside nurse, but a health educator as well, depends her future and the future of English District Nursing.[1]

[1] The following books written by Mary Loane, a graduate nurse, A Queen's Nurse, and at one time Superintendent-General of Queen's Nurses, are well worth reading.
The Queen's Poor—Mary Loane
An Englishman's Castle—Mary Loane

CHAPTER XIII

EARLY VISITING NURSING IN AMERICA

During all these years in which nursing in the Old World had been making such rapid and marvellous progress both in hospitals and in the care of the sick poor in their homes, nothing towards its development had taken place in the new.

Life during the early Colonial period in America was not conducive to the advancement of any of the arts; and nursing, though not yet considered one of them, suffered with the rest.

At the time when the pilgrim fathers left the Old World to seek freedom in the New (1620), nursing as an occupation was almost entirely in the hands of the Roman Catholic sisters, and the care of the sick poor in their homes was only just beginning to be organized in France under the direction of Francis de Sales and Vincent de Paul. It is not likely that the Puritans would have come in contact with any of this work, and had they done so they would have looked upon it as savoring of Romanism. They brought with them, therefore, only the most primitive ideas concerning the care of the sick, and during the early pioneer days in the new land their lives were so filled with the daily struggle for existence as to leave no time for other less pressing needs. Nursing the sick, like cooking or sewing, was supposed to be the work of every woman. If a woman had a special aptitude for it she was called "a born nurse."

When sickness entered the home of the colonist, therefore, the care of the patient devolved entirely upon the wife or the mother of the household, and upon her skill and experience depended the kind of nursing given, whether good or bad. The only outside assistance available was that of the friendly neighbor, who might come in for a few hours each day, or might offer his or her services to watch with the sick at night; and truly, the care given consisted in little more than watching.

The medical knowledge, too, among the early settlers was very crude. It is said that anyone and everyone was permitted to practise medicine, and home remedies largely took the place of professional treatment. The use of herbs and queer compounds made of such strange ingredients as burned toads, boiled snails, and even vipers, was common, and belief in witchcraft prevailed.

Although the knowledge of nursing and of medicine was so limited, the need of both was very great. During the first winter after the landing of the pilgrims at Plymouth Rock nearly all of them fell ill, and before spring came 44 out of 102 had died. Moreover, what with the utter lack of drainage and sanitary measures, the severe winters in the north, and the swamps and heat in the south, sickness of all kinds seems to have been continuous, and we constantly hear of malaria, putrid sore throats and malignant fevers; while terrible epidemics of smallpox and yellow fever followed each other year after year. Boston especially seems to have suffered most severely from these epidemics of smallpox. "Never was it such a time in Boston," writes the Rev. Cotton Mather in 1678; "above 340 have died of the smallpox since it first assaulted the place." And again in 1721 he says, "The town is become almost a hell upon earth." This epidemic of 1721 began in April of that year and ran unchecked for nine months, during which time 6000 people out of a population of 10,500 contracted the disease, 899 of whom died.

Again, in 1784 in a small community of 2000 souls

700 died of the smallpox during a period of three months. At this time we read that the Rev. Cotton Mather Smith and his wife, Temperance Worthington, "spent their entire time in close attendance upon the sick." In fact, a minister's wife was at all times expected to assist not only in the care of the sick, but at births and funerals as well, and it is related of this same lady that "for thirty years it was into her hands that most of the new-born babies of her husband's parish were committed for their first robing."

Yellow fever, too, though generally looked upon as a disease of the South, was not entirely confined to that part of the country, but made its appearance, from time to time, in the North as well, brought in usually by ships and immigrants from the West Indies or the Southern colonies.

One of the most frightful of these yellow fever epidemies in the North broke out in Philadelphia in the summer of 1793. In the four months during which it raged, 4000 people out of a total population of 30,000, died of it, although half of the people had fled the city within a month ofter its outbreak. "The fever swept as a whirlwind through Water Street," says one historian, "leaving none but dead behind it, and spread with horrible speed into every quarter of the town." Poor people burned tar in the street, sprinkled vinegar and carried sprigs of wormwood, hoping thereby to prevent infection and stay the hand of death. The mayor, with the help of a few public spirited and courageous citizens, most of them Quakers, endeavored to organize measures of relief, but there was little they could do. It was impossible to procure suitable nurses—there were none—and the physicians were taxed far beyond their strength. It is said that ten physicians and ten clergymen—two of them Roman Catholic priests—gave up their lives in the fulfilment of their duties, and that to the brave and tranquil charity of the Quakers many stricken sufferers owed their lives.

With the advance in sanitary and quarantine precautions, however, these epidemics were gradually lessened and the health of the people better protected.

During the early days of the Colonies there was not only no proper care of the public health, but there was no organized relief of the poor. At that time the latter, fortunately, was not necessary, for there were no poor, or rather, all were equally poor; all suffered the same hardships and bore the same deprivations. When special loss or hardship visited one of their number there was a general disposition among the others to share with their less fortunate brother any comfort or necessity he might lack. As the Colonies grew, however, and towns and cities began to develop, a disparity in fortunes also developed, and along with the growing wealth of some we find increasing poverty of others. The churches began to distribute charity, and benevolent societies were formed to visit the poor and give relief in food and clothing, shelter and, sometimes, money. For the sick poor, also, some provision began to be made, and along with almshouses and asylums, infirmaries and hospitals began to appear.

The first hospital in America was a little one opened in New York in 1658 by the West India Company for the use of its sick seamen. It was but a little shelter house, nevertheless it provided beds and medical attendance, and was a beginning in the right direction. A little later it was combined with the New York workhouse, and by 1816, having taken the name of Bellevue, furnished quarters not only for the sick and insane, but for able-bodied paupers as well. In fact, it was workhouse, almshouse, insane asylum and orphan asylum, as well as hospital, and the history of its early years is filled with horror.

"The paupers numbered from 1600 to 2000, and
among them were often as many as 200 sick. Epidemics arising from unsanitary conditions and over-
crowding were frequent and severe. Typhus fever,
the sinister companion of filth and misery, now all but
unknown in America, was then common. The physicians were cruelly overworked, for only three were assigned to supervise the whole household, both sick and
well. The nurses (so-called) were detailed from the
prison, and were appointed in the proportion of one
for twenty patients. . . . During many years nothing
but horrors existed at Bellevue." (History of Nursing.
Nutting, vol. II, p. 328) These conditions were
finally brought to the attention of those in authority,
an investigation was instituted, the prisoners and the
insane were removed to separate quarters, other improv-
ments inaugurated, and "Bellevue began its career as
a hospital proper." [1]

The Philadelphia Hospital, afterwards known as
Blockley, was established in 1731. Like so many of
the other early hospitals, it, also, began as the almshouse infirmary. It, too, was overcrowded and unsanitary, and its filth was unspeakable. Such nursing as they had was given by an abandoned, profligate
set of nurses and attendants. It was the old story of
almshouse hospitals all over the world at that time,
and it is little wonder that a horror of hospital care
became deeply rooted in the minds of the poor, and in
many instances has remained to the present day. As a
matter of fact, not only did the poor dislike and fear
the hospitals of those days, but the better class of people
openly acknowledged that this fear was not ungrounded.

In 1786 the Philadelphia Dispensary—the oldest
dispensary in the United States—was opened in "Straw-
berry Alley" for the "medical, surgical and obstetrical
service of the poor in their homes," and an appeal was

[1] Recollection of a Happy Life by E. C. Hobson. p. 77

made to the public for its support. Among the peculiar advantages of this institution were mentioned the following :

First :—The sick may be attended and relieved in their own houses without the pain, discomfort and inconvenience of being separated from their families.

Second :—The sick may be relieved at a much less expense to the public than in a hospital.

The reluctance of the poor and ignorant to enter a hospital, even when seriously ill, gave the new dispensary many patients, and, as physicians were required to visit regularly "such patients as are unable to go abroad on dispensary days," many of the cases were cared for in their own homes.

This brief survey of hospital and nursing conditions in America during the seventeenth, eighteenth and early nineteenth centuries is sufficient to show us that there could have been no nursing among the sick poor in their homes worthy of the name. Undoubtedly there were kindly women who visited the sick poor and ministered to their wants, as there had been in every age, and it may be that many of the church and benevolent societies of those early days counted among their duties that Christian injunction to visit the sick and the poor. If so, however, we have no record of it beyond the single exception of the work done by the Ladies' Benevolent Society of Charleston, South Carolina : and to that small group of earnest workers must we look for an example of possibly similar efforts in other cities.

LADIES' BENEVOLENT SOCIETY OF CHARLESTON, S. C.
1813

Charleston, S. C., is one of the oldest cities in the United States. It was founded in 1670, the first settlement being called Charles Town, in honor of Charles

II, then King of England.   Charles Town soon became
the port of entry for the whole Province of Carolina—
a region then comprising a vast territory, including
what is now North and South Carolina and part of
Georgia—and the little settlement grew rapidly, its
colonists, unlike the pioneers in the North, representing many countries and many classes.   They came,
not only from England, Scotland and Ireland, but
from France and the Netherlands as well, and represented the Church of England, the Roman Catholic
Church, Quakers and Jews.   It was, therefore, a more
cosmopolitan group of colonists than the English or
Dutch settlements in the north, and, as a community,
had a broader religious outlook.

The city grew rapidly, not only in population, but
in wealth.   A large export trade in the cotton, rice and
tobacco raised in the vicinity was established, and its
rice mills and silk mills were the envy of less fortunate cities.   By 1810 the population had risen to
over 24,000, more than half of whom, however, were
negroes, and the position of Charleston ranked high
among the cities of the New World.

Just as her future was most promising and the golden
age of her prosperity seemed to have arrived, came the
Non-Intercourse Act and the Embargo, which at once
brought stagnation to commerce and ruined many of the
Charleston merchants, bringing poverty and suffering
to thousands in city and state.   This was followed by
the war of 1812, in which 5000 South Carolinians
flocked to the colors, leaving behind them wives and
children with no means of support.   And finally, in
1813, came a terrible epidemic of yellow fever, bringing in its wake death, destitution and suffering.   Yellow fever was a frequent visitor to this southern city,
and was always looked upon with dread and horror.
In 1739, during one of its visitations, a merchant of
Charleston in writing to his brother in the North speaks

of "A terrible sickness that has raged and does now . . . the doctors call it a yellow bilious fever, but to me," says he, "it is more like the plague than anything else."

The suffering and distress brought to the poor of their city by these three successive blows did not fail to arouse the interest and sympathy of the kindly and charitably disposed people of Charleston. A "Ladies Benevolent Society" was at once organized, and various efforts undertaken for the "relief of such persons as suffer under the anguish of disease and penury." One of its most important duties was to visit and aid the sick poor. The city was districted, the city ward being taken as the boundary for each district, and a president and a visiting committee of sixteen ladies appointed. The practical work of the society was assigned to this Visiting Committee, which distributed its charity and visited the sick and needy. The ladies were expected to take their turn in visiting for three months, going "when and wherever sent for, with propriety, in the wards of the city allotted to them."

The membership in the Society was not confined to any church or creed, nor were its charities limited as to race or color. The rules and regulations adopted showed a rare wisdom, and were based on many of the principles used today in relief work among the poor. No money was paid out to patients, cases were carefully investigated, and then relieved according to their needs; and an effort was made to furnish work for the unemployed, thereby establishing our modern principle of helping the poor to help themselves.[1]

The material relief distributed was strictly regulated

[1] In January of 1814 we read in the Charleston Courier: "Donations of cotton will be thankfully received by the Ladies' Benevolent Society for the purpose of employing indigent women in spinning, who cannot at this time obtain a sufficiency of work to earn a subsistence."

by printed rule. The following rule bearing on the subject is interesting:

"Patients shall receive weekly one pound of brown sugar (unless the complaint be such as to render white sugar proper, in which case the white shall be substituted): one pound of coffee, or a quarter of a pound of tea: a pint of lamp oil, or one pound of tallow candles: three quarts of grist, or two quarts middling rice: one pound, or 6¼ cents' worth of meat (fresh or salt), or a chicken every day when meat is ordered by the physician. If milk be ordered or preferred to meat, a pint to be allowed: arrowroot or barley, according to the state of the patient: one quarter of a cord of wood, carting and sawing included, to last two weeks in winter: half the quantity in summer: one pound, or 6¼ cents' worth of soap: no money to be given. Flannel and blankets when necessary."

We see from this that substantial aid was distributed. Much sickness, as always, was encountered among the poor and undernourished, and the Ladies did their best to nurse and care for the patients. Especially when yellow fever occurred did they find their hands full. This scourge to mankind appeared frequently, and in the Report of 1839 to the Board of Managers we read the following quaint but pious reference to their work:

"September, 1838, will long be remembered as a mournful era in our history, for then emphatically might we say 'Death is come up into our midst, to cut off the children from without and the young men from our streets'; then was the ear pained by the recital of sickness and suffering and the heart made to bleed for the desolate widow and the orphan children, whose situation was doubly piteous, for they were strangers in the land. But it is just in seasons like this that the beauty and excellence of a society expressly formed for relieving the 'sick poor' is acknowledged and appreciated, and ours, so long the humble instrument of good, in the hands of Him who careth for the poor and needy, became the prominent medium for dispensing comforts and necessaries to many a destitute family."

This Society continued its benevolent activities until the Civil War, during which its members were dispersed and its treasury emptied. No meeting of the Society appears to have been attempted between October 1862 and October 1866. At that time, however, the remaining members of the Society again came together, and it is pathetic to see how bravely they attempted to resume the labors of former days, though their income was but a pittance, being less than $500 all told. This sum was judiciously disbursed by the Visiting Committee for the purchase of wood or flannel or other necessities for the most destitute of the sick poor in their respective wards. In 1868, however, the work was again abandoned, and was not resumed until 1881, when the Society was reorganized on new lines. The care of the sick still remained the especial work of the Association, a supply closet for the supply of bed linen and comforts for the sick was organized, and a "Mother's Basket" established, containing clothing and necessaries for infants. It was not until 1903 that a trained visiting nurse was employed, thus linking this old and well-established charity with the modern movement for public health nursing.

The work of the Ladies' Benevolent Society of Charleston stands alone in the annals of early American charity. To be sure, the part of the work which relates to the care of the sick poor in their homes was little further advanced than that of a similar nature carried on by the ladies of the seventeenth century in France or in England. The motto of the Society was, "I was sick and ye visited Me," and it was the spirit of that motto which animated and controlled all their efforts. To actually *nurse* these poor people was not

so much their intention as to relieve their distress, to
see to it that they had food and clothing, and, when
necessary, medical attention and such sick-room comforts as help to relieve pain and suffering. These
Charleston ladies were not nurses, they were lay visitors, but they did what they could to "aid the sick poor."
Later, when nurses could be procured they did employ
them, from time to time, to care for especially critical
cases; and still later, when trained visiting nursing was
beginning to be established in other cities, they followed
the lead.

The thing that was unusual in the work of this early
society was the modern methods employed. We must
remember that at this time there was no organized
visiting of the sick poor in their homes in any part of
the world, except such as was carried on by the Sisters of Charity, or other religious organizations. We
must remember, also, that material relief was still distributed in most places as it had been for ages past,
that is, without investigation: and that even visitors
of the poor were rarely employed; and, finally, we must
remember that most private charity was limited to some
particular group or church, and that indiscriminate care
of black or white, Jew or Gentile, Protestant or Catholic, was almost unknown in America.

And yet in this old Benevolent Society of the South
we see some of the most modern ideas governing its
work. In the first place, it was entirely undenominational. Its support came from Protestant and Catholic
and Jew, and its charity was supplied to all alike, who
needed help. Another modern principle followed was
that no money should be dispensed. To be sure, there
was a most generous distribution of the things that
money buys, but even this was regulated by well-con-
sidered rules, and from the wording of many of them
we may infer that the distribution was made only
after a certain amount of investigation, or in response

to the doctor's orders, as for instance: "If milk be ordered." The work was systematic and not dependent upon the caprice or sudden impulse of the lady members. The city was districted, each district was in charge of a visiting committee, each member of the committee was obliged to take her turn as visitor to the sick, and during her time of service each visiting lady was expected to respond to every call, and be ready at all times to visit and relieve the sick poor in her particular district. It was a noteworthy charity, and that the Society has continued to the present day and has had the wisdom to adjust itself to the spirit of the times and is now carrying on a good piece of modern public health nursing, is still more noteworthy.

But although this work was the first recorded organized visiting of the sick poor in America, the honor of having employed the first *nurses* to systematically care for the poor in their homes, belongs not to the Charleston Society, but to the Nurse Society of Philadelphia.

THE NURSE SOCIETY OF PHILADELPHIA 1839

In 1828, Dr. Joseph Warrington of Philadelphia, a young physician only 23 years old, conceived the idea of organizing a society to furnish properly qualified medical attendance to poor women in childbirth, and at the same time to establish a school for nurses who could be assigned to certain districts of the city and nurse the patients under the direction of the medical attendant. Four years later (1832) he succeeded in organizing the society, under the name of the "Lying-in-Charity for Attending Indigent Women in Their Homes." The organization consisted of a board of managers; and an *active* board of ladies, who visited the homes of the patients and supplied necessary articles, such as food, clothing and fuel.

In the charter of this organization was granted the right to "provide, sustain and cause to be instructed, as far as possible, pious and prudent women as nurses, it being understood that the association does not confine itself to the supply of monthly nurses only, but for every variety. of sickness of patients." [1]

In order to carry out this part of the program, a second and subsidiary organization, known as the *Nurse Society,* was formed in 1839, and two years later incorporated with the Lying-in-Charity. The work of this Society was unique of its kind in America.

The city was districted, a lady visitor assigned to each district, and a certain number of "women of good habits, quiet, and patient disposition, and with a sense of responsibility" were selected, who were to act as nurses, holding themselves ready to respond to the call of the physician and to care for the patients under his direction and that of the lady visitors.

The work of this Society was not, strictly speaking, visiting nursing, as the nurses did not visit, but remained with their patients, devoting themselves entirely to one case at a time until discharged by the physician in charge, and then going to another. It was, however, nursing care for the sick poor in their homes, and as such resembles district nursing.

The Society not only supplied these women for the care of poor patients, but endeavored at the same time to give them some training to fit them for their work. In the Report of the Society for 1852, thirteen years after its formation, we read that the women selected for nurses were obliged to subject themselves to the scrutiny of a committee of "matronly ladies" from the Executive Board; to undergo a "test of their culinary skill" by the Matron and House

---

[1] It does not appear that this permission to nurse other than maternity cases was ever used.

Committee; and to devote some time to the "disciplinary course of instruction in the duties of a nurse"; and finally, that only at the discretion of the medical chief were they then permitted to attend patients under the care of the medical attendants and lady visitors.

We also read that after this preliminary instruction they were obliged to hold themselves in constant readiness to do nursing service to the amount of *"eighty-four days and nights,"* in the. families of persons, most of whom could scarcely supply them with food and lodging. After this service of eighty-four days had been completed to the satisfaction of the visitors, the physician and the Executive Board, the nurses were "allowed the privilege" of attending on their own account a class of citizens whose means would justify them in "paying no more than three dollars a week," until the sum of such service also amounted to eighty-four more days and nights. After which the poor nurses received a "certificate of honorable discharge from their obligations assumed in entering into connection with the institution," and were free to undertake private nursing on their own account.

From the date of incorporation until 1888 the cost of maintaining the charity was defrayed by those directly interested in the management, each of the managers collecting contributions from his or her personal friends. As the expenses increased, however, it was no longer possible to rely entirely on individual effort for its support, and the nurses were sent to care for pay cases, as well as the poor, the proceeds for their services being devoted to the needs of the organization.

The work of the Nurse Society of Philadelphia is interesting in as much as it united the work of the physicians, the dispensary, and the nurse in the home of the sick poor, and represents one of the first efforts to give some practical training to women in the bedside care of the sick.

13

CHAPTER XIV

THE MISSIONARY NURSES

With the exception of these two early charities—
the Ladies' Benevolent Society of Charleston, and the
Nurse Society of Philadelphia—we have no recorded
account of any systematic home care of the sick poor
in America up to the year 1877.

District nursing as carried on in England seems
practically not to have been known in this country,
certainly it was not followed. Charity extended along
other lines; the giving of material relief without
previous investigation of cases seems to have been
usual, and the care of the sick poor was confined to
such as could be obtained in the hospitals and infirmaries, or to such palliative or desultory care as
might be given by well-meaning, though untrained,
lay visitors. Although, as we have seen, nursing sisters, deaconesses and district nurses had been caring
for the sick poor in their homes for several decades
in Germany, France and England, the work was not
imitated in America. To be sure, in 1839 an effort
had been made to transplant to this country a shoot
of the Kaiserswerth undertaking, and Theodor Fliedner
had himself accompanied two of his deaconesses to
Pittsburgh and endeavored to start the work in that
city. The time was not ripe, however, and for some
reason the undertaking seems not to have prospered.

A few other tentative efforts were also made to
establish nursing sisterhoods and to introduce the Sisters of Charity into the homes of the sick poor;
but none of these efforts was entirely successful,

they failed to arouse the interest and co-operation of the public, and in most cases died of inanition.

Nursing as a profession requiring training was also not recognized in this country as early as in England, and it was not until our Civil War had demonstrated to America, as the Crimean War had to England, the need of a band of trained women to care for the sick, that America developed her first modern training schools for nurses in connection with some of the well-established hospitals of the country; Bellevue, New York. taking the lead in 1872.

NEW YORK CITY MISSION, 1877.

But it is not to her hospitals that we must look for the initiative in starting the first visiting nurse work in America. Rather, we must turn to those followers of the early Apostles who were commanded to go forth and preach the Gospel to all men. In 1877 the Woman's Board of the New York City Mission felt the need of a nurse to go from home to home among the poor, and to minister to their bodily ills, as the missionary did to their spiritual. Whether the idea arose spontaneously, from a growing knowledge of the suffering of the sick among those for whom the Society cared; or whether the idea was suggested by one of the Board members who had lately visited England, and observed the good work being carried on there by nurses and Biblewomen, is not definitely known. However, whatever the animating impulse, the idea was warmly received, and an Executive Committee appointed to put the plan into operation.

A nurse, Miss Frances Root, a graduate of the first class of nurses trained in Bellevue Hospital, was engaged, her salary being paid by Mrs. William H. Osborn of New York. That this first visiting nurse among the poor should thus have been one of the nurses graduated from the first class of the first training school for nurses established in this country is an interesting coincidence, and tends to show that visiting nursing is no new branch of the work, but rather an inherent quality in the very character of nursing itself, and that it was no more possible for the modern trained nurse to confine her service to the wards of the hospital, than it was for her prototype, the nursing Sister, to remain within the convent walls. The new undertaking seems to have prospered from the start and to have received the hearty co-operation of physicians, as well as great material assistance from various groups of lay workers.

In the Annual Report of the Society, published a few months after the nursing work was begun, we read the following: "A new power for good has been introduced this year, the Missionary Nurse. Prepared in the training school, she is thoroughly competent to do all that is necessary in cases of extreme illness, and has been an unspeakable comfort to many who had no one to minister to them."

Like the Biblewomen nurses in England, her work was of a truly religious character, and she was expected not only to nurse the sick, but to use every opportunity possible to introduce godly counsel and words of Christian comfort. Says one of the early reports:—

"The work of the Missionary Nurse is distinct from that of the ordinary missonary, her first thought being for the relief of the body. Yet she does not forget the soul's interest, and when it seems best, after her patient is made comfortable, gives some sweet promise of the Father, or comforting word of the Master to meditate on, and commends to the Great Physician." And again, "If training is needful for her, consecration, not alone to her work, but to the Master, is equally so."

So satisfactory both to the Society and to the public was this experiment that by the end of the second year five nurses were employed, their salaries being guaranteed by five ladies. The physicians, especially, were warm in appreciation of the nurses' work. "I am hopeful of my patient when I see one of your nurses," said one; and, "All I did for Mrs. B. would not have saved her without the nurse's daily care," said another.

The gratitude of the patients, too, was a source of great satisfaction to the nurse, and they loved especially to seek out those who had no one but little children, perhaps, to attend them; or the aged and lonely, who had found "only the one Almighty ear open to their cry," and to whom the visit of the nurse was indeed as the visit of a ministering angel.

The nursing care given by these first American visiting nurses was undoubtedly better than that given by the first district or Biblewomen nurses in England, for they were women trained in the Bellevue Training School, and as expert in their calling as any nurses of that day. The social side of their work, however, was not so well considered, the same errors being found in it as those pointed out by Miss Lees in her survey of the English district nursing, namely, too much material relief, too little instruction in hygiene and sanitation, and little or no supervision. On the other hand, the type of women were of a much higher class, and many of the difficulties encountered in the older country were not found in the new.

Although there was no real instruction given in hygiene and health, an effort was made to teach cleanliness and better living habits. This instruction, however, was based more on the text "Cleanliness is next to Godliness" than on hygienic principles. The nurses also tried to teach the people to nurse their own sick and gave them simple lessons in the preparation of suitable nourishment, such as gruels, beef tea and the like.

Much suffering was relieved by the many sick-room comforts which the nurse was enabled to provide, such as rubber rings, air cushions, blankets, sheets, proper dressings etc., and a constant call was made not only for these articles, but for old linen, jellies and medicines. The cases the nurses cared for were similar to those cared for by the Biblewomen nurses in England—cancer, broken limbs, burns, confinements, rheumatism, the aged and young children. Acute cases, such as typhoid, were transferred to the hospitals.

The work of these missionary nurses was, as their name perhaps indicates, more religious than scientific. Their work was distinctly curative, not preventive, and they could in no way be called Public Health Nurses. Their desire was to relieve suffering and to teach the Word of God. Their first aim, as outlined in their Constitution, was, "To carry the Gospel of Christ to all homes in the lower part of the city"; the subsidary one, "To minister to the sick poor, providing things necessary for their recovery in their homes, or removing them to hospitals, if wise."

There was no accent put on *instruction,* and to *relieve,* not to *prevent* seems to have been the animating motive. The work was no further advanced—not as far, in fact—as that started by Mr. Rathbone some twenty years before; and the fundamental principles for good district nursing laid down in Miss Lees' report, published three or four years before the New York Missionary Society began its work, were evidently unknown. Nevertheless, although this effort was far behind similar work being carried on at the same time in England, it was a beginning, and we speak with pardonable pride of these missionary nurses as the first visiting nurses in America.

The work of this Society in providing nurses for the

A Queen's Nurse.

Outside a cottager's home in rural England.
(Courtesy of the Queen Victoria's Jubilee Institute for Nurses.)

sick poor is still (1922) being carried on. They now employ ten, all of whom are graduates of hospital training schools, and though the work still retains its essentially religious character, it has lined itself up with the modern idea of public health, and its efforts are constructive as well as curative. The following extract from a recent report shows the more modern aspect of its work:—

"She (the nurse) must deal not only with the family as a whole, but with the physical, economic, and social background which forms the setting for the family life. After she has given consideration to defective health, set the machinery in motion necessary to secure glasses for the child with defective vision, dental treatment for the one with defective teeth, surgical care for tonsils, sanatorium treatment for the tuberculous, and institutional care for others—upon liquidating the health debts accumulated in the past—she turns her attention to the physical and spiritual environment as a factor in the future —and that is where our Society differs from some others —it ministers to the spiritual, as well as to the physical."

To minister to the soul through ministry to the body is still the method of their work. The duty of the missionary nurse being to "endeavor by every means in her power to elevate the families, morally and physically, but chiefly to lead souls to Christ."

SOCIETY FOR ETHICAL CULTURE, N. Y., 1878.

A few months after the founding of district nursing by the New York Missionary Society, namely in 1878, a similar piece of work was undertaken by the New York Society for Ethical Culture, at the instigation and through the unwearying efforts of Dr. Felix Adler. The great difference between the work of the Missionary Society and that done by the Ethical Culture Society was that, whereas the former sent out its nurses unsupervised and largely without medical direction, the latter employed nurses to work only in connection with well-recognized dispensaries, and to care for patients under the direct supervision of attending physicians.

It has been erroneously stated that this Society "gave birth in New York to the idea of district nursing." This is not the case, the work of the missionary nurses ante-dating it by several months. It was, however, the first to send out visiting nurses from a dispensary, and in many ways the work was more modern than that done by the New York Missionary Society.

The idea of this work was first suggested to Dr. Adler, as it was to Mr. Rathbone, by the observation of the invaluable services rendered by a trained nurse to a member of his own family during a dangerous illness. He, like his prototype, felt that the poor, when sick, should, so far as possible, receive the same benefit— that their homes should not be broken up, as was so often the case, by removing the mother to the hospital; and that the influence exercised by an educated and refined woman visiting in the tenement homes during illness would have an important and beneficial effect on the condition of the poor.

He knew of the work being done by the New York Mission, but he felt that the Mission regarded sickness merely as an opportunity to introduce religious teachings, and not primarily as an opportunity for health work. Moreover, he believed that the nurse's work could be done more effectively under the direction of dispensary physicians. The first nurse, therefore, Miss Effie Benedict, a graduate of Bellevue Training School, was attached to the DeMilt Dispensary, and cared for the Dispensary patients in their homes.

Later, three more nurses were engaged by the Ethical Society to serve, one with the New York Dispensary, one at the North Western, and one at the Good Samaritan. The supervision of the work was in the hands of a committee of women members of the Ethical Society, and a sewing guild was formed to supply whatever was needed for the sick in the way of linen, clothes, food, or money for special cases.

These nurses did all their visiting in the district of the dispensary which they served, receiving their list of patients and their directions for each patient from the attending physician, and then starting on their round of visits. This method of working under the physician was undoubtedly an improvement on the method followed by the missionary nurses. By receiving their patients directly from the doctors in charge, who knew the exact condition of each patient and told the nurse what treatment should be followed in each case, the nurse knew exactly what to do and could show some member of the family how to continue necessary care during her absence. Meanwhile, she could notice the surroundings and plan what could be done for the general betterment of home and family. No distinction was made on sectarian grounds, and all nationalities were cared for with equal devotion. That much material relief was given goes almost without saying, but that a great effort was made not to give indiscriminately is also true. It was felt that the nurse had exceptional opportunity for discovering the truth as to economic and social conditions, and that all attempts at hypocrisy or deception were rendered futile by her unexpected visits, and keen eyes which were ever on the lookout for imposture, while, on the other hand, she was always ready and anxious to supply all needs, whether material or otherwise, of those who seemed worthy and deserving. The nurses taught that cleanliness is one of the most important measures for health, and they instructed mothers in the proper feeding of infants and children.

This work is still being carried on by the Society, though its staff of nurses has not increased—four still being the number employed.

Slowly was the care of the sick poor in America, as in England, being raised from the kindly, though untrained, care given by benevolent ladies, to that of nurses trained to the performance of their calling, in schools established for that purpose; and slowly were the principles, which changed it from a mere palliative charity to constructive health work, being adopted. England was far in advance of America in the application of the laws of sanitary science, and we see the result reflected in the work of the district nurse. The problem of the poor, too, was an older one in that country, and the method of dealing with it had been longer considered and more thoroughly studied. The work of nursing the sick poor in America at this time compared unfavorably with similar work in England, but the time was soon to come when the young shoot was to show a healthy growth, and to send forth stronger branches and a wider shade than the parent stem in the old world.

CHAPTER XV

TWO PIONEER VISITING NURSE ASSOCIATIONS

And now, at last, we come to the founding of the first Association in America organized for the sole purpose of providing skilled care for the sick poor in their homes. At last, as Miss C. E. A. Somerville has so beautifully put it, "America caught the reflection of England's light" and the era of District, or Visiting, nursing, which was later to be broadened out and given the name of Public Health nursing, began in this country. A quarter of a century was still to elapse before this great step in advance was to be taken, but even in those first early days the seed of the blossom was to be found. England had done well—she had shown the way to constructive health work among the poor and physically weak of her people—she had shown how to combine the age-old charity of caring for the sick poor, with the modern sciences of sanitation and prevention; but America was to go still further. The first District Nursing Association in this country prefixed the word "Instructive," and from that time forward the teaching, not only of home care of the sick, and habits of cleanliness, but of the underlying principles of hygiene, sanitation, disinfection and other health subjects, became a fundamental part of the work of the visiting nurse, until, in some lines, the educational side seemed to over-balance the nursing side, and the care of the public health, to supplant the care of the individual patient. A pendulum must always swing first far to one side and then far to the other, before it finally settles to a steady and perfect balance—

whether the pendulum of public health nursing has yet reached the perfect balance is an open question.

The starting of this first District Nursing Association in Boston, in 1886, was directly due to inspiration gained from the work done in Liverpool, and to the untiring and devoted efforts of two noble-minded women, Miss Abbie C. Howes and Miss Phoebe G. Adam.

Abbie Crowell Howes was born in Boston, August 1st, 1842. In her early womanhood because of the long illness of her mother and the invalidism of her older sister, she was called upon to assume many of the cares and duties incident to a large family and household. These experiences initiated her into a life of service for others, in which she found her satisfaction and her happiness.

When the Associated Charities was organized in Boston, she naturally became a friendly visitor and a worker in the South End Conference, which was nearest her home.

From the knowledge thus gained from the needs of the poor in their homes came her interest in district nursing. She was a member of the Women's Education Association, and actively interested in many of Boston's philanthropic works, devoting herself at all times to the uplift of those who were down, and by her precept and example putting new life and hope into the hearts of those who were discouraged. As a social worker she had no interest in any personal rewards, such as office or leadership for herself, but with rare persistance and tireless enthusiasm gave herself, at all times, to the service of the poor and needy.

It was natural, therefore, that when she heard inadvertently, as she did, of the district nursing being done in Liverpool and elsewhere, she should have become intensely interested, and that her mind should at once have reverted to her own poor friends in Boston, and the desire to give them this added help and comfort should have taken form.

She immediately got in touch with her friend, Miss Adam, and together they planned ways and means for making the dream a reality. Miss Adam was a lady of dominating personality and to some seemed stiff and forbidding, though to those who knew her better, was a loved and revered leader. She had intellectual tastes and had taught school for some years. At the time of which we speak she was connected with the Shaw Day Nursery in Boston, and, having already realized the need of nursing care in the homes of many of her little charges, quickly became interested in Miss Howes' suggestion.

Miss Howes and Miss Adam were both members of the Women's Education Association, whose funds and energies were largely used to promote and support new undertakings of an educative character. At Miss Howes' suggestion, it was determined to approach the Association and ask that it stand behind this new piece of work. The first step necessary was to convince the Committee that the work, which at first sight, seemed to partake only of charity,—was, in fact, largely educational. In this they succeeded, although at first assistance was reluctantly given, and the name *"Instructive* District Nursing" was adopted in order to ally the work with other educational efforts. By the end of the first year, however, ample proof having been obtained that teaching, as well as nursing, was a large part of the work, the undertaking was heartily endorsed.

Before beginning the work, careful examination was made into the methods of nursing among the poor and ignorant in England and also in New York; and an active correspondence with Mr. Rathbone of Liverpool ensued. At the suggestion of Miss Howes, a conference was held with Dr. Hastings of the Boston Dispensary, one of the oldest Dispensaries in the Country, and arrangements made for co-operation between the two organizations. No one knows better than a dispensary physician how hard it is to treat a patient when there is but little to do with, and no one to properly carry out his instructions, and Dr. Hastings cordially welcomed the proffered assistance of nursing care for dispensary patients.

A plan of action was outlined, and rules for the guidance of the nurses adopted. The superintendent of the Dispensary offered a spare corner on the main floor of the Dispensary building as a temporary office, and allowed the committee to partition off another corner in the cellar for its supplies of clothing, bedding and various appliances for the sick-room. The office was quickly furnished, one friend giving a desk, another fitting it up, etc., and, these simple, preliminary arrangements being completed, the first nurse, Miss Amelia Hodgkiss, was engaged and assigned to her work in the South Cove District, on February the 8th, 1886.

So entirely successful was the work from the very beginning that on April first of the same year, a second nurse, Miss C. E. M. Somerville was engaged, and assigned to the Central District; and by November, still a third, who was placed in the North End. During this first year the districts to which the nursing care was extended covered the larger portion of the city proper, comprising what was called the old city limits; but, as the nurses were often unable to reach cases in out-lying districts, it was proposed that a "nurse at large" might be added to the staff, whose work might be so arranged that she could divide her time and care for needy patients in out-lying districts, not under the Dispensary, but under private physicians. A suggestion was also made to secure a woman to supplement the care given by the nurse, by washing, cleaning and

A DISTRICT NURSE OF 1886.

In the early days the nurses did not wear uniforms.
(By courtesy of the Instructive District Nurse Association of
Boston, Massachusetts.)

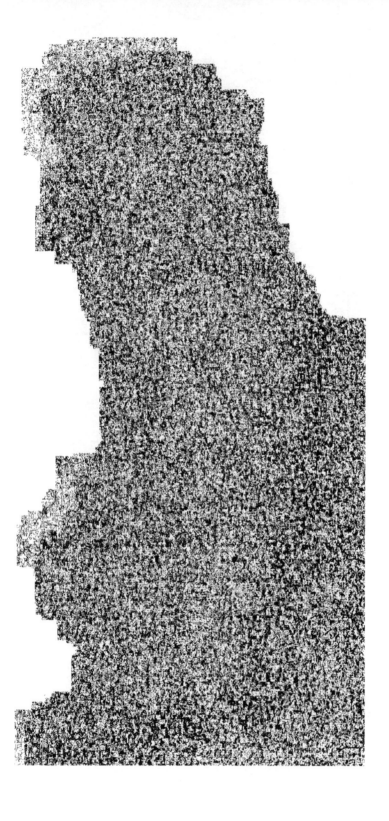

scrubbing where no relative or friend could be found to do this work. The calls from outside physicians, however, proved not sufficient to justify the exclusive attention of one nurse, so the plan for a nurse at large was abandoned.

During the first year there were 707 cases visited, and 7182 calls made; and by the second year, the work had increased to 1836 cases, and 17,066 visits, and covered a field more than twice as broad as in the beginning. In December 1888, the association was incorporated under the name of "The Instructive District Nursing Association," with the two distinct purposes of caring for the sick poor in their homes and giving them instruction in home nursing and health. The precise objects of the Association were stated as follows :

1 : To provide and support thoroughly trained nurses, who, acting under the immediate direction of the out-patient physicians of the Boston Dispensary, shall care for the sick poor in their own homes instead of in hospitals.

2 : By precept and example to give such instruction to the families which they are called upon to visit as shall enable them henceforth to take better care of themselves and their neighbors by observing the rules of wholesome living and by practicing the simple arts of domestic nursing

From the first the idea of instruction, therefore, was prominent; the nurses being expected, not only to relieve suffering, but to teach valuable lessons in the care of the sick, the use of simple remedies, what to do in emergencies, and to insist daily upon the necessity of ventilation, cleanliness and light. The great emphasis put upon instruction was doubtless due, in part, to the fact that it was started under the auspices of the Women's Education Association, although we must remember also that the Boston Association was founded directly upon the priciples of the work carried on in England, and that the teaching of hygiene and sanitation had been especially emphasized by Miss Nightingale, Miss Lees, and other organizers of the English work.

It was a fortunate thing that the first District Nursing Association in America should have laid such stress on the educational side of the work, and as proof that their attitude was accepted by America as the right and proper one, we may cite the words of Isabel Hampton (the late Mrs. Robb) who five years later in an address to the International Congress of Nurses (1893) said; "In District Nursing we are confronted with conditions which require the highest order of work, but the actual nursing of the patient is the least part of what her work and influence should be among the class which the nurse will meet with. To this branch of nursing no more appropriate name can be given than 'Instructive Nursing,' for educational in the best sense of the word it should be." Truly a great advance from the attitude of the missionary nurses so short a time before!

After ten months, "unwilling longer to trespass on the hospitality of the Dispensary," and also for greater convenience, the managers moved their office into a small suite of three rooms at 34 Bennett Street, opposite the Dispensary—one to be used as the office proper, one as a loan room, and one as a room for the use of the nurses when necessary for purposes of disenfecting after caring for cases of contagious disease.

In 1906, the Association moved into a large house at 561 Massachusetts Avenue, for the purpose of securing larger office quarters and to enable it to start a "Training School for District Nurses," [1] the first to

---

[1] An account of this School for District Nurses will be found in Chapter XX.

be started in this country. It still has its headquarters at this address and directs an organization which might well be pointed out as a model of work of its kind.

But we must return to the early day of its existence. The plan of the work was somewhat similar to that in Liverpool. Two lady managers were appointed to each district and the nurse was expected to report once a week to the manager or managers having oversight of the district to which she was assigned, giving all details for record concerning the patients she had cared for during the week, advising with them in regard to special or doubtful questions, or as to the needs of individual patients who might be referred to other organizations for such help as lay outside the service which the nurse herself might give.

This weekly conference with the lady manager of the district was a direct copy of the early Liverpool plan, and took the place of supervision by a trained superintendent, which at that time they did not have. Besides this informal weekly conference, the President met the whole staff once a month to hear their reports, making any necessary criticisms, and informing herself as to the work in all its details. In the week following this meeting of nurses with the President, the regular monthly meeting of the Board of Managers was held, at which time they all had an opportunity of comparing the work in the different districts and becoming acquainted with the Association as a whole. This close contact of the lay people with the work of the nurse gave them a peculiar and intimate understanding of her needs. As was said in one of the early reports: "The Directors find great interest in thus watching the care and cure of this large number of suffering people, who respond so readily and with so much gratitude to the offices of the nurse," and we cannot but feel that this close connection with the active work, the participation, as it were, in the problems and trials of the

14

nurse, was the source of that great enthusiasm which made possible the admirable development of the Boston Association.

At first the nurse, as we have seen, obtained her patients only through the Dispensary physician. This was undoubtedly a wise arrangement. We must remember that in that day there were no telephones, and it would have been a somewhat difficult matter to have found the patient for the nurse, or the nurse for the patient; time would have been lost, and the most needy might have been overlooked. The Dispensary too, was a well-known charity, having been in existence ever since 1796, and only the poorest and most helpless patients applied for aid. The nurse, therefore, was likely to find among them those who needed her care the most, besides being able to take her direction for that care from a physician already in charge of the case. The plan followed was that each nurse should get her orders each morning from the physician in charge of her district, and report to him the work of the previous twenty-four hours. Visits to new patients or to very sick ones were usually made with the doctor, after which she would continue on her round following out the directions given. The rules governing her work were carefully considered and in their essentials have not been changed. They were, in part, as follows:

1: Each nurse shall work for eight hours daily, employment on Sunday and holidays shall be exceptional, also night duty.
2: Nurses must be examples of neatness, cleanliness and sobriety.
3: Nurses attending to contagious diseases shall be subject to special limitation in their attendance on other patients.

7: Nurses shall not interfere with the religious or political opinion of the patient. (This is the first time that we find a suggestion that district nurses might be used for the distribution of political propaganda).

8: Nurses shall not receive presents from patients, nor give money or its equivalent.

We see from these first rules that the Boston Association was based on modern methods, and that most of the principles laid down by the founders of district nursing, and ever since approved, were followed in its work. It was distinctly not a relief-giving society, though it considered carefully the economic condition of its patients and where they were in need of material relief, or any other assistance, the nurse made every effort to refer them to the organization best able to supply the need.

Although the nurses did not teach religious truths directly, and were especially ordered not to interfere with the religious opinion of their patients, they did, unconsciously teach the spirit of true religion, and "the sweet lessons of charity and love which their lives exhibited, could not fail to reach the hearts of those with whom they came in contact." (From the Berkley Beacon, 1889.)

Again, although there were some who felt that it was a waste of generous and refined effort to employ the highest talent and finest culture in the service of those who could not appreciate it, nevertheless the decision of Miss Lees, that only women of breeding should undertake district nursing, was the general decision of the Board of the Boston Association and an effort was made to secure only such women as came up to the standard. "The district nurse," said they, "who can carry into the sick room of the poor, not only the technical skill acquired in the hospitals, but also the delicate instructions and firm conviction of the wellbred woman, can accomplish vastly more in the work of raising the standard of household existence, and in the

way of restoring health to those stricken with disease,"
which was exactly the same conclusion arrived at by
Miss Lees in her survey of English district nursing.

In some points, however, the Boston Association
did not at first come up to standard.   The most obvious
defect being that, although an increasing number of
nurses were employed, there was no supervision of their
work beyond that given by the lady managers.   The
danger of this proceeding was probably minimized by
the fact that all the nursing was done under a dispensary
physician, and that he himself often visited with the
nurses and could see whether or not the care was well
given.   In 1900, however, fourteen years after its inauguration the realization that professional supervision
should be supplied was unanimously reached.

The following extract from the Annual Report published in 1901, shows the reasoning which underlay
the change of method.

"Until last winter, that of 1900, the necessity of
changing the methods of overseeing the nurses had not
impressed itself upon the management, so gradual had
been the growth of the Association, and so efficient
was the work of the Committee on Nurses.   While
there was no more reason than there had ever been for
supervision over the individual nurse, yet the body
of individuals had grown too large and too unwieldly
to be over-seen in the old way.   Someone skilled in
nursing work was needed to see that the best work was
done and to understand the relative working conditions
of each district."

In May of the same year Miss A. E. Beer was engaged as Superintendent of Nurses, being succeeded
in the following year, May 1901, by Miss Martha
Stark, who remained with the Association for eleven
years or until January 1912.   During these years the
Association grew steadily and led the way in
developing many types of special nursing in the com-

munity; first school nursing in 1905, then tuberculosis nursing 1906; followed by nursing for contagious diseases in 1908.   All these types of nursing proved very successful, and were eventually taken over by the city authorities, under whose jurisdiction they are still continued.   Prenatal and child welfare work were developed later.

In 1912, the Association was reorganized with Miss Mary Beard, graduate of the New York Hospital Training School, as Director;[1] Miss M. Grace O'Bryan being engaged as Associate Director in September 1916.   Today the Association has 14 districts, covering the entire city; each district with a Branch Station, which has a supervisor, and assistant supervisor, and a group of public health nurses sufficient to meet the need.   Each nurse is responsible for the work in a given territory.   Connected with each station is a local committee of residents of the district, who are active in making known the work of the nurses to the neighborhood, and in raising money for the support of the nurses.   The chairmen of these district committees serve on a central committee with members of the Board of Managers.

The present staff (October 1, 1921) consists of 116 nurses.   There is a special supervisor for clinics, and one for maternity work, and the positions of orthopedic supervisor and of mental hygiene supervisor have just. been created.   In two districts baby clinics are held, but in other districts such clinics are conducted by another organization.   In four districts two special maternity nurses are on duty to attend confinements at any hour; six nurses have had special training in the muscle treatment of children suffering from .infantile paralysis and treat these cases in all parts of the city.

During 1920, 36,660 patients were cared for by the

[1] Miss Beard resigned as Director of the Boston Association September 1921.

Boston District Nursing Association, this being nearly 10,000 more than in 1919, an increase unprecedented in the history of this or probably any other Association It has been estimated that 23 per cent of the entire service is maternity work, which is carried on by the general visiting nurses under the special maternity supervision.

Were an obstetrician asked: "Is it safe to permit maternity patients to be cared for by nurses who are at the same time caring for other patients, doing surgical dressing, giving bedside care to pneumonia patients, or caring for a child with measles?" The reply would undoubtedly be, "No, it is not safe." And yet this is the method employed with unquestionable success by the district nurses throughout Boston. They have never had a case of cross infection, and have materially reduced the death rate from child-birth. (Boston Instructive District Nursing Association. A Review—by Mary Beard.) The prenatal work also reaches a far greater proportion of mothers, according to population, than are reached in any other large city in the country. This doubtless contributes to the reduction in the death rate.

Altogether this old and well established Association has an enviable reputation and is carrying on a piece of work which may well be imitated by others.

THE VISITING NURSE SOCIETY OF PHILADELPHIA, 1886.

It is a strange but true fact that very often people at a distance from one another will begin similar work at almost the same time, without any apparent connection between the two, and often with no knowledge by the one of the work or idea of the other. Such a coincidence has often happened in connection with the discovery of some new invention or scientific fact, and at times there has been much discussion as to which was first in the field. In tracing the line of thought which led to their discoveries, however, we usually find that the underlying knowledge had long been common property, and that many men had been studying along the same lines for many years. Therefore, it was not so strange after all, that two or more men should almost simultaneously have arrived at the same conclusions, or have made the same discovery.

The same conclusion holds true in the almost simultaneous establishment of district nursing in two different cities of the United States. At the same time that Miss Howes and Miss Adam were starting their first nurse in her work among the sick poor in Boston i. e., in February 1886, Mrs. William Furness Jenks of Philadelphia was endeavoring to establish a similar work in that city. Neither had heard of the efforts of the other, but both had received their inspiration from the work being done in England, and in both cases the founding of the new organization was made possible by a growing appreciation of the suffering of the sick poor, and the knowledge that trained nurses, who could relieve that suffering, were to be had. Let Mrs. Jenks tell us in her own words how the work in Philadelphia had birth:

"It had been a long stormy day in February, 1886, and our guest in our country home, Mrs. Brooke Herford, settled down by the fire after a game of hide and seek all over the house in a romp with my children. She began to tell me of her home in England where she remembered the opening of the first passenger railroad, the one from Manchester to Liverpool—that had been when she was a little girl. Then she spoke of Manchester and its laboring classes, and how, about twenty-five years before there had been an effort made there to aid the poorest people through periods of illness or when suffering from accident, by supplying nurses to care for them.[1]   Mrs. Herford was one of the Committee in charge of this district nursing.   The work, she said, was well systematized and required of her only one morning, or sometimes a whole day, once a week.   It was an entirely new idea to me, but I felt great enthusiasm at once.   I had seen among my country neighbors many cases of the need of just such care, but with the best intention I was powerless to help.   It was difficult to get a doctor, and as his visits cost money they were not requested until the need was great.   The wee ailing baby; the mother out of bed too soon after confinement; the consumptive father sitting 'out of the draft' and feeding his small child alternate spoonfuls with himself from some chance dainty sent to him; the little girl drooping from malarial fever; the scrubwoman who was always wishing that her 'head would only stop aching'; the man restless with the discomforts of a broken limb; these, and many another, needed someone to advise, to warn them of greater dangers, to show them how to be clean, to prevent infection, and to give them comfort such as often they had never imagined possible.   Why had not we in America heard of this work and done it ourselves?"

In turning it over in her mind Mrs. Jenks saw that, dearly as she would have liked to try the experiment near her own home, where she knew the people, it would hardly be possible to do it.   In the country where the patients lived so far apart, and where the wealthy were so few as to make the raising of sufficient funds difficult, the work could not be satisfactorily undertaken.   The city was the place to begin.   Mrs. Jeuks began, therefore, to cast about in her mind as to

[1] It will be remembered that the first district nurse in Manchester had been engaged by Mr. Charles Herford of that city.   See Chapter X.

whom she could find to aid her in the undertaking. Let us again quote her own words:

"The granddaughters of Lucretia Mott ought to be willing to at least consider such a scheme for the assistance of the unfortunate, thought I, so I turned to them. Then my aunt, Mrs. James Furness, would listen for my own sake; so would Mrs. Henry C. Lea, who was both rich and generous; Miss Cornelia Hancock was a public spirited· worker and intimately connected with the Charity Organization, so was Mrs. Peter Lesley, and Miss Anna Hallowell, always deeply interested in public welfare and education, might care for this.

"With these names to start us, we ventured to call a meeting on the invitation of Miss Maria Hopper, granddaughter of Lucretia Mott, at her home, 1206 Spruce Street. At that meeting in February 1886, I laid the idea before these ladies, saying that I would raise $100 (one hundred dollars) and find the nurse to try the experiment for one month. Mrs. Lea promised· to help or to give money. Miss Hallowell said, that in general she did not approve of starting new. charities, there were already so many, often poorly supported, but that in her judgment this plan was good enough to be tried. Mrs. Lesley spoke of the needs of the poor— she knew them well, so did Miss Hancock. The latter said: 'I do not know Mrs. Jeuks but I do know her family, what they undertake they put through.' Miss Hopper declared she had no time to give to outside duties, but that until we could obtain other helpers she would lend a hand.

With this encouragement we began March 1st, 1886. A Board of Directors· was formed, rather loosely at first, and Miss Sarah G. Haydock, a recent graduate from the Woman's Hospital Training School, was engaged as nurse, and an office opened in a back room in Sixth Street near Race Street. We had only the $100, so were very careful of expenditures; a second-hand table at fifty cents would do for a desk, a blank copy-book for our records. Oakum was much used for surgical dressing then, so we bought a bale of that for four dollars, and anyone who needed to write at the table could sit on that.

Then we began a discouraging hunt for patients. No one seemed to need us. We asked the doctors; they said 'Why should a nurse be required? we had better teach the people to be clean, they have done without home nursing heretofore, why suggest it now?' The Seventh Ward Charity Organization declared it had no sick people. We found the whole plan very different from Mrs. Herford's picture of only one day a week devoted to the office. Day after day Miss Hopper and I trudged about to charitable societies, to doctors, to philanthropic friends—no one had ever heard of such a thing as nursing the sick poor, except in hospitals—why begin now? Why give money to a scheme for over-indulging those who could not possibly continue to pay for the luxury? Besides this, we were unknown. To overcome this latter difficulty, at least with the medical profession, we asked some of our leading physicians to sign a circular for our use. This was done by Dr. James Hutchinson, Dr. Ruschenberger, Dr. S. Weir Mitchell, and others and our work increased."

The first regular meeting was held April 20, 1886. By that time the office had been removed to 1203 Race Street, as the first one in Sixth Street had been found too small and too remote. Mrs. Chas. G. Ames was in the Chair and the following Officers were appointed:

Mrs. William F. Jenks, President, Miss Maria Hopper, Treasurer, Miss Groome, Secretary.

The question of charging a small fee to cover carfare was discussed, and it was decided it might be done at the discretion of the nurse. The amount of money from every source thus far collected was only $842.05, of which $239.08 had already been spent.

By the end of May $200 had been collected in the Seventh Ward to be used for a second nurse to work in the southern part of the city. This money was kept separate until exhausted, later all subscriptions were placed under one head. The difficulty of securing patients, however, still continued and toward the end of the year (1886) it was thought worth while to advertise for private patients, those able to pay 50 cents a visit or more; also, as there were now several nurses and attendants, the latter not trained nurses but helpers working under the nurses, it was thought wise to make Miss Haydock Head Nurse.

At first the Society had been called "The District Nurse Society" but it soon became evident that it was difficult to put limits to the work and so the name was changed to that which it bears at present (1922) "The Visiting Nurse Society of Philadelphia."

There had been much doubt and many misgivings, but by February, 1887, the Society felt itself firmly on its feet and held its first annual meeting, February 25, 1887, with such confidence that it resolved to frame a constitution and by-laws; also to print 1000 copies of its first report. The contributions for one year had amounted to $1911.05, the expenses were $1875.39. The patients' fees had brought in $106.57, and there were donations for special cases of $75.64. The patients numbered 380 to whom 5885 visits had been paid.

In October 1887, the Society was incorporated under the name of "The Visiting Nurse Society of Philadelphia" and its purpose stated as follows: "to furnish visiting nurses to those otherwise unable to secure skilled attendance in time of sickness, to teach cleanliness and the proper care of the sick." The management was to be in the hands of twelve Directors or Managers; by-laws were framed and certain notes made for the management by the Board.　During this year, 1887, it was resolved that a uniform for the nurses be adopted, for which the expense was provided by Mrs. Lea, the new President.

The service of the Philadelphia Society was definitely for people of moderate means, who could pay something for the care received, as well as for the poor to whom the service would be given free of cost.　The rules governing this service five years after its inauguration were outlined as follows:

1: For those in comfortable circumstances a visiting nurse can be furnished and the charge must, in such cases, fully cover the expense to the Society, fifty cents or one dollar a visit according to time required.
2: For those able to give no more, the carfare is expected, being generally ten cents a visit.
3: A visiting nurse is furnished without charge to those who are quite unable to pay for her services.
4: Visiting nurses will remain with a patient for the first 24 hours after a major operation and will visit daily after that, as required.　Should a patient need continuous care an outside nurse must be engaged and paid for by the patient.
5: The hours of the nurse are from 9 o'clock in the morning until eight o'clock at night.　After that time they can not respond to calls.
6: The nurse will visit in the morning those cases which have been reported the previous day, while those coming to the office before 12 o'clock will receive attention that afternoon.
7: The nurses are for the use of the public and it is desired that physicians and others interested in the sick shall send for them.　The service should be paid for whenever possible as the Society is supported entirely by voluntary contributions.

It will be seen from the foregoing that the experience, plans and work of the Philadelphia "Visiting

Nurse Society" were quite different from those of the "Instructive District Nursing Association" of Boston. In the first place, although the original idea of the Society in Philadelphia had been to furnish trained nurses for the sick poor, the scope of its work was soon changed and the service opened to all in need of nursing care, the name being changed from "District Nursing" to "Visiting Nursing." In the second place, whereas, the Boston Association, through its connection with the dispensary, had encountered no difficulty in securing patients, the Philadelphia Society had been hampered for some time by the impossibility of making its work understood and appreciated, and the inability to find the sick poor needing its service. Also, the Boston Association, having behind it old and well-known organizations, such as the Boston Dispensary and the Women's Education Association, had no difficulty, from the start, in procuring money for its support; whereas, the Philadelphia Society, being a perfectly new charity, inaugurated by a small group of private individuals, was for some time in great financial straits, and was only kept afloat by the earnest effort and generous support of those immediately connected with it.

In two respects, however, the Philadelphia Society seems to have been in advance of its contemporary, the Boston Association. At the end of the first year it recognized that there should be a Head Nurse, and Miss Haydock was appointed to the position. Although Miss Haydock probably did not supervise the work of the other nurses in quite the same professional way that Miss Stark later did in Boston, some of the workers being only attendants, she held the position of superintendent or Head Nurse, and was, in a way, responsible for the work done by the other nurses. To be sure, the Philadelphia Society employed "attendants," as well as trained nurses, and for that reason a Head was more important than in Boston. Also, as

we have already pointed out, the need of such supervision was not so acutely felt in Boston, because of its
close connection with the Dispensary doctors.   Nevertheless, it is surprising, considering the accent put upon
the professional supervision of nurses in England, that
Boston did not see the need sooner, and that she should
have waited fourteen years before putting the idea into
practice.

Again, the Boston nurses wore no uniform until
1900, whereas, in Philadelphia a uniform was adopted
in 1887.   The question of uniforms for nurses was not
considered a very important one in those early days—
even the uniform for the hospital nurse being in no
way standardized.   Little by little, however, the various
points in its favor began to be appreciated and uniforms
were universally adopted, the dress being of washable
material—usually blue and white striped seersucker,
with white collar and cuffs, and a white apron, to be
carried in the bag and used while tending the patient.
The outside uniform was at first a long cape, or cloak,
and bonnet with veil similar to that worn by the Queen's
nurses, which was later changed to a long blue coat and
a simple hat of straw in summer and felt in winter.

While the work of the Boston Association grew with
leaps and bounds, that of the Philadelphia Society progressed more slowly, though steadily.   Miss Haydock,
who was a faithful and conscientious nurse, with a real
love for the people, (who in return were devoted to
her) resigned her position on the staff, in October 1888.

In 1891, Miss Linda Richards, who is known as the
"first trained nurse in America" was, for a short time,
Head Nurse and did much for the development of the
Society, and whereas, in the first year it was difficult
to procure $2000, for its support, five years later twice
that amount was easily raised.   The financial condition
of the Society was improved also.   Poor patients were
always cared for when necessary, but the nursing of

pay patients was also continued, the income from that source increasing from year to year, until, in 1890, the sum collected amounted to $1000. This pay service was a distinctive and interesting feature of the work in Philadelphia. In England, many years before, the Rev. Septimus Hansard, of the Parish of Bethnal Green, London, had suggested that some such nursing service might be established. "There is a class of poor not actually and legally paupers," said he, "and whom I don't want to make legally paupers—therefore I should suggest that a small fee should be paid by every applicant, exception being made only in cases which had been properly investigated. The result would be that the mass of men and women would get the aid by paying their small fee, and not be or feel degraded nor lose their sense of independence and self-reliance." (Extract from letter sent to the Committee of Inquiry, London 1873.)

This suggestion however, was not followed. In 1887, when the Queen's Institute was established, and for many years afterwards, the English district nurses were furnished entirely free of cost. Later an effort was made in Liverpool—that pioneer city!—to have those patients who, though poor, where able to give something, pay a small fee; and, later still, they established a branch service of the district nursing, which they called the "Visiting Service"; these so called English visiting nurses were, however, more like an American hourly nurse; they could be called upon by anyone, and would remain with a patient for several hours, if necessary, at so much per hour.

At the present time the attitude in England is similar to that in America and a small sum is charged wherever possible.

In 1893, The Boston Association also began to occasionally use the term visiting nurse, instead of district nurse, in reference to nurses not working in connection with the Dispensary—"A visiting nurse is furnished without charge to those who are quite unable to pay" they said, and again :

"A visiting nurse will stay with a patient for the first 24 hours after a major operation."

In 1899 Miss Zilpha D. Smith, Secretary of the Associated Charities of Boston, gave an address at the annual meeting of the Boston District Nursing Association in which she pointed out the danger of giving the service of a nurse to those able to pay for it, but showed at the same time that there was a class of people who, though quite unable to pay for a private nurse, would never be willing to accept nursing service free, or as a charity. For these self-respecting poor she suggested a pay service. "I am quite confident that there is need of such nursing," said she, "and that the demand for it will grow as physicians learn that such service is available, and as one family tells another what the nurse has done for them."

Nevertheless the suggestion of visiting nurses on a pay basis did not progress, and it was not until well on in the beginning of the 20th century that the idea was generally accepted and adopted to any extent by existing Visiting Nurse Associations.

In Philadelphia, however, the idea of a general service available for everyone, had always prevailed, and the money collected from this source had gone far toward supporting the work. As the years went on the amount of money received from patients steadily increased. By 1916, it had reached a total of $6652, by 1917, $9648, and by 1918, $10,260.

In 1919, besides the general pay service, for which a maximum charge of 75 cents per visit was made, a second type of pay or hourly service was opened up for those persons, not able or not desirous of having a nurse resident in the house.

The charge for this service was $1.25 per hour from

8:30 A. M. to 5 P. M. after which hour the charge was increased to $1.75. This charge assures a nurse at approximately the time requested, and for as long a time as needed; whereas, in the general pay service the nurse makes her visit to the patient at whatever time best fits in with her general district work. After the introduction of this second pay service the amount of the fees from patients increased still more rapidly until in 1920 it reached the surprising figure of $25,388.

At the present time (1922) many visiting nurse associations have a regular service on a full pay basis, and most public health nurses—unless paid for by the taxes of the people, as in municipal or county nursing; by a company for its employees; or by an insurance company for its policy holders, as in the Metropolitan Life Insurance Company, are expected to ask a small fee for all their service unless the patient is obviously unable to pay.

These two associations, The Instructive District Nursing Association of Boston, and the Visiting Nurse Society of Philadelphia were the first to be established in this country. They were established almost simultaneously, served as examples for further work in other parts of the country, and should share the honor of having introduced to America one of the most valuable social agencies of modern times.

15

CHAPTER XVI

A PERIOD OF DEVELOPMENT

District Nursing, or Visiting Nursing, as it was soon more generally called, was now well established in the United States. Other cities began slowly to take it up, some following the plan adopted by Boston, others following in the wake of Philadelphia, and still others organizing on new lines worked out to more fully meet local needs.

By the end of the century a great many of the large cities had some form of visiting nursing in their midst and smaller communities were also beginning to take it up. The work was carried on in all sorts of ways. There were visiting nurse associations; there were committees of various charity organizations formed for the purpose of supplying visiting nurses to their especial groups; there were parish visiting nurses; there were visiting nurses connected with hospitals—sometimes only pupil nurses; and there were three visiting nurses working in industry. It would be impossible, in a book of this size, to enumerate all the visiting nurse associations formed during this period. We will content ourselves, therefore, by mentioning only a few of the largest and most important ones.

THE VISITING NURSE ASSOCIATION OF CHICAGO, 1889

The Visiting Nurse Association of Chicago, established in 1889, was the third in point of time, and was the outgrowth of still earlier work of the kind in that city, the first having been begun in 1883, by the Chicago Ethical Culture Society in connection with the Central Free Dispensary affiliated with Rush Medical College.

This work was started at the suggestion of Mr. William N. Salter of Harvard University, (at that date lecturer to the Chicago Ethical Society) who had become interested in the work of the nurse as carried on by the Ethical Society in New York. At the instigation of Mr. Salter, Miss Mary Margaret Etter, a graduate of the Bellevue Training School, was engaged to start the work.

She was accompanied by Miss Benedict, who had been working with the New York Society, and who remained with Miss Etter for three months to assist her in establishing the nursing in Chicago. The annual report of the Central Free Dispensary for 1883, has the following reference to the work: "Since our last annual report there has been established at this Dispensary the headquarters of the system of district nursing for the West Side, inaugurated by the Relief Works, under the auspices of the Society for Ethical Culture. The district nurse attends cases requiring her services, which cases are under the care of the attending physicians. So far the scheme has worked admirably; the work of the physicians has been supplemented, they receive genuine assistance and the patients genuine benefit."

Miss Etter carried on this work for a little over three years with such zeal and earnestness that a great deal was accomplished. She had not, however, the physical strength for such arduous labor and her death, which occurred soon after, was no doubt hastened by it and by the exposure it entailed. The Ethical Society continued to carry on the work for a short time longer, but finding themselves unequal to the task of getting sufficient money, of selecting the right kind of nurses, or supervising the nurses' work, they were finally obliged to give it up.

Shortly after this first attempt had been discontinued, Miss Clarissa Shumway, having become interested in house to house nursing among the poor, as she had seen it carried on in the large cities of Europe, determined to establish a similar system in Chicago. She engaged two nurses, Miss Eleanor M. Brown, graduate of the New Haven Training School, as head nurse, and Miss L. M. Seymour, one of the first graduates of the Illinois Training School, as assistant, and after establishing them in the center of a small section in the congested part of the South Side, called them, in memory of her mother, "The Augusta Memorial Visiting Nurses." Miss Shumway, soon after married Mr. Charles Stedman Hanks, and moved to Boston to live, but for two years continued to support the work. At the end of that time, finding it impossible to carry on work of this kind economically at such long range, she decided to give it up. Some thirty doctors, however, hearing of her decision, united in a petition, urging her not to desert them, saying that the value of the service of the nurses she had supported could not be estimated, and that its loss would be a calamity.

The result was that, although she still adhered to her decision not to carry on the work herself, she asked several of her friends if they could not interest a group of people to form an association and carry on the undertaking in a permanent way. This was done and was the beginning of the present Visiting Nurse Association of Chicago.

A meeting was called by a few of Miss Shumway's friends, the matter thoroughly discussed, and the decision arrived at to establish "An Association to furnish visiting nurses to those otherwise unable to secure skilled assistance in time of illness, and to teach cleanliness and the proper care of the sick."

The Association began very modestly with but one nurse, Miss Seymour, who had previously been one of the Augusta Memorial nurses. Before the first year was over, however, four nurses were at work in different parts of the city, and from that time on the number steadily increased.

This association did not imitate any other; its formation, as we have seen, was in direct response to a call, and the rules which governed it seem to have been formulated from time to time, by the Directors, as the need arose. Several years later a report of the Philadelphia Association fell into the hands of one of the Directors, and interested her so much that she promptly passed it on to others. An interesting correspondence between the two associations ensued, but neither organization seems to have been materially influenced by the policies of the other.

The work in Chicago grew and developed much as it grew and developed in other cities at that time; and, as in most visiting nurse associations, the personal service, time and energy, as well as money, given by the Directors was a big asset and contributed greatly to its power in the community. It has always been governed by a Board of women Directors, with an advisory committee of men since 1911. Seven women, whose names represent the best civic and philanthropic spirit of the city, have held the position of President of the Association. They are: Mrs. E. C. Dudley, Mrs. James L. Houghteling, Mrs. Hugh J. McBirney, Mrs. George S. Payson, Mrs. Henry Hooper, Mrs. Arthur Aldis and Mrs. Joseph M. Cudahy.

These women have, each in turn, given themselves wholly and enthusiastically to the task and the present splendid financial condition of the organization is largely due to their interest and activity.

As time progressed the size of its nursing staff increased; the field of its endeavors broadened; and its

close connection with the health work of the city
strengthened year by year.

On looking back over the annual reports of the Chicago Association, the type and amount of special nursing service rendered to the city stands out prominently.
For instance, during a small-pox epidemic in 1894,
the Association offered to supply all the nursing, if the
city would supply a proper home for the patients. The
Association expected to give three or four nurses; it
ended by giving the full time of twenty-four. It began, also the school nursing, by first giving the time
of one nurse to examine the children in the vacation
schools in the rooms for crippled children, and later in
1908, supervising forty school nurses, paid for by the
Board of Health. It started the first bit of organized
tuberculosis work in the city, by forming in 1902 a
special committee on tuberculosis; and in 1916 began
the special after-care of convalescents from infantile
paralysis, which work has been so extended that at the
present time (1921) the Association maintains a special
staff of eleven nurses and one supervisor, who devote
all their time to work among crippled children.
Another unusual feature of this Association is its large
number of endowed or specially supported nurses, there
being at present on its staff sixty-two *i. e.,* 38 in
general work, 11 giving after-care in infantile paralysis,
and 13 doing full time industrial nursing in seven
large industries. It is interesting to note, too, that it
was the Chicago Visiting Nurse Association which first
used the white maltese cross on the sleeve of the nurse's
uniform. "A fitting emblem," says Miss Somerville,
"of the purity and self-sacrifice of their mission." Unfortunately it was found necessary to discontinue its
use, as various commercial agencies were found using
it for advertising purposes and their work was confused
with that of the visiting nurse.

The Chicago Association has had a long and honor-

EDNA L. FOLEY, R. N.

Superintendent of the Visiting Nurse Association, Chicago, and author of the "Visiting Nurse Manual." President of the National Organization for Public Health Nursing April, 1920 to June, 1921.

able career. During its thirty odd years of existence it has had only three superintendents:

Miss Emily Wakem, of St. Luke's, Chicago, the first superintendent, who inaugurated the work; Miss Harriet Fulmer, also of St. Luke's, who for thirteen years guided the nurses in their new profession, inspiring them with a love for the people, and enthusiasm for their daily task; and Miss Edna L. Foley graduate of Hartford Hospital Training School who is still the superintendent, and whose wise and sympathetic leadership in the field of public health nursing has won for her a loyal and devoted following.

THE BUFFALO DISTRICT NURSING ASSOCIATION, 1891.

The first district nurse in the city of Buffalo was put on duty by Miss Elizabeth Marshall, of the first Presbyterian Church, in the year 1885, as an experiment, in order to ascertain the need of nursing care in the homes of the poor. After proving the need over a short period of time, a committee was formed, funds were asked and a second nurse was appointed.

In 1891, the work was finally established on a firm and progressive basis. In that year the Buffalo District Nursing Association was incorporated, and has operated from that time until the present, with a Board of Managers, and under the same President, Miss Mary A. Lewis. In 1892, there were three nurses in the field, a fourth being added to the staff in 1896. At this time the work was entirely district nursing in the homes of the sick poor, and a diet kitchen was operated by the Association where eggs, broth, fruit, etc. were dispensed. In 1898, five nurses were at work and it was decided that a public appeal should be made to the citizens of Buffalo, for the support of the work and for its advancement. The first Tag Day ever held in the city was for the benefit of the Association.

In May 1909, the services of Miss Ada B. Shaw were secured as Superintendent of Nurses. From the time of Miss Shaw's arrival under her most able management, the work of the Association grew very rapidly, within a few months eleven nurses being employed, as well as an office assistant. The work of the Association at this time included a specialized field for contagious disease nursing, another for tuberculosis nursing and one nurse was loaned to the Baby's Milk Dispensary for infant welfare work. During the next few years the Association was able to demonstrate the effectiveness of tuberculosis nursing within the city so well that the city government decided to take it over, under the Department of Health. A nurse from the staff was loaned for work in the city of Lackawanna, and another for special work with the North American Civic League for immigrants, and an extra number of nurses was placed on duty with the Baby's Milk Dispensary.

In 1915 Miss Shaw resigned as superintendent, at which time there were nineteen nurses on the staff, and the work had become, not only for the sick poor, but also for those of limited means, who might pay a small fee. Mrs. Anne L. Hansen, who succeeded Miss Shaw has been in charge for six years, during which time the work of the Association has developed from a staff of nineteen nurses to one of fifty, including five supervisors and a superintendent's assistant. Five nurses' aides are also used in infant welfare work.

The work today includes general visiting nursing for a small fee, as well as for charity patients; baby welfare work in connection with twenty Well-Baby Clinics throughout the city; and the service of two obstetrical nurses for maternity cases at time of delivery; besides special nursing service for the Central Clinic for sick children and babies, where special diets are prepared under the supervision of the nurse. The Association also does the field follow-up work for the patients attending the Diagnostic Clinic at the Buffalo City Hospital, and also provides nursing service at the Health Centers, with the city physicians, for two hours each afternoon.

The one object the Board of Managers had in mind in the early days was charity to the sick poor, and the annual report shows such items as 100 dozen of eggs, 100 quarts of broth, 1000 lbs. of beef, chickens, etc. distributed by the nurses, or from the diet kitchen. Today the object of the association is:

(a) to provide nursing service in any home where the people are unable to obtain the services of a private duty nurse, or be taken to a hospital, and

(b) to work in very close co-operation with health agencies along the lines of preventive medicine and elimination of disease.

No relief of any description is now handled by the Association, but every nurse is taught to refer to the proper agency cases within her section, requiring material aid.

This work in Buffalo is a good example of the steady growth of most of our large visiting nurse associations, and the development from pure charity, to a democratic service open, on a pay basis, to all self-respecting citizens.

THE VISITING NURSE ASSOCIATION OF KANSAS CITY, MO., 1892.

The Visiting Nurse Association of Kansas City, Missouri, was one of the first associations of the kind in the West and may be looked upon as the parent organization of all such work in its locality. It was the outgrowth of a church society known as the "Ladies Society" of the First Congregational Church, organized in 1891, when the Rev. Henry Hopkins (afterward President of Williams College) was pastor. This Society employed a trained nurse, had a loan closet and reached out to the sick and destitute within its own circle of influence. It was soon recognized, however, that such work would have greater scope for good if it were not confined to one church circle. In the spring of 1892, therefore, a general meeting of the women of the city was called, and as a result, on April 10th of the same year, the Visiting Nurse Association of Kansas City came into being. The Association at once secured the services of two trained nurses, one of whom, Miss Lillie Major, had been the nurse for the church society, and acted as Head Nurse for the new Association until 1906. In speaking of Miss Major, one of the members of the Board recently wrote: "It is not possible to speak too highly of Kansas City's first visiting nurse—for, added to her fine English training, she brought to her task splendid judgment and a sympathy, insight, skill and cheerfulness which were unsurpassed."

By 1909 the work of the Association had so increased that it was found necessary to procure a Superintendent of Nurses. The field of its usefulness steadily extended; it co-operated with other health and social agencies, by securing and supervising in a general way the nurses employed by them, until now (1921) it has on its staff thirty-seven visiting nurses, many of whom are supported by other organizations. This group of *Associate Organizations* includes Roman Catholic, Protestant, Jewish and Non-sectarian societies, showing how well it is that visiting nurse work should at all times be free from sectarian influence.

VISITING NURSE ASSOCIATION OF DETROIT, 1894.

Visiting Nursing in Detroit was started in 1894, by Alice M. Bowen, a graduate of the Farrand Training School for Nurses, Harper Hospital. Miss Bowen had done district nursing in Philadelphia for a year with

Miss Linda Richards, and she returned with her mind so imbued with the idea that the work must be begun in Detroit, that she immediately put into practical operation Florence Nightingale's dictum, "The first duty of a district nurse is *to nurse."*

The needy sick were sought and found through the city physicians and the churches, and to their care and welfare she devoted her time, her energy and her money. She enlisted the interest of a group of young women, who formed the District Nursing Society, and who were active social workers in the homes where Miss Bowen found sickness and want. They met with her weekly for counsel, and to sew garments for the patients and little children. This was the beginning of the supply and loan closet which has never been empty.

A constantly increasing public confidence in the service resulted in the calling of a meeting of interested citizens to co-ordinate the forces supporting the venture that had proven itself, and as a result the Visiting Nurse Association of Detroit was organized. On March 14, 1898, the executive board was formed and the first officers were elected.

Through the auxiliary membership of several training School Alumnae Associations nurses have always been represented on the executive board. The Commissioner of Health is a member of the advisory board, which has fostered the spirit of close co-operation with the Department of Health.

The Association was incorporated in 1901. In 1905, Mrs. Tracy McGregor, a public spirited citizen, built a home for the Association upon a lot which had previously been purchased. After a number of years this building was no longer adequate to house the nurses due to the expansion of the work and so was converted into an office building, providing quarters for the Central Bureau of Nursing, including besides the Visiting Nurse Association, The Babies' Milk Fund, First

District Michigan State Nurses Association, the Home Nursing Association, and headquarters for the State and Local Committee for Red Cross Nursing Service.

Before the inception of post graduate courses for public health nurses, this Association sent representatives to gain knowledge and experience from other established fields of nursing. Tuberculosis nursing, school nursing, infant welfare and county nursing, each, in turn, had its beginning in the Association and was fostered until public appropriations were secured to continue them.

Previous to the federation of philanthropic organizations under the Community Union in 1917, the association was supported by membership dues and private contributions, but since that date an annual budget has been submitted to the Community Union which provides for expenditures in excess of the income. This affiliation with the Community Union is proving invaluable, not only financially but socially and educationally.

The nursing staff comprises a superintendent and assistant; a registrar and statistician; three supervisors; 30 field nurses; six nurses with the Babies Milk Fund engaged in infant welfare, including nursing, instruction and demonstration in the homes and clinics in Hamtramck and River Rouge; one supervisor and seven nurses who give prenatal instruction and care for mothers during confinement; three nurses in the Children's Free Hospital who act as director of social service, an assistant, 'and an orthopedic nurse; one nurse assisting in the general clinic of the United Jewish Charities; one nurse caring for crippled children of Ford Motor Company employees through the company's educational department; three nurses supervising the care of children in the boarding homes of the Children's Aid Society and the Detroit Branch of the Michigan Children's Home Society; two nurses supervising the care of children in the boarding homes of the Society of St. Vincent de Paul, and one nurse doing community nursing in River Rouge, a monthly average of 65 nurses.

The association includes contracts with industrial corporations on the visit basis for the benefit of their employees. For eleven years the Metropolitan Life Insurance Company has had such an arrangement for their industrial policy holders.

Two Detroit hospitals prior to the war affiliated with the Association to give their student nurses experience in visiting nursing, which owing to the shortage of nurses has not been resumed.

With the establishment of a course in public health nursing by the University of Michigan, an affiliation has been effected for the practical instruction of the students in field work with the Detroit Department of Health and the Visiting Nurse Association.

INSTRUCTIVE VISITING NURSE ASSOCIATION OF BALTIMORE, 1896.

The Instructive Visiting Nurse Association of Baltimore is another of the large and important pioneer associations of the country. Whereas, most visiting nursing has been started and established through the initiative and energy of lay people, the work in Baltimore was the result of one nurse's interest and activity. It was started in 1896, by Miss Evelyn Pope, a graduate of Johns Hopkins Training School, who for six months worked alone among the sick poor of the city, giving them the bedside care she was so well qualified to bestow, and doing what she could in connection with the other charities of the city, to relieve their distress. During her vacation her place was taken by another nurse, Miss Anna C. Jack, who became so much interested in the work that when Miss Pope returned from her vacation Miss Jack remained also and together they continued their work in this new field of social service,

Miss Jack for one year and Miss Pope for two years and three months.

In 1898, the work was taken over by an association, organized for the purpose, and Miss Ada M. Carr also a graduate of Johns Hopkins Training School engaged as Head Nurse. Miss Carr held the position for six years, and it is due to her tireless energy, ability and foresight that the new undertaking was so successful and the broad foundation laid which has made possible its work today. In 1903, Miss Mary E. Lent, also a graduate of Johns Hopkins one of the nurses who had been on the staff for two or three years, was appointed to fill her place and retained the position for thirteen years, during which period the work of the Association grew and broadened in many directions.

The development of tuberculosis nursing was one of its most important activities. This service, which began in 1904, with one visiting nurse, supported through the efforts of Mrs. William Osler, steadily increased, until by 1910 there was a staff of six tuberculosis nurses, under the supervision of the Instructive Visiting Nurse Association, carrying all the work in the city. It was felt that this work, however, was a municipal problem, rather than one for a private organization, and so, in that same year, the city created a Tuberculosis Nursing Department and the six tuberculosis nurses, together with the Assistant Superintendent of the Association, Miss Ellen La Motte, as Director were transferred to the City Health Department, which henceforth carried on the work.

Another interesting and novel piece of work was the establishment of classes in hygiene and home nursing. Miss Lent realized the great need that existed for teaching health to young women in industry. She visited department stores and other industrial concerns in Baltimore, gained the permission of the employers to speak to groups of their women workers at the noon hour or other convenient times, and organized classes for those who were willing to learn something of the rules of health and how to give simple care to those who were sick—very much the kind of training indeed, covered by the courses in Home Nursing and Care of the Sick which are given by the Red Cross today. The attendance in these classes often reached over 100. The benefit of these lessons soon became apparent in the district work, and often a visiting nurse, going into a home, would find a patient comfortable and well-cared for, the simple necessities for nursing care ready prepared, and on inquiry would find that the mother or daughter had received instruction at one of these classes.

Still another interesting piece of work was carried out in connection with the Public Athletic League of Baltimore. All lads, before being allowed to take part in the athletics were required to undergo a medical examination, and this examination revealed a very serious state of affairs—defects of the heart, lungs, throat and many others. Over 2000 lads had been found medically unfit and efforts to persuade them to have the necessary physical corrections made had proved unavailing. Faced with these conditions, the Director of the League consulted the Superintendent of the Instructive Visiting Nurse Association as to the best method of getting results with these boys, and she suggested that they should try what a public health nurse could do. After some hesitation the League finally consented, as an experiment, to pay for the services of a member of the visiting nurse staff, employing her from month to month, as her efforts might prove successful. This nurse followed up rejected boys, and in less than two months had succeeded in obtaining 40 per cent of corrections: inside of eight months a record of 95 per cent of corrections had been made. It became a matter of pride with the lads to be in good physical condition, and they soon vied with each other in having their defects removed.

One of the boys, who was going to have his tonsils out brought his pal with him and said: "If you don't kill me, Jim is going to have his out too," and as they didn't kill him he brought, not only his friend Jim, but sixteen others.

The statistics showing the remarkable results achieved by this experiment were quoted at the annual meeting of the National Education Association; and this was probably one of the first systematized efforts to interest a group of young people in their own physical welfare by the kind of methods which are now being so successfully employed with school children.

In 1903 a house at 1123 Madison Avenue was loaned to the Association by Mrs. Bertha Rayner Frank. Later it was given outright as a gift and has ever since been occupied as a Nurses' Home and headquarters for the Association. Extensive additions and a roof garden were later added to the building, the latter being particularly attractive and restful for the nurses in the hot summer weather of Baltimore; many of them being able to sleep in the open air. The Home was a home in every sense of the word, and the atmosphere of happy family life developed in the nurses the best qualities of comradeship and esprit de corps. Miss Lent was greatly beloved by the nurses under her, and retained the position of superintendent until 1916, when she resigned to become Associate Secretary to the National Organization for Public Health Nursing. Miss M. Evelyn Walker is the present Superintendent of the Association.

DISTRICT NURSE ASSOCIATION OF PROVIDENCE, 1900.

The work in Providence, R. I. was begun in June

1900, and was the spontaneous outgrowth of a suddenly perceived need. Miss Eleanor B. Green, a young woman interested in many forms of philanthropy who, in her work among the poor of the city, had noticed how many were without any care when ill, one day met a physician, an acquaintance of hers, on the street. "Doctor," said she, "I think we need district nurses in Providence."

"District nurses!" said he, "what are district nurses?"

Miss Green explained with the result that the doctor's interest was at once aroused, and a meeting planned to be held at his office a few days later. At this meeting the following seven persons were present: Dr. George L. Collins, Dr. Halsey DeWolf, Mr. Charles Morris Smith, Mrs. Henry F. Lippitt, Mrs. John A. Gardner, Miss Amey Vernon and Miss Eleanor B. Green.

Ways and means for starting the work were discussed, and a gift of $500 given by Mrs. Henry F. Lippitt to carry on the work as an experiment for six months.

A temporary committee was formed; an office opened in the Out-Patient-Building of the Rhode Island Hospital; and a nurse, Miss Ellen A. Kenny, engaged to start work in the lower east side of the city.

As usual the new undertaking seemed to meet a great need.

At the end of five months the calls for the service of the nurse were so many that an appeal for funds was made to such persons as might be interested in the work, in order to extend the service to other parts of the city. The response was so quick and generous that a second nurse was at once engaged, and within five years the entire city was covered.

In 1902 the temporary committee was dissolved, and an organization incorporated, under the name of "The

16

Providence District Nursing Association," the purpose
of which was "to provide trained nurses to visit sick
persons deprived of proper care; to care for them in
their homes; to give them such attention as is imper-
atively needed; and to instruct members of the household in the simple rules of hygiene; all of said services to be without compensation."

The rules of the Association asserted that the patient
must be "worthy" and "too poor to pay for a nurse,"
and that a doctor must be in attendance.   This limiting the service to charity patients was an unfortunate
proviso, and rather surprising at that date.   It was,
however, shortly after abolished.   In 1906, the Providence Association began collecting fees for service and
at present pay patients are cared for as well as charity
patients.

In 1905, Miss Mary S. Gardner graduate of New-
port Hospital Rhode Island, was appointed superintendent.   Under her admirable management the work
developed rapidly, new branches of specialized service
being added from time to time.   The Association had
started by furnishing general bedside care.   In April
1905, just previous to the date on which Miss Gardner
assumed the superintendency, the training of pupil
nurses in district work had been begun, one pupil from
one hospital being taken at a time.   The number of
pupils gradually increased until at present eight from
three of the large local hospitals are taken on the staff
at one time for from six weeks to two months and given
supervised instruction in district nursing as a part of
their hospital training.

In 1906, tuberculosis nursing was started; followed
in 1907, by child welfare work; and in 1918, by
venereal disease nursing, special groups of nurses being used for each service.   These various special services are held together and made into one coherent whole
by means of the closest co-operation in their work, free

rotation of nurses, and the daily coming together of all the nurses in the central office of the Association, where exchange of ideas, and a personal knowledge of each other's activities is made possible. This uniting of all the visiting nurse work of the city, except only the school work and contagious disease nursing, under one organization and one head, is a distinctive feature of the Providence Association, and tends to give the work as a whole great unity and strength. Another outstanding feature is the splendid organization of the work, the city being treated as a great out-of-door hospital, the six districts into which it is divided for general work, representing the hospital wards, and the individual patients, the beds. In each district is a head nurse, an assistant head nurse, the requisite number of visiting nurses, and one or more pupil nurses. "The head nurse and her assistant," says Miss Gardner, "exactly correspond to the head and senior nurses of a hospital ward. The head nurse is held responsible for everything in her district, for the records, and reports, and general harmony between co-operating agencies, doctors, etc., the work and health of her nurses, the training of her pupils, economy in use of supplies, as well, of course, of all the purely technical details of nursing." (The Public Health Nurse, vol. V, page 20.)

Certain general principles govern all the work in all the districts, but the head nurses are given a very free hand in the management of details and in method of work, which gives opportunity for personal initiative and the exercise of creative or executive powers.

Moreover in this ward method of administration, with an assistant head, as well as a head nurse, there is a continuous policy carried on in the district, unbroken by the illness or absence of the head nurse, and which assures at all times adequate supervision of the pupils or new nurses, and the proper care of the sick in the district.

Miss Gardner is still superintendent of the Providence Association and is too well known through her book on Public Health Nursing, and her wide-spread and valuable services to the cause, both in this country and abroad, to need further comment.

VISITING NURSE ASSOCIATION, CLEVELAND, 1902.

The visiting nurse work in Cleveland was not begun until 1902. By that time certain well-defined principles for the support and administration of such service had been determined, and the young association was therefore able to avoid some of the pitfalls into which others less fortunate had fallen, and was unhampered by many of the difficulties which had impeded their development. In other words, the Visiting Nurse Association of Cleveland profited by the mistakes of others and was thus enabled to make astonishing progress in its work.

The first impetus given to the idea came in January 1901, when at the monthly meeting of the Graduate Nurses' Association of Cleveland, Mr. Starr Cadwallader, the Superintendent of the Goodrich Social Settlement of that city, made a short address on the origin and development of social settlement work, and spoke at length on the part which nurses were taking in it. In the discussion which followed, the members showed a marked interest, several of them expressing the hope that in the near future their organization might be of practical assistance in providing suitable nursing for the sick poor of the city.

It was over a year, however, before the nurses were able to put their desire into effect. At that time a group of enthusiastic young women called the "Baker's Dozen" (originally a school girls' club) sought the Graduate Nurses' Association and offered them the money in their treasury (not a large sum) and their

MARY S. GARDNER, R. N.

Superintendent of the District Nursing Association of Providence, Rhode Island, and author of "Public Health Nursing." President of the National Organization for Public Health Nursing June, 1913 to May, 1916.

co-operation in founding a visiting nurse association. The suggestion was accepted, an association formed, and four visiting nurses engaged, two of whom were from the Chicago association. Three of these nurses went to work in three different districts of the city, with headquarters in three social settlements,—Goodrich House, Hiram House and Alta House—the fourth acting as superintendent and attending to the work in the central office.

In 1904 Miss Matilda Johnson, graduate of St. Joseph's Hospital, Chicago, who for several years had been on the staff of the Visiting Nurse Association of Chicago, was engaged as Superintendent of Nurses.

Miss Johnson remained with the Association for ten years and won for herself a warm place in the hearts of her co-workers. She was filled with enthusiastic devotion to her profession; was able to inspire her staff with the same high ideals which she herself possessed; and was a powerful influence in the growing movement to develop community health. The esteem in which she was held by the Board of the Visiting Nurse Association was voiced when one of the members said: "The very best that some of us have ever learned has been learned through association with her in her work."

The Cleveland Association was organized on the plan of the Visiting Nurse Assoication of Chicago, adopting its blue and white uniform, with the white cross on the left arm, and incorporating into its Constitution and By-Laws the rules and regulations of the older society. The work grew with amazing rapidity, and the patients came from many sources—through former patients, doctors, friends of the Association, city departments, charity associations and through some of the public schools by securing from teachers each day a list of absent pupils. This last method of obtaining patients was commented upon as follows in the first annual report of the Association January 1903:

"It is a surprise to find that almost unconsciously we have begun work along lines that have been in operation in New York, and in such successful operation, through the efforts of Miss Wald's Settlement, that the matter has been taken up there by city authorities, and an appointment has very recently been made to employ six nurses to care for the sick and instruct families of those pupils absent or dismissed from school on account of sickness. May we not be just as progressive here in Cleveland, and our Association prove as great an aid in helping our municipal authorities maintain a high standard of health?"

By the following year co-operation with the school authorities had become so close that a systematic visiting of the schools in her district by each nurse was not only permitted, but approved, and the teachers had become so interested in the work that they collected from among themselves $456 toward the support of an additional nurse.

The connection of the Association with the social settlements gave it from the first a strong social bent. Two years after its inauguration it co-operated with the Western Reserve Medical College in starting a social dispensary for tuberculosis patients; the following year it made a practical demonstration in school nursing and co-operated with the "Milk Fund Association" in establishing the Babies' Dispensary and in providing a special nursing service for sick babies; and in 1907, took up social nursing for the Maternity Dispensary. These pioneer nursing services were followed by home nursing for the prevention of blindness, nursing supervision of contagious diseases, factory nursing and other special types of social work.

All these varied forms of social nursing originated with the Visiting Nurse Association. There was, therefore, a recognized uniformity of standard, ideal, custom and manner of work which was of inestimable

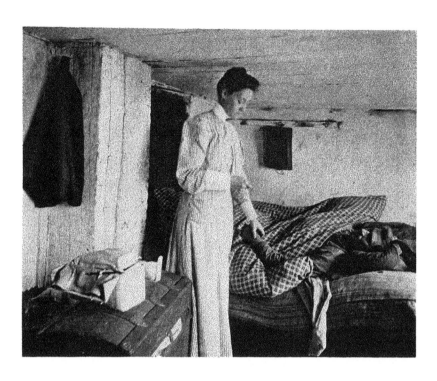

THE VISITING NURSE—1908.

At this time the work of the visiting nurse was almost entirely
with the very poor.
(Courtesy of the Visiting Nurse Association of Cleveland, Ohio.)

value not only to the nurses, but to the work itself. Gradually these groups of special nurses were taken over, paid for and directed by different special organizations—the tuberculosis nurses by the Anti-Tuberculosis League (later by the Department of Health), the baby nurses by the Babies' Dispensary, the school nurses by the School Board, etc., each with a special superintendent, though all the nurses still remained as branch staffs on the central staff of the Visiting Nurse Association. Every visiting nurse had behind her, therefore, not only her own association, but all the medical charities of the city, and because of this inter-relation the advantage of the one became the advantage of all the others.

In speaking of this unity of the visiting nurses of Cleveland, Miss Matilda Johnson, Superintendent at that time, said:

"It seems to us in Cleveland, so important to procure the unity of our visiting nurse staff that there is hardly any feature of the work to which we give more thoughtful attention. It is not an easy matter to safeguard this unity, for it is very natural for the institutions and organizations who employ visiting nurses to separate these branch nurses from the central body. It is only by the closest co-operation between the trustees of these different organizations and their frequent and familiar intercourse with the central office that trouble of this kind does not arise."

The general plan was very simple. All the salaries (except those of the school nurses, and the nurses for contagious disease under the Board of Health), plus a small charge of overhead expenses, were paid by the various organizations into the general treasury of the Visiting Nurse Association, and through it the salaries were paid out to the nurses themselves. The same uniform was used by all the nurses, including the city nurses, and they all met once a week in the rooms of the Association for exchange of ideas and discussion of work.

The Visiting Nurse Association fixed the salary schedule, engaged all nurses, and used its districts as training schools for new nurses without experience in visiting nursing. The plan was to put a new nurse into the district for a few months, in order to give her some social training, before turning her over to any one of the affiliated organizations. This was a splendid method for keeping up the standard of the work done throughout the city; but as the staff of the Visiting Nurse Association was constantly being deprived of its good nurses in order to fill the needs of the other special staffs, and was being replenished by nurses without training or experience, it was sometimes detrimental to the general work in the district, and required much self-sacrifice on the part of the parent organization.

I have described in some detail this method used by the Visiting Nurse Association of Cleveland, because it was unique of its kind and gave the work in Cleveland a unity and high standard often difficult to attain in a large city with varied fields of endeavor and different groups of workers.

As the municipality took over more and more nurses, however, (Cleveland now has 37 school nurses under the Board of Education, and 82 on the staff of the Board of Health), as the number of factories increased; and new organizations were constantly arising and asking for a visiting nurse to help them in their work, the task of supplying them all became too heavy for the Visiting Nurse Association to carry on. *A Central Committee on Visiting Nursing* was therefore formed, which took over most of the duties and responsibilities formerly carried by the Visiting Nurse Association. It acts as a central agency for securing visiting nurses and makes all rules and regulations in regard to salaries, uniforms, standards, etc., though, like the Jubilee Institute in England, it has no power to enforce the acceptance of its rulings and can merely recommend them to its affiliated members. In almost all cases, however, the rulings are at once accepted.

This Central Committee is composed of two members from each organization employing more than one public health nurse (industrial concerns are not at present represented,) one member being a lay person and the other a nurse. There is also a sub-committee on eligibility, consisting of the chairman of the Central Committee and the superintendents of the various large staffs, which investigates the credentials of nurses applying for positions, passes upon their eligibility, and places them in the different organizations according to their needs and the preferences of the nurse herself.

Although the public health nurses of Cleveland no longer form one staff they still co-operate very closely, still preserve the same spirit of unity, and are animated by the same high ideals for the general betterment of community health.

CHAPTER XVII

NURSES' SETTLEMENTS

Most of the well-established early visiting nurse service in the United States was, as we have seen, carried on under the direction of associations especially organized to ɩurnish and control such service, and variously called District or Visiting Nurse Associations, with or without the prefix "Instructive." In 1893, however, a new kind of an association for carrying on the work was organized in the form of a Nurses' Settlement. Miss Lillian D. Wald, a graduate nurse of the New York Hospital Training School for Nurses, impressed by the sight of a woman in a rear tenement sick under unspeakably distressing conditions, conceived the idea of establishing a neighborhood nursing service for the sick in the tenement region of the lower East Side of New York. Up to that time there had been no visiting nursing in that city beyond the limited care given by the nurses of the City Mission and the dispensary nurses of the Ethical Culture Society, and that furnished in a still more limited way by one or two parish nurses working for particular churches.

In Boston, Philadelphia, Chicago and several other of the large cities of the United States, visiting or district nursing associations had already been formed for the sole purpose of furnishing nursing care for the sick poor in their own homes,[1] but New York City

---

[1] According to the Statistical Table II in Miss Waters' book "Visiting Nursing in the United States" (page 365) there were, in 1893, 35 associations employing visiting nurses, eight at least of which had been organized under the specific name of Visiting

like London—and perhaps for the same reason, namely its great size and the immensity of its problem—had failed to follow the great movement to supply nursing care for those unable to procure it for themselves.

Miss Wald was first and foremost a nurse; the sight of this sick woman, lying without care or attention of any kind, aroused her interest and social self-consciousness. "My nurse's instinct revolted," said she, "at the knowledge that nobody had washed the woman, made her bed, or performed any of the offices that every human creature should feel entitled to in like condition."

The thought of this woman and the certainty that countless others were suffering under like conditions haunted Miss Wald, and she could not rest until she had worked out a plan to alleviate their distress by establishing in their midst some kind of a nursing service, free from all denominational or political influence and ready to respond to the call of all the sick in the neighborhood. Filled with the enthusiasm of the young and earnest pioneers of all time, Miss Wald succeeded in interesting two lay people, Mrs. Solomon Loeb and Jacob H. Schiff, in the undertaking, and in persuading another nurse, Miss Mary Brewster, also a graduate of New York Hospital, to join her in the work. The two nurses established themselves in a suite of rooms on the top floor of a tenement in the neighborhood in which they wished to work and began to look about for patients. They started, as Miss Wald has herself said: (Charities Ap. 7, 1906) "with no definite program other than the desire to find the sick and to

or District Nursing Association. Of these 35 associations, Boston employed 9 nurses; Philadelphia 7; Chicago 8; Buffalo 3; while the Ethical Culture Society of New York was furnishing a visiting nurse to 3 dispensaries, and the New York Mission was sending out 10 or more nurses into their district of lower New York. The other associations were, in most cases, employing only one or two nurses. (See Appendix V.)

nurse them." They felt that by actually living in the neighborhood they would the more readily be looked upon as friends, and that by first voluntarily offering their service wherever they might find a sick person they would in time make themselves known and would be called upon by others when sickness invaded their homes. *Neighborliness* was the underlying thought in their work; they wished to be known as friends rather than as paid visitors; they felt that in that light they would more often be called upon in an emergency, and that the advice and suggestions they might give would be more readily followed. Time has proved the validity of their reasoning.

Moreover, they wished to entirely eliminate the idea of charity from the service which they offered. From the very first, therefore, the people paid for it whenever able. That fact revolutionized the relationship of the visiting nurse to the patient. It was the beginning of the broad community service for all which has since become available in many places.

For two years Miss Wald and Miss Brewster lived in their little apartment on the top floor of the tenement house. There they had wide opportunity for forming the friendships they desired, and had many interesting and amusing experiences. It was not an easy thing for two young women, accustomed to all the comforts and luxuries of well-to-do life, to give up their normal way of living and go down to the lower East Side of New York. It took much courage and perseverance to succeed. There must have been many times when the difficulties encountered seemed insurmountable, and when the seeming hopelessness of accomplishing permanent good must have made them almost give up the task. But Miss Wald had seen a vision, and the glory of it led her on. These two years of effort to make her vision come true may have been hard in many ways, but they were filled with the consciousness of daily duty well done. There was refreshment and satisfaction in seeing the sick poor in their neighborhood well cared for and comfortable, and the grateful looks of their humble patients as the nurses left them lying in their clean beds, must have been a stimulus to further effort.

Their "friendliness" was not bounded by nursing service, however; they became deeply interested in all the various problems affecting the neighborhood and their advice was sought for on more subjects than sickness and health.

"In quick succession they were invited into conference by trade unions, by workers in philanthropy, by clergymen and the orthodox rabbis. The unemployed, the anxious parents, the girls in distress, the troublesome boys came as individuals to see them." (Report of Henry St. Settlement, 1898 to 1913.)

At the end of the two years they moved into a house on Henry Street purchased for them by their friend, Mr. Schiff, and were joined by other nurses and social workers. Gradually an organized program of various social and educative activities developed, and the nursing service became only one department of a general social settlement. Nevertheless, the nursing work of the Henry Street Settlement has been at all times its most important and best known feature.

In 1920 the Henry Street visiting nurses made the enormous number of 336,722 visits and cared for 42,902 patients.

The work covers the three boroughs of Manhattan, the Bronx and Richmond, and is a fine example of what one woman's energy and determination may accomplish.

THE NURSES' SETTLEMENT, RICHMOND, VA.,1900.

The idea so satisfactorily worked out by Miss Wald

and her co-workers in the Henry Street Settlement has
not been imitated to any great extent in other cities,
the less complicated organization of a visiting nurse
association being usually preferred.

The only nurses' settlement whose visiting nurse
work is in any way comparable to that done by Henry
Street is the Nurses' Settlement of Richmond, Va.,
though in comparing the two one must remember that
the one was established in the largest and wealthiest
city in the country; while the other was worked out in
a comparatively small community, where money was
proportionately hard to raise.   Moreover, the need for
visiting nursing was not recognized by the citizens of
Richmond for some time, and it was a hard struggle to
get the work established on a sound financial basis.

In a little pamphlet describing the founding of the
Nurses' Settlement of Richmond, the writer says:

"This work is unique, inasmuch as in other places where
such work is done the community has felt the need and
calls the nurse—but here the call came from the nurses,
who in the wards of the hospital had seen the need, and it
took four years of hard struggle on the part of both board
and nurses to make the community recognize the necessity
for such work."

The Settlement was founded in 1900 by a group
of active young nurses from the Old Dominion Hospital, under the leadership and inspiration of Miss
Cabaniss, their superintendent.   For some time these
nurses had realized the need of home care for the sick
poor, and in their off hours had often followed their
discharged patients to their homes, giving them supplementary attention during their convalescence, and
teaching hygiene and the rudiments of home nursing
to the poor mothers.   Their interest in the work so increased that they finally decided to leave the hospital

and rent a house, where they could live independently and carry on settlement work during all their spare hours.

They started "literally without a penny, but with lots of faith; friends rallied round and helped furnish the house, to which each of the 'Settlement Nurses' came as time in the hospital was completed. The rent was met by each nurse paying room rent, regardless of whether she was there or not, and board when there; and by four occupying a room there were some superfluous rooms for lodgers. No servant was kept, partly for economy, and partly for demonstration to the people with whom we worked that it was possible to live decently and do other things, even though we did have our own house to care for. We did all our cooking, and cleaning, except the very heavy part, which was done twice weekly by a scrub-woman. I can feel myself shiver now when I think of how the first one up in the morning must go down to an outer cellar to turn on the water before a drop could be gotten in the house, or else be confronted with jeering tongues of ice from the instantaneous heater in the bath room. After breakfast, dishes must be washed and put away, room straightened, and then we were ready to start on duty at nine A. M." (Pamphlet on The Nurses' Settlement of Richmond, Va.)

Interest in the work increased and, as the nurses grew better acquainted with their patients, various social activities were organized and the house became a centre not only of nursing interests but social interests as well, though nursing of the sick poor in their homes continued to be the most important phase of the work. There was no money to carry on the work, however, except such as the nurses themselves were able to furnish, and the strain upon their pockets and their strength became too great to be longer borne.

"For eighteen months we struggled on, facing misunderstandings, criticisms, and receiving very little sympathy. It was necessary to take pay cases from time to time to keep the pot boiling, but one nurse was always kept ready to respond to calls, receiving a small salary from the group. During this time every minister, or group of ministers, charity organizations, or any individuals who would listen, were interviewed. At last an opportunity was given to read a paper before the Woman's Club, and, as a result of that, Mrs. B. B. Valentine called together a group of women, and formed the Instructive Visiting Nurse Association of the Nurses' Settlement. The three nurses were engaged who had been doing the work as volunteers— Miss Cabaniss of Johns Hopkins, Baltimore, Miss Harvie of St. Luke's, Richmond, and Miss Minor of the Old Dominion, Richmond—at the munificient salary of $37.50 per month, which was what the nurses figured was the least they could live on." (Pamphlet on the Nurses' Settlement of Richmond, Va.)

From this small beginning came the well-organized Instructive Visiting Nurse Association of the Richmond Nurses' Settlement. As the work and interest grew, various means of raising the necessary funds were instituted, among others an annual Tag Day, which was a good means of publicity and gave all the people of Richmond an opportunity to contribute to the support of the work.

During all this time the nurses were gradually increasing the social as well as the nursing side of their work, for they soon realized that every phase of social work seemed to touch that of the visiting nurse—and so they associated themselves with the housing problems, with the Associated Charities, with the movement for playgrounds, and with various medical efforts to combat tuberculosis, infant mortality and the many defects of school children. Industrial nursing was inaugurated in the tobacco factories of the city, and nurses placed in a large railway office and an insurance office. Classes and clubs were started—some for instruction, some merely for recreation—and the work gradually broadened and grew until it embraced all the various social and nursing activities usually found in a nurses' social settlement.

COLLEGE SETTLEMENT—1898
and the
BUREAU OF MUNICIPAL NURSING—1913
LOS ANGELES, CAL.

A few other settlements were started in various parts of the country, with visiting nursing as one of their activities. Among these we may mention the Nurses' Settlement of San Francisco, started by Miss Octavia Briggs in 1898; the Nurses' Settlement of Orange, N. J., which was an outgrowth of the Visiting Nurse Department of the Orange Training School for Nurses; and the College Settlement of Los Angeles, California, which in December 1897 appealed to the City Council to appropriate a monthly allowance for the salary of a visiting nurse. The request was granted, and on March 1st, 1898, the first visiting nurse paid for by a city's public funds started her work in that city, under the direction of a committee of the College Settlement. Los Angeles, therefore, has the distinction of being the first city in America to establish municipal nursing. Six years later, 1904, the first school nurse in Los Angeles was appointed, working under the City Health Department. In 1906 a second school nurse and a second visiting nurse were appointed. In 1907 a third visiting nurse. By 1910 there were five visiting nurses doing general district, as well as tuberculosis, nursing, and two special nurses, one devoting herself to maternity work, and the other

17

to contagious diseases. These nurses all worked under the direction of the College Settlement, but were paid by the city.

The work continued gradually but steadily to increase. The women of the College Settlement began to feel that the supervision of so many nurses was a greater responsibility than they wished to carry, and therefore made a request of the City Council that the work be taken over by the Health Department.

In January 1913 an ordinance was passed creating a Bureau of Municipal Nursing, and the nurses that had up to this time been working under the direction of the College Settlement were taken over by the Health Department.

Still the work continued to grow, ten nurses being added to the staff in 1915 to do tuberculosis nursing only. At this time there were four groups of nurses, one doing general district work, one maternity, one infant welfare, and one tuberculosis, the Board of Education having, in the meanwhile, taken over the school nursing.

In consequence of this division of work there was a constant overlapping, and several nurses might be found working at the same time in the same household, to the no small discomfort and perplexity of the family.

The city recognized that the system was, for some reason or other, unsatisfactory, and in 1916 asked the National Organization for Public Health Nursing to recommend an organizer for the Nursing Division of the Public Health Department of Los Angeles. Miss Mary E. Lent was recommended for this new and important service; she had just been appointed Associate Secretary of the National Organization, but would not take up her duties in that capacity immediately. Miss Lent soon after went to Los Angeles, where she spent six months working out a plan of organization which, for completeness and system, has never been surpassed.

Her entire plan was adopted by the city, and during the five years in which it has been in operation has proved its entire practicability. The original feature of this plan of organization was general nursing in the districts, with *specialized supervision*. Thus, one nurse is placed in each district and cares for all the people in her district, but has special supervisors to whom she can turn for special instruction in the care of her patients. "The obvious advantage of this method," says Miss Lent, "is that it brings constantly to the attention of each nurse all the difficulties and needs of a family group, instead of dividing responsibility for the family among several independent and unrelated individuals." (Report of the Reorganization of Public Health Nursing in Los Angeles.)

At present there is a staff of forty nurses—one chief nurse, one assistant chief nurse, four supervisors, thirty-one staff nurses and three nurses inspecting boarding homes for children, maternity homes and hospitals.

The entire city is divided into districts, with a nurse assigned to each and responsible for all public health nursing in her own district. Each nurse is assigned a certain number of hours each week to the various tuberculosis clinics, venereal clinics, and well-baby conferences.

The city supplies the nurse's bag, fully equipped, pays her carfare while on duty, and furnishes three Ford cars exclusively for the use of the Nursing Division. There are branch offices for the nurses in various parts of the city, and in cases where these, as welfare conferences, are not located in city buildings, the city pays a rental for bungalows to be used for this purpose.

Altogether, it is by far the most extensive and comprehensive system of municipal public health nursing in the country, and seems to be meeting the city's needs satisfactorily.

These various efforts in visiting nursing, and many

others which in a book of this ·size we cannot even enumerate, though differing considerably in detail of management or scope of work, were all established on the well-recognized fundamental principles of visiting nursing. Unfortunately there were many other forms of the same work which were not so well established. Visiting nursing became a popular form of charity. People recognized the great comfort and solace which home care brought to the sick poor, and many would start a nurse out in the field without supervision and often without considering whether or not she were properly trained in the technique of her calling, or whether she had any aptitude for the social side of the work. Many churches would support a nurse to visit the sick poor in their parishes, without recognizing that a social as well as nursing problem was involved. Charity associations would employ visiting nurses, thus combining material relief and free nursing in a way very prejudicial to the use of the service by the self-respecting poor. Private individuals would donate the salary for a nurse to undertake visiting nursing in some small town or rural community, without taking into account that an individually-supported charity will decline or grow according to the degree of enthusiasm of the individual; and that only through the control of an association of many individuals whose interest would be continuous, could a work of that kind be assured of permanent support. Hospitals would send out pupil nurses, without supervision or previous experience, to visit among the sick poor or to follow up discharged patients, and thought that thereby they were doing good visiting nursing and giving their pupils instruction in this new branch of their profession.

In this way did visiting nursing spread and develop throughout the United States, until by 1905 there were 171 associations carrying on some form of visiting nurse work and the number of nurses employed had increased to 445—not a great number considering the great need, and yet showing a steady increase. (Appendix VI.)

From that time on, however, principally owing to the active campaign against tuberculosis, the wide-spread effort to reduce infant mortality, and other preventive activities of like nature, the number of Visiting Nurses, or Public Health Nurses (as they were soon to be called), increased with amazing rapidity; until by 1921 the number reached over 11,000.

CHAPTER XVIII

SPECIALIZED VISITING NURSING

In the beginning of the movement, and for many years afterwards, district nursing in England, and visiting nursing in America, was confined to *general nursing* of the sick poor; in other words, to the giving of bedside care to any poor patient, suffering with any form of disease. In her work in the district the visiting nurse, therefore, cared for the tubercular, as well as for the typhoid patient; for the baby as well as the mother; for the chronic heart or rheumatism case, as well as for acute pneumonia; and for the aged grandparent as well as for the young school child.

Gradually, however, as the work for some one special disease, as tuberculosis, or some one special age, as infancy, grew and developed visiting nurse associations began to appoint special nurses to care for them. This, in time, increased until there were often various large groups of special nurses serving on the general staff of many visiting nurse associations.

From this it was but a step to the formation of separate associations for the care of some one specialty in medical-social work—such as Anti-Tuberculosis Leagues for the care of the tubercular, Maternity Dispensaries for the care of expectant mothers, and Infant Welfare Societies for the prevention of infant mortality and the care of infant life. These various associations would then engage their own nurses, who would devote themselves to some one special line of work—tuberculosis, maternity, child welfare, etc.,—as the case might be—leaving all other work and instruction to the general visiting nurse.

This use of the nurse as home visitor, and especially as health instructor, in the various health problems confronting those interested in preventative medicine greatly increased the demand for her services. "The visiting nurse is the most important figure in the modern movement for the protection of the public health," said Dr. Winslow, and the public began to echo his words.

The activities of the visting nurse, now became more varied, and at the same time more specialized, as group after group of medical and social agencies called for her help, and soon we find her adding a special prefix to her title, as the tuberculosis visiting nurse, the baby visiting nurse, or merely the tuberculosis nurse, the baby nurse, etc.

The effect of these different specialties on the work of the visiting nurse was so important, and contributed so greatly to the evolution of public health nursing, that we must stop a moment and glance back at their origin and growth.

SCHOOL NURSING.

The first special work undertaken by district nurses was undoubtedly school nursing, begun in London in 1892, by the Metropolitan Nursing Association. One year before that time, however, namely in 1891, at the International Congress of Hygiene and Demography, Dr. Malcolm Morris gave as his opinion that "a staff of specially educated nurses should visit the elementary schools regularly to inspect the children." This was the first suggestion for a branch of work that is now considered one of the most important in the whole field of public health nursing.

The idea which led to the actual appointment of a

school nurse, however, originated in the following year during an inquiry into the feeding of London school children, when it was discovered that many of the children were.suffering from the neglect of minor ailments or injuries, and that many others were attending school though obviously unfit to do so by reason of some infectious trouble, or because of some uncleanly or verminous condition.

The suggestion that, were a nurse to visit the school and care for these minor ailments before they became dangerous, much suffering would be avoided, induced Mrs. Leon, a school manager under the School Board, to go to the office of the Metropolitan Nursing Association and ask for a school nurse. Miss Amy Hughes at that time Superintendent of the Queen's Nurses in Bloomsbury Square, herself answered the call, and thus became the first school nurse, visiting daily in one of the Board Schools in Wild Street, Drury Lane, where the children were among the poorest and most neglected in the City of London, and following them to their homes, where the conditions were such as to need medical treatment.

The work done was eminently satisfactory, but was not extended until 1898. At that time Miss Honor Morton, a trained nurse, and also a member of the London School Board, succeeded in interesting a group of individuals in the education and health of school children, and in the formation of a society for the purpose of supplying nurses to the various London schools. Because Miss Morton was a member of the School Board, and was able to secure Lord Breay—Chairman of the Board—as Vice-president of the new society, she easily secured permission to work in the schools and secured, also, the good will of the Board in the undertaking.

This "London School Nurses' Society," as it was called, was a private charity, supported by voluntary subscriptions, and was, of course, entirely unable to cope adequately with the problem of school nursing in a city like London. Nevertheless, it made a noble attempt and blazed the way to further effort.

There were 60,000 school children at that time in London, and only *one* permanent medical officer, therefore, the nurses could hope for little medical assistance. Also there were 500 elementary schools, and only five nurses to start the work. They decided, therefore, to direct their attention at first to the poorest schools only. Each nurse was able to visit about four schools in one day, and to examine about one hundred children, who were sent to her, one by one, by the teachers.

Inflamed eyes, infected cuts and wounds, skin diseases, and dirty conditions of the body or the clothing, were the principal troubles she had to cope with, and the children after being properly attended to were usually able to continue in school without danger to themselves or to others. When the nurse observed serious symptoms in a child, she would follow him to his home and endeavor to persuade his parents to procure the necessary medical attention. The result of this daily ministration was most excellent; attendance in school improved, certain contagious and infectious diseases almost disappeared, and cleanliness among the children "became fashionable."

A report on the School Nursing in Laxon St. School, issued in 1900, in which it said: "The visits of a nurse to this very large infants' school have proved most beneficial to the health of the children, so much so that it could be wished that the School Board might make such visits universal in the schools in poor districts," aroused much interest, and the School Board responded to the suggestion by appointing one nurse of its own. By 1904, the school nurses had so thoroughly demonstrated their usefulness that the entire work was taken over by the London County Council, and the School Nurses' Society was dissolved.

Other cities followed in the wake of London. Liverpool—always alert on the question of nursing—had, through the interest of Mrs. Rathbone, started the experiment in 1895, and engaged a nurse to go to some of the elementary schools to look after the children. Birmingham, Brighton, Widnes, Wimbledon and others followed suit, and the movement progressed rapidly.

At first, of course, objections were raised. The expense would be too great, said some. To this the exponents of school nursing were able to answer that in one school, where a nurse had been employed, the attendance had so improved that the grants from the Government—based on the number of children attending—had increased enough to *pay for the salary of the nurse*. (Report of Jubilee Congress on District Nursing, p. 221.)

Again the people feared that parents would object to having their children examined at school. In answer to this they were able to show that, on the contrary, the work of the nurses was so appreciated that at some of the schools mothers would often be found waiting outside in order to get information as to how to care for their children's ailments. Finally the opponents of the plan asserted that in any case the good done by the nurses would be very small and hardly worth the experiment. But to this objection figures could be brought to show that in one town the number of cases cared for by the nurse was reduced from 23,596 in the first year to 17,924 in the fourth, or a reduction of 5672 cases needing attention—which seemed to show that the work of the nurse had been conducive of great good.

Moreover, the doctors themselves supported the plan, finding that without the aid of the nurse the physician's medical inspection would lead to nothing.

Dr. Hayward, medical inspector at Wimbledon, in his report to the Jubilee Congress in 1909, gave the following testimony in favor of school nurses:

"When I first commenced my duties in Wimbledon it was impossible not to feel exceedingly depressed and hopeless with the work. As a doctor I felt quite stranded in the strange atmosphere of an elementary school, coming into contact, not so much with actual illness as with the primary conditions which produce and foster it. Dirt, neglect, improper feeding, malnutrition, insufficient clothing, suppurating ears, defective sight, verminous conditions, the impossibility of getting information from the children, or a knowledge of their home conditions, and nobody to whom one could give directions, or to help in examining the children. The only means of approaching the parents was to send an official notice that such or such a condition required treatment, and it was impossible, besides being outside my duties, to carry on any treatment at the schools. My duties began and ended with endless notifications—I felt that all this trouble was very useless unless I could get someone to help me professionally in examining the children in the classes, and then, by following up the cases, exert personal influence with the parents in the homes, and report as to home conditions."

The doctor then proceeded to say that he had at last succeeded in persuading the Education Committee to give him two nurses and that now "the nurse gives one the satisfactory feeling that *something will be done.*" (Jubilee Report. p. 233.)

In 1907, the Act for providing medical inspection of school children in England passed, and thereafter the nurse worked in closer co-operation with the physicians.

The teaching of practical hygiene to the children also became one of the important duties of the school nurses. "We have here," said one doctor, "the means of effect-

ing little less than a revolution in matters of personal
cleanliness, hygiene, and all that a proper knowledge
and care of the body involves.   Of far more importance
than as a helper to the doctor, or a treater of minor
ailments is the opportunity now afforded to the nursing profession of becoming a great educational factor
in our social organizations as *teachers of practical hygiene* in the schools and homes." (Dr. Hayward, Jubilee
Report.)

The honor of establishing school nursing in America
is due to Miss Wald, founder of the Henry Street Settlement, who in 1902, suggested the use of nurses to
supplement the work of doctors in the schools of New
York.   Medical inspection of school children had already been carried on for many years, both in New
York and other cities, but medical inspection could
only *exclude* the child, it could do nothing to prevent
the need of exclusion.   Moreover, nobody knew what became of the child during the period of exclusion.   The
assumption was that he went home and was cared for
by his mother.   But in ninety-nine cases out of one
hundred, the mother saw no need of care, when the
child, to all appearances was well, and the consequence
was that most of the children excluded from the school
for infectious condition, unless seriously ill would roam
about the streets, playing with other children, and
transmitting to them the very disease for which they had
been excluded.

In 1902, the health conditions in the New York
schools were so bad that in many of them from fifteen
to twenty children were excluded daily.   When, however, three hundred were excluded from one school in
one day the problem became acute.   What to do with
these three hundred children, and how to get them in
condition to re-enter school became a serious question.

Miss Wald, who had followed the school nursing being done in England, suggested that a nurse in the

school might help to solve the problem and offered the services of a nurse from the Settlement for one month as a demonstration of what might be done.

Miss Lina Rogers was asked to make the experiment, and at the end of the month had definitely proved the usefulness of her service.

In describing this early work Miss Rogers says:

"I selected four schools in the most crowded part of the city, which I visited daily, spending about one hour in each, after which visits were made to the homes. First of all, crude dispensaries were improvised in each school, and these were equipped each day with supplies donated by the Settlement. At the expiration of the experiment the Board of Education furnished the supplies.

"When the doctor examined the children and found it necessary to exclude a number from the others in the class room, until treatment was begun, they were turned over to the nurse. Sometimes thirty children, who under the old system would have been excluded, were taken to the little dispensary and treated, then returned to their class rooms. This treatment was kept up daily until they were cured. The diseases treated in the schools were such as ringworm, scabies, favus, impetigo, eczema and wounds of various kinds. The children with trachoma were allowed to continue school if they could present a properly stamped card showing they were attending an eye dispensary. Children with unclean heads were excluded at once with instructions that they might return as soon as the treatment was begun. Sometimes an hour was all that was lost.

"The children who had previously been excluded were visited and many were found playing on the street, filthy and grimy and spreading their skin diseases to other children. A few demonstrations in the home, with applications of soap and water and an ointment cured these conditions and the children were re-admit-

ted to school.   One child had been out nearly two terms
with a sore on her chin, and another was in school but
once during the term, because her head had never been
properly cared for.   In nearly every instance the parents
were grateful to have some one to go to them, in a
friendly way, or explain why the child could not remain
in school, if the orders were not obeyed.   Others did
not know how to relieve the conditions present and were
glad to be told.''

At the end of this experiment the New York Board
of Health, realizing the value of the nurse in the school,
appointed twelve others to assist in carrying on the
work.   These nurses are sometimes called the first
Public Health Nurses.

The value of the preventive work done by these
school nurses, quite apart from the alleviative, was inestimable.   Children with minor infectious conditions
not only were now able to remain in school with safety,
instead of being excluded, but because of the early
recognition of symptoms and rashes, epidemics of contagious diseases were prevented; and by constant instruction in habits of cleanliness and personal hygiene
the condition and health of the children greatly improved.

Other cities followed in the wake of New York.
Often the Visiting Nurse Association in a city would
inaugurate the work by lending a nurse to demonstrate
its value until the Health Department or the School
Board could be persuaded to take it over.   Gradually
it was realized that the *educative* side of the school
nurses work was perhaps its most important one.   At
first the teaching of hygiene had been more or less
didactic; and had failed to interest the children, therefore the nurse was often unable to get their co-operation.   Little by little she realized that if she was to
teach hygiene to children with any hope of lasting success she must teach it in a way that they would under-

stand, and which would interest them. And so she began to tell them stories about the "Health Fairy" and the "Old Witch of Finger Nail Cave"; kindergarten methods were used, with handkerchief and tooth-brush drills; bright posters illustrated the use of the tooth-brush, the value of good food and fresh air, and the danger from flies and mosquitos, and the children were asked to make their own posters, prizes being offered for the best. Little Mothers' Leagues were organized to teach little girls how to take care of the baby; and Health Crusades were started to teach children how to grow well and strong.

Health education in schools is becoming a great game, and children, teacher and parents are responding with interest.

But in order to carry on this work effectively the school nurse needed special training. And so special courses in school nursing were instituted, and the work became a well-recognized and attractive specialty.

At the present time there are many hundreds of school nurses in the United States. School nursing is often considered the most effective way of introducing public health nursing in a rural community; and in all cities of any importance school nursing is looked upon as one of the most important features of the whole system of public schools.

TUBERCULOSIS NURSING.

No one movement has perhaps had so definite an influence on the work of the visiting nurse as the great fight against tuberculosis. When Robert Koch discovered the tubercule bacillus in 1882, and it was found that consumption was communicable, but, also, that it was curable, it became of the first importance that those suffering with the disease should be taught how to avoid giving it to others, and how so to live as to cure them-

selves.   In this work of instruction the visiting nurse
was found to be the most valuable agent.

The care of the poor consumptive had always been
one of the duties of the district nurse.   He had been
cared for, however, with a heavy heart, because there
seemed to be no hope of doing more than merely to
make him as comfortable as possible until he died.   He
was allowed to sit by the kitchen fire, in a warm, close
room, holding his babies on his knee, kissing and car-
essing them freely, if that were his nature, and cough-
ing and expectorating with no precaution other than
that suggested by cleanliness.

Many physicians and scientists had a vague understanding of the nature and treatment of tuberculosis.
They had known for years that it could be communi-
cated from one person to another—but the knowledge
was so uncertain, the manner and cause of infection so
little understood, that the realization of its infectious
character did not penetrate to the people at large.   The
various modern methods of treating it, too, had been
practiced by many different physicians from time to
time.   As early as 1689, Richard Morton, an English
physician, had recommended fresh air treatment; Prof.
Nathaniel Bowditch in 1808, Dr. Bodington of England in 1840, Hermann Brehmer in Germany in 1856,
and many others had also advocated life in the open
air.   Dr. Dettweiler laid great emphasis on rest; and
many had recommended good food.   But the reason for
this treatment was not understood until, in 1882, Robert Koch showed to the world that a small, but virulent,
germ was the cause of all types of tuberculosis; that
this germ could be transmitted from one person to another through the expectoration of a tubercular patient,
either directly or through the medium of dust, etc.;
and finally that it could be destroyed by sunlight, boiling and other methods, and that, if the lungs were not
already too badly involved, a person suffering from the

disease could be cured by following, for a long period, a regulated life calculated to increase his resistive power.

This definite knowledge put a great responsibility on the medical profession. It now became a duty to discover all cases of tuberculosis in order to prevent its spread, and it also became necessary to find some way of procuring, for poor patients, the proper food, rest and good air required for their recovery. Tuberculosis thus became a social, as well as a medical problem, and required a duplex treatment in order to be properly controlled.

In 1887, Dr. E. U. Philip, head physician of the Victorian Hospital for Consumptives, in Edinburgh, succeeded in establishing in the heart of that city the Victorian Dispensary for Consumptives—the first special tuberculosis dispensary in the world. The effect of this institution was to afford a central place where all poor persons affected with consumption could be directed, helped and supervised. The scope of its work was a large one, and included—(a) the examination and record of patients; (b) the instruction in how to treat themselves and how not to infect others; (c) dispensing of medicine, sputum bottles, and food when necessary; (d) the visitation of patients in their own homes, more especially those confined to the house or bed, and this for the *double* purpose of treatment, and investigation into the state of the dwelling and the general condition of life and consequent risk to others in the neighborhood.

The special tuberculosis nurse, however, is an American product and owes her origin to the interest and influence of Dr. William Osler, one of the greatest physicians of the 19th century.

"Dr. Osler, at that time, (1898), Professor of Medicine at the Johns Hopkins Medical School, in Baltimore, realized that though the medical staff of this dis-

18

pensary diagnosed and treated the patients who had
come there, absolutely nothing was being done to discover their home condition, much less to improve them,
or to use the simplest form of preventive measures
with which we are today familiar. He also realized
that until this could be attempted, the tuberculosis
problem remained practically untouched." (History of
Tuberculosis Nurse—A. M. Carr.)

"The problem of tuberculosis is a home problem,"
said Dr. Osler; this meant that it must be combatted
in the home.

Early in 1899, therefore, one of the women medical
students of Johns Hopkins was appointed to follow up
the dispensary patients to their homes, to investigate
and report upon living conditions, and to teach the
patients and their families the care and precautions
necessary for the proper treatment and prevention of
the disease.   The following year, again through the initiative of Dr. Osler, the Laënnec Society of Baltimore
was established, "to systematize and stimulate the work
in tuberculosis in the hospital, and to diffuse in the
profession and public a knowledge of the disease."

Its first work was to report upon the social and domestic condition of a group of 190 cases of pulmonary
tuberculosis, the first scientific investigation ever made
of the social condition of the tuberculous poor.   (History of Tuberculosis Nurse, Carr.)

The conditions found were appalling. For the first
time the public began to suspect why tuberculosis was
so prevalent, and why a person affected with it rarely
recovered.   Patients, in the last stages of consumption,
were found living with half a dozen other people,
crowded into one or two rooms, with windows tightly
closed, and heated to suffocation, often they slept in
the same bed with one, two, and sometimes three others;
always they ate with the family, sharing the same cups,
spoons and other dishes, and often giving the baby a sip

of coffee from their own cup, or a bite of food from their fork. Was there any wonder that when one case was found, others were almost sure to follow?

Moreover, there was little hope of recovery for a patient once infected—for all the necessary elements were lacking. The medical student could indeed investigate the home condition of the patients and report to the dispensary doctors, but there was no one to follow up the case and see that these home conditions were improved; she could tell the patient that he must live in the open air, eat nourishing food, and rest; and she could leave little printed leaflets of instructions; but there was no one to see that the patient followed the instructions or to help him to obtain the good food, rest and fresh air recommended. Constant watchfulness, encouragement and help were needed if any impression was to be made in reducing tuberculosis.

In December 1903, therefore, a nurse, Miss Reiba Thelin, was appointed to take the place of the medical student, and to devote her entire time to the home care and instruction of tuberculous patients. The names of the cases to be visited were obtained from the history cards in the dispensary, and occasionally from the doctors themselves, though others resented the innovation, and would withhold a definite diagnosis of tuberculosis for fear the patient might resent the visits of the nurse. But they need not have feared that the nurse would be unwelcome. Most of the patients welcomed her as a savior, and were more than anxious to try the new treatment. The patients were necessarily mostly advanced cases, for in those days the methods of early diagnosis were limited. The duties of the nurse, too, were not clearly defined. She was expected to follow the patient to his home; to look up "lost patients," and bring them back to the dispensary; to teach the doctrine of fresh air, good food, and rest; to provide special diet in the shape of milk and eggs, when the patient was unable to obtain it himself; and not only to investigate and report upon home conditions, but to do all in her power, with the help of various relief agencies, to improve them. Besides this she was expected to give bedside care to bed-patients, and to establish the precautions necessary to avoid the infection of others.

This pioneer work took much courage, for not only were the duties vague, but it was felt that the nurse was running a certain danger of contracting the disease herself. The physicians questioned her constantly as to whether she was sleeping with open windows, weighing herself regularly, and taking extra nourishment; for they felt that she was embarking on a dangerous experiment—and worked to protect her by constant watchfulness for early symptoms.

Miss Thelin had never been a visiting nurse; she had had no instruction in social nursing, and the problems that confronted her were difficult and numerous. "I, myself often lost heart," said she, "and as one after another died I would sometimes ask myself, 'Why disturb the poor things and insist on open windows when it doesn't cure them after all?'"

The Hopkins physicians, however, took a great interest in the work and encouraged her to continue. Dr. Osler received her reports; Dr. Thayer gave her minute instructions; and "Dr. Fletcher" wrote Miss Thelin, many years later, "was my head nurse," When she was most discouraged he would cheer her by reminding her that it was the preventive work that counted most, and would say: "Remember that you are working for the *future* generations."

It was not all discouraging however. We quote from a letter recently received from Miss Thelin,—now Mrs. Reed:

"I remember one young girl of eighteen. I went to her home, in a poor section of the city, the day after the diagnosis had been made. She had scrubbed everything in her bedroom, taken her windows entirely out of the frames, and was making arrangements to follow out the fresh air treatment. Much surprised, I asked her who had told her what to do. She answered that she had read about it in the newspapers, and as soon as she heard the doctors say something about 'tuberculosis,' she came home to follow the instructions given to 'consumptives.' That little girl became well enough to resume her work in a department store, but whether it was permanent, who can say?

"Another case I remember, which shows the interest taken in the new work by medical students, nurses and lay people alike, and the co-operation that was beginning to result. A young man, Emil ——, the picture of health, came to the dispensary for a diagnosis. He complained of a continuous fever, which he had contracted, he thought, while on an engineering job in the South. He was found to be definitely tubercular, and put to bed, by the doctor's orders. He and his family were incredulous, and the bed being more than usually irksome to such an active fellow, he eagerly consented to live in a tent, if it could be managed. Everyone helped to manage it—the graduating class in medicine raised the money for the tent, the man who owned the vacant lots near Emil's home gave his permission to have it put up; the nurses contributed warm clothing, socks, mittens, woolen nightgowns; friendly hands built a wooden platform under it; and, as winter came on, put up a small stove; and his devoted mother undertook to carry his meals and nourishment out to him, so that I was able to say "Goodbye" to Emil, feeling that a step had been taken in demonstrating the out-of-doors treatment for tuberculosis."

Miss Thelin continued the work for one year, reporting all cases to Dr. Osler, and also, upon request, making out a separate report on home conditions for the

State Board of Health, for it was felt that if a direct connection could be proved between tuberculosis and poor housing that conditions might be improved. At the end of the year she resigned in order to take up work with the Henry Street Settlement, for she had realized all through the year that some training in visiting nursing would have been a great help to her, and was anxious to obtain that training.

"So much has been learned since those early days," writes Mrs. Reed, "that my efforts, viewed in retrospect, seem very feeble, but it is a great source of satisfaction to me to feel that I did help to make a beginning."

In the meantime another nurse, this time a *visiting nurse*, had been appointed to help in the undertaking.

About six months after Miss Thelin started her home instruction, a public meeting was held in Baltimore in the interest of anti-tuberculosis work, at which Dr. Osler was the principal speaker.

After giving a vivid picture of the prevalence of tuberculosis and the little that was being done to prevent its spread, Dr. Osler raised his voice, and shaking his fist at the audience cried out: "Apathy! apathy! it is apathy on the part of the public that makes it impossible to control tuberculosis!"

After the meeting was over, Mrs. Osler, who was as enthusiastic as the doctor in the anti-tuberculosis movement, hastened across the room to Miss Lent, the Superintendent of the Visiting Nurse Association of Baltimore, and said: "I have an idea. Tomorrow I shall send out letters to every person in Baltimore asking for $1.00 to help support tuberculosis nurses." She was as good as her word, and though she may not have sent a letter to "everyone in Baltimore," she did send out nauy hundreds of them, and money soon began to pour in. As soon as sufficient had been received to warrant the salary, a nurse from the staff of the Visiting Nurse

Association, Miss Nora Holman, was appointed for the special care and instruction of tubercular patients.

For six months Miss Thelin had been covering the entire city, a territory much too large to do good or intensive work. The two nurses now divided the city, Miss Holman taking the cases west of Charles Street, while Miss Thelin continued to carry on the work on the east side.

Gradually other nurses from the Visiting Nurse Association were assigned to special tuberculosis duty, and the work grew, until its size and importance were almost too great to be longer carried by private enterprise.

In 1910, the entire tuberculosis work was taken over by the city Board of Health, and Miss Ellen La Mott appointed as Superintendent of a large staff of special visiting nurses.

The city was divided into districts with one nurse in each district, and each nurse was expected to be responsible for the care of every case of tuberculosis in her district. Tuberculosis dispensaries were opened in different parts of the city, and a systematic method of handling the whole problem was inaugurated.

Other cities quickly followed the example set by Baltimore. In 1904, Cleveland had opened one of the first social dispensaries in the country devoted to the problem of tuberculosis. All during the Summer months Miss Elizabeth Upjohn, one of the nurses belonging to the Cleveland Visiting Nurse Association, had been searching through the city for cases of tuberculosis.[1] By October a large number had been located,

[1] In 1907 Miss Upjohn left Cleveland to organize the tuberculosis visiting nursing of the Out-Patient Department of the Boston Consumptives' Hospital, the first piece of municipal tuberculosis visiting nursing in the country. In 1908 she effected an affiliation between the nursing staff and the Boston School for Social Workers, which was one of the earliest attempts to procure more thorough social training for the public health nurse.

and the dispensary was opened under the auspices of the Medical College of Western Reserve University and the Visiting Nurses Association. In the following year the Anti-Tuberculosis League of Cleveland was organized, and for a number of years this League, with the co-operation of the Medical College, the Visiting Nurse Association, the Associated Charities, and various other local charity organizations, carried on all the anti-tuberculosis work in the city. In 1910, however, a Bureau of Tuberculosis was established and the city took over the entire problem.

Branch dispensaries were opened and a large staff of visiting nurses engaged by the Department of Health to devote themselves to the prophylactic and instructive work among tuberculous patients, bed cases being turned over to the Visiting Nurse Association for bedside care.

The organization of the National Association for the Study and Prevention of Tuberculosis in 1904, had greatly quickened the interest in, and the fight against, tuberculosis all over the country. Between 1895 and 1908, New York City had opened so many different tuberculosis clinics, some private, some municipal, and there was such duplication and overlapping of effort, that it was found necessary to organize an Association of Tuberculosis Clinics in order to co-ordinate and standardize their work. In 1910 the New York Department of Health greatly enlarged its staff of tuberculosis nurses, and became practically responsible for the home supervision of every registered case of tuberculosis in the city under the care of a private physician.

In Chicago the anti-tuberculosis nursing work was started in 1903, by a committee on tuberculosis under the auspices of the Visiting Nurse Association, and later taken over by the Chicago Tuberculosis Institute. The program of the Institute was very wide and comprehensive and included the operation of numerous dispensaries and home visiting by a large staff of special nurses. In 1910, the municipality took over the dispensaries and the tuberculosis visiting nurses, leaving the Institute to continue its activities as "an educational institution for the collection and dissemination of exact knowledge in regard to the causes, prevention and cure of tuberculosis."

But it would be impossible to continue enumerating the various organizations formed to combat the great white plague. In many places the work was inaugurated by the visiting nurse association and the nurse became the accepted agent for the home work. The fight became universal, cities and states took it up; organizations supported by the public funds of city, county or state were formed, and the problem became one for Departments of Health, rather than for private associations. Large staffs of special tuberculosis nurses were employed to visit and instruct the patients, or to help in the tuberculosis dispensaries.

The work was peculiarly *instructive* and *social;* bedside nursing was done by few, the bed-ridden patients usually being cared for by the general district nurse, or, where possible, placed in a hospital or sanitarium.

The prevention of infection and the care of the *public health* became the prime duty of the tuberculosis nurse—she had reached the goal to which Florence Nightingale had pointed, she was working for the health of the nation; she was already a *Public Health Nurse.*

CHAPTER XIX

SPECIALIZED VISITING NURSING,(continued)

THE BABY WELFARE NURSE.

The care of the mother and child is as old as the human race. We have seen how in the early centuries there were seven houses in Alexandria where poor lying-in-women could receive care and attention; and later there were established throughout Europe many foundlings homes, where poor abandoned infants were lovingly cared for under the supervision of the church.

Up to the nineteenth century, however, no thought was given to the care of infants as a class, and that a large proportion of all the children born should die before they reached the age of one year was accepted ·as inevitable. The death rate of infants must, indeed, have been appalling, and only the fact that large families were the rule saved the world from a definite decrease in population. It is said of Queen Anne of England that at the time of her death, in 1714, she had no living children, and yet she had borne her husband some eighteen or nineteen, all of whom had died in infancy, except one, who lived to the age of eleven. If such conditions were possible in the royal family, what must they have been among the poor and ignorant?

Gradually, however, this frightful loss of infant life began to attract the attention of scientists and humanitarians. The first book on the subject was written by an English physician, Dr. John Bunnel Davis, in 1817, under the heavy title: "A Cursory Enquiry into Some of the Principal Causes of Mortality Among Children, with a View to Assist in Ameliorating the State of the

Rising Generation in Health, Morals and Happiness."

This book showed a careful study of the problem of infant mortality, and a good understanding of the general principles underlying its remedy; especially did Dr. Davis advocate maternal nursing. In 1816, he established the first special dispensary for children in London, and suggested the value of home visiting and follow-up work to instruct mothers and report conditions.

"If benevolent ladies," he said, "could be prevailed upon to form district committees to visit and inspect the health of the sick, indigent children, much practical good would result from a medical and moral point of view."

Nothing definite was done, however, for many years, although, after district nursing was established in 1859, the care of maternity cases and small children always formed a large part of the nurse's work, and the development of sanitary science and a better understanding of children's diseases did something toward reducing the loss of infant life.

The first special care of poor babies in modern times was that given by the *créche*—a kind of day nursery—established in 1844 by Marbeau, Mayor of the First Arrondissement of Paris.

"By the aid of private subscriptions a room was secured in a poor district, twelve willow cradles were installed, and the whole placed in charge of a nurse, while a doctor visited the place daily." (Address by L. Emmett Holt, M. D. 1913, Report of Am. Assoc. for the Prevention of Infant Mortality.)

This idea was widely copied all over Europe, but although it did much to arouse public interest in the welfare of infants, it did nothing to really improve their conditions as a class, or to decrease the rate of their mortality.

The next effort, also in Paris, was the establishment

in 1876, of the "Societé d' Allaitment Maternelle," a society for nursing mothers, in which they sought to save the child by caring for the mother—a first attempt at prenatal care and after observation.

"Before confinement, houses or refugees were opened, where poor and destitute women could be sheltered for a few weeks until they were sent to maternity hospitals; and assistance, or partial support, was given to nursing mothers during the first year to make breast feeding possible. This work was supplemented by regular monthly observation of their infants, and visits by social workers." (Holt-Report of 1913.)

These efforts, however, were of little value in solving the great problem of infant mortality. It was clear that the greatest factor in preserving the health of the infant lay in its feeding. If the mother was unable to give it breast milk, then a pure supply of cows' milk should be made available for even the poorest infant. This led to the establishment, in 1889, of the first two milk stations for the distribution of clean milk to the poor, one being opened in New York at the Eastern Dispensary, and the other in the same year in Hamburg, Germany. The milk, however, was for sick babies only—the well babies were still left to struggle on with impure, dirty milk until they, too, fell ill.

All this work was merely preparatory, and did little real good, if not positive harm. To be sure the sick baby received good milk and might recover, but as soon as it was well it was returned to the poor milk— and its last state was worse than its first. Moreover, the free distribution of milk was harmful, as it encouraged weaning, and ran the danger of pauperizing the otherwise independent poor.

These first efforts did, however, focus public attention on the need of mother and child, and led to the formation of the two great organizations which may be said to have laid the foundation for the whole modern movement of child welfare.

These two organizations were the *Consultation de Nourissons,* established in Paris by Budin, in 1892, and the opening of the *Goutte de Lait* in the same city by Dufour in 1894. The first was started in connection with a maternity hospital, thus giving contact with the infant from time of birth. After the mother was discharged the child was brought back regularly for weighing, observation and examination for a period of two years, the mother meanwhile being encouraged to nurse it, and when that was impossible, instructed in the proper way to prepare bottle-feeding.

The Goutte de Lait, opened two years later, was for the purpose of preparing artificial feeding according to formula, under medical supervision, and distributing it, free where necessary, to the poor.

These two forms of prophylactic work, namely the continuous observation of all babies, sick or well, during the first year or two of their life; and the supplying of properly modified milk to those who needed it,—laid the foundation for the modern campaign of prevention in the battle against infant mortality.

In America, however, the milk station, without any general instruction in the homes, still held the field in infant welfare work. The effort to save child life and health appealed to everyone, and many milk station were opened. In 1892, Nathan Straus organized a very definite service for the distribution of pasteurized milk in New York City; in 1899 the Milk Fund Association was formed in Cleveland; and in 1902 the Henry Street Settlement opened its Milk Dispensary. These, and many other like charities, were started in various cities, and milk stations became the accepted way of dealing with the problem. Physicians were usually connected with the undertaking, and sometimes

a nurse was engaged to visit in the homes, but the follow-up work lagged, and special baby nursing was not
organized.

To be sure the general visiting nurse was devoting
much of her time in the district to the care of mothers
and babies, and was doing her utmost to teach the ignorant mother how to care for her child.   Also, in the
summer of 1902, a few special nurses, under the supervision of Dr. Josephine Baker, were sent out to visit
sick babies in the tenement district of New York City;
and in the following summer nurses were sent to visit
every baby whose birth was registered between August
11, 1902, and June 30, 1903, thus watching those infants passing through their first precarious summer,
but both these undertakings were carried on only during the summer months.

In July, 1906, however, a new type of Infants'
Clinic was opened in Cleveland, through the co-operation of the Visiting Nurse Association and the Milk
Fund Association, the object of which was to give continuous attention to babies the year round; to promote breast feeding; to supply good milk to mothers
for their own modification, according to a physician's
direction; to control both by the regular visits of nurses
in the homes, and to aid in improving any conditions
detrimental to the health of the child.   This Clinic,
which in the following autumn was reorganized under
the name of the Babies' Dispensary of Cleveland, was
modeled after the *Säuglings-fuergestellen* in Berlin, and
was the first of its kind in the country.

Like the *Consultation de Nourissons* of Budin, it
aimed to have the mothers bring their babies, even
though well, regularly to the Dispensary for at least
fifteen months, to be weighed and examined by a physician, who would then give the proper advice as to their
care and feeding.

Nurses were supposed to visit these babies in their

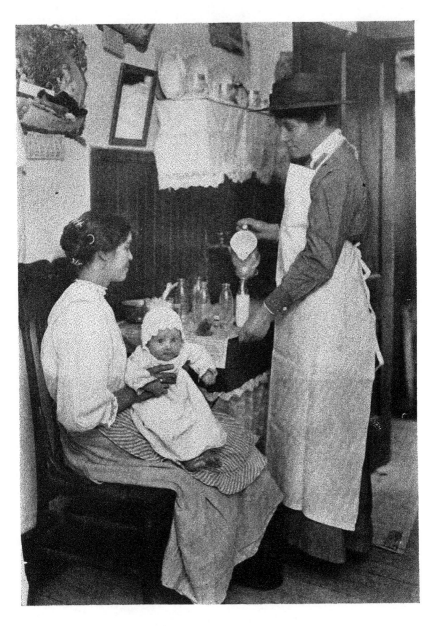

THE BABY WELFARE NURSE.

Showing the mother how to prepare the baby's milk.
(Courtesy of the Baby Welfare Association, Chicago, Illinois.)

homes every two or three weeks, to encourage the mothers in following out the doctor's advice, and to teach them, when necessary, how to modify the milk according to formula.

The work done by this dispensary was epoch-making and was copied throughout the country. As it increased branch dispensaries for well babies were opened in various parts of the city, where mothers could more easily bring their children for the regular weighing and instruction, the central dispensary being used for the care of sick babies only. The work done by the nurses, too, set a new standard for baby welfare—for the first time in history a group of specially trained nurses were giving their entire time to the instruction of mothers in the proper care of their babies. These nurses worked under the direct surveillance of the Medical Director of the Dispensary, Dr. H. J. Gerstenberger, and the able superintendence of Miss Harriet L. Leete, a visiting nurse of forceful personality, who has since earned an international reputation in infant welfare work both in this country and in France.

Little by little the educative possibilities connected with infant welfare work were more and more stressed throughout the country, and the number of visiting nurses employed in this special branch of the work increased from year to year, the home instruction of the mother being looked upon as essential in any effective plan.

In 1908, a great step forward was taken when the New York Department of Health formed the Division of Child Hygiene—the first in the country. This made the care of the child a public concern, and not only enlarged the scope of the work, but gave the nurses more power and authority. It was felt that to successfully combat infant mortality one of the most important factors was the visits of trained nurses to the homes of ignorant mothers as soon after the birth of the child as possible. A large staff of visiting nurses was, therefore, placed under the Division of Child Hygiene, the city divided into eighty-nine districts, and an effort made to have a nurse visit all the new born and sick infants in the poor part of the city.

In spite of all their efforts, however, the rate of infant mortality continued distressingly great. It was estimated that 300,000 deaths of children under one year of age, occurred annually in the United States, and that at least one-half of them were preventable. This was a national problem and could only be properly coped with by a united effort on the part of physicians, nurses and lay people throughout the entire country.

The first distinctive national call to study this problem was made by the American Academy of Medicine at its annual meeting held in Chicago in June, 1908. This was followed by a special conference on the subject held in New Haven in November 1909, at which time the American Association for the Study and Prevention of Infant Mortality was organized, Dr. J. H. Mason Knox, Jr., being elected President, and Miss Gertrude Knipp engaged as executive secretary. The Advisory Committee appointed at the first meeting was composed of physicians, nurses, social workers, and lay people, thus making it the concern of all. The express object of the Association was primarily to direct public attention to the problem, and to bring together the experience of various social agencies dealing with it. The formation of a national society gave a great impetus to the whole subject of child welfare, though the part that the visiting nurse might play in the program did not at once receive attention. During the first year there was no section on nursing, though at the opening meeting in New Haven, Miss Wald in her paper on "The District Nurse's Contribution to the Reduction of Infant Mortality" had called the attention of those present to the value of the visiting nurse in the work and what she was already doing.

"The district nurse is called most frequently for the sick children," said she, "and in the service with which I am identified, two-thirds of the patients, roughly speaking, are infants or children."

At the first annual meeting of the Association, however, a section on Nursing and Social Work was organized, and at the second annual meeting, 1911, Miss Ahrens of Chicago gave what was probably the first paper ever given on the subject of specialized visiting nurse work for babies.

At this meeting a marked advance in the appreciation of the nurses' service was noticeable. Miss Wald in her opening remarks pointed out the responsibility of nurses and social workers in the campaign for the preservation of children, and for the first time pointed out also that a baby welfare nurse was of necessity a social worker.

"Visiting nurses and social workers are, or should be, synonymous terms," said she, "but their training has been distinct,—all nurses and all social workers who are not nurses agree upon the identity of their ultimate purpose, and that their relationship upon the field should be intimate, co-ordinated, and perfectly harmonious. One of the valuable contributions of the trained nurse to medical and social progress is her ability to apply the scientific principles of infant nurture, and the maintenance of health. In her hands have been placed the final responsibility of education in the home, and presenting in simplest form the conclusions of the men and women of science. Humble and important has been her function. She has a broad field and close, first-hand opportunity for observation, which should and does make her testimony of incalculable value." (Opening remarks—Miss Wald—Report of Am. Assoc. for Preventing Infant Mortality, 1911.)

19

Miss Ahrens followed with the paper we have already alluded to. In it she outlined the duties of these specialized nurses in connection with milk stations and babies' dispensaries, and ended by saying: "The nursing profession must see to it that the nurses are made competent to assume the responsibility which is theirs in the campaign to conserve infant life."

The physicians also laid great stress on the necessity of having nurses follow the babies to their homes. "I am sure," said Dr. Knox, "we could not do a thing without the nurse and the home instruction on the part of the nurses." And then he added, "I would specialize a little further and suggest that the care of infants in homes is best done not by the regular visiting nurse, but by a special nurse who gives her whole time to babies and very young children, especially in connection with the milk stations and giving instructions to nursing mothers."

While Dr. Gerstenberger, in speaking of the fundamental assistance of the nurse in a prophylactic dispensary, and of what her qualifications should be, said: "Of course she must be a visiting nurse,—still better is it if she has had a training in the district for a year or so before she enters the service of a babies' dispensary,—and three times better is it for the work if she has had a thorough training in social work previous to her admittance to the staff. She must have the ability and training to ferret out the true material circumstances of the family, whether the parents are, in case of illness of the child, able to afford the service of a private physician, or whether they are, as they constantly claim, too poor. Besides determining the financial standing of the family, it is the duty of the nurse to teach the mothers how to carry out the doctor's orders; to supervise her at regular intervals, at least every two to four weeks until the baby is twelve to fifteen months old; and to encourage her to continue obeying the directions of the physicians with the idea of preventing illness in her infant." (How to Start a Prophylactic Babies' Dispensary. By Dr. H. L. Gerstenberger,—Public Health Nurse Quarterly, July, 1911.)

And so again we see a group of special visiting nurses, whose work, like that of the tuberculosis nurses, was largely, if not entirely, instructive and preventive, and whose chief concern was the preservation of the public health, and again we see the words *Visiting Nurse* and *Public Health* in juxaposition.

It was soon seen that child welfare included many activities beside the care of the child up to the age of one or two years. It included the care of the mother before the birth of the baby, or prenatal work; it concerned itself very much with the problem of midwifery, and a wide campaign was made against the untrained midwife; it had to do with blindness, and special baby nurses devoted themselves to preventing blindness among infants; and finally it took up the supervision of the child of pre-school age.

The Association for the Prevention of Infant Mortality changed its name to the American Child Hygiene Association, and the field of its labors is growing ever wider and more inclusive, but in all its labors the visiting nurse still plays one of the most important rôles.

In 1912 a Children's Bureau was opened by the Federal Government, whose chief work consists in investigating and reporting upon all matters pertaining to the welfare of children, and in studying and comparing the work done in various communities, to decide the best way in which to attack any given problem on the subject.

The Bureau does not keep a staff of visiting nurses, nevertheless the Public Health Nurse has frequently assisted in the various investigations carried on by the

Government and is closely concerned with all its work.

Industrial nursing is one of the newest forms of specialized public health nursing. So new, in fact, that even yet there are many questions concerning its practice over which there is much controversy. Up to 1900 there were, so far as is known, only three nurses employed in industry in this country; the first, engaged by the Vermont Marble Co. in 1895, to visit and nurse its sick employees; the second, in 1897, by the Employees' Benefit Association of John Wanamaker's large department store in New York City; and the third, in 1899, by Frederic Loeser in his department store in Brooklyn, N. Y.

These three pioneer attempts at industrial nursing were each a separate and independent undertaking, started in different ways, and following different methods of work; though all alike were for the benefit of the sick employee, and all were carried on by nurses.

The Vermont Marble Co. engaged its nurse primarily to visit the homes of its sick employees and to give nursing care and first aid to them and their families. In the following year they opened a hospital, and the visiting nursing progressed along purely medical and nursing lines.

The John Wanamaker Nurse, Miss Anna B. Duncan, was first engaged by the Employees' Benefit Association of that company to visit its sick members and to see that its funds were justly distributed. It was felt that a nurse would be better able than a layman to judge as to the condition of the patient, and his right to the sick benefit money.

Miss Duncan, however, soon perceived that there was much more to do than merely to visit the sick employee and report as to his condition.

"She found that she could best be of service by giving first aid when needed; by seeing that the sick and injured had prompt and suitable medical and nursing care; by following up to see that the doctor's orders were carried out; that they returned to the doctor when necessary; that they did not return to work before being able to do so, or while in a condition to be a menace to their associates; and that financial anxieties and family cares did not retard recovery." (The Visiting Nurse in Industrial Welfare Work,—By Florence S. Wright—The Public Health Nurse, Jan. 1917.)

In other words Miss Duncan found that industrial nursing was something more than bedside nursing or investigation. It was nursing work and social work combined—and specialized social work at that.

If it was of importance to nurse the employee when ill, it was of still greater importance to prevent him from becoming ill—to see that slight injuries were attended to at once; that the sanitary condition of the plant where he worked was good; that the worker was protected from all undue hazard; and that the first symptoms of disease should be noticed to prevent future disability. She should know something of factory laws, and a great deal about sanitation, and should make a special study of the hazards of industry.

During the first ten years of the 20th century the growth of the movement was slow; by 1910 there were only 66 firms employing graduate nurses, though there were many others employing practical nurses or social workers to carry out their various forms of welfare work.

In the first year of the war, 1914, sixty new firms adopted the service. In 1916 and 1917 the Federal Government was responsible for stimulating the work in shipyards, also in factories and mills having contracts for war material, and a great impetus was given to the movement. (Industrial Nursing by Yssabella Waters—the Public Health Nurse, Sept. 1919.)

So rapid was its growth that by 1919 there were said
to be 1213 graduate nurses doing industrial nursing
in the United States, for 871 industries.

This work was of various kinds; sometimes it was
simple visiting nursing among the employees of the
company; sometimes it was first aid and dispensary
work, with or without a physician; sometimes it was
social service work of various kinds; sometimes it was
sanitary inspection and the teaching of hygiene; and
sometimes it was a combination of all four.

Some employers called it industrial welfare; others
called it industrial nursing; others again called it visiting nursing, though limiting it to their own employees.
The name and the work varied according to the wish
of the employer or the attitude of the nurse.

In January 1916, Miss Ella Phillips Crandall, in an
address given before a group of welfare managers and
social workers, had said:

"I have been asked to define industrial welfare work
tonight, but, after careful consideration for twenty-four
hours, I do not hesitate to say that it is impossible to
do so. It is absolutely nebulous as yet."

If that were true of industrial welfare in general,
how much more so of the work of the industrial nurse.

She then went on, however, to designate the three
rather definite lines of activity which industrial welfare
usually followed.

"*First,* sanitation of plants, including heating, lighting, ventilation, water supply, toilet and lavatory facilities, proper and adequate janitor service, individual
cups and towels, and many other similar provisions.

"*Second,* health and hygiene of employees, which includes hot lunches, rest rooms, hospitals, dispensaries,
medical examinations and treatment, nursing care,
health education and first aid classes, gymnasium, seats
for women, consideration of bonus and other speed-

ing-up systems in relation to their effects on accidents and inefficiency due to nervous strain.

"*Third,* Social service for employees, including recreation, vacation homes, education, relief and general fitting of the man to the job." (Industrial Welfare— E. P. Crandall—Pub. Health Nurse, April 1916.)

It will be seen from this outline that the trained nurse, especially (and perhaps only) if she has already had some social training, would be the most effective agent to carry on the work. Almost all of it has to do with the health of the employee; it is preventive nursing; it endeavors through sanitation, medical inspection, first aid, and proper recreation to preserve the health of the individual, and therefore becomes a branch of public health nursing. As such it is work for a nurse.

The industrial world is slowly but surely adopting that point of view. The number of concerns calling for nurses to work in their welfare departments continues to increase, and the number of nurses taking up industrial nursing, to multiply.

The variety of this work is still endless, but certain standards are now recognized, and certain principles governing its practice are slowly emerging.

In 1917 Miss Florence Wright, herself an experienced industrial nurse, said: "The nurse in industry is still on trial."

Perhaps even now, in 1922, she is still on trial, but if so she is surely daily proving herself equal to the task, and has definitely joined the great army of Public Health Nurses who are working to prevent disease and to better social conditions.

RURAL NURSING.

Rural nursing can hardly be called a "specialty," inasmuch as it follows no one special line of activity; on the other hand, the large number of rural nurses now working throughout the country districts, from the lonely mountains of North Carolina to the wide plains of Montana, and from the green farm land of central New York to the dry table land of New Mexico, form a distinctive and special group, and the problems they are called upon to solve are peculiar to rural work, and rural conditions.

We who live in cities and see the country only from a train window, or during a summer vacation, do not realize the terrible, unsanitary conditions which often lie behind the quaint farm buildings, nestling beneath the spreading elms. We see the "barefoot boy with cheek of tan" and think of him as a sturdy urchin whose life is cast 'midst healthful surroundings, little dreaming that half his life is perhaps spent in a badly ventilated, badly lighted school room, where the desks are so low and the seats so badly arranged that he stands a great chance of growing up with bowed shoulders and cramped chest.

It is an astounding fact, brought out by the physical examination of thousands of soldier boys, that the country lad is less enduring, more prone to preventable physical disability, than his city brothers. In certain states having a large rural population, the death rate from tuberculosis is greater than in many cities, and typhoid fever may now be looked upon as a *rural disease.*

Over wide stretches of our beautiful land, rural sanitation has been utterly neglected, and the farmer's wife, though with plenty of eggs and milk and fresh vegetables at hand, still feeds the family on salt-pork and fried potatoes.

Strange to say, while city slums were receiving careful attention, and sanitarians, physicians, and visiting nurses were battling with the harmful conditions found in our large industrial centers, practically nothing had been done for the rural population. Rural health was unconsidered, medical attention in the country hard to procure, and rural nursing utterly lacking.

The first attempt to establish a visiting nurse service for a rural district was started by Miss Ellen Morris Wood in Westchester County, New York.

After her graduation from Johns Hopkins Training School in 1896, Miss Wood devoted herself for some time to the care and relief of the sick in the vicinity of her home at Mt. Kisco. When the Spanish-American war broke out, she volunteered for war service, but after the period of her enlistment ended returned home to take up her former duties. Her health, however, never robust, had suffered from the strain and hardship of military life, and shortly after her return she contracted typhoid fever from which she died.

Her work, however, had proved of such great value to the community that after her death it was continued as a memorial of what she had done, and was finally organized as the "District Nursing Association of Westchester County." The first nurse had her headquarters at Mt. Kisco, but worked also in all the nearby villages and intervening countryside.

As the work increased, other nurses were engaged and substations opened up in other villages—Thus was organized the first purely rural visiting nursing association in this country.

Another pioneer effort at rural nursing was started in Connecticut, in 1906, by a resident of Salisbury township, who had seen the work carried on by the Henry Street Settlement and realized how helpful such nursing service would be for her neighbors among the hills and lakes which surrounded her home in that historical and picturesque old township.

So little was the work understood, however, that

"When the nurse arrived no one knew, except in a vague way, what she was to do; even the doctors were without light on the subject."—(Rural Nursing—Henrietta Van Cleft—Public Health Nurse, April 1911.) The District covered by the nurse consisted of three villages, Salisbury, Lakeville and Ore Hill, with the surrounding country. Lakeville and Salisbury contained the homes of many people of means; Ore Hill was a mining village, where the workers were largely Irish, Italian and Polish. At first it was thought that the services of the nurse should be only for the poor, but when well-to-do people began to beg for her, and it began to be seen that a rural nurse should be at the service of the whole community, the well-to-do were visited on a pay basis. These fees were used for running expenses, and by 1910, almost paid the actual cost.

Still another effort to bring nursing service to the neglected and isolated people of the country side, was that inaugurated by Miss Lydia Holman in the mountain districts of North Carolina. Her work has been one of the most beautiful and self-sacrificing of any in the land.

Let us give the account of its beginning in her own words:

"In 1900 a call came to Philadelphia for a nurse who could be trusted with the full responsibility of a typhoid fever case. The place was thirty miles from a railroad station or a regular physician, drugs, etc. It was in a forest, and I received orders to take supplies. The patient, an educated woman of means, was extremely ill in her rough summer home in the mountains at Ledger, North Carolina. . . . I found that I had to be doctor, nurse, cook, housemaid, etc. Fortunately, in six weeks the patient was going about the place recovered. The mountain people were much impressed by this recovery from typhoid fever, for in these isolated communities typhoid is generally fatal. . . . The curiosity and interest of the people were thoroughly aroused, and in a short time many were coming to the house to receive treatment for every conceivable ill.

"In a few months, then, I acquired a fair knowledge of the living, health, industrial and economic conditions of these people. At least enough to disturb my equilibrium. My work took me back to the city slums, but the equilibrium would not be readjusted. The mountain folks, in their terrible isolation and almost changeless lives, from birth to death; the hardships and uncertain chances of motherhood and babyhood; the complaining mothers, many of whom must needs be invalids all their lives, because there was no way to give them hospital treatment; so many sick and deformed babies and children for the same reason; and so many mothers dying of puerperal fever and often butchery in child birth, because these isolated rural communities rarely have good physicians and nurses, and often not even indifferent ones!

"I left the city slums and returned to the mountains."

(Report Holman Assoc. 1911).

For eleven years Miss Holman worked alone, trying to meet the ever-increasing demand for her services. The work soon expanded far beyond the capacity of one woman, be she ever so faithful, and Miss Holman realized that unless she could secure financial aid and more nurses to help carry on the work that her effort to save the people would be fruitless. She returned to Baltimore, and told her friends about the mountain people, of their needs, and of her own desires. The result was the formation of the "Holman Association for the Promotion of Rural Nursing, Hygiene and Social Service."

The Association is still carrying on a beautiful piece of work for "Our Own People"—for the mountaineers of North Carolina and Kentucky are of pure Anglo-Saxon stock, and though ignorant and backward because of their isolation, are the descendants of the early settlers of this country.

RED CROSS TOWN AND COUNTY NURSING SERVICE.

Rural nursing progressed but slowly, however.   With the three exceptions just mentioned, and a few other scattered efforts in various parts of the country, there was practically no nursing service available for the great mass of people living on the farms or in lonely country districts of our great land.

At the second annual meeting of the Association for the Prevention of Infant Mortality, held in 1911, Miss Crandall in an address on "Rural Problems," after dilating on the terrible conditions found in rural districts, on the prevalence of tuberculosis, hook worm, fevers, and worse than all, the frightful conditions attending women in childbirth and the great loss of infant life, compared our indifference in the matter to the attitude of Great Britain, Canada and Australia in providing a nation-wide nursing service for their rural populations.   And then she adds:—

"Why should not our National Red Cross Society, with all its splendid organization and resources, support, direct and operate such a national service during the intervals of time in which there is no need for its emergency duty?"

In 1912, the Red Cross did indeed undertake to establish a nursing service for rural districts, which should provide nurses for the sick, carry instructions in sanitation and hygiene into the homes of the people, and endeavor to improve living conditions in the little villages, and on the lonely farms of the countryside.

The organization of this Red Cross Rural Nursing Service was made possible by a generous gift of $100,000 from Mr. Jacob H. Schiff, and another of $1000 annually from Mrs. Whitelaw Reid, both secured through the devoted efforts of Miss Wald, (Survey—Jan. 18, 1913.)

This money was to be used for administrative and

supervisory expenses, but the salaries of the nurses were to be paid for by the communities which they served.

Miss Fannie Clement was appointed superintendent, and headquarters opened in Washington, D. C. In the following year the name was changed from Rural Nursing Service, to Town and Country Nursing Service, in order to include small towns where no visiting service was found.

The effort met a great need. Nevertheless, it grew but slowly. Many communities, with the inherent American dislike of national supervision over what they considered home affairs, hestitated to call in the aid of the National Red Cross; others could not raise the money for the nurse's salary; and up to 1915, not more than forty or fifty Red Cross public health nurses were employed throughout the whole country. (Report by Miss Clement—Public Health Nurse, Oct. 1915, p. 21.)

By January 1918, the number had increased to ninety-seven. (Town and Country Service, Red Cross Bulletin, January 1918.)

This number however did not represent the whole significance of the work.

The Red Cross had rendered a great service to the cause of public health nursing, first by making it available to many rural communities, where the people, of themselves, would otherwise have been unable to establish it; and, secondly, by insisting that this nursing service should always conform to the highest standard. The theory of the Red Cross was, that only the best equipped public health nurses were good enough for rural work, and it insisted always that before beginning the work a nurse must not only come up to the regular standard set for all Red Cross nurses, but must also have had some experience or special training in public health nursing.

Although this effort did not at first assume the

proportion generally anticipated, the need of rural nursing had been brought to the attention of the public, and gradually State Departments of Health, county authorities, and other local organizations began to employ rural nurses. Laws were enacted in many states, some making the employment of such nurses mandatory, others, permissive, and the number quickly grew.

After the war of 1914–1918, had ended, the Red Cross, desirous of utilizing its great organization, and the interest and enthusiasm of the many men and women formerly enrolled in its war work, decided to organize a country-wide program for public health activities. In 1918, the Town and Country Nursing Service had been reorganized into a Bureau of Public Health Nursing, under the Department of Nursing, Miss Mary S. Gardner as Director, and with Miss Elizabeth Fox a Johns Hopkins graduate as Associate Director. A few months later Miss Gardner resigned and Miss Fox became Director of the Bureau.

The war being over and war activities having ceased, the Red Cross chapters throughout the land were urged to interest themselves in establishing public health nursing in their midst. In this way a great impetus was given to the service, and the number of Red Cross public health nurses increased by leaps and bounds. Just before leaving for Europe on the tour of inspection from which it was destined she should never return, Miss Jane Delano, Director of the Department of Nursing of the Red Cross, wrote:—"One of the first things in the peace program of the Red Cross will be the further development of public health nursing—With the return to civilian communities of about 20,000 graduate nurses released from military duty we hope to extend greatly the town and country nursing service of the Red Cross, and interest nurses in public health activities, so that skilled professional nursing will be available to even the most remote parts of the country."

The program has been carried out with enthusiasm, and although there is still need for more rural work we can at least feel that a splendid start has been made, and that it is not confined to one part of the country only, but extends from east to west, and is found in the most lonely and remote corners of our great land. There are at present (1921) about 1300 public health nurses connected with the Red Cross. In some cases the community supports the work, in others the funds of the Red Cross are used merely to start it. The plan is, that as soon as a community understands its responsibility in the matter, and is able to support the work itself, that the Red Cross will withdraw its funds and surveillance and leave the work to local supervision.

Rural nursing is a combination of all the specialties. It often begins with school work, because that is the easiest road to the home. Once in the home, maternity nursing and child welfare occupy much time, because the need is so pressing. But it cannot end there; the tuberculous son must be taught how to care for himself and protect the family; the father must be made to feel that sanitation in the home is as essential as sanitation in the dairy; and the chronic heart case must be cared for as well as the acute pneumonia. It is a ministry of far-reaching beneficence, and requires a broad understanding.

An ideal rural nurse must needs be a school nurse, a baby nurse, a tuberculosis nurse, and a general visiting nurse; she must know much of rural sanitation and have a good understanding of rural possibilities. She must be strong, for transportation is difficult, and she has often to encounter great difficulties in order to reach her patient; she must be tactful, for country people are peculiarly independent and sensitive; she must be able to co-operate with country doctors, village officials, school and county authorities; and, finally, she should have a real sympathy with rural people in their isolation and ignorance, for only so can she be one with them, and thus accomplish the end in view.

METROPOLITAN NURSING, 1909.

Another type of public health nursing, which, like that of the Red Cross is general in character but carried on under a special administration, is the visiting nursing for the Industrial policy holders of the Metropolitan Life Insurance Company.

In June 1909, at the suggestion of Miss Lillian D. Wald, the Metropolitan Life Insurance Company organized a Visiting Nurse Department, and entered into an agreement with the Henry Street Settlement in New York City, whereby the latter was to furnish the services of its visiting nurses to the company's Industrial policy-holders in a limited section of the Borough of Manhattan.

After three month's trial, the service having proved eminently satisfactory, it was extended to other parts of the city. Two months later it was installed in Baltimore, Md., and in Washington, D. C. By the end of 1909 Boston, Buffalo, Chicago, Cincinnati, Cleveland, Dover, Harrisburg, Philadelphia, St. Louis, Trenton and Worcester were given the privilege of the Service. In 1910 it was installed in Montreal, Canada.

At the close of 1909, there were fourteen of these Metropolitan nursing centers; by 1912, there were 589; and at the present time (1921) there are 1222. Wherever possible the company contracts with the local Visiting Nurse Association to furnish the nursing service at a certain rate per patient; where that is impossible it installs its own nurses, which are under the supervision of its field supervisors. At the present time there are 887 visiting nurse associations whose nurses are carrying on this work, besides 338 individual nurses working alone for the Metropolitan company.

The Nursing Service, which is part of the welfare division under the direction of Dr. Lee K. Frankel and Alexander Fleisher,—is directly under the Superintendent of nursing, Miss Matilda Johnson, who is responsible for its efficient working. She receives reports from the various nursing centers, and visits the larger nursing centers from time to time. There is an assistant superintendent of nursing who performs all the duties generally attached to this office. In addition, there are at the Home Office, two nurses who make professional reviews of the reports submitted by the various nurses in the field, and a clerical force, thirty-five in number. There are also five field supervisors who spend practically their entire time visiting the various nursing centers.

The territory in which the Metropolitan Visiting Nurse Service is established includes the United States and Canada. It is divided into nursing centers. These are towns from which the surrounding districts are worked by the nurses.

The field supervisors already mentioned have the oversight of the several nursing centers in their territories.

The nurses in the various centers perform the usual duties of a visiting nurse in the homes of the policy-holders where there is sickness. There were 290,894 Metropolitan cases in 1920 to which 1,496,109 visits were made. Very careful reports of these cases are made and mailed monthly to the Home Office where they are carefully studied, and from which valuable statistics are constantly being drawn—in fact the Metropolitan Life Insurance Company has contributed more than any other one factor to the standardizing of reports of visiting nursing throughout the country, and to giving them a form from which morbidity statistics can be readily deducted.

20

The Visiting Nurse Service of the Metropolitan has an unique opportunity to perform a widely extended service, owing to the weekly entrance of its agents into the homes of policy-holders having Industrial Insurance. Being in weekly touch with families so insured, these agents learn of illness in their homes promptly and discover cases which would not otherwise be found.

While not part of the official organization of the Visiting Nurse Service these agents are really the first link between a sick policy-holder and the nurse. It is their duty to report such cases as come to their attention to the nurse, and to assist her with such personal history of the family as will help her to work most effectively. They might well be called the "Scouts of the Visiting Nurse Service."

The Welfare or Health Literature is an important adjunct of the Nursing Service although also not directly connected with it. It consists of a series of booklets and circulars on prevalent diseases, simply written and well illustrated. Some of these are in several languages, adding to their efficiency. These booklets are distributed by agents to policy-holders without charge. If there is an epidemic of any kind in a community, the agents promptly begin the distribution of pamphlets bearing upon the disease that is prevalent. The total amount of pamphlets distributed up to dates, since 1911, is over 226,000,000 pieces. For the first six months of 1921, the distribution totaled over 13,000,000 pieces. The distribution is made to policy holders, health associations, public schools and similar institutions and associations.

Perhaps the most outstanding contribution of the Metropolitan to public health nursing is that it advertises it as perhaps it could not be advertised by any other association.

It has brought the public health nurse into homes

where she would not otherwise have been; it has been largely instrumental in removing from visiting nursing the stigma of charity and placing it on a pay basis. In fact we might almost say that the Metropolitan Life Insurance Company has *popularized* public health nursing.

There are other special groups of visiting nurses working along various definite lines of welfare; there are the Hospital Social Service Nurses following the patient from ward or dispensary into their homes; there are those who devote themselves to Mental Hygiene; and those who are helping to combat Venereal Diseases; and there are groups of so-called "Contagious Disease Nurses," who are usually employed by Departments of Health, to visit and instruct in the care of contagious diseases and to establish the necessary precautionary measures against their spread. These nurses seldom give bedside care.

And so we see the work of the visiting nurse ever growing, every widening, until it seems to cover the whole field of public health and social service. The little acorn sown by William Rathbone has become a mighty oak, and nations rest beneath its shade.

CHAPTER XX

EARLY SOCIAL TRAINING FOR NURSES

The last quarter of the 19th century saw, not only great discoveries in the science of medicine, but saw also the development of a new science i. e., that of practical sociology; the former opened up a vast field in preventive work, the latter raised philanthropy to the rank of a profession, and brought about a consequent change in its application as well as its administration. These changes and discoveries had a wide influence on the work of the visiting nurse. No longer could it be looked upon as an independent and separate charity; it was only one of the many forces at work for the benefit and uplift of the masses. Co-operation became the watch-word; social and medical workers came together; the correlation of all charitable and health organization became a necessity.

As in Modern Medicine, so in Modern Philanthropy, the cause, as well as the symptom was studied and it was found that the cause of one fourth of all poverty was directly traceable to sickness. If that were true, the importance of the visiting nurse as a social agent became at once apparent. In fact social problems were seen to be so intimately interwoven with the whole large problem of public health that, in order to relieve the one or the other, it was felt that a general medical-social scheme would have to be evolved, which would eliminate all preventable disease, improve the environment and working conditions of the masses, and place the individual on a stronger and sounder basis, physically, morally and economically.

This change of attitude in regard to social work came about gradually.

In the early days of our country's history the problem of poverty, as we have seen, was very simple. Most of the people were of Anglo Saxon origin, the standard of living was the same, work was plentiful, and the manner of life less complicated than in later times. Such charity as was necessary was administered by voluntary relief societies, benevolent associations and churches. As our cities grew, however, and as the flood of immigrants began to pour into the country, the awful face of Poverty appeared. To relieve this constantly growing distress there slowly developed, side by side with private philanthropy, a system of public charity, known as a city's Out-Door-Relief, supported by taxes and dispensed by city officials. This naturaly led to political manipulation, and as there was little or no investigation of cases applying for relief, the assistance given, in the form of food, shelter, clothing and coal was subject to much abuse and ran the great danger of converting poverty into pauperism.

The evil results of this extensive and indiscriminate relief-giving seem first to have been fully perceived during the industrial depression following the commercial crisis of 1873, which threw multitudes of men out of work and caused a heavy draft upon, not only the public, but the private, benevolent agencies of the day.

The prevailing methods of charity seem already to have been questioned, and for two or three years representatives of the public charities of various states had been meeting, more or less informally, to discuss their various problems. In the summer of 1874, however, following this winter of industrial depression, the first annual conference of the National Association of Charities and Correction took place, at which a paper was read by the delegate from New York, giving an account of the relief administered in that city and of its disastrous effects.

"New York, as is well known," said he, "is a large manufacturng center and employs a great number of artisans and mechanics. It has also a vast number of ordinary day laborers, as well as an unusual number of those who, in the best of times, just keep their heads above water. When the industrial and business panic came upon the city last autumn (1873) it was seen at once by the benevolent and fortunate classes that widespread distress would ensue.—No words can ever praise too warmly the generosity and unselfishness of a large part of the New York community who came forward with their gifts to help meet this distress. Still it was too often a generosity without discretion—" (Report of Charities and Correction.) He then went on to tell how warnings were put forth by persons experienced in work among the poor, and the danger pointed out of creating pauperism by this indiscriminate charity— especially such as soup kitchens, free lodging, etc., which tend to increase idleness, and act as a reward to the improvident. The truth of these warnings was quickly perceived. This indiscriminate charity immediately called into the city the floating vagrants, beggars and paupers, who wander from village to village about the country. The station houses and lodging places were filled with them; street begging became a common thing, and thieving and drunkenness increased.

The evil results were so apparent that some change in the method of administering charity was felt to be essential. "The first duty of a community," said the New York delegate, in suggesting a change, "is not to feed the hungry and clothe the naked, but to *prevent people from becoming hungry and naked.*"

This was a new and modern principle. Gradually the old methods gave way. In 1878, in the dead of winter, the city of Brooklyn ceased giving out-door relief; nevertheless increased suffering did not result, and the burden placed on private charities seemed no heavier. The next year Philadephia followed suit; and gradually official Out-Door-Relief by cities practically disappeared.

Meanwhile private charities were setting their houses in order, and many were being re-organized into one general Charity Oganization. Friendly visitors among the poor were introduced. In 1875, Boston introduced a co-operative society of visitors something on the plan of the Elberfeld system. No visitor was to have more than four "cases" at a time, and lists of needy people were obtained from a physician, who worked from the Provident Association in the congested and poor districts. Similar efforts were made in other cities. Friendly visiting, was looked upon as the best method of establishing human relation between man and man. As a personal friend the visitor was best able to discover the weak points in the family life, its needs and possibilities, and to advise, encourage and assist in a manner which would give permanent and not temporary relief. "Not alms but a friend," became the motto, and the visiting nurse was one of the best of these friends.

But this modern method of administering charity required a high degree of intelligence on the part of the charity worker. The need of food, fuel or clothing, was, according to the new view of charity, merely a symptom of the family's weakness, and it was the part of the social worker to "diagnose" the "case," and to develop some kind of a plan which would put the family on its feet and enable it to lead a normal and independent life. In order to do this properly special training and instruction in the solution of social problems became necessary. A new profession, the profession of the social worker, came into being, and Schools of Philanthropy were opened for her use.

Meanwhile, the visiting nurse continued on her way, grappling manfully with the many great problems confronting her; evolving plans for the better care of her tuberculosis patients; interesting herself in fresh air camps for tired mothers and little children; giving her testimony to strengthen the demand for better housing; and taking her part in all the social problems of the day. Visiting nursing began to be called social nursing by some, and the visiting nurse was looked upon as one of the most important social workers.

In 1904 came the first public recognition of her new position when the National Conference of Charities invited the visiting nurses of the country to join with the "other social workers" at their annual meeting to be held in Portland, Maine.

This was not only the first public recognition of the visiting nurse as a social worker but the first really representative gathering of visiting nurses ever held in this country, and the interest shown and the number of nurses present was greatly in excess of the most sanguine hopes of the promoters. The special invitation, sent out by the President of the Conference on Charities, for visiting nurses to hold meetings at the same time and together with, the other charity workers, gave an added dignity to visiting nursing and, "raised the subject from an isolated one, concerned only with a special body of workers, to its true place among the great philanthropic enterprises earnestly striving together towards the working out of a better social order," (Visiting Nurses at the National Conference of Charities and Corrections—article published in Johns Hopkins Nurses' Alumnæ Magazine, July 1904).

The subjects discussed at this meeting covered a wide range and brought out a great deal of interest and enthusiasm. It was soon apparent, as Miss Hitchcock of the Henry Street Settlement said in her opening address, that nurses were recognizing the benefits to be gained by exchanging ideas and methods with workers in other fields, and were realizing how impossible it was to stand isolated and alone without the help, experience and stimulus that must come by contact with other men and women all striving toward the same end.

The first question discussed, namely: "Should the educational and instructive features of visiting nursing be given such importance as to make skilled nursing only a secondary consideration," was vigorously assailed, and a decided answer in the negative brought out. "Many of us know," said Miss Carr in her report of this meeting "that there has been criticism, and perhaps deservedly so, of district nursing methods. There have been times and occasions when the care of the patient seems to have been somewhat overshadowed by a desire to impart knowledge to the members of the household, and a tendency to let skilled nursing care become secondary to statistics in the way of visits, or to merely instructive work." The danger was pointed out that when the educational and instructive side is too insistently dwelt upon, the real end and aim of visiting nursing, i. e., the providing of adequate and efficient care for the bodily needs of the patient, were likely to be forgotten. The general impression left, was, that the two must go hand in hand, but that, valuable and essential as education and instruction are, they cannot take the place of nursing care. (Report of Visiting Nurse at Charities Conference—Johns Hopkins Magazine, 1904).

Another question vigorously discussed by the nurses present was: "To what extent may the administration of general relief be entrusted to visiting nurses, without reference to investigating societies?" In this connection the necessarily close association of the work of the visiting nurses with that of other organized bodies of social workers was clearly pointed out, and the decision reached that visiting nurses should at all times co-operate with them, and at no time perform duties which other workers or societies were especially equipped to perform.

In considering the last question on the program, namely the advisability of forming a "Federation of Visiting Nurses in America" and adopting a uniform method, both in dress and administration similar to that in use with the Queen's Nurses in England, a vote of "no" was recorded.

"Nurses are already well organized—about as much as they can stand"—one of the members remarked, and further organization for the particular body was voted down.

It was decided, however, that informal meetings should be held annually in connection with the Conference on Charities, instead of at a special conference of their own,—and so, for the present, the question of a National Organization of Visiting Nurses was laid on the table.

"The Conference came to a close after one of the most stirring and helpful sessions in its history, and two new sections were added for the 1905 convention— one on training for social work; and a second on the care of the sick, which was to include two important sub-committees, the first on the campaign against tuberculosis, the other on general visiting nursing." (Charities, July 1904).

The most important truth carried home by the nurses from this first meeting was the necessity of training for themselves in social work. If visiting nursing meant something more than the mere care of the sick; if the nurse was responsible for the social, as well as the physical condition of her patient, then, indeed, did she need instruction in the principles of sociology and the new view of charity.

It was sometime, however, before this additional

training, so ardently desired became available in any adequate degree to visiting nurses.

For some years it had been recognized that hospital training was not sufficient to enable a woman to satisfactorily carry on visiting nursing. A nurse who had done only institutional or private duty nursing, no matter how well trained in hospital technique, found herself quite unable to solve the many problems which confronted her in the district—she even found it difficult to properly carry on her bedside nursing with nearly all the sick room appliances lacking. And so, in order to give hospital graduates, wishing to take up visiting nursing, some experience in district work the custom had long been in vogue of taking nurses inexperienced in social work on to the staffs of well organized visiting nurse associations, and giving them a few months of training under the supervision of an experienced visiting nurse—the feeling being that the hospital nurse, trained in this School of Experience, would soon learn the ways of her new work, and thus be equipped to go out and continue it elsewhere alone. Many of our best and finest visiting nurses received their social training in this way, and have gone forth to inspire and teach others in their turn. However, we must point out that the fine work which they accomplished has not been because of any virtue in this method of teaching, but in spite of it. They reached the goal, not because practical teaching alone can ever equal theory and practice combined, but because they had within themselves the making of a good visiting nurse, i. e., a keen mind, a loving heart, and the spirit of service to mankind, whatever form that service may assume.

The School of Experience however, was the only school to which these pioneer nurses could go for postgraduate instruction, and as a matter of fact, many

a public health nurse is still learning her profession
in that same hard school. When a need is strongly
felt, however, some way of fulfilling it is sure to develop. The first "School of District Nursing" as it
was rather pretentiously called, was started in Boston,
in October 1906, in charge of Miss Charlotte McLeod,
at which was given a course of four months of intensive work in the districts under close supervision, with
daily discussion with the superintendent, and occasional
lectures on the various forms of work the students
were supposed to do. There was no regular theory
taught however, and the lectures were of the most elementary type. The pupils, or students, as they were
called, received no salary, but were given board and
lodging in the Home of the Instructive District Nursing Association of Boston, at 561 Massachusetts Ave.
They were also given car-fare. At the end of four
months they received a diploma of graduation. During the first year thirteen nurses took this course and
graduated, and sixteen others took part of the course.

In 1910 came the first recognition by a college of
the need for special post-graduate work for trained
nurses, by the establishment in Teachers' College, of a
new "Department of Nursing and Health."

In December 1909, the American Journal of Nursing
had made the following announcement: "In response
to the recognized need of training of the social welfare
nurse, that she, in turn, may be a teacher of those to
whom she ministers, as well as a temporary reliever
of their needs, the Teacher's College of Columbia University, through the interest and financial support of
Mrs. Helen Hartley Jenkins, is to broaden its course
in Hospital Economics to include the preparation of
trained nurses in the science and art of hygiene, not
only as school, tuberculosis, and social welfare nurses,
but as sanitary experts, teachers at farmer's Institutes

and instructors of mothers in the care and training of children."

The new department was placed under the direction of Miss Adelaide Nutting, for many years Superintendent of the Johns Hopkins Training School for Nurses, and one of the most experienced, cultured and forceful women in the profession.

In an article on "Nursing and Health" published in the Visiting Nurse Quarterly for April 1910, Miss Nutting said:

"Just as we have spent a half century in developing the science and the art of nursing as applied to sickness and suffering, so must we now forthwith direct ourselves to the study of the larger science and the finer art, that of protecting and cherishing the health of our people. In this direction—that of Health Nursing—there seems to be opening to us a field of truly enormous importance."

After pointing out that, if nursing was to include health as well as sickness, then hygiene became for the visiting nurse a study of paramount importance, and that such fundamental subjects as housing, foods, nutrition, clothing and cleanliness should be studied with thoroughness under expert instruction, she goes on to say:

"In coming to accept the view that all district and visiting nursing worthy the name, no matter what form it may take, is social work and is educational work, as well as that of prevention and relief, we accept also the logical outcome of the view—the necessity of adding to the nurses' training that which will best prepare her for responsibilities. Hygiene and sanitation must be studied in all their respects, from the personal and the household to that of the municipality, and must be as practical as such courses can be made."

Under such leadership the Department of Nursing and

Health was bound to be a success. The course for nurses included:

Hygiene and Sanitation, which dealt with the practical application of sanitary legislation to tenement problems, to the control of food and water supplies, inspection of markets, inspection and regulation of factories, and workshops, etc.

Health Problems, such as the prevention and control of tuberculosis and the reduction of infant mortality, with systematic field work.

Sociology, which included a study of social, industrial and economic conditions both urban and rural, and finally,

Social Psychology, as underlying all social problems.

"Just how this new department of graduate work for nurses will develop," said Miss Nutting, "is not easy at present to conjecture. This much however, is certain, opportunities are before us which we have long coveted—which have long been withheld—it now remains for nurses to show whether or not such further education is really desired by them."

The future showed that not only was it desired, but was eagerly sought.

The following year, that is, in 1911, the Visiting Nurse Association of Cleveland opened up in connection with the Western Reserve University, the first class of Social Training for Nurses which combined theory with practice under competent instructors and supervisors. In speaking of the reasons for establishing this class Miss Belle Sherwin, who was largely instrumental in starting it, said:

"Local organizations are already seeking every means of developing the social sense of their staffs, and of adding to fine nursing technique a knowledge of the principles and methods of treatment of the social questions involved in the care of individual patients. It has been usual to try to get these results by lecture courses, club discussions, and the circulation of books and magazines, in addition to the long day's work of visits, record making, and the analysis of cases with the superintendents. Excellent results have been secured in these ways, and will continue to be so secured. But the time required to see things clearly, and to see them whole, to lay foundations for new thinking and new lines of action, has failed—the number of cases to carry has precluded it.

"In order to give a freer period of more thorough preparation for the various branches of social nursing already maintained in Cleveland, The Visiting Nurse Association has organized a course in the Social Training of Nurses to be opened in September, (1911). The co-operation of the Associated Charities, the Anti-Tuberculosis League, The Babies' Dispensary and Hospital and the Western Reserve University has been offered in the formation of the courses which therefore, affords variety in field work, as well as collegiate lecture courses and class discussion."

The class was conducted under the leadership of Miss Hanna Buchanan, a graduate of the first class in nursing and health at Teachers' College, and required a full academic year for its completion, the first semester being devoted to the History, Theory and Principles of Visiting Nursing; Practical Sociology; and the Principles and Method of Relief; with lectures and field work; and the second to Charities and Corrections, Tuberculosis, its History, Pathology and Control, and Infant Mortality, its causes and control; with extensive field work, and lectures by physicians eminent in their specialities; also a course of lectures on "American Society" as represented by our conglomerate citizenship.

This course, as can be seen, was quite ambitious, and marked a great step in advance in the training and education of visiting nurses.

In the following year, 1912, Henry St. Settlement, ever alert to the need of the visiting nurse, opened its doors to a limited number of nurses for a three months period of practical experience in the field. It was called a "Post Graduate Training Class," weekly instructions being given in connection with the daily nursing work in the districts—for which a one-half salary was paid—and tours of inspection made from time to time to public institutions, Ellis Island, the Department of Health, public schools and the offices of the Charity Organization Society, under the supervision of Miss Hitchcock the Director of the Nursing Service.

In the same year, 1912, the Boston District Nursing Association, in response to the increasing demand of the public for nurses qualified for positions in public health work, offered, besides the four months course, which it had carried ever since 1906, and which had been greatly enlarged, an eight months course, in affiliation with Simmons College and the School for Social Workers.

The aim of this longer course was "to give the knowledge needed for any form of social service, with an insight into special social and industrial problems upon which public health is dependent."

Two-thirds of the Student's time was devoted to work in the school for Social Workers, and one third to practical nursing work with the Instructive District Nursing Association.

During the first year Miss Bessie Lalecheur, Head of the Educational Department of the Association directed both courses; she was followed by Miss Ada Carr who held the position until 1916.[1] In Philadelphia a post-graduate course for nurses was started in 1913 by the Phipps Institute, in affiliation with the Visiting Nurse Society, but was abandoned in 1917.

[1] See Chapter XXV for further notice of Boston Course.

In that same year, however, *i. e.*, 1917 the Pennsylvania School for Social Service at the request of the Public Health Nursing Association of Philadelphia, the Philadelphia League of Nursing Education and the Visiting Nurse Society of Philadelphia realizing that never before had the demand for social training for the nurse been so great, organized a Department of Public Health Nursing and offered a post graduate course of high standard, including, besides such purely social courses as *The View Point of Social Work;* the *Problem of Poverty; Social Case Work;* and *Community Problems;* other more specialized courses in *Public Hygiene; Dietetics;* and *Public Health Nursing,* with carefully supervised field work in the latter.

Besides these and various other early post graduate courses given by Visiting Nurse Associations in affiliation with Schools of Social Science, and Universities, a short two or three months period of undergraduate instruction was given by many hospitals to their senior pupils. These courses were elective and were usually arranged for by affiliation with the local Visiting Nurse Association, who would take two or three hospital pupils at a time and give them practical experience in the districts under the direction of the district Supervisor.

Henry St. Settlement was among the first in this work, in 1893 having taken two nurses from Mt. Sinai Training School for one year to work in their districts. In 1900 students from the Post Graduate Hospital— Margaret Talinestock School, were taken for a four months period of experience at the Henry Street Settlement; and in 1901, a like experience was extended to students from the Brooklyn City Hospital and the Laura Franklin Hospital—while in 1914, training classes for the under-graduate and the graduate nurse were arranged for in affiliation with the courses in Nursing and Health at Teachers' College.

21

In 1905, the District Nursing Association of Providence, undertook the training of pupil nurses in district work, beginning with one pupil from one hospital and gradually extending the opportunity to others; while in 1911, the Cleveland Association arranged to receive two pupil nurses each from three large hospitals, and to give them two months experience in the districts with daily class discussion and six lectures on related topics.

Other associations in other cities followed more or less the same form of procedure. Social training for nurses was at last looked upon as essential for all who intended to take up social nursing. A new profession, not only for social workers but for nurses, had been evolved, and special preparation was considered necessary.[1]

[1] See Chap. XXIV.

CHAPTER XXI

THE NATIONAL ORGANIZATION FOR PUBLIC HEALTH NURSING

For many years the leading nurses of the country had realized that a standard for visiting nursing was greatly needed and that there was great danger in allowing it to increase at the rate it was increasing without some restraining influence, some standardizing organization which might prevent its misuse, and establish and maintain a certain minimum of requirements. In England this need has been recognized, and met by the foundation of the Jubilee Institute, but in this country there was no authoritative council nor association, nor even committee, to protect the homes of the sick poor, by fixing such a standard and defending it against ignorance or wanton commercialism. Any nurse who entered the home of the sick poor to minister to their relief was called a visiting nurse; but there was no standard set for her training; no definite and recognized rules for her observance, and no protection against the practice of visiting nursing by unscrupulous people for exploitation or personal gain.

Moreover, each organization,—we might almost say each visiting nurse,—throughout the country was working alone and independently. Each was obliged to solve its own problems unaided, and the nurse often entered the field with no previous preparation for her work beyond the technical training gained in the hospital wards. She was not always even a graduate nurse, for the standards of nursing education were but vaguely understood by the public, and as lay people, represented by Boards of Trustees or heads of committees, often knowing little or nothing either of nursing or social science, were in the first instance responsible for the type of nurse engaged, the risk of employing badly qualified women was very great. Fortunately the pioneer visiting nurse work in America had been well started, and the large and representative organization of the country had always held to the best nursing technique and ideals. Nevertheless the situation was a dangerous one; the nurses themselves recognized the danger, and felt the need of help and counsel in their work. Many of the leading visiting nurses of the country had been in the habit of corresponding with one another concerning their work, in order to learn what they could from one anothers' experience, and we have seen how eagerly they had responded to the call of the National Conference of Charities to meet together and discuss their problems.

The Cleveland association had tried, in a small way, to meet the need of standardization and an interchange of ideas, first, by securing through the generosity of two of its Trustees a very beautiful seal, as "an outward sign of a common purpose," which it offered to sell at a minimum cost to all associations coming up to a required standard; secondly, by publishing in 1909 a little magazine called *The Visiting Nurse Quarterly,* in which it endeavored, by stories, reports, and contributed articles to let visiting nurses know what others in the field were doing, and by suggestions and advice to help them in their present work and inspire them to new endeavors.

Chicago, too, had tried to bring the visiting nurses of the country together, first in 1906, by publishing a little magazine, also called the *Visiting Nurse Quarterly,* which appeared nine times and then ceased for lack of support;[1] and later, in 1908, by calling a special conference of visiting nurses and directors of Visiting Nurse Associations. This meeting which took place in Chicago on April 25th, 1908, was called together for the special purpose of bringing the work of the visiting nurse before representatives of the various visiting nurse associations of the country, and giving it greater importance in the nursing world.

"For several years," said Miss Fulmer. "We have been represented at meetings of the various nursing bodies, and charity organizations, and while this has been of some advantage it cannot possibly equal that of holding a specific meeting of our own.

"There is great necessity just at this time to awaken interest and enthusiasm among those doing the work, and also among those who might take it up.

"It would be of great advantage to have those who promote the work, also, come together at this time. Officers and Boards of Directors of the various organizations could well benefit by a conference of this kind.

"There are now in the United States about one hundred organized societies, and about seven hundred to eight hundred nurses doing this work. Out of this group if we could have a gathering of perhaps one hundred people we should be very thankful. At this conference we could discuss all the various phases of the work from the nurses' standpoint, and from that of the Directors' and perhaps in this way arrive at a

[1] "The Visiting Nurse Quarterly was discontinued because the nurses could not afford to finance it, and the Board of Directors did not consider it of sufficient value to take it over. With a very limited subscription list (under 200) our income did not anywhere near cover the cost of printing—and we made the deficit out of our own pockets for two years. Every one was interested, but it was too small a publication to succeed. However, all our little effort started the ball rolling and paved the way for bigger things later on." Extract from letter by Harriet Fulmer.

more uniform method of conducting the work in this country."

One of the subjects discussed at this meeting was, the adoption of a common seal or emblem for all visiting nurse associations.

The Cleveland association had submitted three designs for a seal, one of which seemed to embody the real spirit and future of the work. This design was finally adopted, and became the national seal for all visiting nurse associations wishing to use it.

The first definite suggestion for a national association of visiting nurses was made in 1893 by Miss Somerville, then Superintendent of the Boston Instructive District Nursing Association, when, at the International Congress of Nurses, held in Chicago, she made the following remark:

"If the many small societies throughout this broad land were to agree to become one national association, varying the general methods of that organization only in such details as would best suit individual cities, what might we not accomplish!"

But Miss Somerville was ahead of her co-workers. From time to time one would hear suggestions that we needed an organization, like the Victorian Order of Canada, or the Jubilee Institute of England, but nothing was done.

In 1911, however, the desire for national organization began to take definite shape, and the leading nurses of the country to discuss the subject, not in a vague manner merely as something desirable, but with the intention of definite action.

In December of that year Miss Ella Phillips Crandall, at that time Professor in the Department of Public Health and Nursing at Teachers' College, wrote to Miss Gardner, Superintendent of the Providence District Nursing Association, asking her opinion in regard to some form of organization to protect the standards of visiting nursing.   The following reply is characteristic of Miss Gardner's clear thinking:

PROVIDENCE, R. I., DECEMBER 29, 1911.

My dear Miss Crandall:

Your letter quite alarmed me, particularly when it ended with the request for my *convictions.*

However, here are my views as well as I can formulate them in so short a time.

I do think that the standarization of district nursing is extremely important, not only to protect the work of the district nurse, but because I think this branch of the nursing profession is in danger of becoming an open door to the lowering of standards in general.   I mean through the employment of non-graduate nurses for chronic cases, or in some such way as that.   District nursing is not hedged about by the same formalities or restrictions as those surrounding hospital work.   The Boards of Managers are apt to be people with even less experience than hospital Boards, and the importance of the work is often not in the least grasped by the people managing it.   Of course education is the main point, but how to educate is often a problem in the smaller places, and I think some form of national organization is the only thing that will have any permanent effect on the district nursing situation throughout the country.   Little as I am inclined for the multiplication of organizations, this branch of the work is so very highly specilized and has so many problems attending it that I hardly see how a committee of the American Nurses Association, as has been suggested, could be allowed sufficient time at any annual conference to do efficient work.

I would therefore suggest (and yet I have not given the matter sufficient consideration) that a special organization or association be formed, meeting directly after or before and in the same place as the other national nursing association.   I would also suggest that this association have a paid secretary, whose business it would be to answer questions, give advice and set forth standards and principles.   And finally I would suggest that the Quarterly, or some other publication, become a monthly, with articles, news and a letter-box particularly the latter, where questions might be asked.

"I feel most vigorously that concerted action is absolutely necessary among the better associations in order that the poorer and weaker ones may be helped to withstand many things.

"It seems as if I had merely set forth truisms, but to summarize: I am heartily in favor of a National District Nursing Organization; I think strong committee work should be done between meetings, which later should be annual and held directly after or before those of the American Nurses Association and at the same place. I think a paid secretary, giving her entire time to this organization, would double the efficiency of the work done; and I think some publication more frequently issued than the Cleveland Quarterly now is, would also help. I think the paid secretary is largely needed because so many of the Boards of Managers are in total ignorance of the principles involved and because in most instances they would be glad to learn, if they knew how and where to get at information. So often they have no one to turn to, and blunder on, doing not only harm to their own community but retarding the advancement of the whole movement.

"CORDIALLY YOURS,

"(Signed) MARY S. GARDNER."

P. S. "I think the whole question of the proper training of the district nurse should of course go hand in hand with the other things involved, but I am inclined to think it would be greatly furthered by any formal standardization which would in time eliminate the unsuitable nurse."

This letter was typical of the prevailing feeling among nurses at that time and set forth a definite outline for a national organization of visiting nurses.

Soon after this we hear that "a group of prominent

nurses from several parts of the country are now at work devising a policy which will protect the ideals and standards of visiting nursing from enroachment."

This "group of prominent nurses" was, in reality, a joint committee appointed by the American Nurses' Association and the Society of Superintendents of Training Schools, and consisted of Miss Delano, Miss Kerr, and Miss Crandall from the American Nurses' Association and Miss Foley, Miss Beard and Miss Gardner from the Society of Superintendents of Training Schools with Miss Wald as chairman. The committee felt that the standardization of visiting nursing work was important and that the time was ripe for the formation of some kind of a National Visiting Nurse Association.

In order that the subject might be fully and widely discussed a letter was sent to 1092 organizations employing visiting nurses in the United States, setting forth the situation, and asking them to send accredited representatives to a meeting to be held in Chicago, June 5, 1912, in order to consider the subject of organizing such a national association.

The following list gives the distribution of the letter:

Visiting Nurse Associations	205
City and State Boards of Health and Education	156
Private Clubs and Societies	108
Tuberculosis Leagues	107
Hospitals and Dispensaries	87
Business Concerns	38
Settlements and Day Nurseries	35
Churches	28
Charity Organizations	27
Other Organizations	19

Seventy-eight additional letters were sent to the different counties in which the Pennsylvania State Board of Health

nurses were working, and 204 letters to the nurses independently employed by the Metropolitan Life Insurance
Company.

Only 80 replies were received from the 1092 letters,
69 of them contained an agreement to send a delegate.

Most of the answers showed a keen desire on the
part of both nurses and laity for some central organization; only one, a small association employing but
one nurse, expressing the opinion that a national organization was unnecessary.

The Committee had chosen the date of the annual
meeting of the American Nurses' Association as the
date for its own special meeting, feeling that by so
doing they would be assured of a larger attendance.
They were not disappointed. As the hour for the
meeting approached the hall was filled with eager,
expectant faces. It was as if each one present felt
the presage of some great event, and realized that the
coming discussion would be epoch-making.

The chairman, Miss Edna Foley, called the meeting
to order, and requested Miss Gardner to present the
Report of the Joint Committee.

After expressing the feeling of the committee on the
subject under discussion and outlining the work done
by it during the past few months, the Report recorded
two recommendations, *viz:*

First: That a National Visiting Nurse Association be
formed which shall as an organization, become a member of the American Nurses' Association.
Second: That certain standards be upheld and recommended to all organizations employing visiting
nurses.
These standards are as follows:
   (a) That the nurse shall be 25 years of age.
   (b) That she shall be a graduate of a recognized
       general hospital of not less than 50 beds, giving

a course of training of not less than two years, with obstetrics.

(c) That a nurse applying from a state where state registration permits shall be a graduate of a hospital acceptable to State Board of Registration.

(d) That newly organized associations or organizations be urged to secure nurses properly trained for visiting nurse work.

(e) That while it is obviously impossible to state a desirable minimum salary for visiting nurses, owing to the great difference in the cost of living in different parts of the country, all associations are urged to pay such salaries as will secure and retain nurses of the highest grade. It is also recommended that such salaries be increased according to length of service and executive ability.

(f) That Visiting Nurse Associations be recommended to adopt a suitable form of dress for their nurses.

After some discussion, in which, however, the need of a national organization was unanimously expressed, the Report was accepted, and the business of deciding upon a name for the new association came up for consideration.

On this subject the vote of the Committee had not been unanimous, five of the members voting for "The National Visiting Nurse Association," while the other two held out for the name: "Public Health Nursing," as being more all-inclusive.

In opening the discussion Miss Foley said:—

"We are here primarily to organize, and in organizing we want, of course, to choose a name, and want it to be the right name; we want a name that is descriptive and one that is big enough to let in every one who is doing any work we are going to stand for. "Visiting Nurse Association" is not big enough, to my mind, to include all the people—all the nurses who are doing work for social betterment, that is, along public health lines.   There are a good many doing public health work who do not do visiting work primarily; they do it incidentally.   Then, too, would the title "Visiting Nurse Association" mean enough to the public mind? Would it give us large enough scope? It seems to me that "Public Health Nurses' Association," although it is more cumbersome and not so simple, is much more appropriate."

In the long discussion which followed many opinions were expressed, and much earnest thought given the question.

"I feel that we are all visiting nurses, no matter what we are called"; said Miss Lent of Baltimore. "We want the people to get into the habit of thinking of us as visiting nurses, and I believe it would complicate things very much if we were to take any other name."

"In our social service work," said Miss Crowell of New York, "we feel the term 'public health' is much broader and will take in all different lines and branches of nursing work."

Miss Gardner seemed to think the name "visiting nurse" meant one thing in one part of the country and something else in another; while Miss Crandall pointed out that nursing was being carried right along into the very heart of the big health movement, that such nursing often included bedside care, and that *public health* would grow to be more and more the foundation rock in both nursing and medicine.   "We have discussed and considered this most carefully at Teachers' College," said she, "because the diplomas to be issued there had to have a permanent title, and it has seemed quite necessary to use the term *'public health.'* "

Many of the delegates seemed to think that visiting nursing covered the whole field of social or preventive nursing, and that all public health nurses—by which was meant those working under Boards of Health, School Boards, or other public departments—were visiting nurses. Others, again, stated that in their part of the country "visiting nursing" was a restricted term meaning only district nursing, and did not include such forms of work as school nursing, factory nursing, Board of Health work, or even tuberculosis nursing.

The discussion seemed to show that, in general, the title "public health nurse" was broader than "visiting nurse."

"Visiting nursing covers the work done in the large organizations," said Miss Blackington of Connecticut, "but I think in the smaller towns where, in years to come, every bit of work will be covered by the visiting nurse who is supposed to take care of the sick, and do social work, besides district work, the term *public health nurse* would give the nurse a better showing because her work would include all sorts of nursing."

"I think the point made is very good," said Mrs. Gretter of Detroit, "and while there is a good deal of sentiment in all of us as to the name visiting nurse (we all like the title of it),—still the other, in my opinion, is broader and will include in a better way the different classes of work represented by nurses, therefore, I approve the name 'public health.' "

And so the new title was adopted as a generic name for all forms of visiting nursing, which might or might not include bedside care. Henceforth school, factory, tuberculosis, child welfare, or any other form of social nursing—public or private—already existing or as yet undreamed of—would go by the name of public health nursing. It would be known, as not only for the relief of the sick, but for the preservation of the public health as well; not only for the poor, but for all.

Florence Nightingale's dream had become a reality, and visiting nurses were to be known as *Health Nurses*.

After some further discussion a unanimous vote was cast for the name: The National Organization for Public Health Nursing—the words: "for nursing" being used instead of "of Nurses" in order to include lay people as well as nurses.

An organization had at last been founded broad enough to take in all kinds of nursing which had to do with public health or social conditions; liberal enough to include not only nurses, but lay people in its membership; and, best of all, so elastic, that not only the present, but the future was provided for.

In speaking of that wonderful and historic meeting in Chicago, Miss Crandall, so long identified with the Organization which then took form, says:

"Just one thing stands out clearly and sharply in my memory, and that is our two or more hours of discussion regarding a name for the new organization, during which time the selection of each word of the title was made with the greatest care and discrimination. The chief argument in favor of the term "Public Health" was that it was borrowing from or banking on the future, rather than the past or present, and establishing, in anticipation, a vital connection between visiting nursing and public health as it was practically sure to develop in the immediate future. I think it is safe to say that it was this argument that overcame the influence that both tradition and sentiment held in the minds of most of the nurses present."

The new organization did not start on its career empty-handed.

"The real business of the morning being at an end, a beautiful christening present was made to the new baby by the Cleveland Visiting Nurse Association. The seal, a work of art of great beauty, which had for sometime been used by the Cleveland Association, was presented to the National Organization for Public Health Nursing. This most generous gift was received with enthusiastic applause and expressions of appreciation." (Miss Gardner—Visiting Nurses Quarterly, 1912).

The seal, which was at once accepted, is emblematic of the true spirit of visiting nursing. It represents a kneeling woman, the nurse, planting a sturdy, young tree—the knowledge of health,—and beneath is the verse from Proverbs:—

"When the Desire cometh it is a Tree of Life."

The great work to which visiting nurses are dedicated is the emplanting in the hearts and minds of the sick and poor the desire for a better, cleaner, healthier mode of living, and when this desire comes it is indeed a "Tree of Life."

A second gift, also from the Cleveland Association, was the little magazine, the Visiting Nurse Quarterly. In the letter which accompanied its presentation, the Editor said:

"With the establishing of a National Association of Visiting Nurses to guard their high standard, to study their problems and to help solve the same, it has been thought by many that the publication of some regular organ of communication would be advisable.

"The maintenance of a magazine already established is more readily assured than that of a new one yet untried. For this reason the Visiting Nurse Association of Cleveland desires to offer the National Association for its publication, the magazine known as the Visiting Nurse Quarterly, together with its list of nearly 1000 subscribers to the same, its contracts for advertisements and any money remaining to the Quarterly at the time of transfer.

"The Quarterly is now in its fourth year and is more or less well known in all parts of the United States where visiting nurse work is being carried on, and it is hoped that the National Association will see its way to accept the offer of the Cleveland Association and be able to make of the Quarterly a magazine of real influence in the country."

This gift was also accepted, but with the proviso that the officers then in charge should continue its management and publication. For that reason the Editorial Office of the magazine has always been in Cleveland. This magazine has proved one of the most valuable gifts ever received by the National Organization. Its name was at once changed to "The Public Health Nurse Quarterly," and in 1918 it became a monthly, and was included as one of the privileges of membership in the National Organization. It has now (1921) a circulation of about 8000 and is nearly self-supporting.

With the exception of the magazine, the management of, and responsibility for, the new organization was to be left entirely in the hands of the nurses; for, although lay people were to be admitted to membership they were to have no vote on technical questions, or for officers and directors, and were not to sit on the Board of Directors. (Note: In 1918 the Constitution was amended, and four lay members were added to the Directorate.) The wisdom of this policy has been questioned. Lay people had always been closely identified with visiting nursing. In all but a very few instances the work had been inaugurated by lay men and women, and the administration and financing of its affairs had been in their hands—nurses, as a class, have had little training in business methods or the financing of large undertakings. It is quite conceivable that had lay people been admitted on more of an equality with nurses, the division of labor and responsibility would have been made in such a manner as to still have left the financial and business responsibility to the laity, while all questions pertaining to nursing standards, eligibility, ethics, etc. would have been entirely in the hands of the nurses. On the other hand the Organization had been established primarily to safeguard the standards of visiting nursing; lay people were astonishingly ignorant of what those standards should be; they had, in more instances than one, already imperilled the status of the work, and had they been given a vote on any question which pertained to nursing they might easily have negatived the value of the Organization. Nurses were rightly jealous of the prerogatives and influence of their profession, and hestitated to hand over to unprofessional members any power which might endanger the high standing which that profession holds—we cannot but feel therefore that their decision to keep it a "close corporation," as it were, was a wise one.

The officers and directors elected were:

Officers

President: Miss Lillian D. Wald, R. N., Head Resident, Henry Street Nurses' Settlement, New York.

Vice-President: Miss Edna L. Foley, R. N., Supt. Visiting Nurse Association, Chicago, Ill.

Secretary: Miss Ella Phillips Crandall, R. N., Instructor, Department of Nursing and Health, Teachers' College, Columbia University, New York.

Treasurer: (Temporary) Miss Mary E. Lent, R. N., Supt. Instructive District Nursing Association, Baltimore, Md.

Directors.

Miss Mary Beard, Supt. Instructive District Nursing Association, Boston, Mass.

Miss Jane A. Delano, Chairman National Committee, Red Cross Nursing Service, Washington, D. C.

Miss Mary M. Fletcher, Secretary State Board of
    Registration, Virginia, Charlottesville, Va.
Miss Mary S. Gardner, Supt. Visiting Nurse Associa-
    tion, Providence, R. I.
Miss Flora M. Glenn, Supt. of Nurses, Municipal
    Tuberculosis Sanatorium, Dispensary De-
    partment, Chicago, Ill.
Miss Annie L. Hanson, Domestic Educator, Immigrants'
    League, Buffalo, N. Y.
Miss Sarah B. Helbert, School Instructor and Nurse,
    Anti-Tuberculosis League, Cincinnati, Ohio.
Mrs. Edith M. Hickey, School Nurse, Seattle, Wash.
Miss Lydia A. Holman, Supt. Holman Association, Alta
    Pass, N. C.
Miss Matilda L. Johnson, Supt. Visiting Nurse Asso-
    ciation, Cleveland, Ohio.
Miss Anna W. Kerr, Supt. School Nurses, Dept. of
    Health, New York City.
Miss Ellen N. La Motte, Supt. Tuberculosis Nurses,
    Baltimore, Md.
Miss Harriet L. Leete, Supt. of Nurses, Babies' Dispen-
    sary and Hospital, Cleveland, Ohio.
Miss Minnie P. Patterson, Supt. Visiting Nurses,
    Minneapolis, Minn.
Miss Julia C. Stimson, Head Worker, Social Service
    Dept., Washington University Hospital, St.
    Louis, Mo.

It will be seen from this list that all parts of the
country were well represented, and that the officers and
directors elected were the strongest and most influential
in the field.

The first important business of the National Organization was the appointment of Miss Ella Phillips
Crandall as Executive Secretary.

In its Constitution the object of the Organization was
said to be:—

"To stimulate the general public and the visiting nurse
associations in the extension and support of public health

ELLA PHILLIPS CRANDALL, R. N.

Executive Secretary of the National Organization for Public
Health Nursing June, 1912 to May, 1920.

nursing service to facilitate harmonious co-operation among the workers and supporters, and to develop a standard of ethics and technique. Also to act as a clearing house for information for those interested in such work."

In order to accomplish this purpose it was important that a field secretary should be employed who could devote her entire time to the work, and who, by spending much of this time in traveling about the country could keep in close touch with all the visiting nurse work throughout the land.

There were at that time over 1000 organizations, employing, some, one visiting nurse, some a large staff of visiting nurses, and it was thought that a secretary who could continually carry from one centre to another needful help, advice and information would rapidly effect the standardization of method and quality desired, and that her presence and enthusiastic assistance, when needed, would greatly help in stimulating the public in the extension and support of public health nursing.

No better selection for the position could have been made than that of Miss Crandall. Her enthusiasm, devotion and constant self-sacrifice to the cause she had so close to her heart did much to establish the prestige of the National Organization and to increase the spread of public health nursing.

At the end of the first year, the Quarterly, speaking of the year's work, says:

"How many of us really know or realize what our Executive Secretary, Miss Crandall, has meant to this Organization in this first year of its existence? Only those who have come within the radius of her personality can understand her capacity for giving tirelessly, unflaggingly of herself, not for an eight-hour day but for the long day which takes from the early morning and late evening treasures of unrecorded time which only that invisible recording angel, which we all believe in as seated somewhere in the midst of this bright firmament, will ever commit to any kind of a ledger.

"Besides this over-gift of time those who know our Secretary will feel that her quickness of understanding, warm human sympathy and an ability to see impartially the equal claims of all associations, makes her very truly the one to resolve differences into accord, and unrelated parts into the harmony of a national whole whose spirit shall transcend and preserve the letter which embodies it."

During this year a flood of work poured into the main office which had been opened in New York City. Hundreds of visiting nurse associations turned to the National Organization for help in solving their problems. Some of these problems included the entire reorganization of the visiting nurse service of a city; others had to do with the raising of the standard of work; others, again, were questions concerning the establishment of some new phase of work; and still others sought to prevent duplication, or to safeguard municipal nursing against political manipulation.

Early in the year, Miss Crandall made a trip through the Southern States, visiting the historic association in Charleston, the Nurses' Settlement in Richmond, and tramping over the mountains of North Carolina with Miss Holman to visit the mountaineers in their cabin homes and to help devise some means for the further amelioration of their condition.

It would be impossible to express what the understanding sympathy and wise counsel of Miss Crandall meant to these and many other lonely workers. It seemed as though, all at once, they were not alone, they had each and all become one with a great band of other workers, all striving toward the same end, each meeting the same perplexities. All at once they knew what their sisters in the field were doing, how they had met and solved the same difficulties which they were meeting, how they were increasing and improving their methods of work.

This interchange of ideas, this drawing together of isolated groups and individuals was one of the most important sides of the work of the National Organization. As the years progressed, the need of the Organization became more and more apparent; the appeals made for help and counsel increased, and the Executive Secretary soon found that a good half of her time was spent in traveling over the country. In the year 1915 these travels covered a distance of 82,021 miles, and Miss Crandall gave 83 public addresses in towns and cities throughout the length and breadth of the United States.

It would be impossible to estimate the value of these personal interviews and these intimate conferences on local conditions.

Also, as schools and colleges began to offer special courses in Public Health Nursing, they would turn to the National Organization for counsel in arranging them. There were many requirements, both in theory and field practice, which were considered essential to a full and satisfactory course of instruction. If a course was endorsed by the National Organization it was known to meet these requirements; if this endorsement was withheld, it indicated that something was lacking—either the theory given was not up to the standard, or, more often, that the field of practical demonstration—the laboratory of work, so to speak—was restricted or not properly supervised. A desire on the part of schools, associations or universities to procure this endorsement for their courses usually led to a change in methods to meet demands, and this in itself helped to uphold the standard of public health nursing.

There were three types of membership in the National

Organization, *i. e.*, nurses, lay people, and corporate members. A nurse, to be eligible, was obliged to be a graduate of a recognized hospital training school; any lay person, or a nurse not eligibl₂ as a nurse, could become a member with a limited vote; and any organization engaged in public health nursing could become a corporate member, provided it conformed to certain standards in the nurses employed.

This also safe-guarded the standard of public health nursing, and many nurses at first ineligible, added to their training in order to become members in the National Organization.

It is interesting to note the difference between the American National Organization and the Queen's Jubilee Institute for Nurses in England. Both were founded for the purpose of raising the standard and extending the field of District or Visiting Nursing, and both have succeeded in their endeavors, though following different lines and with different results.

The government of the American organization rests, as we have seen, in the hands of professional nurses; that of the English Institute in a Council composed mostly of lay people, a few nurses of high training and ability being directly employed by the Institute as Superintendents and Inspectors.

The English Institute maintains its standard by requiring that every Queen's Nurse shall be a graduate of a three years' course in a hospital, with a subsequent six months' special training at some one of the large training centres, supervised by the Jubilee Institute; and that its affiliated associations must come up to a certain standard outlined in its form of affiliation. (See Appendix VII.)

The American organization, in the same way, requires all nurse members to be graduates of a recognized training school, but does not require supplementary training, though it approves of it.

The standard of this supplementary training, or post-graduate work, however, is much higher in America than in England. In the latter, it consists of a six months' residence in one of the nursing homes, with district work under supervision, and special lectures on hygiene, maternity nursing, tuberculosis, and six lectures on social subjects connected with district nursing; also a few special lectures on eyes, ears and throat, drugs, and the early recognition of infectious diseases.

Many of the American courses, on the other hand, entitle the student to a college certificate, and include, beside practical field work under supervision, a high standard of theoretical work in such studies as chemistry, bacteriology, economics, psychology, sociology, hygiene and sanitation, etc.

The greatest difference between the English and the American organizations, however, is that the one is an *administrative body,* training and supervising district nurses; whereas the other is a *consultant body,* working out standards and principles for those in the field to follow, and furnishing expert consultants who are ready at any time to give help or advice on all subjects pertaining to public health nursing.

The method employed in England has worked out well in that country. However, it has tended to confine their work to the original type of district nursing among the poor, and it is only lately that the Queen's Nurses have included general public health and instruction in this district work.

In America the original idea for an organization was similar to the English idea. Miss Somerville wanted "to gather into one standardized system all the unrelated work of the country," and the Jubilee Institute, with its affiliated associations, did "gather into one standardized system all the district work of the Kingdom, making the cause a truly national one."

But the American spirit of independence seems to

have prevailed at that first great meeting of nurses. They were willing, indeed, they were anxious, to unite in membership for mutual benefit, but they desired no supervision, no direction from a centralized council. Each member wanted to be independent, with equal rights in discussion, and with an equal vote. It was founded on purely democratic principles, and as such it has grown and broadened steadily in its work and influence.

Certain suggestions for extending the franchise of the Organization are at present being considered. But whatever changes may come, the governing power will still be in the hands of the nurses; it will still preserve its democratic and professional character; and its primary function will still be to protect the standard of public health nursing.

CHAPTER XXII

WAR AND THE PUBLIC HEALTH NURSE

UNITED STATES.

When, in 1917, the United States entered the great war which was raging in Europe, it faced many problems, many difficulties. Men and women from every class came forward to help meet and solve them. Everyone wanted to do his or her "bit" to help win the war. Prominent business men left their private affairs, and became the so-called "Dollar-a-year men" in the employ of the government; society women left their drawing-rooms and devoted themselves to Red Cross work; young girls served in canteens, or became nurses' aides, or joined the Red Cross for reconstruction work abroad; while doctors and nurses volunteered their services for the overseas hospitals, or for duty in the great training camps at home.

There was plenty for everyone to do, and everyone wanted to do his part.

In the early days of this general enlistment for war service a lady, who for many years had been actively interested in medical and social charities, and especially in the advancement and support of public health nursing, was asked, "and what are you going to take up as your war work?"

"I shall try to devote myself more closely than ever to my special interests," said she, "for I feel that never before was it so important to guard the public health, and never before were public health nurses so necessary."

And she was right. A country at war has a two-

fold duty; it must not only support and care for the
man at the front, it must also uphold and strengthen
the worker at home; not only guard the health of the
soldier, but protect and watch over the health of the
civilian.

The problems which the war created for nurses
went far beyond the care of men wounded in battle, or
sick in the concentration camps—they included the care
of the wives and children left at home; the safeguarding
of the great army of industrial workers in the ship-
yards and munition plants and other factories; and
especially the protection of child-life, which the abnormal conditions of war times endanger.

War had no sooner been declared than the nurses of
the country realized that a call had come for them, as
well as for the young men of the land. That this call
was unofficial made it none the less imperative. The
response was instantaneous. Within a few months
no less than 13,500 nurses were enlisted for Red Cross
work at home and abroad. These nurses, however, were
all enrolled for military service. To care for our
wounded boys "over there" seemed our first duty; to
nurse the sick soldiers in the great camp hospitals over
here, the next. Few thought of the civilian at home.
Although public health nursing was popular as a peace
time activity, its value as a war service was not recognized.

Public health nurses, and the National Organization which represented them, "faced war with no war
status," and it looked as though the work so carefully
established throughout the land would suffer, not only
for lack of support, but also from depleted ranks, for
public health nurses, filled with a desire to render
patriotic service, were flocking to the Red Cross standard in ever increasing numbers.

The officers of the National Organization, and a few
other leading nurses, saw the danger and immediately

took steps to secure suitable recognition for the special
service which they realized public health nurses were
prepared to render.

Their efforts led to the appointment of three committees on nursing, under the Council of National Defense. These committees were; two under the Medical Board, *i. e.*:

*1. A General Committee on Nursing. Miss Nutting,
Chairman.*

This Committee was (a) to ascertain through a census
the actual nursing resources of the country, and (b) to
increase the supply of nurses by every means possible.

*2. A Sub-Committee on Public Health Nursing of the
Committee on Hygiene and Sanitation. Miss Beard,
Chairman.*

This Committee was (a) to collect information regarding the disastrous effects of the past three years of war on
the community health of the European nations at war:
(b) to show how various progressive public health activities, in many of which the public health nurse was the active agent, would help to prevent these disasters; and (c)
to recommend the universal establishment of such public
health activities.

And, one under the Committee on Labor.

3. A Committee on Home Nursing. Miss Wald, Chairman.

This Committee was (a) to furnish information
concerning all industrial nursing service throughout the
country; (b) to stimulate such service; (c) to see that
home nursing care was available for all industrial workers, especially for those engaged in war work.

In order to correlate the work, Miss Crandall, Executive Secretary of the National Organization for
Public Health Nursing, was made Secretary to all three
of the Committees, the National Organization paying
her salary and other expenses. For nineteen months,
or until the close of the war made her presence un-

necessary, Miss Crandall gave herself unsparingly to this arduous war service.

The amount of work done by those three committees was stupendous, and wonderful results followed in the wake of the public attention and interest which they aroused.

One of their first efforts was directed toward gathering statistics regarding the actual nursing strength in the United States. It was found that there were 79,000 registered nurses, and about 120,000 others, some trained, some untrained, mostly engaged in private nursing. This made a total of nearly 200,000, only 6000 of whom were Public Health Nurses. The danger of depleting this already insufficient number spurred the workers on in a renewed effort to conserve, so far as possible, this limited number for the protection of public health at home or abroad.

The Red Cross had already made a ruling that nurses employed in the Red Cross Town and Country Nursing Service should not be called upon for work outside their community. The Committee on Public Health Nursing felt that a modification of this policy should apply to all public health nurses. They were willing that, when necessary, public health nurses should be called upon for overseas work of a purely public health nature, but felt that they should not be called upon for military service, this entailing a distinct loss of the special service they were fitted to render.

This policy was finally adopted, and a special Red Cross enrollment of public health nurses, exclusively for public health work, was secured, together with special service chevrons for such patriotic duty. In order to obtain as many nurses as possible, however, for overseas duty letters were sent out to hundreds of visiting nurse associations asking if they had in their employ any nurses who, in case of need, could be spared from their local work for military service. By this method they were enabled to secure some three hundred public health nurses for war duty without seriously disrupting local health activities.

Also, of course, many public health nurses continued to enlist voluntarily for overseas service, feeling that only by ministering to the soldiers at the front could they satisfy their desire to help in the war.

This recognition by the Red Cross, however, gave the public health nurses at home the war status which they desired, and their value as war workers became recognized by the public. The result was immediately felt. Visiting nurse associations and other organizations employing public health nurses began to increase their activities, and new work of various kinds was undertaken.

The Red Cross had organized a Department of Civilian Relief, the work of which consisted in looking after the needy families of soldiers and sailors. In this work the visiting nurse associations in the various cities cooperated by caring for the sick, as they were reported to them, and in giving their service to many families which, in ordinary times, would not have appealed to them.

Camp life, and the vicissitudes of military duty, had developed many cases of latent tuberculosis. These cases were returned to their homes, and the danger of an increased infection from the great white plague became imminent. In France, tuberculosis had increased in an appalling manner during the first two years of the war, and it was only by the most stringent methods that it was at last brought under control.

In order to avoid this menace renewed activities in anti-tuberculosis measures became necessary, and here, of course, the public health nurse was needed in great numbers.

The physical examination of the soldiers had disclosed the great prevalence of the so-called *social dis-*

eases, and a special campaign was started by the Government to cope with this world-old problem. A Division of Veneral Diseases was established by the U. S. Public Health Service, and $1,000,000 appropriated for the first year's work, and a nation-wide program to combat the scourge was inaugurated. In this program—which included, besides scientific studies and medical measures, the establishment of special clinics and the education of the people by means of pamphlets, exhibits, placards and lectures—the public health nurse played an important part.

Again, the danger to child life arising from war conditions was well recognized, and a special campaign for child welfare was undertaken.

In England, during the first year of the war there had been a startling increase in the rate of infant mortality, due, doubtless, to the fact that many mothers were entering industry, that the price of milk was soaring, that the babies were left without proper food or attention, and that, because of the war, general medical and district nursing care was limited. Stringent steps were immediately taken, however, to mitigate these dangers. Home visiting was resumed; health centers for consultation were opened; nursing mothers in industry were given special consideration; until, by the second year of the war, the death rate of infants had decreased to below that of pre-war times.

America took warning by England's experience. All existing child welfare activities were greatly increased and many new ones started. The Federal Children's Bureau inaugurated a campaign for the conservation of child life, and named the year 1918 "Children's Year." The slogan was "1,000,000 infant lives saved in 1918," each State being expected to save its quota by preventive measures.

A wide and comprehensive program of work was outlined by the Bureau, and a series of leaflets bearing on the subject was printed and distributed in great numbers. About 17,000 local or community committees did the actual work. The first activity, and one that aroused a great deal of interest, was the weighing and measuring of babies throughout the land. This was done by doctors and nurses in some central place, health centers, schools, club rooms, etc., being usually selected for the purpose. For rural districts traveling clinics were furnished by "Baby Specials," i. e., a motor truck fitted up to carry the equipment necessary for the weighing and measuring tests, and manned by one or more doctors and public health nurses. A record card was furnished to each child after being weighed and measured. Nearly 7,000,000 of these cards were distributed, which gives some idea of the extent of the work done.

Naturally, this campaign aroused much enthusiasm, not only among the mothers themselves, but throughout the entire community wherever a clinic was held. The public began to perceive that the conservation of child life was not only a war measure, to be carried on for one year, but a peace measure for all time. State Departments of Health began to organize Divisions of Child Hygiene, and to support public health nurses; cities and counties did the same; and by the end of the year 24 States had appointed new groups of public health nurses for the special duty of child welfare.[1]

During the first few months following the entrance of the United States into the war the output of factories and industrial plants was greatly increased. Especially was this true of munition plants, ship-yards and other industries furnishing war equipment. The

[1] The conservation of Child Life meant, not only work with children, especially baby clinics, health centers and nutrition work, but also the care of the mother, and tremendous emphasis was placed on all phases of maternity work, including pre-natal, confinement, and post-natal care.

success of the army of soldiers at the front was dependent on the huge army of workers at home, and it was incumbent on the Government to keep this home army "fit." Nor was this an easy task. The strain to a nation, peaceful for many years, plunged suddenly into war, was quite as serious for the man at the machine as for the man at the front. A large per cent. of the young and able-bodied men had been drafted into the army, and yet the demand for laborers was greater than ever before. The result was that many men of poor physique, or too old for hard work, entered the industrial field. Women, too, replaced men in many industries, and the system of "speeding up" caused a strain on all. The best way in which to readjust industry so as to meet these changed conditions and safeguard the health of the worker became a serious problem.

The history of the first year of the war in England's munition plants was one of suffering and strain, demanding a human endurance almost undreamed of. "For seven days a week thousands of ill-nourished, poorly housed, well-nigh physically exhausted men, women and children started on their long hours of work at daylight, replacing night shifts equally underfed, equally poorly housed, each one trying to meet the peril of unpreparedness. Then the reaction of that first year's frantic effort came, and nature rebelled. Output decreased and many working days were lost through sickness." (Safeguarding the Worker as a War Economy. By Florence B. Downing. Public Health Nurse, Sept. 1918.)

The English nation at last awoke to the necessity of protecting the health of its workers. Hours were shortened; rest periods inaugurated; facilities for hot noon-day meals and healthful recreation established; and with these rational changes the output again increased, and England was able to furnish a steady and continuous supply of products from the factory to the soldier in the line throughout the war.

Again America determined to take warning from England's bitter experience. Employers in all parts of the country began to install medical and social welfare departments in their plants. A clarion cry was sent forth for industrial nurses. The demand greatly exceeded the supply. A serious effort was made to recruit them from the field of public health nurses, as it was felt, with reason, that the social training of a public health nurse would be a great asset in the industrial field. It was impossible, however, to obtain a sufficient number, and many nurses with no previous social experience undertook the work. The result was that the standard of industrial nursing varied according to the personality and training of those carrying it on.

At the beginning of the war there had been only a few nurses in a limited number of industries; by September 1919 there were 1213 graduate nurses employed in this field, not counting practical nurses and those of inferior training.

By far the most interesting piece of work undertaken by public health nurses, however, was that carried on in the Extra-Cantonment Sanitary Zones under the Federal Public Health Service. For the first time in history public health nurses were employed by the Federal Government, and a precedent established for future health work.

When the United States entered the great world war, one of the first problems which confronted her was the opening up and preparing of suitable camps for the vast army of soldiers which she was suddenly called upon to train. After a careful survey of the country certain camp sites were selected in various parts of the country, and equipped with everything that modern science could suggest for the proper care and protection of the men. The establishment of camps, and the

23

steps taken to insure, as far as possible, the health and comfort of the soldiers quartered in them is a fairly old business, and the military authorities were equipped to carry on the work. When, however, they began to consider the various dangers to health which menaced the soldier, once he stepped outside the camp boundaries, it was a different matter.

In the past, the sanitary activities concerning the army had centered in the camp proper; now it was realized that to have camp sanitation effective these activities must reach out into the surrounding country through which the soldiers might wander in search of recreation, or from which his food supplies, etc. might be procured. There was little use in protecting the soldiers from impure water in the camp if any day he could go into the nearby town and drink contaminated water from the public supply; if the soldier was to be kept free from communicable diseases, the civilian with whom he came in contact must also be kept from contracting and spreading them.

The problem of camp sanitation naturally developed upon the military authorities; but the problem of the sanitation of the surrounding country was one for the public. On whose shoulders should it rest? The problem was seen and it had to be met. "Rural communities which for generations had employed the most rudimentary methods of excrement disposal, had to be led into the paths of sanitary righteousness; areas whose names were a by-word for malaria, had to be rendered free of mosquitoes; the water supply, sewage disposal apparatus, and scavenging systems of large cities had to be put into an efficient state. Who should assume the responsibility?" (Surgeon-General Blue, National Geographic.) The health departments of the rural districts and small towns were usually too poor, both in money and men, to undertake so heavy a burden; the state appropriations for sanitary purposes had already been made, and the State Boards of Health had, in many cases, no money to apply to new work. Therefore, the minds of men turned naturally to the Federal Government. The health authorities felt that this new and far-reaching work was a proper function of the general government, and that the United States Public Health Service, in co-operation with the munici-palities, counties and states, should undertake the per-formance of the task.

A plan of operation was, therefore, outlined, and a Bureau of Sanitary Service created, with headquarters in Washington, and an officer of the Public Health Service placed in charge. The American Red Cross, feeling that it was its duty to assist in this work for the protection of the soldiers' health, came foward with offers of assistance, and operations were soon in full swing. Sanitary zones, surrounding encampments for a distance of five to 100 miles, were established, and a group of workers placed in each zone.

The method of procedure was for the Red Cross to form a sanitary unit, of which the Public Health Service Officer in charge of the sanitary zone was director; sanitary inspectors, bacteriologists, public health nurses and clerks were then appointed to carry on operations. The undertaking included work in rural districts, as well as in the towns and districts adjacent to the camps. In establishing this work the Federal Public Health Service endeavored to let the local health authorities continue their own activities and responsibilities as far as possible, the Federal Service taking over only such work as was not already adequately provided for.

Of course conditions varied in the various sections of the country, and the needs of one sanitary zone varied from the needs of another. Nevertheless, there were certain fundamental things which had to be in-vestigated in all alike.

(1) The water supply, both public and private, had to be investigated, analyzed and standardized. (2) The milk analyzed and dairies inspected. (3) The sewage disposal facilities, both in town and country districts, investigated and proper facilities installed. (4) Adequate garbage disposal arranged for and protection against disease-bearing insects assured, which included the draining of malarial districts, oiling of stagnant ponds, etc. (5) Arrangement for adequate housing facilities and the enforcement of proper housing laws and clean food laws; and (6) finally, a survey of all school children, in order to prevent possible epidemics of communicable or contagious diseases.

The work of the public health nurse in this scheme of action was mostly investigative, instructive and educational. She was expected to provide proper care for those suffering with dangerous and contagious diseases, but actual bedside nursing was not a part of her work. The duty of the Public Health Service— city, state or national—was conceived to be to protect the public health, not to give individual bedside care; the actual care of the sick, therefore, became a problem for the private organizations already existing in the various communities; and a co-ordination of the work done by the nurses under the U. S. Public Health Service and by those engaged in local work became a necessity.

In order to bring about this co-ordination of public health nursing forces, and also, where none existed, to establish and standardize such work in the various extra-cantonment sanitary zones, it was decided to appoint a general supervising nurse under the Federal Public Health Service, and Miss Mary E. Lent, on nomination by the Red Cross, was appointed to the position. Miss Lent was at that time Associate Secretary to the National Organization for Public Health Nursing, taking the place of Miss Crandall, who had been "loaned" to the Nursing Committees under the

Council of National Defense. With patriotic unselfishness, however, and though thereby seriously crippling its office force, the National Organization willingly freed Miss Lent for this new war work, and in November 1917 she became an officer of the U. S. Public Health Service. She immediately started out on a tour of inspection of the public health nursing in the various sanitary zones throughout the country. During the first nine months of her service she travelled nearly 12,000 miles.

The problems found in the various zones were manifold. In some places there were numerous organizations employing public health nurses, but they were often seriously duplicating each other's work, while at the same time leaving certain branches of the work utterly unattended to. In such cases it was the duty of the supervising nurse to confer with the different groups of workers and assist them in establishing a more comprehensive and practical organization of their work. Again, there might be one or two nurses working along one line, as school work, maternity work, etc. In such cases it was thought wise to have them work with the public health nurses of the Sanitary Unit and under the control of the Federal officer. In still other zones, no public health nursing had ever been attempted, and the development of the work was slow and discouraging. In every case Miss Lent endeavored to co-operate with the local agencies, and to educate the people of the community to an understanding of the problems involved and their own responsibility in the matter. "We have tried so far as possible," says she, in the report of her work given at the annual convention of the National Organization for Public Health Nursing, May 1918, "to co-ordinate all the nursing agencies in a community—the Associated Charities, the Social Service Bureau, the Visiting Nurse Association, Board of Education and city nurses doing school or other types of public health work, and the local Red Cross.   These, and the nurses under the United States Public Health Service, have usually all united and put their work under the direction of the directing officer of the Public Health Service.   The city and county communities that were within the particular zone were then divided into districts, and a nurse placed in charge of each particular district."

Besides organizing the nursing work in the various zones, assistance was also given in regard to systematic records, and rules for nurses were established in order to standardize the work.

The inspection of school children formed one of the most valuable pieces of work carried on by these nurses, many important facts being brought to light and several incipient epidemics of contagious diseases prevented.   In one a typhoid epidemic, which had been running unchecked for some time, fifteen to eighteen new cases developing each week, was investigated, the source of the infection discovered and the epidemic at once stopped.   In another case smallpox threatened the community, but, by energetic measures of isolation and vaccination, was curbed before it had fairly started. In many instances unsuspected cases of measles and mumps were discovered by the nurses, and by prompt precautionary measures prevented from spreading to others and infecting the soldiers.

By January 1919, when Miss Lent resigned her position, the war being over, she had organized the nursing work in thirty-seven zones and had under her direction a staff of two hundred nurses. (Public Health Nurse, 1919, p. 15)

"For the first time in history," said Surgeon-General Blue in speaking of this work, "the U. S. Public Health Service organized a division of Public Health Nursing.   The work which these nurses performed was inestimable.   It is not too much to say that without

MARY E. LENT, R. N.

Supervising Nurse, Extra Cantonment Zones, under the U. S.
Public Health Service November, 1917 to January, 1919. Former
Associate Secretary of the National Organization for Public Health
Nursing.

their aid our success in keeping down sickness in the Extra-Cantonment Zones, and in making the venereal disease rate in our army lower than that of any other army in modern times, could not have been achieved."

But the work during the war and for the army was not the only, nor in fact, the greatest part of this special war service.

"Miss Lent's work," said Miss Crandall at the end of the war, "is unquestionably the greatest single war service rendered by the National Organization for Public Health Nursing to the Government and to the public —*its permanent influence is incalculable.*"

Gradually the zones were closed, the Federal officers withdrew, and the continuance of the nursing work was left in the hands of local organizations. But the minds of the people had been awakened; whereas before the war the public health nursing, in most of these communities, had been poorly and insufficiently carried on—or not carried on at all—it was now well established, and it was not likely that the people would ever give it up. It was this organizing of standardized public health nursing in widely-separated and often out-of-the-way districts, throughout the United States, that made Miss Lent's work in the Extra-Cantonment Zones of such great value, and, although the results have not in all cases come up to expectation, still its influence has been widespread, and it is this influence as much as any other single achievement, which has increased the demand for public health nurses, and set a standard of work throughout the land.

CHAPTER XXIII

WAR AND THE PUBLIC HEALTH NURSE
(continued)

FRANCE.

But the war work of the public health nurse was not confined to this country. Even before America entered the great conflict many of them had already enlisted as Red Cross nurses and had gone abroad to do their part in caring for the sick or wounded soldiers, both at the front and in the great base hospitals behind the firing line.

Very soon, however, it was seen that in these war-racked countries not only the soldier but the civilian needed looking after and that France and the other nations were in dire need of public health care. In the devastated sections of Europe where for many months the people had been living in shell-torn houses or underground, without proper shelter, without proper food, in constant terror of the enemy, the health conditions were deplorable. The suffering among the children was especially appealing. The death rate of infants became alarming; little children forgot how to play and looked on at the horrors about them with mute terror; the older ones were stunned or dazed; all were white, and pinched and undernourished. Nor was the suffering of the very old less pitiful. They, too, felt the lack of food and warm hearth-side; they, too, were dazed and bewildered; and, added to their bewilderment, was fear for their absent sons.

As the months passed a new problem arose in the

care of the refugees and repatriés from the occupied regions. For weeks they poured into France through the doorway of Switzerland, at the rate of hundreds, sometimes thousands, a day. Many of them were old and helpless; many of them children separated from their parents; many of them were so dazed that they did not know where they came from; and all were weak, and sick, and in need of medical care.

The cities, moreover, were crowded; housing inadequate; food scarce and expensive. Every condition for poor health and sickness was present, and means to cope with them lacking. The majority of the dispensaries were closed; half the civil hospitals had been converted into military hospitals; physicians were overworked; and visiting nursing, except on a very small scale in one district in Paris, was unknown. Public health work of every kind was necessary, if the future citizens of France were to be saved and the nation kept fit for its present Herculean task. The American Red Cross was not long in recognizing the peculiar fitness of the public health nurse for this work.

One of the first tasks undertaken was the care of babies. In August 1917 a Children's Bureau was established by the American Red Cross, with Dr. William Lucas in charge, and Miss Harriet Leete (who had been serving in one of the military hospitals) as chief of nurses.[1] Dr. Lucas at once set to work to organize a plan whereby the American Red Cross could get into touch with the different French Associations already existing for the reduction of infant mortality, such as the *Consultation de Nourrissons,* the *Crèches,* etc. His efforts met with hearty co-operation. Health centres were opened in various cities; traveling dispensaries

[1] At this time Miss Leete's title was chief nurse, and Miss Elizabeth Ashe was director of nurses. Later Miss Leete devoted her time to certain specialized work and Miss Ashe assumed the title of chief nurse.

were operated for the villages and country districts; children's hospitals and convalescent homes established and a far-reaching campaign for child welfare inaugurated. As usual, the public health nurse was one of the most necessary agents in the campaign, and many who had previously done baby work in America now joined the Red Cross in France.

A campaign against tuberculosis was also undertaken by the Red Cross in conjunction with the Rockefeller Foundation Miss Clara L. Shackford being chief nurse for the Red Cross, while Miss Elizabeth Crowell held the same position under the Rockefeller Commission. Tuberculosis clinics were started in Paris and other cities; home visiting and instruction instituted; and again the public health nurse was in demand.

One of the most interesting undertakings was the work for the refugees and repatriés. Only the old, the feeble, and the helpless children were sent back from the occupied regions, the able-bodied women being kept by the Germans to work in the fields or on the roads. It was necessary, therefore, to open up hospitals and homes for their reception, and to establish a thorough system of medical examination and care, in order to prevent their becoming a menace to the health of those among whom they would later be distributed. A letter from Miss Elizabeth Ashe, written from Evian, one of the receiving centres, gives a concise, but vivid picture of this work:

"Again I witnessed that ever tragic and moving sight," says she, "train loads of people arriving in France after an absence of three years. The train moves in slowly, the buglers play, eager faces appear at the windows; men, women and children weep as they shout 'Vive la France!' Our ambulance men tenderly lift the ill and feeble from the cars into wheeled chairs or on to stretchers. Many feeble men and tottering women refuse to be carried in the ambulance. They do not want to enter France in that helpless way, they wish to march with the crowd, shouting as they go, 'Vive la France!' Afterwards they are served a good hot meal, while the band plays patriotic airs. The dinner and music is followed by a medical inspection. We have a doctor and four nurses who undress and examine the children. Our ambulances are waiting to receive the hopital cases. After the medical examination every-one takes a hot shower bath, which is thoroughly en-joyed, clothes are disinfected, clean things given, and the history of each person carefully recorded. When the children are convalescent, they are transferred to our convalescent home, a wonderful place near Lyons."

In this work, as in the infant welfare and tuberculo-sis work, public health nurses were much interested and took their part. In this way, the work of the public health nurse was gradually introduced into France and visiting nursing became popular.

In order, however, to penetrate effectively into the homes of the poor, and especially in order to con-tinne the work after the Americans had withdrawn from the country, it was necessary to have *French* public health nurses. These did not exist. In fact, with the exception of a few notable examples, trained nurses, such as we know them in America and England, did not exist.[1] Much of the care of the sick in France was still in the hands of the Sisters, who, though kind and tender and with some experience in nursing, were not trained in the modern sense of the word; while the ordinary infermières were usually ignorant and in-capable women.

It was decided, therefore, to select a certain number of intelligent French ladies, who had, perhaps, been doing some nursing among the soldiers during the war, and to give them a course in medical-social subjects in

[1] "The Public Health Nurse," Vol. XI, p. 283, "What we Need in France," by Anna Hamilton, M.D.

order to fit them for such simple home visiting and instruction as was deemed necessary.

These courses were to cover a period of, some four, some ten, months of intensive work; after which an examination would be held and the successful candidate be given a certificate as *Visiteuse d'Hygiène,* (Health Visitor) or *Visiteuse d'Enfants,* (Children's Visitor), as the case might be. It was originally intended to call the graduates of these courses "nurses," but Miss Leete held that such short, incomplete training did not entitle a woman to the name of nurse, and insisted that they be called "visitors" instead. Her suggestion was finally agreed to.

The course for the *Visiteuse d'Hygiène* was given in Paris by the Rockefeller Commission for Tuberculosis and the Red Cross Children's Bureau combined. The pupils first had two months of theoretical and practical work, either in a tuberculosis or a children's hospital. This hospital course was followed by two months in a dispensary which had, in conjunction with the medical work, a supervised home nursing service. The home visiting was conducted on the family unit plan, with both tuberculosis and child supervision, the former being under Miss Elizabeth Crowell of the Tuberculosis Commission, the latter under Miss Marie Phelan of the Children's Bureau. Besides this ten months' course there was a shorter one of four months' special training in the care of children, which entitled the students to a certificate as *Visiteuse d' Enfants.* These *Visiteuses* were employed exclusively in the campaign to conserve child life.[1]

Another effort at training French women as *Visiteuses,* to follow up the children in their homes and to give instruction to the mothers, was undertaken in Lyons,

1 (The outline of these courses is given in a Report by Miss Leete in The Public Health Nurse, August 1918.)

—1918

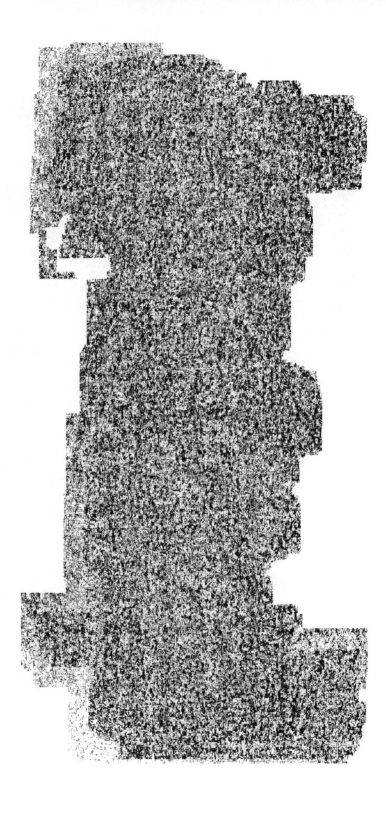

where the Children's Bureau of the Red Cross, in co-
operation with a local committee of French citizens, had
for some time been carrying on a fine piece of work
among the sick and debilitated repatriés children.[1]   A
group of intelligent French women, who had been doing
nursing during the war, and who therefore had some
idea of ordinary nursing care, were chosen, and a course
of four months theoretical and practical work given
them.   Lectures on obstetrics and pediatrics were given
each day by French physicians, the students also making the rounds with the doctors in the children's and the
obstetric wards, and assisting at the public clinic for
babies.   The practical demonstration and teaching was
given in the homes of the people by the American
nurses.   This course, planned and supervised by Dr.
Clifford G. Grulee and Miss Sophie Nelson, also entitled the student to a certificate of *Visiteuse d'Hygiéne*.

These various short courses in public health nursing
were of course far from adequate, but the emergency
was great and a compromise was necessary to meet the
need.   The French people quickly became intensely interested in the public health nurse and saw the value
of her work, physicians co-operated whole-heartedly.
Patriotic and philanthropic women arose to support
the movement, and many young French girls offered
themselves for the training and entered with enthusiasm upon the new effort toward the restoration of their
country's health.

After the war was ended public health nursing in
France was not abandoned, the American Red Cross
continuing to give it aid, and to supplement the work
of the French wherever needed.

The Rockefeller Foundation also continued its assistance, helping to establish health centers and tuberculo-

[1] The American Red Cross introduced visiting nurses in Lyons
in 1917.   There are now (1921) ten times as many visiting
nurses there as there were two years ago.

sis clinics throughout France, and co-operating in the
organization of short two year courses of training for
both bedside nurses and public health visitors, Miss
Crowell remaining in charge of the work.

In a recent report on the anti-tuberculosis work in
France (Bulletin of the League of Red Cross Societies,
December 1921) Dr. Bruno, of the Rockefeller Commission, speaking of the application of American methods in this campaign said that within three years
the number of tuberculosis dispensaries in France had
increased from 22 to 312, while 99 others were in proc-
ess of organization. The short two year courses in
training are also being extended to different parts of
the country.

One piece of post-war work of great interest is that being carried on by the American Committee for Devastated France.

Through its nursing service, which was directed by
Mrs. Breckenridge and Miss Evelyn Walker, an extensive system of public health nursing was established
shortly after the war.

This work which began in May, 1919, with one American nurse, working in the one little village of Vic, in
the Department of the Aisne, grew rapidly until by
September 1921 it extended to one hundred and six
villages and to two large towns, Soissons in the Aisne,
and Rheims in the Marne, and was carried on by twenty-
seven nurses—most of whom were French graduate
nurses trained in public health work.

In speaking of the work carried on in the Department
of the Aisne a recent report says: "Each nurse has a
certain number of villages under her care and in those
villages she knows all the children from birth to 14
years, all the pregnant mothers, and all the sick people. Her calls come to her from the mayor, the priest,
the schoolmaster and the people themselves, and of

course the doctor, though it is more often she who calls the doctor. She visits every village every two weeks to weigh the babies and look after the child of pre-school age; she arranges the medical examinations of the school children, helps the doctor and does the follow up work; she advises the pregnant woman and helps her to make arrangements for her confinement, and she cares for the sick and injured—for we still have many shell accidents. Each nurse has a Ford camionette at her disposal, otherwise she could not cover a quarter of the territory, for which she is responsible."

This work which includes weekly clinics for sick and well babies and prenatal work as well as school work and general home nursing is already beginning to show very decided results. The French statistics on infant mortality for 1921 in the Aisne show 89 per thousand as the rate of infant mortality for the whole department and only 35 per thousand in the territory of the four counties covered by the work of the public health nurses. Moreover the capital of the department, Laon, a town of about 15,000 inhabitants where no baby hygiene nursing service has been installed, shows an infant mortality rate of 110 per 1000; while in Soissons, a town of the same size,. but with a well established child hygiene service, the rate is only 54 per 1000 —a most astonishing showing.

This work, as can be seen, has been from the first largely carried on by French workers with American assistance.

It is intended to withdraw the American nurses in the near future leaving the continuance of this work entirely in the hands of the French people. In fact this is the policy of all the various American organizations which have been assisting the French during and since the war, and already most of the actual field work is conducted by them, a few Americans remaining merely to offer advice and counsel in administration and supervising matters.

The essential weakness in all the French public health nursing work is the lack of a proper hospital training foundation for the nurses. There is danger that, in their enthusiasm, women will be encouraged to take up public health work when their real training in nursing is negligible from a nurse's point of view. If this superstructure of public health work is built up without the solid foundation which we in this country deem so essential, there is great danger that public heal h nursing in France will become wholly confused wi:h mere social service, and that the French public health nurse of the future will become a combination charity agent and sanitary inspector, with an admixture of dispensary or first aid worker in accident cases.

One of the most encouraging auguries for the future of public health nursing in France is, that at the Bordeaux Hospital Training School, now known as the Florence Nightingale School and endowed by American nurses, an opportunity is being offered, not only for theoretical training in public health nursing but for extensive practice in the field as well. The American Red Cross is still keeping very close in touch with the work there and is still paying the salary of the head nurse of the visiting nurse work, Miss Hay.

The following description of the special accommodations erected for these French visiting nurses is interesting.

"In the garden attached to the *Maison de Santé Protestante* stands an attractive little brick building— put up by the American Red Cross, and used as a special office for the visiting nurses. The most perfect order reigns throughout these three small rooms. In the first are kept the bicycles, with which in spite of winter's mud and summer's sun the nurses make their daily rounds in

French Visiting Nurses with Their Bicycles, Bordeaux, France.

the town and suburbs. Little baskets are fastened to the handle-bars, miraculously filled with everything necessary for the care of the patients. In the second room one finds the medical supplies, stored in two glass cupboards of American origin; also the registry, where is kept a card catalogue of the cases carried and care given. The third room is to be used for a milk dispensary."

(Translated from a pamphlet on "Example de Florence Nightingale" by Chas. D. Morris.)

The French people have become keenly interested in public health nursing and it is hoped that in time France will have a well-organized public health nursing service of her own.

ITALY

In the latter part of 1918 the American Red Cross appointed a Commission to go to Italy and there assist the Italian people in their fight against tuberculosis. A new feature in this Commission was a Bureau of Public Health Nursing, consisting of about fifteen nurses, with Miss Mary S. Gardner at the head as Director. On arriving in Italy the Commission found the country in the throes of the Spanish Influenza, that terrible epidemic which swept over both Europe and America during the years of 1918 and 1919, as the Black Plague had swept over Europe many centuries earlier.

This unexpected encounter somewhat delayed the original plan of work, but, on the other hand, it gave the nurses, especially, an exceptional opportunity for the very thing which they most desired, namely, an entrance into the homes of the people and a working knowledge of home conditions.

After the first intensive work in combating the epidemic and in caring for the influenza patients was over, a careful study of conditions was made and a general plan of work outlined, the main feature of which was

24

to help establish an organization for anti-tuberculosis work which should be national in character and which, being entirely in the hands of the Italians themselves, would give the undertaking the permanency which was necessary and make it possible to continue the work long after the American Commission had returned to its own country.

In this scheme the need of the public health nurse was made apparent. Now in Italy, as in France, public health nursing as understood in England and America was non-existent. The first thing the Bureau of Public Health Nursing did, therefore, was to try to understand nursing conditions in Italy, and to arouse a desire on the part of the people for the service which a public health nurse could give. For this purpose three surveys, or local studies, were made, one in Milan in the North, another in Aquila in the Abruzzi region; and a third in Naples in the South. It was felt that the conditions found in these three widely separated localities would be fairly indicative of conditions throughout the country.

The result of this painstaking inquiry seemed to establish the fact that there were few graduate nurses, that the care of the sick was largely in the hands of untaught nurses, or *infermieries* (a common and ignorant type of woman) and that there were several groups of partially trained women, such as the Italian Red Cross nurses, who had taken lessons in nursing under the Red Cross; and the Samaritana nurses, who had taken short courses in the Scuola Samaritana.

The effort to arouse a desire for public health nursing was not difficult. The emergency work which the American nurses had done in connection with the influenza had been an *Open Sesame,* and the people welcomed them with open arms. It would have been a simple matter to have placed a few American nurses in various Italian towns and cities, and thus to have established public health nursing in the country.

But such a procedure would have been but a temporary arrangement. Miss Gardner, with wise forethought, realized that unless the work were placed in the hands of the Italians themselves, and women were trained to continue it after the Americans withdrew, that no permanent benefit would result, and that it would be but a passing war measure which would terminate with the close of the war.

It was therefore decided to place a very limited number of American nurses in what might be called *holding positions,* which could be held and developed by them until such times as Italian students could be educated to replace them.

These American nurses entered upon their work with enthusiasm, and were soon stationed in various cities and towns, these being selected according to the peculiar needs of the people or the work.

The second step was to educate the Italian workers who were later to supplant the American Nurses. For this purpose two schools for *Infermierie Visitatrici* were opened, the one in Rome, on March 17th, 1919; the other in Genoa in April of the same year; still later a third course was planned and started in Florence, Miss Elnora Thomson having supervision over all the schools.

One American nurse was placed in local charge of each school. Miss Mary Davis and Miss Ethel Nichols in Genoa, Miss Pearl Kamera in Rome, and Miss Ruth Houlton in Florence, while six others in each city acted as instructors in dispensary work and home visiting. Lectures were given by Italian doctors, and a few by American doctors with interpreters, and conferences were held by American nurses. The lectures were planned by Miss Elnora Thomson, the subjects taught being: History of Public Health Nursing, Theory and Methods of Public Health Work, Tuberculosis

Nursing, Child Welfare Nursing, School Hygiene Nursing, Obstetrical Nursing, Dietetics, Sanitation, Housing.

The courses were to last four months, the first three being divided between lectures and field work, and the last given over entirely to field work.

The most difficult part of the plan was arranging for supervised field work. This, however, was accomplished through the employment of the American nurses as district supervisors, the students accompanying them to the homes of the patients and assisting in the work.

A report of the cases visited by these Italian pupils, given out by Signorina Gina Fadda, who succeeded Miss Kamera as Director of the School at Rome, shows that they encountered the same problems met with by their sisters in this country, and that they are learning to meet and solve them in the same spirit of constructive philanthropy.   (Public Health Nurse, vol. 12, p. 945)

The Italians have shown a keen interest from the first, in public health nursing, and are now carrying it on by themselves in a manner which augurs well for the future.   Since the war several Italian ladies have visited this country, to study our work and methods, in order to return and introduce these same methods in their own work.   We feel, therefore, that public health nursing is well started in Italy, and that its spread and development is only a matter of time.

The work done in France and that done in Italy was dissimilar.   That carried on in France during the war was not homogeneous, it was not planned in advance, and carried on under the supervision of one organization (the Red Cross), as was the similar work undertaken in Italy, but was the result of a pressing need, perceived gradually as the war advanced and undertaken by several different organizations to meet different needs. Various forms of specialized work were undertaken at various times, under various groups of people. It lacked, therefore, something of the unity of purpose and standard of organization, which prevailed in Italy. In the latter country the work was all organized under one group—the American Red Cross— in affiliation with local Italians—and each center was established under the same supervision and on the same general principles in training and work.

In Italy as in France, however, some kind of training for the work has seemed to be the first necessity. In both countries, therefore, short courses have been introduced to meet the need. As the work progresses, however, and as nursing as a profession is more widely recognized in these countries, it is hoped that these short courses will be superseded by thorough hospital training which will include, or be supplemented by, the training and study necessary for successful public health work.

Into many other countries also has public health nursing been introduced through the exigencies of the great war. The various Relief Commissions sent out by the governments of America and England, and by the American Red Cross, to help carry relief to the famine stricken countries of Central Europe, Russia and the Near East, have usually combined some medical and health work with their other activities, and in this work the nurse has taken her part. In this way public health nursing has been introduced into Greece, Roumania, Serbia, Russia, Poland, and many other lands where, heretofore, it has been utterly unknown, and although we cannot say that the work is as yet organized, still the seed has been planted and later will, we hope, bear fruit.

Immediately after the war a *League of Red Cross Societies* was organized, in which most of the civilized countries of the world are represented. The primary object of this League is "the development of National

Red Cross Societies for community service in the field of public health" (Bulletin of the League of Red Cross Societies, July-August, 1921. P. 481). This service places special emphasis on child welfare, tuberculosis, and venereal disease, and urges popular instruction and the employment of public health nurses. As there were no such nurses in these various countries, the first step was to create them. An International Course in Public Health Nursing, planned by Miss Alice Fitzgerald, Director of the Department of Nursing of the League of Red Cross Societies, was therefore established at King's College, London, and free scholarships offered by the League to the National Red Cross Societies of ten countries, chosen because of their post-war conditions, or because the local Red Cross Society of the country was not sufficiently developed to carry the responsibility itself. Other students paid for themselves. The result was that nineteen young women from eighteen different countries attended the first year (1920). These students were women of birth and breeding, and represented the best intellectual class. They had all received the best training for nurses offered in their own particular country, usually under the Red Cross Societies, and had rendered splendid nursing service during the war. The countries represented in this first class were; Belgium, Canada, Czecho-Slovakia, Denmark, France, Great Britain, Greece, Italy, Peru, Poland, Portugal, Roumania, Russia, Servia, Sweden, Switzerland, United States, Venezuela.

These young women have now all returned to their homes and are endeavoring to establish a new method and a new standard in nursing and health work in their own lands.

The work varies in the different countries. In Belgium the accent has been chiefly laid on child welfare work, and very encouraging results have already been obtained, especially in the reduction of infant mortality. Czecho-Slovakia has also entered upon a quite ambitous program of child conservation, twenty-two infant welfare stations having been opened in various parts of the country, each under the direction of an American Red Cross nurse, a social worker and a doctor. Poland has a peculiarly difficult task. "If Poland is to live," says the Bulletin of the League of Red Cross Societies (1921), "she must save her infants who, deprived of maternal milk, are exposed to the scourge of tuberculosis." A great effort, therefore, is being made to open health centres throughout the country, where medical examination by local Polish doctors will be available for children, and where a milk station may be established.

In Serbia the work is wholly rural. Ten health centres have been established, with local doctors and two American Red Cross nurses in charge. One nurse is expected to confine herself to school work, while the other devotes herself to home nursing. A recent report of this work says: "These dispensaries serve a large country-side . . . and average four to five hundred patients a month with thirty to sixty home visits (often to far distant hamlets), and the examination of from two to three hundred school children." (The Public Health Nurse, January 1922.)

It is difficult to estimate what the establishment of all this various health work may mean to the wide-spread dissemination of public health nursing. In countries where, hitherto, there was little knowledge of preventive health work, and practically no knowledge of modern nursing, there will now be established public health nursing, and this not by strangers, or for a short period only, but by their own people and in the way which will best apply to their own peculiar needs.

Miss Katherine Olmsted, who occupies the position of

Associate Director of the Department of Nursing of the League of Red Cross Societies (1921), in speaking of this course says:

"The experiment of bringing together students from many countries for a course in public health nursing; the standardizing of their methods, and points of view; the sending back to many countries of a strongly equipped advocate of nursing standards, is so sure to be of success and value that another course is being planned for next year."

The best of this method of introducing public health nursing into a country as yet without it, is, that it *begins with education,* and is undertaken and carried on by the countries themselves, with their hearty consent and understanding.

And so, out of a world-wide cataclysm may come a world-wide benefit; and health and "health nursing" be available to all nations.

CHAPTER XXIV

AFTERMATH OF THE WAR

The effect of the great war on public health nursing was epoch making. In England, and in America the prevalence of preventable disease, disclosed through the physical examination of hundreds of thousands of soldiers, aroused a national consciousness in regard to public health which years of didactic preaching could not have achieved. The health of the individual, both at the front and behind the line, became a matter of definite and practical concern, and public health work on a scale almost inconceivable was undertaken and made possible by the immense sums of money which war times possess—and which peace times have the dreary rôle of repaying. But the interest aroused by this advertisement of our damaged human stock was not transitory; it created an enduring impression which has remained as an inspiration and incentive for future work.

ENGLAND.

The Ministry of Health

In England the effect was almost revolutionary. Not only was the work already being carried on, increased and stimulated, but an entire reorganization of the administration of all national public health activities was inaugurated, and a new department of the Government created to have jurisdiction over them.

The realization that concentration of energy and elimination of all waste effort was vital to military success, reacted upon civil departments, and led to an examination of their work with a view to greater efficiency and economy of time. In July 1917 there was appointed a sub-committee of the Reconstruction Committee, known as the "Machinery of Government Committee," whose business it was to inquire into the various departments of the Central Government, and advise as to how their various functions might best be exercised.

In the Report of this sub-committee a special section was devoted to the Health Service, which included "all those activities of the Central Government which are directed to maintaining or improving the physical well-being of the population at large." These activities at that time rested in the hands of a number of separate departments, each exercising jurisdiction over a portion of the province of public health. The committee expressed its belief that, in order to facilitate the work then being carried on by these various departments, and to increase their activities, there should be a concentration of all health services in one department under a Minister of Health.

This was revolutionary. Many difficulties, however, had to be overcome before the functions and responsibilities of the new Ministry, and its relationship to the various government departments which touched, in more or less degree, upon matters of health, could be defined.

On February 7th, 1919, however, a bill to establish a Ministry of Health was introduced in the House of Commons, and, after the usual lengthy discussion, was finally passed, and received the Royal Assent on June 3rd, 1919, Dr. Christopher Addison being appointed as the first Minister of Health.

The formation of this Ministry marked the change of attitude which had gradually been taking place in England toward the whole question of health and sickness; the very title, Ministry of *Health,* marked the new conception of a national and governmental responsibility to prevent disease and preserve the health of the people.

English nurses were, from the first, keenly alive to the importance of this new Ministry, and its bearing on the nursing profession. Hardly had the Ministry been formed, indeed, before it was able to show its close relationship to nursing matters by action in regard to nursing registration. For many years English nurses had been making strenuous efforts to have a bill passed to provide state registration, but diverse interests were involved and their efforts had been unsuccessful. One of the first actions on the part of Dr. Addison, therefore, was to draft a bill which would incorporate what the Government was prepared to give, and at the same time should embody the main principles advocated by the Society for State Registration of Trained Nurses. This bill was approved by the nursing profession, was passed by Parliament, and received the Royal Assent December 23rd, 1919, thereby giving to English nurses the protection they have so long sought.

The effect of the new Ministry of Health on the work of the district nurse has been particularly far-reaching. The term "Public Health Nurse" has not yet been generally adopted by England, except for those nurses acting specifically under the direction of some one department of public health service; for, though the Queen's Nurses have been concerning themselves more and more with educative and public health matters, and have been doing child welfare work, maternity work, teaching the tuberculous patient, etc., for many years, nevertheless the district is still looked upon as her special province, and the care of the sick as her chief activity.

However, as the nurse is the universally accepted agent for carrying out a large part of the program of Preventive Medicine, and as the district nurse was already in the field, there has necessarily been a very close connection between the Ministry of Health and the Queen's Nurses.

"For more than thirty years," said the *Daily Telegraph,* "the Queen's Institute has been fighting against disease, bad conditions, and the other enemies of a healthy race, until at the present time (1921) it has over 5000 nurses engaged in curative, preventive and educative work in the homes of Great Britain and Ireland."

It was natural, therefore, that this large force of trained workers, already familiar in the homes of the people, should have been used whenever possible by the Ministry of Health in carrying out its program of health work. Especially has this been done in the maternity and child welfare service, and in the school medical service.[1]

The School Medical Service comprises:

(a) The medical inspection of children and young persons in public elementary, secondary and continuation schools;

(b) the medical and dental treatment of those requiring it;

(c) hygiene and physical training in training colleges and elementary, secondary and continuation schools;

(d) the administration of the Education (Provision of Meals) Acts;

(e) special schools for blind, deaf, defective and subnormal children;

(f) nursery schools;

(g) restrictions on the employment of children;

(h) the control of infective disease in schools.

[1] The Ministry of Health is responsible to Parliament for this latter, which, however, is carried out under the Board of Education.

A Queen's Nurse of Today—1922.

The staff of the local education authorities is responsible for the carrying out of the program, and includes (Report of 1919-1920) 1575 whole time, and 452 part time school nurses, whose duties, as can be seen from the foregoing outline, are very similar to those of school nurses in the United States.

No function of the Ministry of Health, however, is more important than that which has to do with maternity and child welfare, and to this task of preserving the lives and health of her mothers and children England has set herself with strong and well directed energy. Here, of course, the Queen's Nurses have found a familiar and congenial field of work, and have taken a large part in its performance. A great number of Queen's Nurses are certified midwives and are, therefore, able to attend patients in that capacity, as well as to help in the Schools for Mothers and the Infant Welfare Centres, which are being established everywhere throughout the Kingdom.

The good results of this active campaign for the health of mother and child are already seen in the reduction of the rate of infant mortality, which, for 1919, was 89 per 1000 births for England and Wales, the lowest on record.

In this work of child welfare the effort is directed mainly towards:

    (a) Health Visiting.
    (b) Infant Welfare Centres.

In April 1920 the number of "Health Visitors" was 3359, of which only 1130 were district nurses.

Unfortunately, according to American ideas, a health visitor is not necessarily a trained nurse—although training in nursing is recognized as a desirable background, if supplemented by training in public health work. In other words, England has recognized, as has America, that hospital training alone does not qualify a nurse as a teacher of hygiene among the people, and that qualities and instruction other than those found necessary for good bedside nursing are essential if the message of health and the lesson of how to attain and preserve it is to be gotten over to the masses.

In America we have endeavored to meet this need by additional training, insisting on a nurse's training as the fundamental requirement; we have, therefore, the Public Health Nurse.   In England, they have tried to meet the need by employing one agent—the nurse—for bedside care (and when possible for health work also); and another—the Health Visitor—for purely educative and instructive work.   Which of the two methods will prove the best, time alone will show.

As early as 1908 the need was felt in England for additional women to act as teachers of the people in matters pertaining to health, and an Act was passed sanctioning the employment in London of suitable women as health visitors, the qualifications, duties, salary, etc. of these health visitors being regulated by the Local Government Board.   Not having at that time the experience necessary for the establishment of a special training course, the Board laid down the following requirements for those who sought to qualify as health visitors:—

(a) A medical degree; or
(b) the full training of a nurse; or
(c) the certificate of the Central Midwives Board; or
(d) some training in nursing and the Health Visitor's Certificate of a society approved by the Board; or
(e) the previous discharge of duties of a similar character in the service of a Local Authority.[1]

[1] Annual Report of Chief Medical Officer, Ministry of Health. 1919–1920.

As time went on, and the number of health visitors increased in London and elsewhere, various short courses of instruction were organized, by means of which students could gain certificates or diplomas in health visiting. But it was not until 1919 that a standard training was officially prescribed. At that time the Board of Education, with the concurrence of the Ministry of Health, issued regulations covering two courses of training: a two-year course for persons 18 years and over, who are not qualified nurses; and a one-year course for trained nurses. These courses are provided by the following institutions:—

King's College for Women, University of London.
Battersea Polytechnic.
Bedford College for women (University of London).
University College of South Wales and Monmouthshire.
Liverpool School of Hygiene.
(Note Appendix VII)

The official point of view regarding the training of health visitors is expressed in the following statement, taken from the Annual Report of the Chief Medical Officer of the Board of Education (1919):

"Health visiting is social, educational, and preventive work. It is not in the narrow sense remedial or curative. The training given in a general hospital is not designed to equip a woman to become a health visitor. It was, therefore, considered that, in view of their primary function, health visitors need not be required to possess full nursing qualifications, though there are clearly many advantages in a sound understanding of nursing, and the habits of duty, discipline, and devotion acquired in the course of a hospital training is in itself a valuable acquisition quite apart from the technical knowledge gained. Yet, by general consent, the hospital trained nurse requires further instruction in the prevention of disease to give her the outlook and attitude of mind which the health visitor should have."

The training of health visitors appears to be still in a somewhat experimental stage, however, and recent statements indicate that the present prescribed training has not proved altogether satisfactory. That the training of a nurse, as the foundation of preparation for health visiting, is proving its value would also seem to be the case. England and the United States alike have realized that *health teaching* is the basis of *health living;* both have seen in the training of the nurse many of the fundamental requisites for the training of the health teacher, both as regards the formation of character and the kind of knowledge and ability acquired; both have seen also that, in as much as the training in the hospital ward deals with the sick and not with the well—with the abnormal instead of with the normal—it requires modification and addition to make it the ideal preparation for those whose chief value must be in their ability to teach how to preserve the normal condition of life, which is health. Recognizing these facts, each country in her own way is striving to discover the best means to mould the instrument which shall meet her own needs and her own conditions. With the greater and greater accent on the education of the nurse, and with the greater division of her work into specialties, it would seem to us that the logical outcome of the experiment in England would be that the large force of district nurses already carrying on such fine home work throughout the country, should add to their present qualifications the training so necessary for successful public health work, and thus fit themselves for the enormous possibilities opening before them. On the shoulders of these home visitors, whoever they be, associated with the National Health Service, will depend the education of the people in habits of healthful living: it is hoped that the Queen's Nurses will see their opportunity and embrace it.

AMERICA.

The Education of the Public Health Nurse

In America the effect of the war on public health work was not so radical as in England, nevertheless, it increased that already begun and greatly stimulated public health nursing. One of the most important effects on the nursing situation was the increased interest which it aroused in nursing education. During those strenuous days when the Nursing Committees of the Council of National Defense were endeavoring, by every means possible, to stimulate the output of nurses; and when community after community called in vain for nursing aid, it was realized that in order to meet the shortage various short courses for the training of nurses might be introduced, thereby endangering the high standards so long and so proudly held in this country.

As a reaction against this fear, much stress was laid on the benefit to a nurse of a thorough high school, or even college, education before entering upon her hospital training, and the necessity of a full course in such a training before a woman would be competent to practice the profession of nursing, or to take into her hands the responsibility of the care of the sick.

The realization, by nurses and lay people alike, however, that the long period required for such thorough training—especially if it were to include four years in college, three in hospital, and perhaps a year of postgraduate work in some specialty—might deter desirable young women from entering the profession, led to the discussion of many possible compromises, such as:

    (a) A combined five year course, consisting of three years of college and two of hospital.

    (b) A three year course in hospital, the third year to be devoted to some specialty, such as hospital administration, public health nursing, etc.

25

In all such discussions, however, the great need of special training for public health nurses was made apparent, and an unprecedented demand for opportunities for this training arose. To meet this demand, colleges all over the country began to consider introducing courses in public health nursing into their curricula.

In 1916 a Department of Public Health Nursing was established in Simmons College, Boston, under which the earlier eight months' course of the District Nursing Association was placed, with Miss Anne H. Strong as Director, holding the title of Assistant Professor of Public Health Nursing. The four months' course continued to be given by the District Nursing Association, being also directed by Miss Strong, who had succeeded Miss Carr as Head of the Educational Department of the Association. There was no organic connection between the two courses.

This form of organization was not, however, altogether satisfactory; in 1918, therefore, the Department of Nursing of Simmons College was changed to the "School of Public Health Nursing," in order to conform more closely to the other schools of the College, and Miss Strong's title became "Director of the School and Professor of Public Health Nursing." In order, however, to preserve the close connection always maintained with the District Nursing Association, the School was placed under the joint direction of Simmons College and the Association.

Coincident with the opening of this school in 1918 a second course of five years, leading to the degree of Bachelor of Science, was announced. At the present time there are 25 students taking this course.

In the same year in which Simmons College opened its Department of Public Health Nursing, namely, 1916, Cleveland enlarged its "Class" into a "Special Course for Public Health Nurses," which became a constituent part of the School of Social Science of Western Reserve University, with Miss Cecilia Evans as Director. This Course, like others of its kind, was designed to give a basis for social work, and to relate the work of the public health nurse to other social activities, with an understanding of their common method and goal. Approximately half time was given to lectures, reading and class work; and half time to field work. At first this field work was carried on, as formerly, in the districts of the Visiting Nurse Association, under the direction of the District Supervisor. It gradually became apparent, however, that a District Supervisor is too busy with her other duties to act as special instructor to a class of inexperienced students; also, that in order to get the full benefit of the work done in the class-room, the theory already learned must be more closely related to the practical work being done in the districts.

A certain section of the city, therefore, offering a great variety of problems for study and treatment was set aside as a "Teaching District," the work in which was carried on entirely by the students, under the direction of Miss Evans and a staff of specially qualified instructors. The idea back of this Teaching District was, that in public health training, as in hospital training, the theory learned must be made applicable to practice before the very eyes of the students; that they must not only know, theoretically, that such and such a thing should be done, but must know how to do the thing themselves, and must have practice in doing it. In other words, a Teaching District is a laboratory, where the student can put her knowledge into practice, under the direction of her instructor.

The instruction given in the University Teaching District in Cleveland was very thorough and painstaking. In describing this work, Dr. Haven Emerson, in the Report of the Cleveland Hospital and Health Survey, 1920, says:

"When students begin their field work they are taken out, one at a time (very occasionally two at a time), by the Instructor, who gives the instruction in the home and does the work required, while the student observes. A thorough discussion of the visit follows. On a subsequent visit the rôles are reversed, the Instructor observing, whilst the student conducts the visit. This procedure is repeated with different types of visits, such as to prenatal cases, communicable disease cases, and so on, until the student has been gradually introduced to the various types of work usually encountered in the district."

(Cleveland Hospital and Health Survey. Nursing, Part IX.)

As the skill and knowledge of the student develop she is held increasingly responsible for the cases under her care, until at last she is able to carry full responsibility.

The idea of special teaching districts is gaining ground, other cities now following the Cleveland plan and reserving certain sections for this purpose.

Besides Simmons College and Western Reserve, other colleges, in ever increasing numbers, began to plan for courses in public health nursing and to write to the National Organization for information on the subject.

The special education .of the public health nurse became a burning question, and one which had to be judiciously dealt with, for, unless some standard were set and some supervision installed to see that the standard was conformed to, these courses might do more harm than good, and the last condition of the student be worse than the first, in that she would feel herself properly trained, whether she were or not.

In 1917 the Committee on Education of the National Organization for Public Health Nursing met in Philadelphia to formulate a standard for post-graduate work —a subject they had been working over for two years; and early in 1918 the Organization appointed Mrs.

Bessie Ammerman Haasis as Educational Secretary to assist in maintaining a standard and in developing public health nursing education throughout the country.   The great difficulty to be met was that many universities, anxious to be in the fore-front of this popular movement for nursing education, wished to establish courses in public health nursing, without having any idea of the real requirements necessary, or the dangers into which they might fall.

In speaking of this danger Mrs. Haasis said:

"As many as four Universities have written to the National Organization for Public Health Nursing within the past two months stating their intention or desire of starting courses for public health nurses.   Now in some places the University may not realize that through the lack of field work in their neighborhood it would be very undesirable for them to start a course, because all they could offer, although it might be good, would be theory, and we do feel strongly that field work is absolutely essential to any preparation, no matter how short."

In fact, good and adequate field work, under proper supervision, that is, under a supervisor who can *teach* as well as *supervise*—is considered quite as important, if not more so, than theory.   The field is the laboratory where the student can put her theory into practice, and learn by experience, as well as by instruction, the fundamental principles underlying her new profession; it is an absolutely necessary adjunct to class work.

During the time that Mrs. Haasis was Educational Secretary, she travelled almost constantly throughout the country, visiting the various universities or associations where the courses in public health nursing were being formed, and helping and advising in regard to them.   In most cases her suggestions were received with gratitude, and acted upon whenever possible.   A full course consisted of one collegiate year of work, or from eight to nine months, the time usually being divided equally between theory in the class room, and practice in the field, at the termination of which a certificate was to be given.

A few short courses of four months were also established, but for these the Educational Committee advised that no certificate be given. They consisted usually of field work, with interpretative class-room talks, certain lectures, and specified readings. These short courses were a concession to the great demand for public health nurses, and the pressing need of offering some standardized post graduate work to those who could not afford a full year for additional training, and yet desired to start their work with a proper general conception of the principles involved, and the methods of work followed.

By the fall of 1918 there were some fifteen standardized post-graduate courses in public health nursing being given in various parts of the country, most of them connected with Universities or Schools for Social Service, and covering a period of eight or nine months, with a certificate presented upon the completion of the course.

By 1921 there were twenty-four university courses in public health nursing,[1] all but four of which were endorsed by the National Organization. These courses form part of the regular post-graduate work offered by the colleges and the credits given may be applied toward requirements for a full B. S. degree.

The program of studies offered varies in different colleges, but usually includes biology, bacteriology, dietetics, practical sociology and preventive medicine and hygiene, besides different special courses in tuberculosis, mental hygiene, industrial hygiene, etc. The field work is supposed to include all branches of public health nursing, and is usually secured through affili-

[1] Three have recently been discontinued owing to lack of funds.

ation with the local visiting nurse association, or other special associations or groups of workers representing child welfare, tuberculosis, rural, school or industrial nursing; or, in some places, as we have already described, in a special section of the city set apart for the purpose.

These courses are now available to nurses in many parts of the country, some being located in the far west, some in the south, some in the middle west, as well as those older ones in the eastern and central states.

Special education of the nurse for public health work has been accepted as a desirable, if not yet as an absolutely necessary preparation for the task of public health nursing, and America leads the way in its attainment. (See also Chapter XX—Early Social Training for Nurses.)

Another effect of the war on public health nursing was the great extension of full pay service to those who were able to pay for it.

For many years far-sighted men and women among the workers for public health had emphasized the great need of dis-associating visiting nurses from charity and had urged that the pay service should be greatly extended. Visiting nurse associations themselves had also long realized that there was a vast field, vaguely called the "middle class," that needed their service— people either not able to pay for the full time of a private duty nurse, or those whose living conditions in small apartments, hotels, or boarding houses made the accommodation of a full time nurse difficult, and yet who would never think of receiving free care from a charity organization.

During the war, and especially during the influenza epidemic of 1917 and 1918, when the shortage of nurses was most acutely felt, a great many visiting nurse associations opened up what they called "A Pay Service Department," and furnished visiting nurses on a full pay basis at so much an hour to anyone needing nursing care. This service has in many cases been continued and extended, and is usually carried on by ` the regular staff nurse, in addition to her general district work. The main difference between this service and the so-called hourly nursing carried on by many private duty nurses is that in most cities it cannot be given at any specified time, but must be fitted in with the other daily work of the district in such a way as to best conserve the time and energy of the nurse. For this reason the price asked is usually much below that asked by a regular hourly nurse, being calculated to just cover the actual expense of the visit.[1]

This pay service is becoming very popular and as its great usefulness and availability becomes better known and understood by the public will doubtless form one of the main branches of visiting nursing in the future.

[1] This is not always the case. In Providence, for instance, a nurse is sent at any home asked for; and in Philadelphia also, by adding six nurses to the staff the Visiting Nurse Society has been able practically always to meet the approximate time desired. (See Chapter XV.)

CHAPTER XXV

PUBLIC HEALTH NURSING TODAY

One of the most conspicuous changes in the status of public health nursing today—and this also we may attribute to the war, and especially to Children's Year —is the increasing number of public health nurses found working under state and city health departments, which means the increasing use of public funds and taxes for their employment. No longer can the public health.nurse be called the "Servant of the Poor"—she has become a "public servant." City, county, state and federal governments are seeking her service. Her work, too, is becoming more and more instructive and preventive; it lies not only in the home, but in the school, the factory, the shop—even the street. It embraces not only the health of the family, but the health of the entire community.

The first city to pay for the service of a visiting nurse from public funds was, as we have seen, Los Angeles, who in 1898 paid the salary of the nurse, while the College Settlement directed her activities. In 1902 New York City undertook to pay for and direct the school nursing in that city. Later tuberculosis nurses and baby welfare nurses were taken over by Boards of Health in many cities. At present almost every city of any size in the county is carrying on some form of municipal public health nursing, either under its Board of Health or its Board of Education, and in some cities a complete service has been established. (See Chap. XVII, Los Angeles.)

State public health nursing is also making great

strides.   There are at present some 29 states directly
employing nurses through their state departments of
health.   In some of these states there are divisions or
bureaus of public health nursing; in others, bureaus of
child hygiene or of tuberculosis; in some the state employs merely one nurse as director, who supervises locally supported public health nurses; in others, again,
there is a large staff, consisting of director, supervisors
and field nurses.   Some assume full financial responsibility for the work; others are assisted, or entirely
financed by the Red Cross or Anti-Tuberculosis Associations.   There seems to be a general desire among all
the states to carry on some form of public health nursing in connection with their state health departments,
and many who have not yet organized a division of
nursing have expressed their hope of so doing in the
near future.

In reply to a circular letter recently sent out to
the departments of health of the 48 states of the Union,
asking their opinion in regard to the value of a division
of public health nursing, all but three out of 44 answers
expressed the opinion that a division of public health
nursing was of vital importance.   Of the three who
thought otherwise, one wrote that he did not consider
a department of public health nursing of vital importance, and went on to say: "There is danger in trying
to educate people."   [Letter from J. H. Hurty M. D.
Sec'y of the State Board of Health, Indiana—P. H.
Nurse, Oct. 1920.]   This state has, since, however,
established a division of public health nursing in its
State Board of Health.

Another wrote: "I have no doubt about the value
of a public health nurse, but the more she nurses the
less she will be worth to a Department of Health."
This latter attitude which would make of a public health
nurse merely a teacher of hygiene and deprive her
of exercising the greatest power she has for enforcing

her teaching and making it acceptable—namely, bedside nursing—seems to us short-sighted.

We are glad to contrast these opinions with those of the Secretary of the Department of Health of New York State, who says: "There is hardly any more important division in the State Department of Health than the Division of Public Health Nursing." This Division has a director and twenty-six supervisors, who assist and supervise the local, rural and small town nurses throughout the state. In the past ten years the number of public health nurses in New York State, outside of New York City, has increased from 87 to over 1000.

The main objects in most of the state divisions or bureaus of public health nursing are to encourage local communities to organize and support the service in their own midst, and especially to assist in the development of child welfare, prenatal work, or anti-tuberculosis measures. In some states they can only give supervision and advice; in others, they can also finance the work, in whole or in part.

Much of this work, most of it in fact, is carried on in small towns or rural communities, in which the county is usually the geographical unit for the service. Health centers are organized, clinics held, and school inspection instituted, besides general home visiting.

This extension of county and small town public health nursing has been greatly assisted by the so-called Peace Program of the Red Cross. When the war ended, the Red Cross found itself with a splendid organization of local chapters extending over the whole country. The cessation of war activities left these groups of enthusiastic men and women without employment, and they would naturally soon have dispersed. The Red Cross felt, however, that it was unwise to lose the interest and co-operation of an already well organized group of active people, when there were so many other activities needing their help; and so planned what was known as its Peace Program. This program included, as one of its most important features, the development of public health nursing in localities where it did not already exist, and in co-operation with other health organizations already in the field. Miss Elizabeth Fox, Director of the Bureau of Public Health Nursing of the Red Cross, in speaking of this program said:—

"Because of its extensive chapter organization the Red Cross feels that it may be able to promote the establishment of these activities in territories which otherwise might not be able to introduce such service for some time to come, and may thus make a distinct contribution to the progress of public health nursing throughout the country."

The expectation has been more than realized: great enthusiasm was at once aroused, and committees on nursing activities were organized by the various chapters in all parts of the country.

Because of its policy to initiate work only in communities where no public health nursing already existed, most of the Red Cross activities in this line were confined to small towns or rural districts. By 1920 there were 701 Red Cross nurses in this service, employed in 629 different places; by 1921 there were 1311 employed in 1200 different places. The great majority of these nurses were employed by Red Cross chapters, the rest were maintained in part or wholly by state, county, or town, or by local organizations in affiliation with Red Cross chapters, supervised by Red Cross supervising nurses.

At the present time Red Cross public health nurses are to be found in all of the forty-eight states, as well as in Alaska, the Virgin Islands, and Porto Rico. In most cases, as we have already said, the county is the unit of work, and wherever possible the service is carried on and supported in co-operation with local organizations or health authorities.

In one county, for instance, there may be a large and flourishing health service, partly supported by the Red Cross local chapter and partly by county funds. Here we may find a large staff of from ten to fifteen nurses, including one or more supervisors. The main policy in the work here would be so to stimulate local interest in, and understanding of, public health nursing by demonstration and education that the community would desire to assume full financial responsibility without further help from the Red Cross. School nursing would be one of the first activities entered into in order to arouse this interest; clinics for general public health, dental work, orthopedic, child welfare and maternity work would be instituted; and home nursing would be carried on in such a way as to demonstrate effectively the value of a permanent nursing service. Talks on health matters would be given before groups of mothers, women's clubs, farm associations, churches, school boards, etc., and various committees would be appointed to interest themselves in such problems as that of transportation for the nurse, the opening of clinics, or, finally, the introduction of Bills that would authorize the use of local public funds for the employment of nurses. As the community became interested, funds would be voted for the salary of a nurse, and in the end the Red Cross would withdraw and the work in the county be taken over entirely by county or state health authorities.

In another county, on the other hand, the nursing service might be entirely supported by the Red Cross chapter, and only one nurse available for the entire field. As a county often covers thousands of square miles, with several small towns and many villages, or, as in the far western states, many isolated ranches and widely separated towns, it is self-evident that the service given by one nurse must be more or less limited in scope.   As a usual thing the work in such a county is generalized, with perhaps special emphasis on child welfare or school nursing.   In fact, the school nursing is usually assumed to be the best entering wedge in a new community, allowing as it does the opening of health centers, clinics, giving of talks and home visiting.   Other types of public health nursing are entered into as the local interest is awakened and funds become available.   In other words, the special work of the Red Cross in this field is to demonstrate to a community the value of a nurse, until that community itself is able to take full charge.   The main object is to point the way toward the eventual building up of a complete and adequate county nursing service which will provide all forms of public health nursing, including the care of the sick.   What the benefits of such a service will be to the health of the country at large is incalculable.

Not only have city, state and county been demonstrating the value of the nurse in public health work, but the Federal Government as well has continued to employ her.   The activity of the U. S. Public Health Service during the war was, as we have seen, very great, and the employment of the public health nurse in the Extra-Cantonment Zones opened the way to several new fields of work.   Many of the war-time activities were necessarily abandoned after peace made their continuation no longer needful; while, in other cases, the local community assumed the responsibility for the work which the U. S. Public Health Service could no longer maintain.   Nevertheless, the usefulness of the public health nurse had been so thoroughly demonstrated that the Bureau wished to continue her service in various divisions of its work.

In the Extra-Cantonment Zones the work had in most places been in co-operation with local health authorities, and had been greatly in the nature of demonstration and assistance. After the war it was found that where such demonstration had resulted in the establishment of local full health service the health work progressed satisfactorily; where not, it retrograded steadily. This fact justified the Federal Service in starting what is called the *Co-operative Rural Health Plan.* Through the co-operation of the U. S. Public Health Service with local health authorities, the Red Cross, the Tuberculosis Association, etc., a whole time health service is established in a geographical unit—usually a county or a group of townships or towns—including general sanitary and hygienic measures, school inspection, anti-tuberculosis work, child welfare and maternity, and industrial hygiene. In all this work the public health nurse is, of course, an active agent. This service, as will be seen, is purely co-operative, and as yet is not very extensive, owing to the lack of funds for the purpose. There are, however, some thirty public health nurses engaged in it, about fifty per cent. of whom are carried on the pay roll of the U. S. Public Health Service and directly responsible to it. These nurses assist the various officers in carrying out the measures for the prevention of disease and the promotion of health, holding clinics, inspecting school children and giving general advisory instruction. They do not give bedside care. As with State and Red Cross county work, a special feature is the promotion of infant welfare and maternity hygiene.

During 1921, besides the many other duties connected with general health activities, these few nurses made 9035 home visits to demonstrate hygienic measures for the protection of infant life, and 3161 visits to prenatal cases to advise with and assist expectant mothers; besides 12,000 visits to communicable disease cases.

From the view point of the future of public health nursing, this phase of the work of the Federal Government is most interesting, because it leads directly, as does the State and Red Cross public health nursing work, toward the further development of the service throughout the country.

"This demonstration rural health work of the Public Health Service," says a recent report, "has succeeded to such a degree that it now should be put on a co-operative basis, so that any rural community in the United States ready to do its proper part might receive from the Federal Government due and logical assistance in the development and maintenance of reasonably adequate local health work."

Besides the nurses in the Co-operative Rural Health-work, the Federal Service is also supplying a few public health nurses in the follow-up work with disabled soldiers. After the war it was found that many men were being discharged from hospitals as arrested cases of tuberculosis, others were leaving the hospitals contrary to medical advice; and while the former did not, perhaps, need active hospital care they did need health instruction and supervision. There were also many mental cases in dire need of help and advice, if not of hospital care. To meet, in part, this great need, a section of public health nursing follow-up work was established in the Fourth District of the Federal Public Health Service, comprising the states of Maryland, Virginia and West Virginia, with a Chief Nurse in Washington, and one nurse in the office of each State Supervisor in the three states. The interest and co-operation of the Red Cross, the state, county and city nursing organizations, and other associations, were solicited and a general scheme worked out by means of which any ex-soldier needing nursing care or supervision or advice in health matters could be taken care of through local co-operating nurses.

It was found that within the three states comprising the Fourth Division there were some 300 public health nurses, belonging to state, county, Red Cross, visiting nurse associations, or tuberculosis associations, all of which expressed their willingness to co-operate in every way with the Federal Service. This follow-up work has proved to be of great value. Many cases of tuberculosis and of unsuspected mental disease have been discovered and timely instruction and assistance given; health literature published by the U. S. Public Health Service has been distributed, and, when necessary, sanitary sputum outfits have been furnished. When a tuberculosis patient is bedridden he is referred to the local visiting nurse association for care, while those suffering from mental disorders are visited at intervals of from thitry to sixty days, according to their condition.

During the first seven months of this follow-up work in the Fourth District, 3226 visits were made by the nurses of the U. S. Public Health Service and 342 by nurses of the various co-operating agencies, making a total of 3568. When we remember that these men were all ex-soldiers, whose physical ill-health was in most cases the result of their war-time experiences in the service of their country, we cannot be too thankful that at least something is being done for their relief.

Besides these two distinct types of public health nursing service, the Federal Bureau is also supplying advisory public health nursing service in connection with its Division of Venereal Diseases.

The passing of the so-called "Maternity Bill" in November 1921 will no doubt exercise a far-reaching effect on public health and public health nursing. This bill provides for federal co-operation with the states in promoting the welfare of maternity and infancy; the administration of the act is given to the Children's Bureau of the U. S. Department of Labor, and the Chief of this Bureau is made the Executive Officer. A Board

26

of Maternity and Infant Hygiene, consisting of the Chief of the Children's Bureau, the Surgeon-General of the U. S. Public Health Service, and the U. S. Commissioner of Education, is given certain powers of review and approval. A total appropriation of $1,480,-000 is authorized for the current fiscal year, and an appropriation of $1,240,000. for each of five years thereafter, this money, except for a very small percentage to be used for administrative purposes, to be divided among the states accepting the provisions of the act, to be used, together with state funds, for promoting the welfare and hygiene of maternity and infancy. At least five states have already passed laws accepting the act.

That public health nursing is gradually being looked upon more and more as a public function, to be paid for by state, county, city, or even federal taxes, and made available for all, is certain.

Yet this does not mean that the need for the work of the private associations is disappearing; rather, are their activities and opportunities increasing and broadening. Everywhere we see visiting nurse associations co-operating with and supplementing public services. The foundation of their work is still bedside nursing in the home, but in almost every act in the technique of bedside care the true visiting nurse is planting the seed of prevention and giving instruction in the principles of public health. Again, the private organization is necessarily the laboratory where new pieces of work are tried and tested for an experimental period—its part has ever been, to demonstrate the value and practicability of a thing and to carry it through that period of life when the mortality of good things is highest which, of course, is precisely the same period as for human infants—the first few months of existence.

Thus new developments and extension of work to meet new needs are constantly being nurtured by these associations, until such time as, their value being proven, they can properly and logically be taken over by the public service.   And since the field of the public health nurse is constantly enlarging, the demands upon the old visiting nurse associations have been steadily increasing—their experience, their standards have helped to mould and influence every type of public health nursing work in the country; and they have been largely the training ground from which have gone forth the workers who have sown the seed of other harvests.

CHAPTER XXVI

BRITISH DOMINIONS AND ELSEWHERE
CANADA.

We have followed the devolpment of district nursing in England and in the United States. We must turn now for a moment to glance at what is being done along this line in Canada and elsewhere.

Under the British North American Act of 1867, health and education were made the responsibility of each province, a principle which still applies to the nine provinces now included in the Dominion of Canada.

It was not until 1897, however, that an attempt was made nationally to standardize visiting nursing. Records of isolated organizations believed to exist prior to that date have not yet been compiled. In 1897 suggestions were received by the National Council of Women from the far eastern and western provinces that a national organization should be created to provide a visiting nurse service for Canada. Under the leadership of Lady Aberdeen, wife of the Governor-General of that time, the Victorian Order of Nurses was established as a National Memorial of the Diamond Jubilee of Queen Victoria. A royal charter was procured under which the objects of the Order were defined as follows:

1: To supply nurses thoroughly trained in hospitals and district nursing, and subject to one central authority, for the nursing of the sick who are otherwise unable to obtain trained nursing in their own homes, both in town and country.

2: To bring local association for supplying district nursing into association by affiliation with the Order, and to give grants or other assistance to such associations.

3: To maintain, as a first necessity, a high standard of efficiency for all district nursing.

4: To assist in providing small cottage hospitals or homes.

The whole scheme was, as one can readily see, based on the plan of the Jubilee Institute, only such changes being introduced as better fitted it for the new country. Special permission was granted to the Victorian Order of nurses to wear the same uniform and insignia as the Queen's Nurses, the insignia merely having the name "Victorian Order of Nurses for Canada" around the edge; and the type of work carried on by the Queen's Nurses was followed by their sisters across the sea. The one outstanding difference between the two organizations was that, whereas in England no fees were asked, in Canada, from the first, a small charge was made wherever possible. This was probably due to the fact that the service was not confined to the very poor, but was also supplied to the independent and sturdy pioneers in the sparsely settled regions of the country, where little or no medical or nursing care was then available.

The central authority for the Order was placed in the hands of a Board of Governors, consisting of five members appointed by the Governor-General of Canada, one or more representatives from each of the affiliated local associations, and one representative from each Provincial Medical Association. This made a very representative body, every part of the country having a voice in the affairs of the Order, and being able to bring before the Board for discussion any local matters needing adjustment.

Besides this Central Board of Governors, local committees were appointed which, like the local committees in England, have full power in the community which they represent.

The first action of the Order was to appoint a Superintendent of Nurses; the second to assist in organizing local associations for the purpose of supplying district nursing in the various communities, and to give the training in district work felt to be essential. Training Homes for this purpose were established at various times in Ottawa, Montreal, Toronto, Halifax, Winnipeg, and Vancouver.

The standard of nursing was the highest possible. To be admitted to the Order it was necessary for the nurse to be a graduate of a hospital training school, approved by the executive council, and to take a four months' training in district nursing in one of the Training Homes of the Order. Upon the completion of the four months of service and instruction, and upon the recommendation of the Chief Superintendent, the nurse was given a diploma, and a medal of the Order, which she was expected to wear during her service.

The wife of each succeeding Governor-General is recognized as head of the Order, and in 1900 Lady Minto started a Fund which was known as the "Lady Minto Cottage Hospital Fund," the interest from which was to be used toward the building of small hospitals in parts of the country where the need was greatest. Many of the large hospitals now operating in the cities of the west were started as little cottage hospitals, and owe their high standard of efficiency to the Victorian Order of Nurses.

A still further expansion of the work took place through the establishment of Lady Grey's "Country District Nursing Scheme," by which District Associations were formed which included large areas of country-side and through which trained nurses could be supplied to the homesteads, ranches, or farms lying many miles away. These nurses were obliged to combine continuous nursing with their district work, for when a patient is very ill it is impossible to limit the service, and the distances were too great to permit repeated visits day after day. Maternity cases formed a large part of the work carried, and many of these women working in remote parts of the country were midwives as well as nurses.

During the pioneer years, the Victorian Order of Nurses held an ideal of nursing standards which would not have been posible without the central control provided by the Order. To that leadership Canada owes the fact that visiting nursing is carried on, with few exceptions, by graduate nurses.

Gradually, however, Provincial Associations of Graduate Nurses came into existence—the first about 1904 and the last in 1921;—and the Canadian National Association of Trained Nurses was organized in 1908, with the result that nursing standards throughout the Dominion have been raised, and the training offered by hospital schools has been steadily advanced and to some extent standardized.

The recent rapid devolopment of provincial health movements and nursing organizations at first threatened to isolate to a certain degree the nurses of the Victorian Order, who were more strongly influenced by the national charter and by central control than by local nursing development. In 1918 it was discovered that only sixteen of the Victorian Order nurses were identified with provincial nursing associations. This, however, is being rapidly overcome. In 1921 the Victorian Order discontinued its pioneer training centres, and granted 31 scholarships to nurses enrolled for public health courses in the provincial universities. In the

same year recommendations were made by the nurses
of the Order that the Royal Charter should be amended,
authorizing them to continue the health teaching which
had been added in some communities to their visiting
nursing.   This was done, the first clause of the Charter
now reading:

"The objects of the Order are: (1) to supply nurses
thoroughly trained in hospitals *and public health nursing,*
and subject to one central authority, for the nursing of
the sick, *the prevention of disease, and the promotion of
health."*

And to still futher elucidate the meaning of "public
health nursing" the following paragraph has been added:

"Public health nursing is a branch of nursing service
which includes all phases of work concerned with family
and community welfare, with bedside nursing as a fundamental principle, and developing from it all forms of
educational and administrative work that tends to prevent
disease and raise the standard of the health of the community."

The Canadian National Association of Trained
Nurses made a survey in 1915 of public health nursing
in the nine provinces, and discovered 372 nurses engaged
in some form of public health work, 184 of whom were
identified with the Victorian Order.

The last survey, in 1921, showed a grand total of
999 nurses engaged in every possible type of public
health nursing, including that carried on under departments of health, departments of education, the Department of Soldiers' Civil Re-Establishment, as well as under the Victorian Order and other private agencies.
The number of Victorian Order nurses included in the
survey was 422.

Bedside nursing has been so long recognized as the special field of the Victorian Order of Nurses that the work of the departments of health and education tends to be limited to the preventive aspects of health work. In Manitoba and Alberta, however, the Provincial Departments of Health have appointed nurses for the care of the sick in rural areas.   The municipal hospital schemes of Alberta and Saskatchewan provide for graduate nurses to visit in the homes of the outpost communities, and it is not unusual for municipalities in other provinces to employ private nurses in the homes of the poor when adequate hospital care is not available.

The most rapid growth is in the work being done by the public departments, a result which is largely due to the encouragement offered by the private agencies. The standard of nurse education required by the Departments of Public Health and Education is the highest possible in each province, and the salaries paid are, with few exceptions, equal to or larger than those paid by private agencies.   There is no evidence that the selection of nurses appointed by public departments will come under unfavorable influences.   This condition is attributed to the fact that medical officers of health do not change with changing political parties.

The tradition is becoming well established in Canada that public health departments should take a leading part in public health nursing.

One of the private agencies responsible for this tradition is the Canadian Red Cross Society.   The Provincial divisions of that Society began in 1920 to assist in the development of health nursing as part of their peace time program.   Nurses have been appointed by them to work in connection with public departments in eight provinces, and grants have been made to universities, enabling them to organize post graduate courses for nurses.   When public health or hospital work has been undertaken in the name of the Red Cross Society, it has been in co-operation with the departments of public health.

The development of the nursing services of departments of health and education created a demand for post graduate courses in public health nursing which has been met by six universities, *i. e.*

The University of British Columbia, Vancouver, B. C.
Dalhousie University, Halifax, N. S.
University of Toronto, Toronto, Ont.
McGill University, Montreal, Quebec.
Western University, London, Ont.
University of Alberta, Edmonton, Alberta.

A four months' course was started under the joint management of the Victorian Order of Nurses and the Red Cross Society, and the University of New Brunswick, St. John, N. B., undertook to grant certificates to the successful students.

Beginnings are being made throughout Canada towards the introduction of health nursing into the hospital training schools. In some communities theory alone is given, but in others practical experience is possible with public health organizations. In Toronto, over eighty students selected by the superintendents of all the training schools of the city were given two months' practical experience in connection with the Division of Public Health Nursing of the Department of Public Health.

The Canadian National Association of Trained Nurses organized a Public Health Section in 1920 with the object in view of developing an esprit de corps amongst the varied and scattered groups of public health nurses, in order that the standards of training and of service might be advanced throughout all the provinces of the Dominion.

NEW ZEALAND

In the young and comparatively small country of New Zealand public health nursing is organized in a way that would probably not be possible for larger countries or those with less centralized governments. The whole group of islands which compose the Dominion of New Zealand is only 1000 miles in length and 180 miles at the widest part; while the entire country, as one writer has put it, is "like a big family," and a general spirit of co-operation and neighborly interest in the small, intimate concerns of the community prevails. (Infant Mortality Series No. 2, published by the U. S. Department of Labor, Children's Bureau.)

Moreover, government assistance is available for all benevolent activities. The central organization for nursing and preventive care of the public health is placed in the Division of Nursing of the Department of Health, which is staffed by fully trained nurses, under a Director who is also a nurse.

Through this Division are carried on various phases of work pertaining to nursing, such as the examination and registration of nurses and midwives, [1] inspection of training schools, inspection of hospitals and midwives, etc. The country is divided into 37 hospital districts, each controlled by its own Board, which is expected to provide for outside nursing in the district,—as well as in the institution,—for which the Government pays a subsidy. It is often difficult, however, to find a sufficient number of nurses prepared to go to the *back blocks* (as the interior rural districts are called) and, when found, it is equally difficult to find suitable living accommodations for them.

These nurses are appointed by the Health Depart-

---

[1] The registration of midwives in New Zealand is compulsory. Persons not registered as midwives who practise or use the name of midwife are liable to a fine not exceeding thirty pounds ($146).

ment for district nursing generally and for district midwifery, district midwives being placed only where there
are no private midwives and where one would be unable
to make a living without a settled salary. They are
expected to give ante-and post-natal advice to mothers, as well as to attend them at time of delivery. In
several towns the St. John's Ambulance Association has
established trained nurses for the poor, and the hospitals in a few cases have nurses doing this town work.

For the most part these district nurses are sent to
the remote country districts—the back blocks—where
their services, both as nurses and as midwives, are
greatly needed.

"The reports from the Government district nurses
show that a rugged and varied service is often demanded. For instance, a call may come from the bush
at midnight, perhaps a case of accident, when delay
would be serious. The nurse is called upon to mount
a horse and to ride in darkness for miles, over muddy,
slippery roads, often so narrow that every step brings
danger of a fall over a precipice. In the swamps her
horse gets bogged, or, after a rain, has to swim a way
out. The responsibility of the nurse in districts far
from hospitals or medical aid has often developed an
almost heroic initiative and courage." (Infant Mortality Series No. 2, published by U. S. Children's Bureau.)

Public health nursing was first introduced into New
Zealand by Dr. Truby King, who, being much impressed
by the high rate of infant mortality prevailing in all
countries, and believing that, were proper preventive
measures established it would not exceed 3 per cent, succeeded in arousing public interest and establishing in
1907 a Society for the Promotion of the Health of Mothers and Children. He himself provided the first infant welfare nurse to carry on and demonstrate the
value of the work. This was the beginning of the pres-

ent splendid service which has made of New Zealand the "place where babies seldom die."

In starting this work Dr. King was fortunate in securing the interest and co-operation of the Governor and Lady Plunket; the former issuing a pamphlet describing the work and calling on all classes to join the Society; and the latter showing her great interest by lecturing, demonstrating and personally instructing mothers in matters of health. Committees were appointed in various parts of the country, infant welfare centres and clinics were established, and nurses, known as the "Plunket Nurses," were appointed to carry on the work. These nurses were "to give sound, reliable, instructive advice and assistance gratis to any member of the community desiring such service, on matters affecting the health and well-being of women, especially during pregnancy and while nursing infants; and on matters affecting the health and well-being of children; and also to endeavor to educate and help parents and others in a practical way in domestic hygiene in general."

The work of the Society is mainly educational, and while the services of the nurse are free to any member of the community, rich or poor, those who are able are expected to pay something toward the support and extension of the Society.

The result of this intensive effort in child welfare and maternity care has been to reduce the rate of infant mortality in New Zealand to four per cent.—the lowest rate in the world.

In 1920 a Child Welfare Division of the Health Department was established and Dr. King made Director of the same. At present the work of the Society for the Health of Mothers and Children is largely subsidized by the Government and is practically under its direction. There is also a Division of School Hygiene of the Department of Health under which school medical officers and nurses are gradually developing school medical service; as well as a Division of Dental Hygiene, started in 1920, which is at present training a number of assistants called dental nurses to work under qualified dental officers among the growing children.

Altogether, it looks as if New Zealand would soon be one of the foremost countries in the world in the extent and quality of her public health nursing.

AUSTRALIA.

In Australia *Bush Nursing,* which is the local name for a certain form of rural public health nursing, has beeen carried on for over a decade. It was first started by the Countess of Dudley, who formed a committee with the intention of organizing a large association, something like the Victorian Order, to cover the whole of Australia and furnish nursing care to the isolated people in the back country. This original scheme was too large, however, and failed to materialize; but the idea was so sound and the need of nursing service for the lonely pioneers so pressing that the plan was finally taken up on a smaller scale and independent associations were organized in some of the states.

The method usually followed is, first to form a Central Council, with headquarters in the largest town, which shall have charge of all the business and work of the association and help establish and finance nursing service in various local districts throughout the state. Centres are opened and a nurse placed in charge. Most of these centres are run on a co-operative basis, the head of a household paying a certain yearly subscription, which entitles him and the members of his family, up to the age of eighteen years, to ordinary nursing care, midwifery cases being charged extra, and non-members paying full professional fees.

Although the Centre pays the salary of the nurse, and in some cases furnishes a small cottage for her residence, there are many other expenses which are borne by the Central Council, such as payments for overlapping days when nurses are transferred from one centre to another, insuring the nurses, advertising for them, and providing the initial equipment for the centres; besides the general overhead expense of the Central Council and the salary and travelling expenses of the Superintendent Nurse.

The work of the Bush Nurse varies greatly, including all kinds of bedside nursing and some public health work; but by far the greater part and the most important is that of midwifery and the care of infants and children.   Because of the accent on midwifery all nurses are required to be registered midwives.

Another important part of the nurses' work is that of first aid, which often enables the victim of an accident to travel in comparative safety—often in the care of the nurse—to the nearest medical man, who may be many miles away.

Still another important part of her work lies in connection with the schools.   She is expected to assist the school medical officer, to inspect the hygienic conditions of school children and school; to teach hygiene; and to correlate the school work with that of the home and the community, for which the Bush Nurse has unusual opportunities.

In maternity cases or in cases of serious illness, where her persence is greatly needed, a nurse may remain for ten days with a patient, but it is especially stated that she shall not be required to do the house work.

The amount of work done by these Bush Nurses is immense and the ground covered often very great.   In one district a nurse in visiting her patients actually travelled 6740 miles in one year.

Bush nursing not only brings a feeling of comfort and security to thousands of people in the back lands, unreachable by railroads and without medical aid or hospital service—but it also carries on a systematic propaganda of health teaching and demonstration, and is well adapted to the needs of the country which it serves.

In the cities of Australia little public health nursing is being done, although with the recent establishment of the Public Health Association of Australia (August 1920) the work in the cities will doubtless also be extended. The Association is entirely free from political, departmental or official connection and has a branch in each state. Its special object is to promote personal and public health and to correlate all health activities in every state. In a recent account of this Association (Public Health Association of Australia —Australian Nurses Journal, June 15, 1921) special mention was made of Bush Nursing in connection with public health and the value of the work of the health official, "whether he or she be a health inspector, baby clinic nurse, district nurse or medical officer of health"; which seems to line up public health nurses with the other active agents of public health work in Australia.

SOUTH AFRICA.

District nursing, or public health nursing, is as yet little understood in South Africa, although even there a start has been made, the King Edward VII Order of Nurses, organized by Lady Gladstone as a memorial to her husband, having been carrying on a certain amount of rural nursing for some years. Hitherto it has not, however, been extended to large towns— a reversal of conditions in older countries.

We are glad to know, however, that Johannesburg has lately organized a District Nursing Association, in affiliation with the King Edward VII Order of Nurses, and hope that other cities will follow her lead.

The work is being established on purely modern principles, it being required of the nurse that she shall have had some social training, so that she may efficiently cooperate with the health visitor, school nurse or other social worker and work intelligently with other social organizations; also, that her work must be educational and preventive, and absolutely non-political, non-racial, and non-sectarian.

In many other countries also public health nursing of different kinds is being carried on under various names and under varying conditions. In some it is still confined to district nursing among the poor, often carried on by deaconesses or religious communities; in others it is carried on in co-operation with public health agencies. In some the nursing given is general bedside care; in others again it is confined to some specific health problem, such as tuberculosis, child welfare, or maternity work. In most countries outside of these we have mentioned the training of the so called "nurse" falls far below that required in the Anglo-Saxon countries; whereas in one or two the agent employed is given a highly specialized and technical training.

The Government Specialists in Obstetrics in Holland are required to have had at least three years of High School or its equivalent, and the special training given is as follows:

1st year—College work only—Subjects: Anatomy and physiology, bacteriology and pathology, physics and chemistry. Also algebra, geometry, geography, history and Dutch.

2nd year—Student attends clinics and laboratories, is also present at deliveries—Before finishing the sec-

27

ond year's training the student must have cared for at least twenty cases herself and a complete history must have been written of each case.

3rd year—Practical work in various wards, prenatal as well as postpartum, confinement room, aperating theater, and incubating room.

All over the world, however, preventive medicine is making its way, and hand in hand with preventive medicine must go the public health nurse.

CHAPTER XXVII

CONCLUSION

And so at last we see the public health nurse firmly established as one of the most important agents in the whole modern movement for the conservation of the public health. We have watched her slow evolution through the centuries; we have seen her as the deaconess of the early church; as the Lady Bountiful of the middle ages; as the district nurse of modern times; and, finally, as the highly trained public health nurse of today. No longer is she content to give only passing relief; she aims to give permanent cure; no longer does she confine her attention to the individual and the poor; she takes the whole community under her care.

To be sure, there have been some variants and fluctuations in the type, but on the whole the changes have been fewer than one might imagine. In fact, in looking back upon the evolution of public health nursing it is surprising to see how few changes have been made in its methods and principles since the days when it was introduced under the more limited name of district nursing. It has merely kept pace with the progress of time, showing that it is a living organism, responsive to the influences about it—growing with the growth of scientific knowledge—changing with the changing needs of humanity—fitting itself to meet the opportunities of its environment; and yet holding ever at the centre of its being the purpose for which it was born—service to mankind.

Probably the greatest changes in its practice have been the increased accent on health instruction, and the

419

extension of the service to those who can pay; and yet even these are not so much a change as a growth.

The public health nurse of today represents the prevention of disease through instruction and supervision, not only in families where illness exists, but throughout the entire community. Her work is preeminently constructive, and if her training as a nurse is essential, her ability as a teacher is equally so.

It has been said that the public health nurse is a product of modern times; and yet this modern, highly specialized public health nurse is the same visiting nurse of early days. Though the accent of her work is on health, it still takes her to the bedside of the sick; and though instruction is the key note of her effort, it should go hand in hand with nursing care.

The future is hidden, but whatever it may hold, the place of the public health nurse is established. She must go forward, and her progress will be along the lines of science and of health.

But as every age presents new perils, just as it presents new opportunities, so in this age the danger of becoming a scientist and a teacher at the expense of tender ministration may well threaten the best of public health nurses. Let her never forget her glorious past. The work of the public health nurse is founded in Christian charity. It is not merely a profession—it is a vocation; not merely a gainful occupation, but a ministry. The truly great physician, sees in his patient not only the case, but the human being. So with the nurse. The professional, the scientific, the purely business side of her work must never over-shadow the warm, human side; she must still be not only a teacher, but a friend, so that those who are to benefit by her teaching and her care will say, not "There goes the public health teacher"—but, "There goes *Our Nurse.*"

APPENDIX I

There is much controversy as to whether or not there were deaconesses in the Western Church (Rome). If so, they were certainly not as much needed as in the Eastern Church (Constantinople), nor as numerous, there being at the time of Chrysostom 40 deaconesses in Constantinople alone. To be sure, the Fathers of the Western Church made no specific mention of *Deaconesses* in their writings, though, on the other hand, the word "widow" which is used with much frequency by the Latin Fathers, may apply to the same group of workers; for in the Apostolic Constitution it is commanded that the deaconess be "a pure virgin, or a *widow* once married" and of the many Roman ladies whose charitable work, as described by the early writers, seems to resemble that of the deaconess, practically all were either virgins or widows once married. Ludlow, in "Women's Work in the Church," p. 25, says: "In the Latin Church the distinction between the deaconess and the church widow and between the latter and the church virgin, appears to have been early obliterated." All of which makes it quite permissible to assume that the deaconess was to be found in the city of Rome.

Moreover, it is generally accepted that one of the first deaconesses was Phoebe, "a servant of the Church at Cenchrea" (Rom. xiv, i). If that supposition is correct and Phoebe as deaconess (here translated *servant*) and an acknowledged official representative of the Church, visited Rome on "business" for which St. Paul asks assistance, is it not natural to suppose that the order which she represented would have been introduced

by her into the Roman Church, and the work which she
represented as "a succorer of many" have been followed
by her fellow-laborers in that city?

Be that as it may, the Roman women were no less
active in good works than their sisters in the East, and
their care of the sick poor and their dependence upon the
Church for aid was the same; therefore, it matters little whether their official title was "deaconess" or
"widow" or merely "Christian worker." Their work
was the same, they visited the sick in the same spirit
of Christian charity; and as the Rome of that period
is more familiar to the average reader than Constantinople or other Eastern cities, I have taken Rome as
the background for my picture of the primitive deaconess.

APPENDIX II

EAST LONDON NURSING SOCIETY

RULES FOR NURSES.

1. The nurse to wear Society's uniform all days
   except when she has leave of a holiday or goes
   right out of her district.
2. The nurse is supposed to rest after 4 o'clock in the
   afternoon; and work done after this is done by her
   own free will.
3. The district nurse not to do night duty unless she
   wishes to give a night now and then.
4. She is not to attend confinement cases in the character of a midwife, but she may bathe the baby and
   help the mother afterwards.
5. She is to have a fortnight's holiday every year with
   her wages going on.
6. The matron can give any district nurse leave to
   go out for an afternoon once a fortnight from one

o'clock, but the nurse must inform the Superintendent when she goes.

7. The nurse to attend once every Sunday in the Parish Church and sit in the nurses' seat.

RULES FOR PATIENTS.

Ventilation or the due admission of fresh air to the room, punctuality in giving medicine or food, and perfect cleanliness of the bed-room and person being so absolutely necessary to the well-being and recovery of sick persons, you are expected to aid the efforts of your medical man and the Society's nurse by strict attention to the following rules:

1. Strict attention to the direction of your medical man as to the manner and time of giving medicines and other particulars relating to the sick-room.
2. Particular care as to the cleanliness of the sick, both in person and clothing.
3. The immediate removal of all things offensive both from the bed and room and care to keep the sick-room quite clean and fresh at all times.
4. It is part of the nurse's duty in her visits to see that necessary things are properly carried out and she will give the suitable advice and directions in these and all other particulars concerning the proper care of the sick person. Neglect of these instructions will make the nurse's visit useless and she will not continue them.

APPENDIX III

Questions asked in letter sent to clergy by Committee of Inquiry.

1. Has the want of trained nurses for the sick poor been long felt in your district?
2. Is there a nurse at work in your district not as a midwife but to help the sick poor?
3. Has she been regularly trained in a hospital?

4. Is she connected with any or what Society?
5. Please state whether there are any reports or available particulars of the Society in which the nurse has been trained.
6. How have funds been provided? For payment of the nurse? For the medical comforts?
7. If no such trained nurse exists, can you give the Committee any reason to expect aid in your district either personal or pecuniary?
8. Can you give the Committee any suggestions as to the special requirements of your district in regard to nursing?

APPENDIX IV

Rules for District Nursing Associations in affiliation with the Queen's Institute.

1. The services of the nurse shall be for cases of sick persons in their own homes without distinction of creed, it being understood that free nursing is given in cases of necessity. Patients, however, may be attended whom, although unable to incur the expense of a private nurse, are able to make some contribution to the funds of the Association, provided that the full performance of her primary duty leaves the nurse time for such work. (Patients, when able, should be encouraged to give a donation to the Association, however small.)
2. The general sick nursing of the patient should be carried out under the direction of the medical practitioners.
3. Application for the services of the nurse may be made direct to her or otherwise. The nurse may attend a patient on application or in emergency, but must not continue to visit without informing a medical man and receiving his instructions, if any. Should a nurse advise that a patient should have a doctor and the advice be not accepted, the nurse may not attend this patient except in case

of fresh emergency. She must report the matter to her Secretary.

4. The nurse shall not dispense for her patients any such drugs as should only be prescribed by a medical man.

5. The nurse shall in no case attempt to influence a patient in the choice of a doctor.

6. A midwife shall not accept an engagement without first asking the patient to state and herself registering the name of the doctor to be called in should any emergency arise.

7. The nurse is strictly forbidden to interfere in any way with the religious opinions of patients or of members of their families.

8. The nurse shall not act as almsgiver, or, except in cases of urgent necessity, herself distribute nourishment or other relief. She shall at once report any such case to the Hon. Secretary or other proper authority. (When private gifts are received to assist a special case, the patient should be informed that this comes from a private source and not from the Association. All such gifts should be acknowledged in the Annual Report.)

SUGGESTED BY-LAWS FOR NURSES.

1. The general sick nursing of the patients shall be carried out under the direction of the medical practitioners.

2. The nurse is strictly forbidden to interfere in any way with the religious opinions of patients or of members of their families.

3. The nurse shall not act as almsgiver, or except in cases of urgent necessity, herself distribute nourishment or other relief. She shall at once report any such case to the Hon. Secretary or other proper authority. (When private gifts are received to assist a special case, the patient should be informed that this comes from a private source and not from the Association.)

4. The nurse shall not dispense for her patients any drugs as should only be prescribed by a medical man.

5. The nurse shall in no case attempt to influence a patient in the choice of a doctor.

6. The nurse may not attend infectious cases unless with the sanction of the medical men and Committee.

7. The nurse shall be responsible to the Committee of the Association, and shall keep in the form prescribed a register of patients, time and case books, and shall report regularly to the Committee upon her work.

8. The nurse is not to be on duty more than eight hours daily, except under special circumstances. On Sunday she shall only attend cases requiring special or immediate attention. Night duty shall only be undertaken under exceptional circumstances, when due provision can be made for the other cases under her care. She shall be entitled to a month's holiday in the year, and shall have, if possible, half a day off duty at least every fortnight.

9. The nurse shall be punctual in going to and returning from her district, at the times appointed by the Committee, and shall leave word at her room where she is likely to be found. Any messages or instructions for the nurse shall be given in writing, so as to avoid leaving verbal messages with patients or others. A slate should be provided at the nurse's rooms on which messages may be written when she is out. When the nurse has anything to communicate to the doctor she shall do so in writing, and it is hoped that the doctor will do the same to avoid leaving verbal messages with patients or their friends.

10. The nurse shall be in her rooms from 3–4 o'clock on ——— every week in order to meet the Hon. Secretary or any members of the Committee who may desire to see her.

11. The nurse when on duty shall wear the uniform dress and no ornaments.

12. The nurse shall not accept any presents from patients or their friends.

13. The nurse shall be responsible for all appliances, clothing, etc. lent to her patients, and shall see as far as possible that they are turned in in good condition.

14. The nurse shall be responsible for the personal cleanliness of her patients. She shall endeavor to improve their general surroundings, and when the relations of the patients can be taught how to keep the room in nursing order, they should be encouraged to do so.

ADDITIONAL BY-LAWS FOR ASSOCIATIONS.

The following suggested additional by-laws for Associations employing nurses as midwives explain themselves. The only essential point not covered is that it is absolutely necessary to make some arrangements by which the services of a medical man can be secured in emergencies and to provide by a definite rule whether the Association shall in such cases be responsible for the doctor's fee or whether the midwife's fee shall be returned.

1. The midwife shall not accept an engagement without first asking the patient to state and herself registering the name of the doctor to be called in should any emergency arise.

2. Applications for the services of the midwife shall be made at least three months before the date when she will be required.

3. One-half the fee shall be paid at the time of booking, and the remainder at least a fortnight before the confinement.

4. A card shall be given to the applicant upon which her payments shall be entered as they are made. This card must be sent to the midwife by some trustworthy messenger when her services are required.

5. The midwife shall enter the cases and the amount
   of any fees received by her in a book. The book
   shall be shown to the Hon. Secretary at her weekly
   visit, and the fee given to her.
6. The midwife must keep the register required by
   the Central Midwives Board. (A special case
   book is also desirable.)
7. The midwife must work in accordance with the
   rules of the Central Midwives Board.
8. The midwife shall be responsible for the care of
   mother and infant during the lying-in period *i. e.,*
   during the time of labour and for ten days after
   or for longer, if necessary). She shall visit each
   case at the end of the month to see if the mother
   has made good convalescence and the child is in
   good health.

APPENDIX V

Table showing growth of the Visiting Nurse Movement throughout the United States from 1877 to 1892
inclusive.

"In 1890 there were but 21 associations in all the
United States, the greater number of these employing
but one nurse." (Visiting Nursing in the U. S.—
Waters, page 14.) By 1893 the number had increased
to 35 (ibid Table II p. 365) and the number of nurses
employed by the ten largest of these associations—most
of them organized for the sole purpose of employing
visiting nurses—was distributed as follows:—

Boston....................................9
Brooklyn..................................1
Buffalo...................................3
Chicago...................................8
Denver....................................1
Ethical Society, N. Y.....................3

APPENDIX VI

Chronological list of the establishment of Visiting Nurse Associations in
the United States from 1877 to 1905—(not including a large number
of churches and hospitals and small committees employing nurses).

Date	Place	Name of Association	Remarks
1877	New York City	New York City Mission	
1878	New York City	Society for Ethical Culture	
1886	Boston, Mass.	Instructive District Nursing Ass'n.	First nurse began work Feb. 8th. 1886 Incorporated 1889.
	Philadelphia. Pa.	Visiting Nurse Society	
1887	New Bedford. Mass.	Instructive Nursing Ass'n.	
1889	Chicago. Ill.	Visiting Nurse Ass'n.	Visiting nursing established 1883 Ass'n formed 1889 Incorporated 1891
1890	Brooklyn, N. Y.	District Nursing Com. of the Bureau of Charities.	
	Buffalo, N. Y.	District Nursing Association	
1891	Kansas City,	Visiting Nurse Association	Work began by church in 1891
1892	Denver, Colo.	Visiting Nurse Ass'n of Denver	Flower Mission employed visiting nurse V. N. A. organized 1900
1893	New York City	Henry Street Settlement	
	Worcester. Mass.	Society for District Nursing	
	Grand Rapids. Mich.	Dist. Nursing Ass'n	Connected with Charity Ass'n
1894	Detroit, Mich.	Visiting Nurse Ass'n.	Organized 1897 Incorporated 1901

Allegheny Pa. Visiting Nurse Ass'n.
St. Louis, Mo. Provident Ass'n.   V. N. A. formed 1911

1895   Pittsburg, Pa. The   East   End   Visiting
                   Nurse Aid Ass'n
       New York,   V. N. Department of the
       N. Y.   Charity Org. Society

1896   Baltimore. Md. Visiting Nurse Association
       Omaha, Nebr. Visiting Nurse Ass'n.
       Albany. N. Y. Albany Guild for the Sick   Formed in 1880 as a
                                                 Flower and Fruit
                                                 Mission

       Marblehead.   Visiting Nurse Ass'n.
       Mass.
       Syracuse, N .Y. Visiting Nurse Association

1897   New York City John Wanamaker's Bene-
                     ficial Ass'n
       Groton, Mass. Visiting Nurse Ass'n
       Newburgh,   The Visiting Nurse Society
       N. Y.

1898   San Francisco. Nurses' Settlement
       Calif.
       Los Angeles, Instructive District Nursing   1898 to 1913 work
         Calif.   Ass'n   directed by College
                                                     Settlement.   Re-or-
                                                     ganized under Bd. of
                                                     Health in 1913

1898   Evanston. Ill. Visiting Nurse Committee
       Newton. Mass. Newton   District   Nursing
                       Ass'n.
       Manchester,   Manchester District Nursing
         N. H.   Ass'n.
       Westchester.   Visiting Nurse Ass'n of West-   Begun by Miss Ellen
         N. Y.   chester Co.   Wood 1896

       Drifton, Pa.   Visiting Nurse of Drifton
       Columbus,   Instructive Visiting Nursing
         Ohio.   Ass'n.

1899   Natick, Mass. Visiting Nurse Ass'n
       Winchester.   Winchester Visiting Nurse
         Mass.   Ass'n
       Concord. N. H. District Nurse Ass'n
       Harrisburg,   Visiting Nurse Ass'n
         Pa.
       Malden, Mass. V. N. of the Industrial Aid   Ass'n formed 1900
                       Society

       San Francisco, Dept. of V. N. of the As-   Work   started   by
         Cal.   sociated Charities   Flower Mission 1897

1900   Providence,   District Nurse Ass'n
         R. I.
       Middletown,   District Nurse Ass'n
         Conn.
       Fort Wayne.   Visiting Nurse League
         Ind.

Canton, Mass. Canton Nursing Ass'n
Medford, Mass. Medford Visiting Nurse Ass'n
Waltham,   Waltham   District   Nurse
Mass.   Ass'n
Orange. N. J. Visiting Nurses' Settlement
Toledo, Ohio. Toledo   District   Nursing
               Ass'n
Washington,   The   Instructive   Visiting
D. C.   Nurse Ass'n
Richmond, Va. Instructive Visiting Nurse
               Ass'n
1901 Hartford,   Visiting Nurse Ass'n
       Conn.

Davenport, Ia. Visiting Nurse Ass'n
Framingham,   District Nurse Ass'n
Mass.
Pittsfield.   Pittsfield Visiting Nurse
Elmira, N. Y. Visiting Nurse Ass'n
Oakmont, Pa. Oakmont   District   Nursing
               Ass'n

1902 South Bend,   Visiting Nurse Ass'n
       Ind.
      Bridgewater,   Bridgewater Visiting Nurse
       Mass.   Ass'n
      Watertown.   District Nurse Ass'n
       Mass.
      Newark, N. J. Visiting Nurse Ass'n.
      Lake Placid,   Visiting Nursing Fund
       N. Y.
      Cleveland.   Visiting Nurse Ass'n.
       Ohio.
      Portland, Ore. Visiting Nurse Ass'n
      Pittsburgh,   Irene Kaufman Settlement
       Pa.
      Charleston,   Ladies' Benevolent Society
       N. C.
      Altapass, N. C. Miss Holman's Rural Work. Society founded. Hol-
                                                man Ass'n estab-
                                                lished 1911.
      Colorado
      Springs, Colo. Visiting Nurse Ass'n   Started by Associ-
                                                ated Charities 1902.
      New York City N. Y. Health Dept. Visiting Schools and   Child
                     Nurses   Welfare 1903. Con-
                                                tagious Nursing 1904.
                                                Tuberculosis Nurs-
                                                ing.

1903 Waterbury,   Visiting Nurse Ass'n
       Conn.
      Brockton,   Visiting Nurse Ass'n
       Mass.
      Milton, Mass. Milton Visiting Nurse
      Minneapolis,   Instructive V. N. Com. of
       Minn.   Assoc. Charities
      Berlin, N. H. Berlin Instructive V. N. A. Founded by Berlin
                                                Mills Co.
      Bernardsville, Visiting Nurse Ass'n
       N. J.
      Eau Claire,   Visiting Nurse Ass'n
       Wisc.
      Dayton, Ohio. Visiting Nurse Ass'n.   Work   started   by
                                                Flower and Fruit
                                                Mission.
      San Francisco.V. N. Telegraph Hill   Settlement established
                     Neighborhood House.   1890

1904	Derby, Conn.	D. N. A. of Derby, Ansonia and Shelton
	New Haven. Conn.	Visiting Nurse Ass'n
	Eastport, Maine.	Eastport District Nursing
	Portland, Maine.	Portland District Nursing
	Arlington, Mass..	District Nursing Ass'n
	Cambridge, Mass.	Visiting Nurse Ass'n
	Auburn, N. Y.	Visiting Nurse Ass'n
	Walpole. N. H.	District Nurse
	Summit, N. H.	Visiting Nurse Ass'n
	Wilmington, N. C.	Visiting Nurse
	Youngstown, Ohio.	Visiting Nurse Ass'n
1905	Bloomingdale, N. Y.	District Nurse Ass'n
	Carlisle, Pa.	Visiting Nurse Ass'n
	Naugatuck. Conn.	Naugatuck Visiting Nurse
	New Britain, Conn.	Visiting Nurse Ass'n
	Muskegon, Mich.	Visiting Nurse Ass'n

By 1905 there were 171 associations in different parts of the country employing 445 visiting nurses. From this time on the work grew with leaps and bounds until by 1921 there are over 11,000 public health nurses carrying on different phases of the work.

APPENDIX VII

The following brief account of the training given at Battersea Polytechnic indicates the type of instruction provided for Health Visitors.

(a) The shortened one-year course for fully trained nurses, and women with a considerable amount of experience rendering them fit to profit by the shortened one-year course;

(b) The full two-years course for students with no special previous knowledge, but having a good general education. She is usually a younger student, but full of energy and enthusiasm. The theoretical instruction given is similar for the students taking the one-year or two years' training, though the two-year students have the advantage of being prepared for the Examination of the Sanitary Inspectors' Examination Board, in addition to the Health Visitors' Diploma Examination, thus passing out with a broader outlook on, and knowledge of public health questions. Lectures and practical laboratory teaching where possible, are given on Maternity, Infant and Child Welfare, Hygiene, Sanitation, Elementary Science in its application to Hygiene, Social Science, Elementary Physiology, Sanitary Law and the Law relating to the Protection of Women and Children, Cookery and Household Management, and Needlework.

Students attend for Clinical Demonstrations by a medical woman on Infants and Children at the Victoria Hospital for Children, and at Infant Welfare Centres, and thus a good practical knowledge of both the healthy and sick child is gained.

Great importance is attached to the practical teaching. It varies somewhat for the one-year student, depending on her previous training, experience and knowledge, but always includes practical experience at a Maternity and Child Welfare Centre, School Nursing, and may include Maternity Nursing and Tuberculosis Visiting.

The two-year students all gain practical experience in Maternity and Child Welfare Centres, in Maternity Nursing on the District, with two afternoons at a Lying-in-Hospital, in School Nursing, and Minor Ailment Centres, in Tuberculosis Visiting, and in Social Training. About four-fifths of practical training is undertaken in the second year. (Brd. Ed. Rpt. Chief Md. Off. 1919)

28

INDEX

29